# THE
# ESSENTIAL JOHN ARLOTT

# THE ESSENTIAL
# JOHN ARLOTT

## FORTY YEARS OF CLASSIC CRICKET WRITING

EDITED BY
DAVID RAYVERN ALLEN

WILLOW BOOKS
COLLINS
8 GRAFTON STREET, LONDON W1
1989

Willow Books
William Collins Sons & Co Ltd
London · Glasgow . Sydney . Auckland
Toronto · Johannesburg

First published 1989
© John Arlott 1989

British Library Cataloguing In Publication Data

Arlott, John, *1914-*
The essential John Arlott
1. Cricket. Stories, anecdotes
I. Title
796.35′8

ISBN 0–00–218308–0

Set in Plantin Light by Bookworm Typesetting, Manchester
Printed and bound by Mackays of Chatham PLC

# Contents

Author's Preface    vii

Editor's Introduction    ix

1    Looking at the Game    11

2    Early Excursions    37

3    International Figures    97

4    International Discourse    118

5    Test Grounds    158

6    Notes from the Diary    168

7    Jottings from the Journal    177

8    Three from Three Makes Nine    191

9    Hants and All That    219

10    Obituaries    236

11    Reflecting the Game    253

12    Cricket Writers and Books    266

13    Poets and Peasants    296

Index    314

# Author's Preface

To be described as 'essential' would be an extravagant claim for any writer, and this one certainly would not lay claim to it. In fact, this collection is quite humbly the result of something rather more than an ambition. It would be stupid to say that a provincial police constable of the late 1930s aspired to be a writer. In those days to read, to collect books – often at prices beyond the reason of his salary – was everything, or at least nearly everything, for playing and watching cricket, too, were something of an obsession.

It was a slow, unforeseen progress, even to the point of daring to suggest making a collection – in fact, an anthology of topographical poetry – to a senior editor and a publisher and, solely by a freak accident, contributing to it. When, in the course of time, by a strange series of coincidences, invitations came – or, more accurately, offerings were accepted – it all seemed unreal. Surely it could not last. To find oneself actually paid for writing verse and reviews and, soon, for watching, broadcasting and writing about cricket, seemed a pipe dream. That feeling was never really overcome: if ever a man was completely happy in his work, this book is a memorial to that happiness.

To write a book is one thing; it is an operation that stays in the mind. To write a piece of verse – it would be extravagant to call it poetry – or an article is equally to concentrate effort but, because it is more brief, it does not stay in the mind. Therefore, to read through David Rayvern Allen's thoughtful, kind and thorough collection was in itself a separate pleasure.

This is, by implication, an autobiography, for it marks the life progress of one who was, in fact, carried along by the tide of events; rarely, if ever, planning or foreseeing the developments which made up his professional life. Indeed, it is almost an exaggeration to call it professional, for he seemed simply to follow a series of accidental opportunities which led him to a point where, as now, he looked back in amazement. To have spent the best part of a lifetime doing not only what he liked most, but something which he never dreamt he might achieve, is a striking happiness for anyone.

More than one piece to be found here was at the time something of an effort – even an effort which seemed to face him with the insurmountable; yet the pleasure never evaporated. That is the unifying quality of all this writing – that it was done for pleasure and with a perpetual sensation of amazement that the work was printed; as it now is equally surprising that it should be collected. It consists, in a way, of two separate pleasures; that of writing, which was first expressed in verses, and then that of watching, enjoying and striving to understand the remarkable and ever-renewing game of cricket.

'Essential' is a big word in terms of ambition, but the contents of this book were essential in their time to the writer – but, while he cannot claim that they will be that to a reader, he wishes everyone who does read them something of the pleasure he had from writing them.

John Arlott
Alderney
*May* 1989

# Editor's Introduction

No excuse is made or needed for rummaging further through the Arlott cricket repository. The supplies available, seemingly inexhaustible like the needles for the Desert Island discs, make the search the exact opposite – to stick with the metaphor – of the one in the proverbial haystack. An anthologist is soon, so easily, allured by all sorts of riches and, usually later rather than sooner, seeks the self-imposed discipline of chapter categorization to bring a sense of order. But the huge choice remains . . . Wonderful!

Naturally enough, this volume reflects John's thoughts on cricket and cricketers during forty years and more as the definitive communicator; the reflection of the game itself and its exponents, of course, being six times that length. His ideas and views on certain subjects and issues, understandably, may or may not have changed in the course of a working lifetime and therefore one has sought a balance between retrospective glances and copy of the moment. Occasionally, a fact has been outdistanced by time and in such a vast output, understandably, a degree of repetition occurs. Throughout, however, the range of experience integral to the text never fails to illuminate. We can share the glee of early discovery or become engrossed in a philosophical thesis on cricket's aesthetic qualities or we can greedily enjoy both.

Contained within are many pen portraits of famous figures and figures that many thought should have been – famous, that is. There is a treatise of compelling insight on the day-to-day existence of professional players; Spectators' Notes for two seasons, 1949 and 1950; surveys of English Test arenas; international assessments; Jottings from a Journal for *The Cricketer* and diary entries for *Playfair Cricket* during the 1960s; pieces for *Cricket Spotlight* in the 1970s and articles for *Wisden Cricket Monthly* and *The Guardian* within the 1980s.

The vicissitudes of Hampshire cricket are covered comprehensively – as is to be expected from a fellow countryman – and impressions are gained of those who have represented the game on canvas and through the photographer's lens. A novelty item comes in the form of a narration to a short film depicting a typical village cricket match in the Cotswolds; both for this and the script of the radio talk on Albert Craig, 'the Surrey Poet', readers will notice a departure from the norms of literary prose form to that of the spoken word. In the historical halls of broadcasting, John Arlott joins a select group in a very small room.

For these offerings and much else, I would like to express my gratitude to those who gave permission for reproduction and to those who gave assistance in other ways. Geoffrey Copinger, devoted cricket bibliophile, was enormously helpful in providing copies of articles from the now-defunct *South Wales Cricketers' Magazine*. Geoffrey Whitelock also was enormously helpful, though probably unaware of the fact: his manuscript listings of John Arlott's writing led the way directly to many forgotten areas. Ken Murphy at *The Guardian* went to a great deal of trouble with library material, as did Tony Mitchener with back numbers of the *Hampshire Handbook*. Howard Milton was kind enough to send an early essay and Harry Croxford a late one – it is not their fault that neither made the final edition. David Frith, editor of *Wisden Cricket Monthly*, for which John has written on a regular basis ever since that splendid magazine was launched over a decade ago, readily gave clearance for three articles that he first commissioned, and Christopher Martin-Jenkins, quietly authoritative commentator and 'voice' of *The Cricketer*, equally readily allowed use of a number of pieces that appeared in print a score and more years ago. My thanks also to Imogen Grosberg for *Goodbye* and to Michael Doggart, Graham Hart and 'Bunty' Ireland for making my illegibilities legible.

Acknowledgments are due as well to E.W. 'Jim' Swanton: *Barclay's World of Cricket*; the BBC; Burke's Peerage Marketing Ltd; Cassell (Macmillan), London; Davis-Poynter Ltd; Eyre and Spottiswoode Ltd; Glamorgan CCC; *The Guardian*; John Haig and Co. – Trans World International Film Library; Hampshire CCC; *Hampshire – the County Magazine*; Hodder and Stoughton Ltd; *London Calling*; Longmans, Green and Co.; Lutterworth Press; *The Observer*; *The Spectator*; *The Weekend Australian*; and Worcestershire CCC.

Finally, a massive vote of thanks to John himself, not only for allowing me to pester him with all manner of questions to which he had long ago sensibly forgotten the answers, but, most importantly, for writing all this in the first place.

David Rayvern Allen
Chorleywood
*April* 1989

# –1–

# Looking at the Game

## One Day of Enlightenment that Shaped a Lifetime

*January* 1988. It was an extremely persistent, if not positively pestiferous twelve-year-old who, on Saturday 14 August 1926, nagged his parents into letting him to The Oval for the first day of the fifth and final match of the Test series between England and Australia.

He had never seen a first-class match in his life. There was, of course, no television, no radio commentaries and he saw little of newsreel cricket. His head, though, was crammed with journalese about the leading cricketers.

Over the years that followed he was to immerse himself deeply in cricket and this was the occasion which fired that interest. It was also the match in which England regained The Ashes John Douglas had lost in Australia in 1920–21. It was, from the viewpoint of 1988, less than halfway in the history of those matches.

With words of warning still in his ears about those who swindled small boys over lemonade, and armed with sandwiches and two shillings, he set off from the Victorian house his parents had borrowed from his uncle for the family holiday.

He had found himself a seat on a bench in the front row, eaten his sandwiches, drunk a glass of fizzy lemonade and, most important, bought a scorecard long before play started.

That scorecard remains still ingrained in his memory. England had Jack Hobbs, Herbert Sutcliffe, Frank Woolley, 'Patsy' Hendren, Percy Chapman, Greville Stevens, Wilfred Rhodes, George Geary, Maurice Tate, Harold Larwood and Bert Strudwick. Many of them, though he could not then have dreamt it, became friends in later years. Between them those men eventually had played 243 times against

Australia – not mere Test matches but the real occasions against the old enemy – over the years from 1899 to 1934.

Australia had Bill Woodfull, Warren Bardsley, Charlie Macartney, Bill Ponsford, Tommy Andrews, Herbie Collins, Arthur Richardson, Jack Gregory, Bertie Oldfield, Clarrie Grimmett and Arthur Mailey. They played, in all, 238 times against England between 1909 and 1926. This was a body of great players.

Because the four previous matches of the series had been drawn, this was to be played to a finish, however long it took. He was not to know that it was to prove a historic match, nor that Harold Lake, under the pen-name of John Marchant, managed to get out a book on the game called *The Greatest Test Match* in time for the Christmas market.

It was a once and for all day. He was not to watch any more of the match, but he had the immense good fortune to see, briefly or long, all the major contestants on each side. Percy Chapman, who had taken over as captain on this match from Arthur Carr, won the toss and England batted. The boy pinched himself in disbelief as he saw the one and only Jack Hobbs come out to bat with Herbert Sutcliffe.

Jack Hobbs remains England's most successful batsman against Australia and it must be stressed that over the years this has been the main test of English cricketers. He scored 3636 runs against them with twelve centuries and an average of 54.26. More than anyone else the boy was ever to see, Jack hobbs *felt* bowling; understood it with a sympathy that was like an extra sense. he was, though, more than a maker of runs. He was a man of gentle manners, consideration and wisdom.

He put on more than 100 for the first wicket against Australia eleven times with Herbert Sutcliffe, the carefully groomed Yorkshire professional with the social air of an amateur. Herbert could be as dour as any; relentless in his defence, a fearless hooker and a faithful maker of runs for his county and his country in all conditions.

The pair made 53 at about a run a minute before Mailey, the Australian leg-spin and googly bowler, whom Neville Cardus described as a 'spendthrift', bowled Hobbs with a dipping full toss. Both batsman and bowler burst out laughing.

The tall Frank Woolley came next, a left-hand batsman of immense style. In his early days a considerable all-rounder (slow left-arm), he once took over in an emergency as England's wicket-keeper which, for a man of his height, was a considerable physical test. He did not in this innings last very long. Neither did the stubby-nosed, droll little batsman and lively outfield, Patsy Hendren, who was bowled by Gregory.

Jack Gregory, of a great cricketing family, was an Australian idol. A tall, strong, right-arm fast bowler and left-hand bat, he still holds the record for the fastest of all Test centuries, made in 70 minutes against South Africa at Johannesburg in 1921–22.

Percy Chapman of Kent came next. Tall, fair-haired, athletic and an almost miraculous close fieldsman, he was a bold and mighty left-handed hitter who, after all too short a period, was defeated by his employment as a liquor salesman. He took the bull by the horns and hit. He just missed his fifty, pulled down the pitch by Mailey's flight and stumped by the unobtrusively neat Bertie Oldfield.

Greville Stevens, the good-looking, fair-haired Oxford all-rounder, also put a bold bat to ball before Mailey fooled him, too. Then Sutcliffe, after a sound, craftsmanlike innings, edged a ball from Mailey on to his nose and did not seem to see the next ball, a leg-spinner, which bowled him.

Wilfred Rhodes, the shrewd Yorkshireman who took more wickets – 4187 – than anyone else who ever played, and shared with Jack Hobbs in the record opening partnership (323) in England v Australia matches, was now almost forty. He played his last Test when he was well past fifty-two.

Many stories, some of them quite funny, but more relating to his tactical perception and skill were – and still are – told about the man whom all Yorkshire referred to simply as 'Wilfred'. He plodded and, briefly, Maurice Tate swung lustily, but the England innings expired for 280 before Mailey and Clarrie Grimmett.

Before they were all out there was a chance to watch the bowling of Charlie Macartney who, in his day, had been a great slow left-armer, and Arthur Richardson, who played in spectacles, bowled off-spin and came to the Lancashire League.

Maurice Tate opened the England bowling. Strong in shoulders, legs and feet (the cartoonists' delight), his reputation was for 'pace off the pitch'. If he was fast-medium through the air, he often beat people by what he called 'fizz'. A rosy, cheerful extrovert, he had the stamina to take two hundred wickets and score a thousand runs in a season.

Tate's opening partner was Harold Larwood, the short, strong-shouldered Nottinghamshire miner and bowler whose extra yard of pace probably represented the difference between the two sides. Douglas Jardine's Bodyline series of 1932–33 was to defeat Australia–

above all, to defeat Don Bradman – but it was substantially the end of Larwood's career.

There was no doubt about him. For half a dozen years he was the fastest of bowlers and superbly controlled. He frightened lesser batsmen. Now he had the stalwart left-hander, Warren Bardsley, caught at the wicket. Then Woodfull, most obdurate of batsmen, was joined by Charlie Macartney.

That former all-rounder and splendid stroke-maker had scored a century before lunch at Leeds. He was dropped first ball at slip off Tate by Arthur Carr, who thereby, no doubt, lost the England captaincy. Stevens bowled Macartney through a bad stroke to a bad ball and Ponsford, the mighty record-breaker and forerunner of Bradman, was run out.

A mighty Larwood breakback bowled Andrews, and Herbie Collins, the Australian captain known as 'Horseshoe' because of his alleged luck in the game, saw out the day with the patient Woodfull to 60 for four.

The boy saw no more of it in the flesh, but in his imagination he watched it down to the finish and England's win by 289 runs at the end of the fourth day. It was a mighty cricketing occasion and, as a tiny by-product, it made at least one little boy a cricket addict for the rest of his days.

*The Guardian*

# The Pleasures of Cricket

Stand behind the bowler's arm. The morning sun is warm, but it has not yet dried the last of the dew from the twenty-two grass yards that run from one prim set of bail-capped stumps to the other. The lines that mark the creases stand out brusquely in startling white against the ground's lively greenness. The first ball of the morning leaves a hand urged by a straight-swung arm which, in its turn, is powered from a mighty down-plunge of body-swing. The ball is so new that you may catch the flicker of the gold stamp on its gleaming redness. It moves straight for the first half of its course, then, as if an invisible string were tugging at it, it swings away towards the off-side of the wicket: it pitches and, because of that dewy life still in the turf, its seam, striking the cushion of grass, flings it back on to the line of the stumps. The bat, until now poised with all the anxious wariness which is bred by the fear of a 'first-baller' – the fear of great batsmen as of lesser – sweeps down along its ordered pendulum and the full 'meat' of the blade places the ball firmly away to a fieldsman standing a few yards off. He, unhurriedly, picks it up and lobs it gently back to the bowler who, surveying it with proprietorial care, identifies the spot where the blow of the bat has marred its shininess and rubs that part of it against his flannels as he walks relaxedly back to his mark.

Soon, he feels, his muscles will have warmed to the point where his swing is at its fiercest: then the ball will leap from the pitch before the batsman can move to smother it. He does not consider the moment, some ten or twelve overs hence, when the first freshness will have passed, when that long, eager run will be slowed, when the fine prodigality of effort which is the fast bowler's glory and the fierce stamp of the pounding lever of his left foot will have brought his hair flapping over his face, the sweat surging through his shirt, the long-ago-torn muscle jabbing him into the slightest limp. Nor, when that time comes, will he think it a heavy price to pay for four good wickets and, as he settles his sweater about him at the end of his spell, there will be in him the warmth of a man whose day's work has not shamed his pride of craft.

At the other end, the batsman, already twice the man for the vibration that passed comfortingly through the bat to his hands as that first ball squarely met its middle, finds a new ease in his stance. The problems of the morning – problems of pace and swing, spin and flight – lie ahead in all their complexity and all their nagging insistence, but he has overcome them before on such a day as this. He looks round the field with more of an eye to avenues for the scoring stroke than he had dared to assume before that vital first ball.

First slip has relaxed into the easy slouch he assumes between the spells of poised alertness as each ball is being bowled; the finger-tips of his well-made, certain hands are barely touching: any moment may produce that demand, rapid as the flicker of an eye, which calls years of judgement into the stretch of an arm; yet he wears, as to the manner born, the distrait air which is his disguise.

Away in the deep field, third man, middle-aged, never a good player but pleasant to play or talk or travel with, pulls himself yet again to his highest pitch of preparedness and dreams of performing such feats as twenty-five years of failure have proved to be beyond his powers.

Behind him, an older man stretches in his deck chair, pulls richly upon his pipe and gives himself up for the remainder of the day to watching the pattern of men in white against a backcloth of green. Under the distant hedge, a boy in knickerbockers watches the players – and the fast bowler in particular – with an intentness necessary if you are going to 'be' that fast bowler, down to the last mannerism, in tomorrow's play with your fellows.

The appeal of cricket, the qualities which make it, for its devotees, one of the pleasures of life – while for the uninitiated it is a virtually incomprehensible physical hardship – are not easily analysed. Certainly it has an immense contemplative quality, or it could not give such genuine and long-lasting pleasure: even the player of great physical endeavours savours his labours in a subsequent pleasant languor. The game has a physical appeal and it can satisfy pride; yet its attraction, so far as can be judged, does not depend upon, or vary with, the ability of the player. It is not solely an adult pleasure; it has not even confined its delights to those who play or have played: some of the most earnest lovers of cricket have never, or hardly ever, handled a bat. As a cottage sport profoundly played, it became a cottage craft and, just as much of the early cottage pottery is now recognized as primitive art, so the playing of the game of cricket has achieved not only a very high technical standard but also a poetic and epic standing.

Much of the true quality of the game, present today as formerly, can be hidden from the eyes of those who do not play themselves and who are forced to take their cricket at second hand. It is, indeed, the function of newspapers to present *news*. Thus, that a man spent one of the happiest days of his life fishing is not news if he caught only three small fish, yet it is of the true stuff of angling. That another man hooked a young whale *is* news, and is reported. Who shall blame the new editors if their readers infer therefrom that angling is a matter of freak catches? The angler knows better, but the newspaper man may reasonably hesitate to assume the role of instructor in the basic and contemplative values of angling. Thus we may read of the strange events in the lives of Test cricketers or be harangued on the deficiencies of our national cricket team; but we ought not to confuse these topical issues with the unbroken humanity of the game which has given them off as so much unnecessary froth. Yet again, as a not unjustifiable counterblast to the lack of proportion which the followers of cricket share with all other enthusiasts, there is a tendency on the part of the uninitiated to cry down cricket on the grounds that a mere game ought not to be allowed to assume great importance in the life of any man. It should be admitted at once that under the influence of topical sensationalism the defeats of Test teams have been greeted as national disasters, to the annoyance of those disinterested observers who, reasonably, doubt the sense of values of those who think that the result of a cricket match *means* anything at all outside its immediate circle.

The sceptics, and not the cricket followers, are probably largely right in this particular instance. It would undoubtedly be possible for England – as I write, a losing side in Test cricket – to produce a team which would win Test matches by methods which would ruin cricket as a pleasure. Regimentation and organization could produce regularly, from our large population, the winning teams which normally occur about once in each generation on the coincidence of four or five really great players. On the other hand, our cricket can be perfectly healthy – that is to say some numbers of men, of their own free will, and in their own manner, can play and enjoy the game – without *necessarily* producing players who possess some huge streak of genius for bowling or striking or catching a leather ball.

That greatness is within the sphere of the sportsman is not to be doubted. The fact has never been better demonstrated than by William Hazlitt at the conclusion of his essay 'On the Indian Jugglers' when he quoted his obituary notice of Cavanagh, the fives player. So true is Hazlitt's analysis, and so rounded his judgement that although concerned specifically with the game of fives, the passage achieves complete validity for any game to which a man of great aptitude for it may give himself wholeheartedly. No apology, therefore, is needed for inserting it here for, much and well as men have written of cricket, few have ever conceived it necessary to justify their own estimate of the importance of the game. Moreover, when so great a pen as Hazlitt's has been turned to a task, it is difficult to imagine any subsequent author writing with comparable style and effect. Here, indeed, is the perfect picture of a great games player:

'When a person dies, who does any one thing better than any one else in the world, which so many others are trying to do well, it leaves a gap in society. It is not likely that any one will now see the game of fives played in its perfection for many years to come – for Cavanagh is dead, and has not left his peer behind him. It may be said that there are things of more importance than striking a ball against a wall – there are things indeed which make more noise and do as little good, such as making war and peace, making speeches and answering them, making verses and blotting them; making money and throwing it away. But the game of fives is what no one despises who has ever played at it. It is the finest exercise for the body, and the best relaxation for the mind. . . . He who takes to playing at fives is twice young. . . . He has no other wish, no other thought, from the moment the game begins, but that of striking the ball, of placing it, of *making* it! This Cavanagh was sure to do. Whenever he touched the ball, there was an end of the chase. His eye was certain, his hand fatal, his presence of mind complete. He could do what he pleased, and he always knew exactly what to do. He saw the whole game, and played it; took instant advantage of his adversary's weakness, and recovered balls, as if by a miracle and from sudden thought, that every one gave for lost. He had equal power and skill, quickness, and judgement. He could either out-wit his antagonist by finesse, or beat him by main strength. Sometimes, when he seemed preparing to send the ball with the full swing of his arm, he would by a slight turn of his wrist drop it within an inch of the line. In general, the ball came from his hand, as if from a racket, in a straight horizontal line; so that it was in vain to attempt to overtake or stop it. As it was said of a great orator that he never was at a loss for a word, and for the properest word, so Cavanagh always could tell the degree of force necessary to be given to a ball, and the precise direction in which it should be sent. He did his work with the greatest ease; never took more pains than was necessary; and while others were fagging themselves to death, was as cool and collected as if he had just entered the court. His style of play was as remarkable as his power of execution. He had no affectation, no trifling. He did not throw away the game to show off an attitude, or try an experiment. He was a fine, sensible, manly player, who did what he could, but that was more than any one else could even affect to do. . . . Cobbett and Junius together would have made a Cavanagh. He was the best *up-hill* player in the world; even when his adversary was fourteen, he would play on the same or better, and as he never flung away the game through carelessness and conceit, he never gave it up through laziness or want of heart. The only peculiarity of his play was that he never *volleyed*, but let the balls hop; but if they rose an inch from the ground, he never missed having them. There was not only nobody equal, but nobody second to him. It is supposed that he could give any other player half the game, or beat him with his left hand. His service was tremendous. He once played Woodward and Meredith together (two of the best players in England) in the Fives-court, St Martin's-street, and made seven and twenty aces following by services alone – a thing unheard of. He another time played Peru, who was considered a first-rate fives-player, a match of the best out of five games, and in the three first games, which of course decided the match, Peru got only one ace. Cavanagh was an Irishman by birth, and a house-painter by profession. He had once laid aside his working-dress and walked up, in his smartest clothes, to the Rosemary Branch to have an afternoon's pleasure. A person accosted him, and asked him if he would have a game. So they agreed to play for half-a-crown a game, and a bottle of cider. The first game began – it was seven, eight, ten, thirteen, fourteen, all. Cavanagh won it. The next was the same. They played on, and each game was hardly contested. "There," said the unconscious fives-player, "there was a stroke that Cavanagh could not take: I never played better in my life, and yet I can't win a game. I don't know how it is." However, they played on, Cavanagh winning every game, and the by-standers drinking the cider, and laughing all the time. In the twelfth game, when Cavanagh was only four, and the stranger thirteen, a person came in, and said, "What! are you here, Cavanagh?" The words were no sooner pronounced than the astonished player let the ball drop from his hand, and saying "What! have I been breaking my heart all this time to beat Cavanagh?" refused to make another effort. "And yet, I give you my word," said Cavanagh, telling the story with some triumph, "I played all the while with my clenched fist." He used frequently to play matches at Copenhagen-house for wagers and dinners. The wall against which they play is the same that supports the kitchen-chimney, and when the wall resounded louder than usual, the cooks exclaimed, "Those are the Irishman's balls," and the joints trembled on the spit! – Goldsmith consoled himself that there were places where he too was admired: and Cavanagh was the admiration of all the fives-courts, where he ever played. . . . He was a young fellow of sense, humour, and courage. In a word, there are hundreds at this day, who cannot mention his name without admiration, as the best fives-player that perhaps ever lived (the greatest excellence of which they have any notion) – and the noisy shout of the ring happily stood him in stead of the unheard voice of posterity!'

(William Hazlitt, Table Talk, 1821)

For cricket itself, the best word had been said some eighty years earlier, in 1739 – before the day of satisfactorily recorded cricket – by Mary Turner of East Hoathly, in a letter to her son who was at Brighthelmstone on holiday. Her words have been much and well quoted, for they hold the essential quality of the game with which they are concerned, in that they light a rural simplicity with a fire which, if not divine, nevertheless burns to the full of human warmth.

> 'Last Mundaye youre Father was at Mr Payn's and plaid Cricket, and came home please anuf for he struck the best ball in the game and whishd he had not anything else to do he ould play at Cricket all his life.'

Cricket, Burke, 1953

# Cricket for Breakfast

Cricket is pre-eminently the breakfast-time sport, recognized and enjoyed all over the world, though nowhere quite so deeply nor so frequently as in England. In the life of the English county cricketer, breakfast is in many ways the symbol of his achievement. While other men are choking down a cup of tea and dashing out to be at work at eight or nine o'clock, the county cricketer is at his leisure. At away matches he strolls downstairs in the hotel without hurry – though not always to the entire approval of the dining-room staff – with the ease of a man who does not have to start work until half-past eleven. True, some captains call for a half-past ten report on the ground but even that leaves time for relaxation, a three-course meal, an extra cup of coffee at the end; and above all, the paper.

You may always identify a county cricket team at breakfast in an English hotel because they are all reading the morning newspapers; not simply one apiece but passing them round so that they all see them all. They are, of course, reading the cricket scores and reports so that, by the end of the meal, most of them know – without consciously committing it to memory but from sheer interest – just what every team and individual did in the previous day's play. Being a county cricketer is not simply playing for a county; it is following all the other counties. These are the ultimate 'shop' men.

The conversation stirred by this morning study has an established and traditional form. 'I see' – comment on anything read in the paper always begins with 'I see' – 'I see old Fred got a hundred against Derbyshire; must have been a beautiful track for him to get runs against Alan Ward.' 'But perhaps Alan wasn't really fit –?' 'Must have been, they gave him eighteen overs.' Every game is weighed up. They have not missed a trick. 'I see old Eddie got another star [a not out] against Sussex; bet that made Snowball mad.'

They know who is fit, who is playing well; they notice tactical details a hundred miles away: 'Why did Brian only bowl a dozen overs yesterday if it's a turner at Weston, then?' 'Why did he keep Skinny on for forty overs when he only took one?'

The difference between the first-class cricketers and their followers is that the players have longer to go about this delightful morning pursuit. Other games, such as football, produce morning reading only once or twice a week – and anyway it is not quite the same on Sundays. England is the best breakfast-cricket country because every day in the season there is a match to be reported somewhere. Since my childhood the special flavour of summer has always been the cricket scores in the morning. There was one brief period when, living in north Hampshire where the local club is called Basingstoke and North Hants, I thought we had two county teams – Hampshire and Northants – and was relieved of the anguish of not knowing which to support in a match between the two only by my father's explanation.

Like millions of other small boys, I knew all the county cricketers from the morning papers before I ever saw any of them play. There was no television then; cricketers were to be seen only in the papers – photographs and Tom Webster, then in the heyday of his economic, laughing line – on cigarette cards, or in the mind. There were not even any evening scores on the wireless, so that the rumour someone had heard from a man who saw it in the Stop Press of an evening paper, that Mead had been 77 not out in the afternoon, left us in a state of agonized suspense until next morning's news confirmed that he had scored his century (he usually did, though several of us were rendered uneasy for years after he got out in the nineties twice during the same fortnight).

Test matches in Australia were tantalizing; in the years before the relayed commentaries there was a terrible wait for the morning editions of the evening papers: they did not arrive until we had gone to school, there was no chance of a glimpse of one in the mid-morning break and it was horrid not to know even the worst until lunch-time.

It is never quite the same after one has grown up. Of course, many breakfast-table cricketers follow their native counties faithfully all the summer through the morning reports. For them, though, the players themselves are not distant and unattainable; they simply do not bother to go to the matches when they might. For us as boys, remote from the county grounds, the morning paper was the only link with those splendid creatures. The heavy tread of Armstrong's Australians echoed through England in that blazing summer and, all at once, though their game was not even a distant relation of our rough-ground skirmishes, they spellbound me. So each breakfast-time, when my father had gone out to work, leaving the paper, there was regular news of the great: Jack Hobbs (until he fell ill), Hendren, Hearne, Russell, Woolley, Sandham, Tyldesley (E.), Freeman, White, Macaulay, Rhodes, Parker, the destroying Australian fast bowlers Gregory and McDonald, the splendid Macartney – and, of course, *all* the Hampshire players, but especially Tennyson, Mead and Brown, who almost alone defied the Australians. All of these I was to see, and many of them I later came to know personally.

Many others, though, remain fresh in my mind, cricketers I followed through those distant summers, men I never set eyes upon, but whom I still remember (initials as well, if pressed) in the pictures my mind made of them all those years ago: Wells, Murdin and Buswell; Curgenven, Cadman and Bestwick; Coventry, Preece and Tarbox; Mounteney, Coe and Benskin; Gillingham, Perrin and Farnfield; and, from the 'new' county, Whittington, Hacker, Creber, O'Bree and Pinch. Do cricketers ever realize, I wonder – to how many millions of people they will never know – they are breakfast-table heroes?

*Twelfth Man, Cassell*, 1971

# The Professional Cricketer

*December* 1949. The few hundred professional cricketers of Britain form only a very small section of the community. They are not organized in the trade union sense and lack, apparently, both spokesman and the inclination to state a case. There have been a few isolated instances of special pleading by both employers and employed but the complete assessment of the situation has never been written and it may well prove that the factor which has so far precluded the production of a full and objective report will always do so. This factor is the intricate blend of the economic and romantic ingredients of the problem. Of the two types of person likely to attempt the analysis, the expert social reporter will inevitably over-emphasize the former aspect, the cricket enthusiast the latter.

Mr Learie Constantine, the West Indies cricketer, has pleaded the cause of the league club, of Lancashire League calibre, as the only fair employer of the professional cricketer in that it pays him a wage based on his value as a public entertainer. This argument, powerful as it must appear to the disinterested spectator, is not supported by the cricketers concerned because it fatally ignores the romantic element of their position.

There is no orderly approach to the actual economic state of the professional cricketer because there is no guarantee, little likelihood even, of any degree of uniformity in the treatment of players of any two clubs, even though the clubs be of apparently identical standing.

The first problem is to identify the 'professional' cricketer. For this purpose I shall ignore, as not germane to my argument rather than as *de facto* excluded from it, the player who retains amateur status while either holding a sinecure position in the pay of a wealthy patron of his club, or being paid by the club itself, nominally for a post other than that of player. The most important professional cricket players from the point of view of the general public are those employed by the MCC and the seventeen counties of the County Cricket Championship.

Far outnumbering these, however, are the other paid cricketers – the professionals of the minor counties, of the competitive leagues of the North and the Midlands, of the factory and non-competitive clubs of England and Wales, and, to a lesser degree, those of Scotland and Ireland. Their number cannot be accurately gauged but is probably not less than twelve hundred. The MCC and the seventeen first-class counties, on the other hand, probably employ less than five hundred players in all.

The position of the school 'pro' is more closely akin to that of the coach and the umpire – a subsequent development from the normal status of the cricket professional and one which must receive attention later.

Because there is no uniformity of treatment, I propose not to trace the development of any one player, since no one player could be truly representative, but to examine, from the earliest possible age, the standing of various types of individuals falling within my compass.

### THE BOY CRICKETER

The boy cricketer has always received attention in some counties but his status is one of importance in an increasing number of centres. The fact of his importance being limited to centres is a vital one and must condition even the earliest remarks about him. The boy cricketer in one of the twenty-two counties not playing 'first-class' cricket, or in Scotland, or even in the rural areas of the senior cricketing counties, stands considerably little chance of being noticed. The boy cricketer at a public school is almost certain to be seen and coached but is unlikely to become a professional. In the main centres of cricket, however, and almost anywhere in Yorkshire, the fourteen- or fifteen-year-old player of talent will receive encouragement and advice and will be watched by the county cricket club. If he is exceptionally good he may be offered a post on the county groundstaff when he leaves school.

There is no accepted standard of payment or treatment of these lads. Some are taken on as groundboys, labouring on the ground, selling scorecards and running errands during the season; in winter they may continue labouring work or be found a minor post in a business undertaking owned by a patron of the club; a few of them are given clerical work in the county club office. Engagement is rarely longer than for the professional season which runs from April to the beginning of September. In the case of many of these youths their promise has been unfulfilled by the time they are seventeen or eighteen and their contracts are terminated, leaving them untrained for any rewarding post. Only too often in the past these youths have been allowed to labour on the ground and bowl to members, but have been left to work out their own salvation as cricketers, with little more than the fortuitious kindness of some established player for advice, and that advice is not always infallible. It was all too common to see public schoolboy members of the county club being bowled to at the nets by the bowling-staff boys and receiving the coaching which the young professionals might better and more profitably have received.

In most cases, however, these lads, of the last few years, have been more carefully coached. As a rule even the *atmosphere* of a good cricket headquarters develops considerable ability in any youth who is physically fit and has enthusiasm and some aptitude for the game. This means that no definite decision as to his unfitness for county cricket can be taken until he is twenty-three or twenty-four. The groundstaff youth of nineteen will earn, through the five-month season only, a wage comparable with that of a labourer in industry. In some counties he is assured of winter work, but only in a minority of cases is there anything nearer a guarantee of this than a verbal expression of willingness to find it if possible.

The rough average age of a young man's entry into county cricket comes between twenty and twenty-four. He may come on to the professional strength of a county by any one of three routes. He may be a groundstaff lad who has worked his way up to the first team; he may be a successful club cricketer found, after trial, to be worthy of a place; or he may, if wise and in the position to command sufficient leisure and financial independence, be a man who has played as an amateur with the county side until both he and the country authority are satisfied of the wisdom of his engagement. Here again the position of the players varies. The groundstaff lad, for instance, will in most counties receive his contracted groundstaff wages plus match-money. The man newly accepted as of county status will be given a specific contract. Any county eleven will contain some 'capped' and some 'uncapped' professionals, and 'caps' are notoriously harder to win for professional than for amateur players.

## FINANCIAL REWARDS

The 'cap' is the cricket professional's guarantee of the greatest security he can know. It is upon the financial rewards of the 'capped' professional player of the 'first-class' county that I now propose to concentrate. The MCC staff I shall deal with subsequently as a unique phenomenon. No two of the seventeen counties have identical terms for their players. The terms offered to a player are decided solely and unrestrictedly by the committee of the county club. There is no arbitrator: the player may argue, but eventually he must accept the committee's final offer or go. One county pays every capped player £520 per annum, Test-match players and newly capped youths alike, and then pays match expenses, talent money and match bonus. It provides, for all who care to take it, employment on the county ground during the winter in repairing structure and seating, painting and so forth at an additional £4 a week. This is one of the highest, and probably the fairest, payment made. Yorkshire is the most generous of all counties towards its players – who must be Yorkshire-born (no other county enforces such a rule). There is a guaranteed yearly wage for a man whether fit or not, whether in or out of the side; there is a generous talent-money system and, the county's 'home' games being played at various centres within the county, hotel accommodation at those centres is supplied for every member of the team. In other counties the standing rule is that no expenses are paid for a 'home' match even though the player may live the length of the county from the town in which it is being played. It may be safely said that an established member of the Yorkshire county team will receive about £700 a year. In other counties either of two methods of payment may be adopted: one is that of the yearly salary, paid monthly throughout the year, the other the match-money system. Match-money may or may not be additional to a very small wage or subject to a yearly guaranteed minimum payment, but an increasing number of counties now give a guaranteed figure below which the player's income cannot fall. Again, match-money varies according to whether or not players are expected to pay their own expenses. One county pays £22 for every four-day match (Saturday, Monday and Tuesday, but involving Sunday) and £18 for every three-day match (Wednesday, Thursday, Friday). This applies whether the game be 'home' or 'out'; when 'out' the player is expected to pay his own expenses. Another county pays £12 for a four-day match, £10 for a three-day match and pays £1 per day for expenses on 'out' matches. A county plays roughly twenty-six matches per year. Of the salary-paying counties some 'grade' their players, the star players receiving £550 a year, the lower-graded men £450. Most counties pay 'talent' money, which is now generally awarded on a points system. The captain or the county committee awards points for meritorious performances – runs scored, wickets taken, catches and stumpings in the case of a wicket-keeper. In some cases the awards are automatic: so many points for a hundred runs, so many for fifty, a certain number of points for every wicket taken over five, or for every catch or stumping. Other committees, following more enlightened methods, award points for the match importance of the performance, so that twenty runs scored by a normally poor batsman, which serve to win a match, will receive at least the same reward as an easy century scored when the game is not in hazard. Several counties now pay match bonus, some £2 per man for a win, £1 for a first-innings lead, others £1 for a win only. Expenses for 'out' matches vary from payment of all railway fares and hotel bills to third-class fares and ten shillings per day. Guaranteed minimum yearly salaries vary between county and county from £300 to £550. In other words, Test and tour payments apart, a county cricketer's income depends less upon his excellence as a player than upon the financial soundness of his county club and the attitude towards payment adopted by his county committee.

About twelve star players in the country at any time will earn substantially more than these wages. These are the professional players who may expect to be selected in about three years out of four as members of the touring sides playing cricket overseas during the winter. Such a tour, with all travelling and hotel expenses provided, will be worth between £500 and £1000 in cash, saving on normal household expenses and gifts in kind. Of these star players about half will obtain further additions to their income by highly-paid newspaper articles, books of memoirs or instruction, or from publicity schemes. A few players on the rank immediately below these stars might expect a minor tour perhaps once in five years, with a resultant profit of appreciably less than £500, or winter coaching engagements overseas worth possibly £500. The remaining hundred and thirty capped county professionals cannot expect to earn anything from cricket between September and April. Some of them also play association football as professionals but the overlapping of the two seasons and the elaborate nature of preliminary pre-season training in each sport makes this increasingly difficult. Most of them are not content to exist through the long cricket close-season on the wages of the actual season but take up work which they can do nothing to retain between April and September. Some of them do rough work on the county grounds. Some report soccer matches for provincial papers; others who have had the capital to start businesses return to them during the winter; but they are few. Most earn a small wage for unskilled work.

## THE BENEFIT MATCH

The cricketer's benefit is often discussed by non-cricketers with some degree of awe or envy. The facts of it, in the main, tend to rate it as less important than is generally believed. In the matter of a player's benefit, the county cricket club committee, through, or under the direction of, its secretary according to the actual seat of power, acts completely at its own discretion. It is generally accepted that a county cricketer is entitled to a benefit after he has been a regular member of the county side for ten years. But the gift of a benefit is at the discretion of the committee.

Often it happens that, with the almost simultaneous retirement of a number of senior players from a county team (which is a frequent occurrence), several young players come into the side together. If there are four of them, they may, all four, be eligible for a benefit in the same year. It is, however, an unwritten rule that no two players of a county shall have a benefit match in the same year. In this case the most outstanding of the four players will be given a benefit in his eleventh year, the next in order of merit in the twelfth, the next in the thirteenth. Thus the least accomplished of the four may have to wait until the fourteenth year for his turn. He has the longest period to wait and is the one most likely to lose his place in the side before that period elapses. This circumstance arises so frequently that the average player is often in a state of considerable anxiety as to whether or not he will ever receive a benefit match.

In 1947 several players with nine years of service, *excluding* the war years, sixteen years after their entry into county cricket and hard upon forty years of age, had received painfully plain intimation that their contracts would not be renewed and that they need not expect to remain on the county strength to receive a benefit. This incidence of seven non-cricketing years has been very hard on several fastish bowlers, the type of cricketers to show the effect of age earliest. A batsman may, often does, play until he is comfortably turned forty; the pace bowler rarely remains in big cricket to the age of forty.

A benefit match, within the gift of the county committee, is often withheld on various grounds. Some of the poorer counties have made a rule that one blank season shall come between any two benefit matches. Once again the ruling on benefit matches varies from county to county. The scheme is, roughly, that the proceeds of one match during a season shall be allotted to a player as his benefit match. The match must be selected by the player before the season commences. A number of counties will not allow a Bank Holiday match to be chosen, because this will, normally, be their most profitable match of the season. (The granting of the match between Lancashire and the Australian touring side in 1948, to Washbrook, is the only example known to the writer of a game with the tourists being awarded as a benefit.) The player takes the risk of weather ruining the match. If he wishes he may, at his own expense, insure privately, at ten per cent, against a daily revenue below that of a match, comparable in ground, opponents and time of year, in the preceding season. County rulings, however, even apart from comparative size of attendances, combine to make the value of a benefit match to a player widely different as between county and county. Some counties ask the player to pay, from the receipts, all expenses of the match, such as ground and turnstile staff, pavilion meals and match-money. Others demand that he find also the expenses for the next, or the corresponding 'out' match.

But of recent years there has been a considerable move in the direction of making the entire season of his benefit match, in effect, the player's benefit season. For instance, the county players play matches with local clubs on Sundays or in the evenings, the proceeds going to the beneficiary. County committees allow collections, probably one per match at home games. Raffles and entertainments are organized, subscription cards are hung in every county club. It is the custom for each visiting county team to contribute five shillings per member to the current benefit fund in the county they visit. A Yorkshire county player's benefit has been as high as £8000. No other county, however, approaches this figure. A few years ago a Test-match batsman who played for an unimportant county had a benefit at about the same time as the most obscure member of a great county side. The final figure of the Test player's benefit was less than a third of that of the other player.

A benefit, like wages, depends not upon the eminence of the player but upon the county for which he plays. Its success also depends upon the player's popularity within his own county; popularity is the most certain guarantee of a good return from the local public. One great point in favour of the benefit match, however, is that the proceeds are regarded as charitable gifts and are not subject to income tax.

## THE CRICKETER'S CAREER

The life of a professional cricketer in the first-class game is possibly twenty years, sometimes more in the case of the great, often less in the case of the average player. Often the period is less dependent upon the prowess of the player than upon the availability of an adequate successor, a circumstance beyond forecast.

Other qualifications than those required to be a satisfactory player of the game are required for the posts normally filled by retired county cricketers. Therefore it will be fair to balance the account at this point.

Although the discrepancies already pointed out make an average figure impossible, and although, in addition, the great changes in money values before and after the Second World War make the savings of pre-1939 relatively worthless, some rough figure of income ought to be struck. Let us say, erring on the side of generosity, that the forty-two-year-old county cricketer retiring from the game in 1947 earned, from sixteen years of cricket (allowing for a 'cap' unduly early, at the age of twenty) including a benefit and one overseas tour, £10,000. Of this he will have spent at least £7000 on frugal living over this period. During the war period his earnings may have been £3500. Again the figure is a generous one. Let us now examine the expenditure he will have incurred which is peculiar to the cricketer. His expenditure on flannels, shirts, socks, caps, pads, bats, bags and the very heavy dry-cleaning and laundry bills of cricket players, will have been at least £60 per year. Living in hotels, living in the easy company of sportsmen, inevitably means expenditure on entertainment, drinks for friends, and cinemas. Only the few stars receive their gear free and are entertained wherever they go. My own experience when travelling with a county team was that I spent at least £1 per day beyond strict expenses without any extravagance. This accounts for a further £88 per year. Doctors' bills are impossible to estimate. The average county cricketer suffers countless strains and twists in the course of a season. Sometimes these are treated at the expense of the county club, in other cases the player pays. Often such an injury, under the match-pay system, can cost a player £200 in income in a season. Few players have survived even ten years of first-class cricket without serious injury or illness.

The popular idea of some county cricketers as lazy or over-indulgent is a foolish one to anyone who has ever fielded-out through a whole day, 11.30 a.m. to 6.30 p.m., with forty minutes for lunch and a quarter of an hour for tea. In the heat of the summer, particularly on renownedly tiring grounds such as The Oval, this is a trial of the fittest constitution. By about five o'clock, when the feet are bruised almost raw with the jolting on the hard ground, when the whole body aches from the tension-to-the-toes with the delivery of every ball, when muscles behind the eyes ache and tug almost to screaming point and still the player must be keyed for the brief chance which may turn the game, first-class cricket is purgatory. Then, when the sharp stroke is played, just out of reach and you dive for it, miss it, and fall to the ground, the temptation is almost overwhelming to stay there and shut the eyes, just to rest. But you feel the sweat rushing through the shirt, through even the thick white flannels, and you know that in another second the sweat will be soaking the dust into the cloth as mud and there will be another dry-cleaner's bill. You get up, chase after the ball and come back to fit again, accurately as a piece of machinery into the plan of captain or bowler – in which your defection may spell long- or short-term damage to the standing or finances of the bowler.

There is always a last chance for a cricketer and a first chance in the climb to higher fame, and any member of his team can make or mar that chance. The player is at the mercy of his team-mates and his captain. A captain is always in a position to ask for a player to be dropped or dismissed, and then the committee must choose between the captain or the player. The dissension may be purely personal but the problem is the same and, for the sake of vital team discipline, the decision to drop one or the other must be taken. There have been some famous compromises on this score; all of them have proved disastrous.

But our non-existent average county player has endured the strain and survived these trials and has come to the end of his playing days. Let us be optimistic once again and say that he has escaped also the occupational diseases of the cricketer. These are several and common. Only one long-serving first-class wicket-keeper of my acquaintance has eight fingers and two thumbs which work properly! None has escaped fracture. The continual jar of playing back upon the point between the bases of the thumb and index finger has malformed the operative hand of most batsmen. Few pace bowlers retire from the game with sound knees or feet. Tom Wass of Notts, that phenomenon who bowled the fast leg-break and took Nottinghamshire to the Championship before the 1914 war, has two fingers immovably wedged in the palm of his hand.

### THE AFTERMATH

Our cricketer, however, is reasonably fit. What choices of employment are open to him? He may become an umpire – one of the twenty odd on the first-class 'list' – but he is usually expected to serve first an ill-paid season as a minor counties umpire. The MCC, benevolently, has recognized the financial inadequacy of the financial rewards received by cricketers and, where it has control, has striven to rectify the position. Thus in Test matches players are paid £60 per match and it has fixed first-class umpires' salaries at £12 per match for all matches plus £1 a day hotel expenses and third-class railway fare. Umpires are reported upon by the captains in every match and many good cricketers cannot, as they grow old, maintain sharpness of wit and calmness of judgement through a daily six hours. The number of first-class umpires is small – twenty-two – but they are changed year by year as the strain becomes too severe or they prove unsatisfactory. A first-class umpire, forbidden to umpire a match in his own county, is much from home, and his life as an umpire will rarely exceed ten years. Coaching, at a school, a club, or overseas, is available for those temperamentally suited to the work and prepared to work for the prevailing low wages and for only five months of the year.

If our player has been careful and has the unusually high savings of £5000 in either cash, shares, property or a business, a few years of umpiring will tide him over until he can settle down to live on capital.

Some older players go to league cricket as Saturday afternoon professionals, but in the highly-paid leagues there is a demand for speed, albeit only for a long 'half-day' per week as opposed to six days a week, which does not usually allow the man whose age has driven him from county cricket to last more than two or three years there. There are, again, the non-competitive clubs, but with them, as in coaching, wages are extremely low, duties usually include the arduous task of the preparation of wickets and menial work about the pavilions and again, the period of cricket is five months of the year.

If the player has founded a business on his capital, his good name in the county and an aptitude for commercial dealings may enable him to retire to business without regretting his life as a cricketer. If he has worked steadily during the winters and trained himself for other work, he may go back to that. Many cricketers have achieved considerable financial security after their playing days are over. Others, in instances usually widely publicized, have not done so.

A series of 'Talks With Old Yorkshire Cricketers', contributed by 'Old Ebor' (A.W. Pullin) to the *Yorkshire Evening Post* in 1897–98, revealed that many of the greatest Yorkshire players of the middle and early second half of the last century were then in a state of abject poverty bordering, in some cases, on starvation. The general all-round social improvement has raised the lowest standards above those there reported, but the principle, since admirably rectified in the case of the Yorkshire club (which alone runs an adequate social security and provident fund for its players), still applies in most other counties.

## THERE IS NO SECURITY

Neither the MCC nor the separate County Cricket Advisory Committee has imposed, or can hope to impose, any ruling as to payment, insurance, benefits or method of contracting players, because of the varying financial positions of the counties. Several county clubs have to dispense with players whom they would otherwise retain against future development solely because their finances do not permit of an adequate pay-roll. Other counties, Lancashire and Yorkshire at least, are able to maintain quite large staffs. The MCC has again adopted an enlightened attitude which its comparative wealth allows it to implement. The MCC bowling staff of youngsters of promise and players beyond their county-cricket days is paid wisely. The lads are paid commission on the sale of scorecards, and considerable care is taken for their close-season welfare. The young players, when developed, are invariably willingly released to play county cricket – Bowes of Yorkshire, Goddard of Gloucester, Compton and Edrich of Middlesex are among famous modern players so trained and released. A concession to the difficult economic position of the cricketer has been made in the discretional relaxation of the twelve or twenty-four months residential qualification period formerly required for county cricket. This facilitates the transfer by 'Special registration' of a player not required by his own county from it to another county able to find him a place in its team.

But none of these considerations, nor the generosity of individual county committees to individual players, can alter the situation of the county cricket professional. He has no trade union. He can be dismissed without reason on personal grounds. He can be denied a benefit which he has morally earned but which he has no right to claim. There is no guarantee of his security should he be injured or ill for any appreciable period beyond the end of his contract. He can draw crowds running into thousands and fill the headlines of the press of an empire yet be living on less than the wages of a good artisan. His career is over before he is fifty and he must make his own provision for his subsequent years.

It is small wonder that many promising, and many fully developed cricketers of the highest powers refuse, on financial grounds, to play professional first-class cricket. And no protest, not even the sincere argument of Mr Constantine, who points out the entertainment value of the great cricketer in terms of gate-money, can change the state of some county exchequers. Many other men, clerks, scorers, groundstaff, net-bowlers, turnstile attendants, printers, pavilion attendants *and* ten other good cricketers, besides those being trained-on, must be paid to maintain one great cricketer at the crease. The poorer counties can pay, in many cases, not a farthing more than they pay now. The richer counties cannot fairly further exaggerate the difference between their players and the sometimes more accomplished players of poorer counties. The answer is, of course, a central pool of a fixed percentage of all gate receipts. Then, a number should be fixed of the permitted extent of each county's colts and capped players and a same and agreed wage paid to every player, with a bonus based upon performances and assessed on a standard basis.

I have dealt with the six-day-a-week county cricket professional specifically, because his problems are not shared by any other player. The Saturday League professional is invariably earning a living by some other work; it may be coaching or ground attendance but it is quite as often some completely different form of work so that his Saturday match and evening coaching at the club nets are merely earning him money 'on the side'. The same applies to the minor counties professionals almost without exception, and, in any case, their playing lives are appreciably longer than in the first-class competition. The factory professional is a factory employee whose post is the better and the better-paid for his cricket ability. To these men cricket is a sideline. They are not true professional cricketers.

### THE ROMANTIC PRO

Why then does the county 'pro' take up the game as a living, why does he endure it?

The answer lies at the opposite pole to the attitude which asks why in the name of heaven the county cricketer does not go into the Lancashire League and earn more in one day than he will earn in six for a county. The playing of county cricket is not a living, it is a life. The county pro's reason is purely romantic in almost every case. This would be denied by almost every one of them in speech if the question were put to him – but their behaviour every minute of the summer and for most of the winter too is proof of my argument. There are so many aspects of this romantic approach that they contend for importance, varying in their order of precedence from player to player.

The man who has known cricket well enough to excel at it has realized its complexity, its all-absorbing interest, the infinite subtlety of the contest. This very subtlety sends a man to many weeks of practice to perfect the slightest deception in the action of the bowling hand. Precision born of years of practice added to great natural gifts allows a great bowler to pitch a ball at a range of seventeen yards plumb in a heel-print or the dent made by a bat on the pitch. The speed of the fast bowler baffles even the reflex action of the practised batsman. Only great concentration maintains a batsman unwavering in face of subtle and unrelenting attack for six hours. Constant practice produces the anticipation of the fieldsman who catches the apparently uncatchable ten yards from his starting point.

All these perfections are attainable only by daily application, and that means full-time first-class cricket. And, as the greatest players have admitted, even when at their greatest, there is the unpredictable heady luck of the game. The games are to be played out before great crowds, often under the attention of four countries. The attraction of fame and popularity has often not been resisted by philosophers of repute. The man who has taken delight in matching his limbs and brain against another's may be forgiven for preferring fame to the obscurity of a steady job in an office or factory. And it would be unwise to underestimate, particularly in the case of Yorkshiremen but to some degree in men of every county, the pride of a young man at being asked to 'play for the county'.

The average county cricket professional, rarely recruited after the age of twenty-two, usually earlier, is frequently from one of the more humdrum callings – a clerk, perhaps, or a junior or apprenticed artisan. Let him sample county cricket, even for two or three matches. I first stayed at a hotel with wash-basins in its bedrooms as a member (twelfth man) of a county cricket team. The company is that of men who are enthusiasts – county cricketers rarely talk anything but shop. The cricketers are local idols; they will be invited to dinners and to dances, small boys will ask for their autographs. Wealthy and important men will talk to them with some respect for their proficiency in a sport which is a religion to a larger proportion of the population than is recognized in some circles. The professional cricketer travels the country as he might otherwise never have done. Before 1939 he did so by car (four players to a car amply maintained it). He is well-fed and waited upon by hotel servants. And, after a day's play, in an atmosphere of sun and fresh air, which the office or the factory denied him while his inclinations led him to it, he relishes his tiredness in complete relaxation and food. The old stories, funny only to those versed in the technicalities and the personalities of the game, are brought out once again for the newcomer; the rest, who have heard every one of the stories fifty times before, listen gravely, prompting or laughing precisely as well-trained actors. He is among his own kind. Give him one breath of success and he will throw away security for what must appear a modern equivalent of the tourney.

The step between being a good county cricketer and a Test-match player has been taken before now by men whom no one believed capable of it. That goal has led many a man away from financial security.

On a sane and economic level no argument can be adduced for a man becoming a county cricketer; he is valuable to the student of social history only as an example of the incurable romantic – but it is difficult indeed to deny him sympathy, perhaps even envy.

*Pilot Papers, Vol.2 No.4*, 1949

# Early Excursions

## The 1946 Indians

*May* 1982.   It must be difficult for anyone who did not experience it to appreciate the quality, the intense, romantic feeling, of the English cricket season of 1946.

Since it took place more than a generation ago those who remember it clearly now are in a minority. It was, in its way, historic; the restart of first-class cricket in England after six summers blacked out by war and the last Test series played by an 'All India' team. Partition took place in 1947, and Abdul Hafeez Kardar was to return as captain of Pakistan in 1954.

It was certainly not, by the highest standards, a great season. The two following summers, in their separate ways, were more important and the Test cricket was of a higher quality. They could not, though, quite match the euphoria of 1946 when, for so many, cricket was the symbol of the post-war return to normalcy.

For those returning to play the game at any level, to watch it – always a serious pursuit in peacetime England – to report it, seemed at first barely credible. To me, the rawest of raw commentators, this summer on tour with the Indians was joy beyond any conceivable ambition. Much of the delight in it stemmed from its very simplicity – even triviality – and the fact that its values were not constantly those of life or death.

That may – indeed, to those who never experienced it, must – seem an extravagant statement, yet there are figures to support it. The weather of that summer was grim, initially cruelly cold; for much of the rest, wet, windy and bleak.

Reg Hayter, entering into his element and covering the tour for *Wisden*, wrote: 'In anything like reasonable weather crowds every-where flocked to India's matches. A profit of £4500 in such a dreary summer told eloquently of their popularity.' Such a financial return in the time of the shilling gate, so many lost days, and when any but an Australian tour could show a loss without arousing comment, argues considerable success.

The first day of the tour at Worcester was quite savagely cold yet more than 8000 people – more even than Bradman used to draw for the opening game – turned up to watch.

The Indians' two Bank Holiday matches with Glamorgan attracted remarkable crowds, especially at Cardiff where rain halved the first and last days. On the Tuesday, John Clay, captain of Glamorgan, was at the wicket when their last man, Peter Judge, was bowled by Chandu Sarwate and, all out 149 – 227 behind – they were invited to follow on.

Clay, feeling the crowd had already been sufficiently frustrated by the late start, suggested that they should continue batting without the usual interval between innings. Vijay Merchant, acting captain of India, agreed. Sarwate picked up the ball and instantly clean bowled Peter Judge again, to share with him a – surely – unique record of a man being bowled out twice within a minute in a first-class match. The second fixture at Swansea set a record for a match in Wales with an attendance of 50,000 and gate money over £5000.

England had had no first-class play at all during the war, unlike the other Test-playing countries, who had been free from the constant air attack which made wartime life in Britain so insecure and so destructive of the enclaves of normality, even in civilian life, that any kind of serious cricket was neither practically nor psychologically possible. So the English game, in terms of playing strength, was still virtually its pre-war self, though six years older.

Familiar, too, on the Indian side was the Nawab of Pataudi, formerly of Worcestershire and England; nowadays accorded the appendage 'senior', father of the subsequent 'Noob' who also captained his country. Merchant and Mustaq Ali had opened the innings so successfully in the Old Trafford Test in 1936; C. S. Nayudu, younger brother of the great 'C.K.', Lala Amarnath and the sturdy, perky Dattu Hindlekar had all been juniors on that tour.

England were happy enough to win this first post-war rubber, of three three-day matches, by taking the first by ten wickets; the Indian last-wicket pair, Ranga Sohoni and Hindlekar, batted through the final quarter-hour to save the second, and the third was ruined by rain.

Given hard, dry wickets (as they rarely were) the Indians were a powerful batting side. Merchant, who missed only one match, showed himself a world-class batsman with 2385 runs at 74.53, an average bettered only by Wally Hammond in the season.

Hazare was almost as dogged; Mushtaq Ali, fitfully brilliant; Modi and the Nawab made useful runs. Their main strength lay in the two all-rounders, Vinoo Mankad and Amarnath.

Mankad, slow left-arm bowler, competent right-hand bat, was a tireless and combative craftsman who performed the 'double' with 1120 runs (28.00) and 129 wickets (20.76) and hung on to some good catches. He and Amarnath, immaculate, medium-pace, right-arm, and wily, formed by far the strongest bowling combination of the series.

They won eleven and lost four of their twenty-nine first-class matches; and that record could have been markedly better but for their quite prodigal waste of catching opportunities, especially off Amarnath and Shute Banerjee, close to the wicket.

Joe Hardstaff's 205 not out at Lord's made him the most successful English batsman, though Denis Compton, averaging 73, and Hammond, whose major scores were made in the county game, with 39, Washbrook (36.50) and Len Hutton (30.75) created a superior run aggregate.

The man who gave England the winning advantage, though, was the newcomer, Alec Bedser, one of the twins who had appeared, without distinction, for Surrey against the two Universities in 1939.

Now, towering, mighty-limbed, phlegmatic, apparently tireless, he stepped at once into the Test-match duty he was to discharge, with much sweat and distinction, for a decade. From a relatively short but adequate run, he bowled, in those days, almost slavish in-swing but the delivery-hammer of his huge left foot put devil in the pace of the ball from the pitch.

His was a prodigous first Test. On an initially sluggish, and never truly difficult, Trent Bridge wicket, he bowled 61 overs to take seven for 49 and four for 96. Joe Hardstaff, on his native pitch, created England's advantage in runs but Bedser gave them the margin of ten wickets.

That match set Alec Bedser's cricketing standards. As he will tell you now – and he is careful with his figures – 343 overs were bowled; 951 runs were scored; thirty wickets fell; and the game was over by lunch on the third day. That represents rates of 25.4 overs, and 70.5 runs, an hour. Small wonder that the big fellow contemplates so sardonically the progress of modern Test matches.

He sent down 51 overs (four for 41 and seven for 52) at Old Trafford;

32 (two for 60) in the mud of The Oval. His fourteen wickets at 12.41 set him commandingly at the head of the English bowling figures: Dick Pollard, with seven, was next.

In the last Test, an ebullient young former boxer from Kent, Godfrey Evans, took the place of Paul Gibb as wicket-keeper to the diversion of the crowd and the surprise of those who had not seen him before. He, Jack Ikin, Frank Smailes, Pollard and Peter Smith began their Test careers in the series; Smailes (also), Bill Bowes, Jim Langridge and Alf Gover ended theirs. Another four – Hammond, Bill Voce, Laurie Fishlock and Gibb – did not survive the following winter's series in Australia.

For that one year, though, they were there; a comfortingly familiar part of home, before the younger generation moved in to create the post-war scene.

The Indians constantly produced surprises. They lost at Worcester in the coldest weather most of them had ever endured in a cricket match. For Oxford University, Martin Donnelly showed himself a world quality left-hander; while the heavily built Hindlekar, at home both film star and wicket-keeper, caught five and stumped one.

Then to The Oval where, after Bedser and Jack Parker had reduced them to 205 for nine, Sarwate (124 not out) and Banerjee (121), coming together before either had scored, set an English last-wicket record of 249 and for the first time in cricket history, numbers ten and eleven both scored centuries. Incidentally, they had both opened the innings for strong sides in India, though they never again did so well in 1946. 'C.S.' of the prodigious leg-spin performed the hat-trick and India won by nine wickets.

The tall, slim, quiet Parsee, Modi, batted stylishly and well in the early days before constant cricket wearied him. The unruffable Merchant simply reeled off big scores. Merciless killer of the bad ball, he never tired of making runs.

Scotland were baffled by Sarwate's mixture of leg- and off-breaks – he took twelve for 72, including the hat-trick – but Hodge, the Scottish white hope fast bowler, proved no danger.

So to Lord's and a strong MCC side, which included ten amateurs. Merchant, Modi, Hazare and Hindlekar built a towering 438 on Saturday and, after weekend rain, Amarnath (seven for 83) and Mankad (ten for 77) bowled them to a win by an innings and 194 runs. That was the high peak of their tour.

Then, when Merchant and the Nawab this time made the runs

Banerjee, Amarnath, Mankad and Sarwate bowled out Lancashire for victory by eight wickets. Yorkshire avenged the north, however.

Arthur Booth, the elderly resurrected slow left-arm bowler, was wrily amused to take ten wickets, and although after Hutton had scored 183 not out, Nayudu spun out five for 27, the tourists were well beaten by an innings and 82.

Handsome all-round cricket by Dick Howorth – 114, and nine for 72, which probably won him a Test cap in the following summer – could not prevent a draw in the final match at Scarborough where there were 12,000 spectators on Saturday and 14,000 on Monday. They had a last sight of the cat-like fielding of Gul Mahomed, the lively wrist-spin of Sadu Shinde; the prodigious effort of the burly Banerjee as a pace bowler; and the neat handling of the humorous Hindlekar.

Too many of the players in that match are now dead for the scoresheet to be contemplated without sadness. Indeed, the entire tour was soon pushed into the background of English memories by the Compton–Edrich–South African season of 1947, and Bradman's 1948 Australians. For a few who lived it through, though, it is still utterly sharp in the memory.

*The Guardian*

# Compton, Edrich and Middlesex

Looking back now on the cricket season of 1947 is to recall, warmly and gratefully, an enjoyment that seemed like magic. If the cricket of 1946 had been a symbol of relief after the war, 1947 was, by a happy accident of history, vintage cricket by any standard, its quality heightened by a back-drop of remembered war.

No single ingredient made the summer. Error might lie in the attempt to analyse it – to explain in hard terms something which countless people in England that summer *felt* beyond all argument. There were so many contributions – the day-after-day sun of the late weeks; a Test series fought hard between two teams who ended the series, as they had played it, in admiration and friendship. Up and down the country in a County Championship of twists, turns and dramatic decision, old players and new demonstrated their skill and delight in the game.

The season, however, was epitomized by two cricketers; yet they would not stand so gloriously in memory if it were not for the supporting cast which both challenged, and set off, their triumphs. Denis Compton and Bill Edrich were and are two vastly different cricketers and men. Had they been too much alike they would not so have captured the imagination. They are not to be compared; rather their differences should be relished, for the contrast between them made their dual performances the more absorbing. Yet they had, simply but importantly, in common that they were both, at about thirty, old enough to be mature as players, yet with enough of youth in them to relish and reflect a pleasure in playing; for this *was* pleasure. Cricketers have become jaded through constant cricket. But those of 1947 played with the eagerness of men who had lost to war six years of the game that was their living. Compton and Edrich were, too, a partnership – for their county and country; and in the same summer they both reached the peak of their cricket. It was as if history had conspired to produce them in this perfect setting.

Denis Compton became twenty-nine years old in May 1947. At fourteen he had joined the staff of MCC; at eighteen he first played for Middlesex and scored a thousand runs in the season; at nineteen he became the youngest man to score a century for England against Australia. This was in the first Test at Trent Bridge in 1938; it was also his first match for England.

By 1947 he was an experienced cricketer, hardened by a tour of Australia in the previous winter, yet still with the keen eye which enabled him to take what, in older players, would have been impracticable liberties against good bowling. Above all, he retained the zest of a spontaneous batsman, one to whom batting came like second nature, who had an inborn ball-sense and remained so unsophisticated in approach that he still batted as if he were inventing the craft as he went along.

This boyishness, and his general attitude to life, led some to give him the facile label of a 'playboy', which did him considerable injustice. Compton would not have been a fraction of the player he was if he had not been a fighter. The finest innings he ever played were against the run of a game, after injury, or almost single-handed against the full bowling power of a more powerful side. Compton's cricket bespoke his nature: to him it was always a game – but a game at which he gave no man best.

He had a genuine human fallibility; but that, though it could be exposed, was not easy to exploit. He would set off down the wicket before the ball was bowled, in a bid to unsettle the bowler. An old hand would then bowl a high full toss – or a wide ball – or a short one which was a good length to a man three or four yards down the pitch. Then Compton would play a tennis shot, or dive back and cut, or stand firm and play a defensive stroke of impeccable rectitude – and then scuttle back to his crease with the guilty haste of a small boy caught stealing jam.

There have been greater batsmen than Denis Compton, but few of the great have played the game with such obvious joy: Victor Trumper, by definition; Jack Hobbs in his quieter, twinkling way; no others made so many runs with such unmistakable happiness.

In technique he was deficient in the straight, or near-straight, drive. But his control through the two wider arcs was such that he would tantalize a slow left-arm bowler's cover field, or the leg-side setting of an off-spinner, with a degree of control few men have ever bettered. At need he had all the strokes, and if his left foot often seemed further from the ball than the purists would approve, that gave him greater room to power his strokes, and his superb eye kept him out of such trouble as would have beset lesser cricketers who thus deviated from the text book.

Challenge brought out the best in him. Year after year he conceived it his duty to entertain the Whit Monday crowd at the Sussex match at Lord's, which was usually played for the benefit of one of his Middlesex colleagues; and he rarely failed.

By 1947 he had thickened physically. Before the war he had been comparatively slight; in subsequent years he developed a tendency to inconvenient weight. In that great summer he had come to maximum power with unimpaired mobility: powerful of shoulder and trunk, muscular in arms and legs, yet with a lazy looseness of movement and, for all his negligent air, quick and balanced on his feet.

No part of his equipment was more deceptive than his speed – particularly in readjustment. He would move out to drive through the covers; the ball would, unexpectedly, move on to him and, with a mock-desperate wrench of body and arms, he would flick it down to long leg. Or, in impish mischief, he would rock on to his back foot and, with an immensely powerful twist of the forearms – or, in even narrower space, of the wrists – drive a ball coming into his leg stump through the covers. At need he could be decorous in defence; that was never any trouble, for the germ of orthodoxy was in him, even at his most unorthodox; or, when he had abandoned the anchors, his superb natural eye and balance would retrieve the situation for him. He was an instinctively perfect timer of the ball. But the facet of his cricket which went to the heart of the average club player who watched him was his improvisation, which rectified such error as, in ordinary men, would have been fatal. It must, however, be admitted that he was an incredibly bad judge of a run. Walter Robins once said – with a grin, but more than a little justification – that anyone batting with Compton should regard his 'yes' or 'no' as no more than a basis for negotiation.

Originally a change bowler of orthodox, slow left-arm spin, he suddenly changed his method in 1947. From a shambling approach and in off-hand fashion, he bowled the 'Chinaman', not with consistent accuracy, but with sufficient spin often to turn widely, and with a googly so well hidden as to deceive some good batsmen: he took 73 wickets – 51 more than in any previous season. Moreover – and perhaps there is no greater single example of his natural cricketing ability – in the Cape Town Test of 1949, he bowled orthodox slow left-arm and in a long and accurate spell – 25 overs – took five for 70, and changed the course of the match.

For years he moved at a roll that was faster than it looked in the outfield, threw well and caught safely. As a soccer outside-left he played for England in wartime and 'Victory' internationals and won an FA Cup medal with Arsenal. He could, and did, forget almost anything: he was once late for a Test match. It has been credibly related that he once went in to bat wearing shirt, boots, socks, pads and gloves belonging to five different members of the Middlesex team. His cricket bag held a frightening jumble of unopened correspondence and assorted gear. He was probably the most popular cricketer of his day.

W.J. (Bill) Edrich was already unmistakably a cricketer of appreciable stature in 1935, but the two-year qualification period after he left his native (minor) county of Norfolk for Middlesex delayed his entry into regular first-class play until 1937. He scored over two thousand runs in that first full season; a thousand in May the following year, when he won his first England cap – against Australia. In Test cricket, however, he did not produce figures to match his ability until his 219 in the unfinished 'play-to-a-finish' Test at Durban in 1939.

After war service in the RAF – where, as a bomber pilot, he rose to the rank of Squadron-Leader and received the immediate award of the DFC for a low-level attack on a power station near Cologne – cricket might have seemed a relatively unimportant matter. It was, however, the essence of Bill Edrich that nothing he ever did was, to him, anything but *all*-important. There is in him an unfailing combative streak. Short and wiry, with wide shoulders, he was never content to be a small man. His stride was longer than seemed natural; the back-lift of his bat was unusually high; and he feared no one. He was vibrant, consumed; when he played cricket he gave it, as he gave everything else in life, a furious utmost of concentration and energy.

No man, in fact, can be successful on the top level of cricket – or any other game – if he devotes to it less than his full effort. Both Compton and Edrich played their cricket to the full. Compton looked carefree; Edrich was always, and obviously, at full bore.

His technique was quite his own. Extremely fast on his feet and well balanced, he played both forward and back with considerable facility, though his strokes had an unorthodox bottom-hand emphasis. His defence, at crisis an affair of intense, tiptoe awareness, was fiercely efficient. His most exciting attacking stroke was probably his straight drive against fast bowling – he played one such off McCormick immediately before he was out in his second innings of the Lord's Test of 1938 – a blow so thrilling as to remain indelibly in the memory.

The hook was a stroke essential to a man of his nature; it was the counter-thrust to the fast bowler, and he played it from the heart. It often cost Edrich his wicket in his early days but over the years he improved his control of it without losing his enthusiasm, or motive, for using it; and in due course, it brought him many, and deeply relished, runs. He was a tidy cutter and had a highly profitable chop through gully. His most characteristic stroke, however, was the pulled drive – often lofted – which he employed with savage effect against off-spinners, but also against fast bowlers. It seemed, somehow, to personify Bill Edrich's batting – he would leap down the wicket with that improbably long stride, bat swung far back, and go through unhesitatingly with the stroke; time after time, the ball would pass for six between the pavilion and the Clock Tower at Lord's.

Bill Edrich was pre-eminently a cricketer of guts. When his side was in a corner, especially on a bad wicket, he bristled with resistance. On a typically evil Brisbane 'sticky' in 1946, he batted with moving courage and quick-footed skill. Against Valentine and Ramadhin at Lord's in 1950, a protracted innings of only 8 cost him his England place, but earned him less than his due for the determination he showed against spin that was baffling him. At other times he took considerable risks to hit off a bowler who looked dangerous.

In a rich period, it would be difficult to rate Bill Edrich as an outstanding fast bowler. Yet it is doubtful if anyone in the English county cricket of 1947 was faster. Certainly no one had a more spectacular action. He ran up at a full and furious gallop, threw his body back so far that his cocked right hand almost brushed the ground, and then, with a furious heave, catapulted the ball down the pitch and followed through with a violence that threatened to tug him off his feet. His delivery was too low to allow him the lift and seam-movement of the pace bowlers with actions nearer the classical ideal, and his control was not always sure. But he had a little in-swing and an occasional body-action off-break; he was not frightened to put the ball up to yorker length and was always likely to surprise – and beat – good batsmen when they were well set by the extra pace of sheer enthusiasm. In any other age he would not have opened the bowling for England. He did so in 1947, at first as a convenience of selection and a bonus to his batting; subsequently because he was extremely effective. He took more wickets in the series – sixteen – than any other bowler except Wright, and eleven of them were those of batsmen in the first six places of the South African batting order. It was, in truth, a triumph of mind over method. It could not last. The excessive effort always threatened to tear his muscles apart; and in August 1947, it did so. He never bowled really fast again; but he had made his point.

His speed made him at first a brilliant outfield; later, he became a neat and certain slip-catcher. Like Compton, he was a soccer outside-left; for several seasons he was on the staff of Tottenham Hotspur, but never gained any success at first-class level.

In 1947 Edrich became an amateur and, duly, one of the few who have played for both Gentlemen and Players at Lord's. He became joint captain of Middlesex with Compton in 1951 and 1952, and sole captain from 1953 to 1957. In his forties he went back to Norfolk, still an extremely valuable player and a wise and helpful captain.

The Middlesex team of 1947 was strong: undoubtedly, but not overwhelmingly, the best in England. It was not well balanced. The batting was so strong that it could easily have proved top-heavy, while the bowling was limited. The Championship, indeed, might not have been won but for the captaincy of Robins. He played in only nineteen of the twenty-six Championship matches, but he missed none of the key games.

Walter Robins was now forty-one. As a younger man – leg-break bowler of sharp spin and well-hidden googly, aggressive batsman – he was a somewhat individualistic and highly competitive player. Now, though still an enthusiast, he had developed a wider outlook: he took a broad view of cricket in general, and he saw his task as captain as solely that of steering the side objectively towards winning matches. This may seem a truism; but many captains lose sight of this primary aim, if only through reluctance to lose. Of the five occasions when Middlesex were beaten in 1947, three were through continuing to attack a large fourth-innings objective rather than accept a 'safe' draw. Conclusively, however, of the nine matches they played at less than full strength – on occasions Young and Robertson were taken for Test matches as well as Compton and Edrich – they won seven.

A lean, wiry, active man, Robins remained alert and safe in the field; though he made no long scores, he played important innings in at least four matches and, for all his reluctance to bowl himself, he took some useful wickets. His chief importance, however, was as a captain – we might almost say a pilot, for he knew, of old, the shoals and currents – constantly anxious, by encouragement or advice, to draw the greatest possible *effect* from his players.

The opening batsmen, Jack Robertson and Sid Brown, nine times made a hundred for the first wicket and, with 310 against Notts at Lord's, set a new Middlesex record.

Jack Robertson, a neatly made, trimly turned-out, unobtrusive man, was considered in the county dressing-rooms the finest player of the new ball in England at this time. A craftsman of stylish method and neat footwork, he was quick to move on to the back foot and force the short ball while, when he went forward, his defensive play and driving were equally correct. Always keen to seize the initiative from bowlers, he scored more quickly than most opening batsmen because of his all-round power, to on and off, forward and back. For all his modest bearing, he batted, especially against fast-medium bowling, with an air of brisk mastery, and against Notts at Trent Bridge in 1947 he scored a century before lunch. He was a tidy outfield, but the action with which he bowled his slow off-breaks displeased some.

Sid Brown, a stockily built right-hand bat, was, like Edrich, Compton and Robertson, trained on the Lord's staff and, like them, came to his batting prime in 1947. He was less of a stylist than Robertson, but he was watchful, strong off the back foot, quick to move into position to cut or hook, and powerful through the whole off-side arc. Certain of the quality to follow him, he could afford to go for his strokes and often he and Robertson made the way easy for

Edrich and Compton. Brown was one of the finest outfields in the country, quick, safe and an immaculate thrower.

Robertson, Brown, Edrich and Compton between them made 12,193 runs in 1947 – 8213 for Middlesex in Championship matches. They had all the support they needed from George Mann, who captained the side in the absence of Robins; Leslie Compton, who kept wicket for most of the season but, at the side's need, opened the bowling; Alec Thompson, who played at least one match-winning innings; Alan Fairbairn, a left-hander from Haileybury; Fred Price, reserve wicket-keeper to Leslie Compton; and Harry Sharp, who was unlucky to play in only three Championship games.

Jack Young, the stocky, slow, left-arm bowler, was top of the county's bowling averages with twenty-two more Championship wickets than anyone else. He was a jaunty, optimistic cricketer of considerable competence. He first appeared for Middlesex in 1933 when he was twenty, but did not gain a regular place, or his cap, until 1946. He had a perky run-up, a low arc of flight, kept a good length, and spun the ball honestly. At need, he could bowl defensively with considerable economy, while on a turning pitch he took wickets quickly and gave away nothing. At times in 1947 he was even called upon to take the new ball, with which he bowled tidy, medium-pace swingers.

Jim Sims, although he was out of the side with injury for a period, took a hundred wickets with his leg-breaks and googlies. Wise in the game, he gave the ball a little more air than of old and, especially through his artfully concealed googly, took good wickets on batsmen's pitches. Laurie Gray was the classic willing horse: fast-medium and straight, he bowled some achingly long stints, suffered all the ill luck that was going, and was still plodding away at the end. The bowling economy was really balanced by Edrich – 67 wickets before he was injured in August – and Compton, 73. Robins, Ian Bedford,* the young leg-spinner, and, in a brief period before he split his hand, Norman Hever, helped out.

Add eager fielding – tight on the ground, at times superb in the close catching positions – and the ability of the batting to score at headlong

---

*Given his Middlesex cap at eighteen, Ian Bedford played most of his subsequent cricket for Finchley; but he returned to captain Middlesex humanly and modestly through the 1961 and 1962 seasons. He died at the wicket – batting for Finchley against Buckhurst Hill – in 1966, only thirty-six years old.

pace, and the power of the side is apparent. It may be noted, also, that they were magnificent at shove-ha'penny.

*Vintage Summer: 1947, Eyre & Spottiswoode*, 1967

# The Invaders in Baggy Caps

*June* 1981.   Post-war first-class cricket here had been launched with the Indian tour of 1946, followed by the South Africans, whose bowlers were pillaged in the high noon of the 1947 summer of Compton and Edrich. It was a delayed yet profound post-war euphoria that beguiled the cricket followers of that year.

India, even South Africa, were all very well in their way – especially when they were beaten and beaten, in the latter case at least with enough panache to stir the blood but Australia were the real opponents: theirs was always the classic year; now, too, a symbol of the return to the good life. Bradman was more than ever the prime box-office attraction, both to those who had watched him in the thirties, and, perhaps even more, to those they had bored with their stories of his performances.

Soon, though, he was to be challenged, though never outdone, by new adversary–heroes. Indeed, Australians filled all five places in *Wisden*'s Cricketers of the Year. Of Bradman's team, he and Bill Brown had been chosen before the war – no one is featured there twice. Now Lindsay Hassett, Ray Lindwall, Arthur Morris, Bill Johnston and Don Tallon were the chosen five; but the editor tacitly admitted that even that did not do full justice to such a powerful team.

To the bewilderment of many, the belligerent Sidney Barnes, an impressive second in the batting averages, the youthful Neil Harvey and, most amazingly, the flamboyantly brilliant Keith Miller, had to wait their turns. In the official citation, 'grounds other than cricket' were to prevent Barnes returning to lay his otherwise undeniable claim to that distinction.

The sanguine hopes of English supporters were gradually extinguished by the relentless progress of a side which, unbeaten on the tour, won more matches than any previous Australian team in England and set a new record with four wins in a Test series here.

If their batting put them constantly, but dishearteningly, beyond the reach of England, it still fascinated the home crowds; but it was Bradman whom they came to see. Third in average to Morris and Barnes, second in aggregate to Morris in the Tests, he was clear ahead, by 506, in total of any other Australian, and by a street top, 13 ahead in the first-class averages including home and touring players.

On grounds of health there had been doubts about his appearing after the war; on form, about his Test place; and he was rising forty, almost decrepit by Australian standards, when he made this tour, which was to prove such a triumphant progress as no cricketer ever knew before or since.

The opening match, then established at Worcester – a tradition sadly allowed to lapse – was regarded as a fixed occasion in the Bradman calendar. There on his three previous visits he had scored 236 in 1930 – his first innings in England; 206 in 1934; 258 in 1938: that daunting kind of challenge a young man sets the old.

Bleak, windy and showery weather (not only the Australians enjoyed the fire in their dressing-room) could not chill the enthusiasm of the crowds. Although it was a Wednesday–Thursday–Friday fixture, the attendance of 32,000 – 15,000 on the day Bradman batted – contributed a record for the Worcester ground.

The centre of attraction was held tantalizingly back from the first-day crowd when Worcestershire batted and Lindwall took a wicket with his second ball in England. Charles Palmer, driving wristily and easily, produced one of the best innings played against the touring team with thirteen fours and a six in his 85; Eddie Cooper and Dick Howorth helped towards Worcestershire's 233. Even on the second day, the crowd had to wait until Barnes and the left-handed Morris put on 79 for the first wicket before Bradman appeared.

Short, dapper, baggy green capped, square-shouldered, stockier than we remembered, he walked unhurriedly to the crease. Howorth – slow left-arm – bowled to him; and Bradman, surely more anxious than of old, defended with exaggerated care.

Once he went back, almost on to his stumps; the ball dropped from his dead bat and rolled slowly on.

There was a gasp round the ground as he came quickly down on it and kept it out of his stumps. A single to Morris and Bradman, with the familiar pounce, pulled Peter Jackson wide of mid-on for four. Suddenly it was just as of old: the sharp-eyed, quick-footed destroyer of bowling.

His century took him no more than two and a quarter hours; and no one on the ground doubted that the second was there for his taking when he played, for him, casually round a ball from Jackson and bustled off to the warmth of the pavilion.

Australia won by an innings and 17 runs. Morris, one of the nicest men ever to set foot on a cricket field, made 138; Bradman only 107; but there was no doubt who – for the fourth time on as many tours – seized the imagination of the Worcester crowd.

In the next match, against Leicestershire, Bradman was bowled for a mere 83 by a young seam bowler from the Lord's staff named Etherington. It was his first wicket in the first-class game and he should cherish it, for he took only two more before illness ended his county career.

Keith Miller, coming in at number three when the crowd was expecting Bradman, bowed ironically as their applause faded, and then proceeded to score an explosive 202 not out in another innings win.

England cherished hope when the touring side, without Bradman, went to Bradford, where Smailes and Wardle harried them to their narrowest escape from defeat on the entire tour. Yorkshire were beaten, by only four wickets, through the late resistance of Harvey and Tallon, the wicket-keeper.

Any suggestion of vulnerability in the batting was immediately dispelled at The Oval: Barnes 176, Bradman 146, Hassett 110; Laker one for 137, McMahon four for 210, in a total 632; won by an innings and 296. At Cambridge the reserves were given a run: Brown 200, Hamence 92; 414 for four declared; an innings and 51.

So to Southend and the most amazing carnage. Tom Pearce, the shrewd, amiable philosopher who captained Essex, was made a member of the Purchasers for being the first captain to get the Australians out in a day. They were all out, in fact, by twenty-two minutes past six. Brown 153, Bradman, who batted with tigerish ferocity, 187 (in 125 minutes), Loxton 120, Saggers 104 not out; only Miller, withdrawing his bat from a straight ball – bowled Bailey 0 – refrained from pillage; four Essex bowlers, too, were credited with centuries. The Australian 721 remains the record total for a six-hour day.

Although it was over – by an innings and 451 – in two days, the attendance and receipts were both county records.

Meanwhile, one of the most dramatic and penetrative attacks of all cricket history was limbering up in the shadow of that batting.

*The Guardian*

# The Golden Summer of Lindwall and Miller

*June* 1981.    Armchair selectors may ponder this passage:

> The labours of the cricket selection committee today should not
> be heavy, for there is an obvious nucleus – Hutton, Washbrook,
> Compton, Wright, Evans and Edrich – and the remaining players
> of the England team can be found without too much discrimina-
> tion from 20 or 30 other honest artisans now engaged in county
> cricket.
>
> The names might as well be drawn from a hat containing
> Young, Howorth, Pollard, Woodhead, Robertson, Simpson,
> Hardstaff, Fagg, Barnett, Bedser, Cranston, Fishlock, Palmer –
> the technical product will remain much the same.... But the
> nucleus is so good that no England captain could ask for much
> better.

Neville Cardus was writing before the start of the 1948 England–
Australia series: no one disagreed with him. Indeed, the English
cricket follower of 1981 can but covet such richness of talent as
included five who made cricket history; and to whom were added
during the season Jim Laker, Eric Hollies, Allan Watkins and Tom
Dollery.

Yet that side lost to Bradman's Australians by four Tests to none, a
record margin for a series in England. Many professional observers at
the time, while respecting the weight of the Australian batting, thought
it suspect against finger spin and, on the evidence early available, that
their bowling might lack the penetration on the good wickets expected
for the Tests, to put out the apparently strong English batting twice in
time to win Test matches.

Already, after the second Test, Sir Neville was writing:

> When the selection committee meet again today to choose the
> England team to play the Australians at Manchester ... they can
> argue that as the rubber is already more or less beyond our reach,
> and must be counted a dead loss, the future policy in Tests should
> encourage young blood, and begin at once to build and train our
> international cricketers of tomorrow.

Between the two Cardus judgements an historic Australian attack
emerged from the towering overhang of the Bradman-centred batting.

Not long before, the gates had been closed on the first day of their fixture with MCC at Lord's, which was their seventh innings win out of eight matches.

In the main the leg-spinner McCool, off-spinner Johnson or the left-arm stock Johnston or Toshack had taken the wickets. Then suddenly, against Nottinghamshire (six for 14) and Sussex (six for 34 and five for 25), Ray Lindwall, after nursing himself until his muscles were warm, revealed the qualities of a great fast bowler.

An eruptive five for 25 against Hampshire announced Miller ready to partner him and all at once England and their followers looked into the face of stark defeat.

Memory calls back that magnificent, indeed legendary, pair as they dawned on the English cricket of 1948. In that summer the twenty-six-year-old Lindwall, with the cool mind of a thoughtful, as well as physically talented, cricketer, nursed himself through the chills of May, avoiding the possibility of pulls or strains as he worked up steadily to his high peak of pace.

No taller than five feet eleven inches, with powerful, sloping shoulders, deep chest, wide hips and strong legs, he was most admirably built for the job. He had outgrown the excesses of youth, and was too wise to attempt to bowl too fast.

The keynotes of his bowling were variety and control. The purists thought his arm too low, but he could nevertheless, in apparent contradiction of that fact, bowl sharp in-swing as variation to the perfectly lined and pitched late out-swinger which was his deadliest weapon.

His run-up was one of smooth, sweeping acceleration to a sideways-on delivery. He bowled the ball that left the bat at extremely lively pace, had in reserve a faster one which disturbed even the best of batsmen, and a slower one so artfully concealed as often to deceive cricketers when they were well set.

Tom Graveney will ruefully confirm that he could deliver his yorker as the first ball of the morning. He had a quite startling bouncer, which he used sparingly, but which he could feint so that it brought him many a wicket of batsmen who, 'looking for it', were bowled by one of good length.

All in all, he was the complete fast bowler: a craftsman with immense application and concentration, fit enough to be a Test opening bowler at thirty-nine. There have been faster bowlers in the post-war era, but no better fast bowler.

Lindwall was a good enough batsman and fieldsman to be termed an all-rounder. Keith Miller, though, was a great all-rounder, technically as talented in all departments as any in modern times, except perhaps Garfield Sobers, and with an elan unexcelled in any period.

Strong, athletic, mobile, rapid in response, prodigal of energy, he was an outstanding athlete in any pursuit that engaged his interest. He was, too, one of the characters of cricket, adored by the young women cricket enthusiasts of two – if not three – generations.

'Nugget' seemed the epitome of Australian masculinity: hard, bold, a gambler, yet contradictorily, a serious and perceptive enthusiast for classical music. A lovable, loyal, generous – extravagant – man.

As a batsman he could be perplexed by spin bowling on a difficult pitch, but when the ball came through he was one of the mightiest drivers and most exciting cutters, a batsman capable of picking up a game and remoulding it to his purpose. It is difficult to believe that any slip fieldsman ever covered a wider area than he with his amazing speed of reaction and spectacular diving.

Though unpredictable, at his best he was a shatteringly fast bowler. Once in the first over of a Test match he came up as at full pace and suddenly dealt Len Hutton a blind length googly. Again in a Test, he dropped the ball during his run-up, bent, picked it up, continued his approach and bowled a rather faster ball than usual. Often, too, as he turned to walk to his mark, he would suddenly check, toss back his heavy mane of hair, spin round, and off no more than a three-yard approach, bowl at his fiercest speed.

While Lindwall was a swing bowler of much resource, Miller was essentially a seam bowler, possessed of high pace and, in 'green' condition, sharp movement off the pitch. He had considerable variety, not only the extravagant googly but a surprising range of speeds. He could toss in a startling round-arm slinger, a fierce body-action break-back, finger-spun off-break and, as alarmed more than one batsman, a quite lethal and perfectly disguised bouncer.

English cricket had not seen such pace in post-war years; crowds were awed by this dramatically destructive pair. Indeed, for those who watched that series, Miller and Lindwall – even more than Bradman and his massive batting – personified the Australian dominance.

So deep an impression did they make when in double harness – reducing vast crowds to breath-holding silence – that although, decisively, they took forty wickets between them at less than 21 each, it is deceptively easy to forget how little they bowled together in Tests.

In the first, at Trent Bridge, Lindwall sustained a thigh injury and did not bowl in the second innings. The pair had virtually won the match in the first, though, when with support from Bill Johnston, they reduced England to 74 for eight.

A back condition stemming from war service meant that Miller could not bowl at Lord's nor until the second innings at Old Trafford. At Headingley they stuck to a hard task and, although their six wickets were expensive, they were also crucial.

Finally and unforgettably at The Oval, they rose above the sodden, sluggish pitch and savaged the English batting to take thirteen wickets for 97 runs, putting out England for 52 and 188 for an overwhelming win, by an innings and 149 runs.

The memory must remain vivid for everyone who watched them in that epic season. The spectators at Trent Bridge, understandably, did not appreciate it – indeed they protested angrily – when Miller hurled a series of hostilely steep bouncers at Hutton. Otherwise, English crowds were compelled to admiration even in defeat.

*The Guardian*

# Bradman's Human Steamroller

*June* 1981.   The English cricket season of 1948 surely is, for all who knew it, the most deeply cherished of modern times. It was for many a return to sanity after the stresses of wartime life. That summer endures so richly, though, mainly because the cricket was of such epic quality.

It has been argued that Bradman's side of 1948 was the strongest Australia ever sent to England. Certainly the English team, of greater strength than most, was roundly beaten. The names of most of the Australians come readily to mind for those who recall that cricket.

Among the batsmen, Bradman himself, the prolific left-handed Morris, the belligerent Barnes, the dapper Hassett and the boy Harvey, were not only heavy scorers, but players of positive and memorable character. Many forget that Bill Brown, a considerable Test batsman in pre-war days, was with the side. Indeed, he scored eight centuries and averaged 57.92 on the tour but could get into the team for only two Tests.

The bowling had an even greater embarrassment of riches. Everyone remembers the mighty pairing of Miller and Lindwall. Few, though, now recall Bill Johnston; surely the most under-rated Test cricketer of the post-war period. In less than eight years of international cricket he took 160 wickets – more than all but seven other Australian bowlers, all of whom had longer Test careers than his.

In addition to being one of the most humorous and companionable of cricketers, he was a left-arm bowler of immense skill and range. Well over six feet tall, he bowled over or round the wicket, slowish spin, medium-pace stock, cut, swing and, when he liked, an extremely lively pace with impressive life off the pitch. To his great amusement he used often to dismiss well-set batsmen with a huge late in-swinger which hit the leg stump through a confident cover drive.

He was a man of jokes, none richer than his batting. His last-wicket partnership with Ernie Toshack could convulse the play on the field and in the dressing-rooms as well as spectators. As his arch joke, in 1953, quite grotesquely, he was top of the tour batting averages with an aggregate of 102 runs, because of his seventeen innings sixteen were not-outs. (Vic Cannings of Hampshire claimed that rare wicket.)

At Scarborough, at the end of the tour, he was saved by Jack Hill's match-winning six from having to face a humorously planned but menacing attempt to destroy that fantastic figure.

In 1948 he bowled more overs than any other Australian in Tests, to take twenty-seven wickets – the same number as Lindwall – at the economic figure of 23.33. Toshack, the eminently steady, slow-medium left-arm, over-the-wicket stock bowler, was the stopgap between one new ball and the next. He knew what he had to do, and did it.

On any other tour, Sam Loxton – once described as 'the poor girl's Keith Miller' – would have commanded a regular Test place as fast-medium bowler, busy batsman and safe field. In 1948, despite a 93 at Leeds, he played only two. Returning home he became an MP in the party of that arch cricket enthusiast, Sir Robert Menzies.

Ian Johnson, an off-spinner who did not turn – not even at Old Trafford in 1956 when Jim Laker took nineteen wickets – was lucky to keep his place with seven wickets at 61 in four Tests. Lucky indeed, when as good a wrist-spinner all-rounder as Colin McCool was never chosen; and Doug Ring played only once.

Its strength is clear in the 4–0 win over England in the rubber; but the margin is emphasized by the comparative runs-per-wicket figure: theirs cost England 44; they took England's for 29 apiece. Yet the Tests were never uneventful; if the win was overwhelming it was never the dull, steamroller affairs of some modern series.

The first Test, at Trent Bridge, was all but decided on the first morning when the initial break by Miller and Lindwall, supported by Johnston, cut down England to 74 for eight. Evans, Laker and Bedser hauled it up to 165 but that was a trifle by comparison with the Australian 509 (Bradman 138, Hassett 137).

Even Compton's 184 – ended when he turned on a bouncer from Miller and fell on his stumps – could not set Australia more to win than 98, which they scored for two wickets.

Compton and Miller were not merely good, but close, friends off the field and, as one of the best bowlers and batsmen of their respective sides, fierce keen rivals on it. Compton respected Miller. He did not fear his bouncer but Miller knew its value as a surprise, so he used it, as he judged, at the right moment, succeeded and tilted the match.

At Lord's, 350 and 460 for seven by Australia enabled Bradman to set England a somewhat sadistic 596 to win. Lindwall, Johnston and Toshack left them 409 short of that objective.

It was now apparent, as scoresheets cannot show, that the English batting was in psychological as well as technical distress. The fact was that English batsmen had not faced such pace since the war and, like their predecessors of 1921 before Gregory and McDonald, when Miller or Lindwall switched to top speed they were at a loss. For a time they could soldier through, but at the pinch they lacked the experience to cope with such speed sustained over after over.

So, for Old Trafford, the selectors left out one of the best two English batsmen, Len Hutton. His replacement, Emmett of Gloucestershire, was twice swept aside by Lindwall.

Compton, though, with 145 not out, and supported gamely by Yardley, Evans and Bedser as the wickets ran out, set England's sights unexpectedly high at 363. That looked better than ever when Bedser, and the game, red-headed, Lancashire fast-medium bowler, Pollard, worked their way through Australia for 221.

On Saturday Bradman threw in the only partly fit Miller with Lindwall but, after Emmett went at 1 for one, Washbrook and Edrich built the innings. England's 174 for three of Saturday night was suspended by rain which wiped out Monday and delayed Tuesday play until after lunch. Then Yardley declared, setting Australia 317 to win, but Morris and Bradman coolly saw out the day to an utterly safe draw.

Leeds was both the high point of English hope and the pit of their disappointment. By historic demand, Hutton was recalled. (He made 81, 57, 30 out of 52 – and 64 out of 188 – in his remaining four innings of the series.) He, Washbrook, Edrich and Bedser led England to 496. Australia, largely through Miller, Harvey, Loxton and Lindwall, mustered 458.

Hutton and Washbrook's second century opening stand of the match saw England on the way to 365 for eight, when Yardley declared and set Australia 404 to win in 345 minutes. It was said that he had batted into the last morning in order to use the heavy roller to break up the pitch to the advantage of his spin bowlers.

Yardley used not only Laker, with his off-breaks, but the occasional wrist spin of Compton, who took a wicket, and Hutton, who did not. Catches went down. Laker, as at Lord's, was especially unlucky, but he still had much to learn. To the anguish of listening England, Morris (182) and Bradman (173 not out) carried Australia so far clear that they had a quarter of an hour and seven wickets to spare when they won and took the rubber.

Lest there could have been any doubt of their superiority in the fourth Test, Australia took the fifth by the towering margin of an innings and 149 runs. Miller and Lindwall bustled England uncere-moniously out for 52. Hutton was last out, for 30, brilliantly caught down the leg side by Tallon off Lindwall.

With the series already decided, the story that always attaches to it is of Bradman's last Test dismissal. When Eric Hollies, the Warwickshire leg-spinner, had Barnes caught at the wicket, Bradman came in, at 117 for one and, since there was no little likelihood that he would need to bat again, this was the cue for a farewell on his last Test innings.

The Oval crowd did not stint him; and the English team stood in salute. Hollies' first ball to Bradman was, so far as could be ascertained, straight; he played it calmly, defensively. The next ball, a typically accurately pitched Hollies googly, passed through the gate of Bradman's hesitant forward push and bowled him for 0. Had he scored four runs he would have totalled 7000 runs – and averaged 100 runs an innings – in Test cricket. Hollies used to grin about it.

His feat made no difference to the result. Australia (Morris run out 196) made 389. Miller, Lindwall and Johnston put the English innings tidily into past history and a contradictorily paradoxical, one-sided but exciting rubber.

*The Guardian*

# Spectator's Notes

MAY 1949

The start of a new season is always exciting. The whole County Championship may be reorientated merely by the settling down of a side whose previous performances have been indifferent; players on the edge of the top class for years may suddenly make the vital step which puts them into a Test team; meanwhile, conversely, established teams and players may suddenly falter under the burden of age. So much may happen – and something always does.

It is never possible to think of the outcome of the County Championship without taking Yorkshire into consideration. They always maintain a uniformly high standard and are always likely to beat any side in the country. They produced an eleven of established players against New Zealand, in a game which they almost won. It is not easy to criticize a county which has come out on top against a side so strong as Hadlee's men nor, indeed, can it be said with certainty that Yorkshire will not again win the Championship. Nevertheless I cannot escape the feeling that the present Yorkshire team contains too many young players who have made virtually no advance since they first came into the eleven and that there may therefore be major team changes in Yorkshire before the season ends. Against New Zealand, Lester played a good hitting innings – he will always be a force on fast wickets. Lester should not be criticized, as some of the folk in his own county criticize him, for being precisely what he is – a strong attacking forward player. On fast true wickets he will, obviously, make a lot of runs, because he hits very hard and very straight. In defence his back-play is suspect and may betray him on damp wickets where the ball turns. On the other hand, his speed of scoring will win matches which might otherwise have been drawn.

Aspinall, who has had such a brilliant opening to his season, is a powerfully built fast-medium bowler. He is faster than Bedser and, if his control is not absolutely accurate, he often bowls a very dangerous ball which moves late and with life off the pitch. He is strong and keen and one of our few improving pace bowlers.

The tourists are going to be a popular side with spectators everywhere. This New Zealand party has come to play cricket – and enjoy it. I doubt if they will win a Test – but then I doubt if England will do so either; these are two very strong batting sides to be got out twice in three days for a headable aggregate. There was a genuine spirit of adventure about the batting of Wallace and Donnelly against Yorkshire on the morning of the third day. New Zealand were hard pressed. Their batting virtually ends at number five; three wickets down, and Wallace and Donnelly represented the last line of proved defence. Lunch was near and the time had come when the shrewder of our county batsmen put their heads down and bat for half-past one. But Wallace and Donnelly regard a half-volley as a half-volley whatever the clock says, and I felt almost guilty at my exhilaration when at 1.28 the ball was hit steeple-high into the empty outfield to bounce over the boundary. The batting is full of handsome strokes, with Scott, its sheet-anchor, catching the pervading sense of adventure to score faster than his reputation promised; Rabone looks likely to make a useful defensive batsman at number six – with more experience. He can bowl too, and his off-breaks will be useful. The bowling, I believe, will be Hadlee's main anxiety – Cowie is going to be a very tired man by August for he does not spare himself, and such is the quality of his fast-medium bowling that Hadlee will probably not be able to spare him either. Cresswell, I fancy, match in, match out, will take most wickets, and take them fairly economically. He is just too fast for batsmen to run out to him, and he cuts the ball off the spot. The fielding is sound – with three good cover-points in the side and a general keenness which promises to last the season through. Hadlee is a thoughtful skipper, considerate to his bowlers and keen in his field-placing. Everyone who watches them is going to like this side; it is a real cricketing party.

The three days allotted to the Tests with New Zealand will mean that there will be less interruption than in 1947 and 1948 with our domestic cricket. The Championship looks very open. Particularly if the season is a dry one, I fancy Lancashire will win it, but a year of damp wicket should see another Glamorgan win. Surrey, Warwickshire and Middlesex should all be near the top – the young Surrey and Warwick elevens will improve all the time. Middlesex without Whitcombe and Bedford seem to lack penetration in their bowling and Jim Sims cannot bowl at both ends nor all the time. The question of Denis Compton's bowling, how much he can be used without adverse effect on his batting, is a difficult one for George Mann to solve – it will become desperate if one of the main bowlers should become unfit. One match-winning bowler and this Middlesex side, with the batting of Edrich, Compton, Robertson and Brown, would be almost invincible.

The Lord's match with Nottingham revealed just how good the Notts bowling of Butler and Jepson is, until they become tired. Notts are woefully short of bowlers and have only, substantially, the similar bowling of Woodhead to offer as long-spell relief of the two openers. Butler is, I am convinced, the best pace bowler in England. Clumsy as his run may seem, he has an almost perfect action, which gives him great pace off the pitch. He is faster than most through the air, too, and he moves the ball late and spitefully. It is unfortunate that injuries at crucial moments in his career – before the fifth Test with the South Africans, in the West Indies and during last summer – should have robbed him of opportunities to establish himself. Jepson may yet force his way into an England side; he bowls the now relatively uncommon out-swing to a good length and at clinking pace. These two bowlers, unless young Harvey, the leg-spinner, comes off, will have to be bowled and bowled and bowled again this year until much of their attacking edge must be lost in the process. I am sure that no one was more surprised than Bill Sime, the Notts skipper, when he himself, going on to bowl after Butler's injury, took the four wickets which put Middlesex struggling. It was a keen, exciting match between two good sides, but I doubt the 'devil' in their bowling will last to August.

One of the most refreshing cricket events for years was the magnificent start made by Northants. Freddie Brown, their new skipper, should have a dually good effect. He is a fine cricketer who turns the leg-break and googly sharply, at fair pace for a bowler of that type, as a forcing bat – at his brilliant best he might turn the course of any game – and he is a capable fieldsman. Brown has a quick brain which will not miss the qualities of the men under him and, above all, he has immense gusto. The Northants players, particularly Broderick, Oldfield, Brookes, Nutter and Fiddling, are too good to be at the bottom of the table. Barron, Clarke, Timms, Garlick and Davis are all useful and one has been forced to the conclusion of recent years that only the drive was lacking to have the side winning as many games as it lost. Garlick is back into form which he barely showed last season, Nutter and Oldfield should be settling into three-day cricket and Northants' prospects must be better than for years past.

Our selectors this season will be looking keenly for three specific players – one pace bowler, a slow left-arm bowler and an all-rounder. There is no doubt that any one of these places is wide open for some young player to occupy. Of the pace bowlers, Gladwin, who improved vastly in South Africa, must be regarded as first choice at the moment, but his county-mate Jackson, Jepson of Notts, Aspinall and P.A. Whitcombe of Oxford University and Middlesex must all be considered. The position of slow left-arm bowler is at the moment held by Jack Young and it seems that, unless Broderick improves his fielding or Wardle develops greater accuracy, neither of them can take the place from him. Any one of the three Lancashire slow left-arm bowlers – Roberts, Hilton or Berry – may have to do enough to keep a place in Lancashire's side to compel their selection for England. Meanwhile there are probably no two bowlers of the type in the country better than Bailey of Hampshire and Hazell of Somerset, but both of them are too old to be considered for a side which will provide the basis of our next touring party to Australia.

There is a desperate famine of all-rounders. With the retirement of George Pope, we have no one who can make hundreds and fairly be given the role of stock bowler. It may be that Rhodes of Derby will make a stronger claim this year or that Jenkins may repeat his South African bowling and maintain his early batting form of this season. Otherwise the position is so wide open that some of our bowlers may well commence to take serious batting practice, or Allan Watkins turn successfully to his bowling – if he were just twenty-five per cent better as a bowler he would have no competition for his Test place.

*South Wales Cricketers' Magazine*


JUNE 1949

So the Test Trial is over and the English team selected, though it is difficult to see much connection between the two. Our eleven has been picked on current county-match form – which is reasonable enough in itself but, if current county form was to be the basis of selection, if the outstanding performances of the trial – Jackson's six for 37 and Jack Robertson's century – were not sufficient to win them a place in the team, why on earth play a trial match at all? Of the new Test players, Bailey has lacked little but the stark determination of the great Test players since his early appearances in wartime cricket; he bowls at fairish speed, is a useful fieldsman and has some good strokes. Wharton is an attractive bat of the type wanted in three-day cricket, a very fast outfield and he can bowl a little, right-arm, if wanted.

Mann supersedes Yardley on the strength of his vital innings and zealous captaincy in South Africa. Allan Watkins' not out 46 was not sufficient to win him a place despite his good record in South Africa, but if Wharton does not come off then Watkins must, surely, be recalled. The failure of Bailey or Mann must lead to serious consideration of Wilfred Wooller. As a captain he is one of the few cricketers now in the game fit to stand up to the Australians, one of our finest close-fieldsmen and, at his reduced pace, bowling better this season than at any time since his unfortunately few but magnificent spells for Glamorgan in 1939. At medium pace he is 'doing' more with the ball and, on damp wickets, his off-cutter may well prove deadly. Indeed, on his present form he should achieve the 'double' this season. If not quite so dangerous a bowler as Bailey, he is nevertheless a serious candidate for the post of England's all-rounder in a period demonstrably short of all-rounders – and certainly as worthy of the place as Cranston of Lancashire who played against the South Africans and the Australians.

Wooller's innings at Cardiff against the New Zealanders was a remarkable one; its speed would have been commendable in any circumstances, but on the Cardiff wicket as it was that day, it was a remarkable feat – beyond, apparently, even such accomplished batsmen as Wallace, Hadlee, Donnelly and Sutcliffe. The wicket precluded any hope of a finish, in that it made defensive batting virtually the only course; so slowly did the ball come on to the bat that any attempt at stroke-making from any ball short of half-volley length was likely to spoon the ball up. A run of such wickets at Cardiff could easily cost Glamorgan their hopes of the Championship this season. They have already been unlucky with the weather but for which they might have had twenty more points, and if the Cardiff wicket is going to produce a sequence of drawn games, Lord's and The Oval are not, and Glamorgan will suffer. Not only will they lose points, but such crowds as attended the tourists' match will not continually come to watch drawn games.

Perhaps the most encouraging feature of the Bank Holiday game was the bowling of Maurice Robinson. Formerly a leg-spinner, he banged the ball into the ground at fair pace and, despite the dead wicket, extracted enough life from it to promise some useful spells of change bowling on greener wickets. Clift, unfortunately, batted only long enough to confirm the high opinions which Bradman's Australians had formed on his promise before he too was out in attempting to force the pace. Once again Muncer showed what a good batsman he is to be going in so late – and in his partnership with Hever for the last wicket he gave its chief point to the match in the attempt to gain a first-innings lead.

The New Zealanders' previous game was against Somerset – a much improved side under the single captaincy of George Woodhouse, with Gimblett in form and Hill promising to make him a steady opening partner. This factor of stable captaincy always contributes to the happiness of a side, and the Somerset players have been much unsettled since the war by continued changes in captaincy, the team and the batting order. It seemed that those days were over until Buse, one of the most useful all-rounders in the country, was dropped from the side to play Gloucester. Gimblett is currently playing so well that he must be a candidate for the England side. He has developed a sound defence but he still hits the bad ball as hard as ever and, once he is under way, he can rip an attack to pieces. Rogers, a wartime Cambridge blue and a Highgate player, adds power to the lower half of the Somerset batting; particularly for one who holds his bat so low on the handle, he hits very powerfully and, like Gimblett, he does not stand on ceremony. Indeed, with Gimblett, Rogers, Tremlett and Wellard, Somerset's batting can be most entertaining. Wellard, moving into the late forties, bowls nowadays at slightly reduced pace but he does much with the ball, swinging late and 'seaming' dangerously. Tremlett has bowled consistently well with the old ball this season – well enough to emphasize that he should have been given more bowling in South Africa.

My first view of the new Northants side under Freddie Brown came in their game against Lancashire. Brown himself, with the third finger of his right hand rubbed raw from spinning his leg-breaks, bowled slow off-breaks most accurately and, in the circumstances, impressively. In the absense of Broderick, Ablack, playing his second county match (the other was against Glamorgan in 1946), bowled slow left-arm and had heart-rending luck in the course of some very long spells of bowling – an average club cricketer should have caught at least two of the chances given off him. R.W. Clarke, who bowls left-arm fast-medium, was by no means impressive on the rather easy-paced Peterborough wicket. He appears to need some assistance from the pitch to be dangerous. Nutter, on the other hand, was never easy to deal with; he bowls very straight and is always 'after' the batsman.

For Lancashire that very competent batsman Winston Place made a sound century, doubly valuable in the absence of Washbrook, and Wharton came to take advantage of the good start with a forcing hundred. He tends to spar at the rising ball outside the off stump but his eye is good enough for him to get away with it on a slow pitch. He hit several sixes to mid-wicket with a stroke reminiscent of Haydn Davies' short-arm pull and, above all, he missed no opportunity of scoring.

After four matches with the New Zealanders it seems reasonable to attempt some serious evaluation of Hadlee's party. They are keen, they play bright cricket and they have been amazingly popular with their county opponents. Maurice Tremlett said to me, quite without prompting, 'It's a real pleasure to field out to these chaps.' That they can win a Test is doubtful but it is certain that they have the batsmen capable of making runs very quickly to win a three-day Test. Wallace, apart from being their most prolific run-getter, is one of the most handsome off-side players I have ever seen. He hits the ball between mid-off and cover with a perfection of footwork and timing which has impressed everyone who has watched him make one of his big scores, and once set he moves easily at fifty runs an hour. Donnelly has not yet completely found the form which made him such an outstanding batsman in 1946 but he gives glimpses of it and, if he gets set in a Test match, he has such gifts as to punish the England bowling mercilessly. Hadlee, the captain, handles the game well, and as a batsman devotes himself to the needs of the particular match. Against Surrey, on a difficult wicket, he played a superb defensive innings and scored a century when the next highest score in the side was 20. He can drive powerfully when runs are wanted quickly and, as at Cardiff, will risk his wicket in an attempt to push the score along. Scott is solid and undisturbed by anything. Sutcliffe, expected to be the success of the tour, has yet to come off; he, too, is a handsome stroke-maker, but he has repeatedly got himself out through playing strokes too early in his innings. His two innings at Cardiff represented an attempt to play himself back into run-scoring, but he was a victim of the wicket each time, in playing a forcing stroke. Cowie, the veteran of the side, is doing a lot of bowling at the moment and will, I fear, be a very tired man by July. He bowls remarkably straight for a new-ball bowler and at Cardiff he got more life from the wicket than any other bowler on either side, and moved the ball dangerously off the pitch. His long bowling spells are more remarkable for the fact that he has played only about three three-day matches a year since he came to England last, in 1937. Burtt, the slow left-arm bowler, is consistent and steady, Cresswell, who bowls slow-medium cutters, has had some good spells, and Cave bowls out-swingers at fast-medium pace with a comfortable high action. These three with Cowie will probably shoulder the brunt of the Test bowling. Apart from Cowie, however, Hadlee's main hope of getting out England's best batsmen must be Hayes, not yet recovered from a muscle injury but, when fit, as fast as any bowler in England. He is erratic and relatively inexperienced, but his speed and enthusiasm are very positive qualities.

One thing is certain of the first Test – which will be over by the time you read this – the two captains have the will to finish it in three days and, as nearly as possible, the right men for a quick finish; but, as at Cardiff, the last word may be with the groundsman.

*South Wales Cricketers' Magazine*

JULY 1949

Since my last set of notes, two Tests have been drawn – as most of us expected. There is some degree of truth in the allegation that we have not bowlers of such high quality as of old, but there is more in it than that – so much more as to indicate that the bowlers are not so *very* far short of their predecessors. To be sure, Test matches in the past *were* finished in three days – even between the greatest of the cricketing giants. There are, however, factors which mitigate against a three-day finish today, factors so powerful that they are not to be swept aside, as some of the older generation would do, by an airy 'play cricket'.

Let us examine these factors, and we shall not only see the reasons for three-day Tests being drawn but we shall also come to appreciate our contemporary players nearer to their deserts. The first factor is the vastly improved technique of defensive play – a technique enforced by the development of the late swing. The pace ball which moves in the air late in its flight places back-play at a premium and makes it virtually certain that the player who throws his bat at the ball outside the off stump in the old manner will be out very cheaply. Indeed, the only modern attacking batsman to make consistently good scores by the attacking method is Frank Woolley – it would be stupid to say that Woolley could not play the new ball, but it is significant that he usually went in at number four where he was not likely to find the ball absolutely new nor the pace bowlers absolutely fresh while he was getting his eye in. The attacking batsmen who went in first, Denis Smith, Charlie Barnett and Harold Gimblett, had steep ups and downs when they attacked early, and they were all capable of leaving the off-ball alone – as indeed the opening batsman *must* do today. This technique is the batsman's defence against early dismissal. On the other hand, the bowler employs it in reverse; that is to say, he bowls in such a manner as to enforce the defensive technique. Now, it might appear from this argument that I am attempting to argue in favour of modern batsmen scoring more slowly than their predecessors. In fact, scoring is as fast now as of old. Turn up the records of the Test matches of the Golden Age of cricket – the day of Trumper, Clem Hill, Ranji, C.B. Fry, F.S. Jackson, Abel, Hayward, even Jessop – and you will find that the rate of scoring in runs per over has barely changed. If anything, scoring at times nowadays touches higher rates than of old – sides going for a win in the fourth innings are topping 120 runs an hour in a way that was most rare fifty years ago.

Again, and arguing to the end of the unfinished three-day Test, wickets nowadays are vastly more *dead* than they were. Certainly wickets at the turn of the century were uniformly *true* but they did not deprive the bowler of all pace from the wicket. The modern bowler, deprived of assistance from the pitch and given, in place, assistance from the seam of the renewed ball, has employed swing instead of spin from the pitch – and the circle is complete. The pitch, then, compels defensive bowling, and the modern batsman has an extensive defensive batting technique and can defend his wicket over a long period when things are going badly for his side. Yet, given wickets with more life, a Test *can* be finished in three days, but if our wickets are to be prepared to last for five days and to prolong a Test against Australia for those five days so as to earn the maximum gate money, then the groundsman cannot in a year change the character of his wicket to give a three-day wicket. Our only hope of a finish to any match in this series appears to be rain – in other words an accidental livening of the wicket.

The whole question of wickets today is a vexed one. At Trent Bridge now the groundsman is the man who formerly produced those perfect turf slabs for Sir Julian Cahn. At Trent Bridge the current plumb wicket is most to be experienced at its deadest. Given fine weather, the only hope of any life in the wicket is at the very start of the match when the water used in preparation may make it a little 'green'. That, I should say at long range, was the reason why Wilfred Wooller put Notts in at Trent Bridge. The wicket, he might reasonably expect, would go on getting easier; if he could take two or three early wickets cheaply he had an outside chance of forcing a win, if he did not he knew what total he had to head.

Something of the same conditions existed at Lord's for the second Test – it was 'a good wicket to lose the toss on'. The wicket never again gave the assistance to the bowlers that it gave to Cowie in particular on the first morning. Cowie used it so well that England were always fighting back, even to the first hundred runs of their second innings. That innings was a difficult experience for two batsmen, Jack Robertson and Allan Watkins, both of whom came in as replacements for injured players. If either failed, he might easily be written off. The state of the game was such that a draw was inevitable, so no pace of scoring was dictated, as it usually is, by the shape of the match. So each had to work out his own salvation, and each did so very capably – but to what extent will the selectors say that each made his runs easily because 'it did not matter'? Nevertheless, in the continued absence of Washbrook, each may well get a further opportunity – Robertson virtually certainly, and Watkins, because of his fielding, a likely choice in the absence of any left-hander of clearly higher standard.

In current selection the choice of Wilfred Wooller for the Gents against the Players reminds that he is likely to be the first amateur since the war to complete the 'double' of a hundred wickets and a thousand runs. Had there been an overseas tour this winter he must have been a certainty for it.

The cricket of the last few weeks leaves me with the impression that England may have a shock from a return to form of the two New Zealanders Sutcliffe and Wallace, two magnificent punishing stroke-players who may easily enforce changes among our bowlers. Already Bailey and Gladwin by their bowling at Lord's have reduced the certainty of their further selection, and Jackson of Derby and, if he is fit, Ridgway of Kent must be considered. It might even be worth the selectors' while to 'blood' such a promising young all-rounder as Close of Yorkshire or, especially if wickets continue hard, Tom Graveney of Gloucester, a batsman whose class is unmistakable. These young players are a reassuring sign of renewed health in English cricket, and so are the young opening batsmen who promise, if not to make Test class, at least to provide the backbone of their counties' batting – men like Smith of Sussex, Hill of Somerset, Martin Young of Gloucester and Phil Clift. Perhaps my 'discovery' of the month is young Arthur Milton of Gloucester, who bears the stamp of a natural ball-games player – he is already on the Arsenal's books as a footballer – he can use the new ball neatly, can field outstandingly anywhere and looks a class batsman already. Eve of Essex, whom I have also seen for the first time, is another good young county player. He not only makes runs but probably saves as many as any other outfieldsman in the country. Essex, however, are delaying, because of his injury, the reappearance of Ken Preston, their fast bowler – but it will not have escaped notice that he has bowled in deadly fashion for their second eleven. Here, with Trueman of Yorkshire, is one of our major fast-bowling 'hopes', no more than a hope yet, but a hope which will die hard.

*South Wales Cricketers' Magazine*

AUGUST 1949

The third Test, as I suggested in my last notes would be the case, has gone the inevitable way of any match limited to three days between an England side temporarily weak in bowling, and a strong New Zealand batting side on a plumb wicket. Once again, at Old Trafford, early greenness in the wicket gave the seam bowlers a chance on the first morning while, on the third day, there was some degree of dust which made it just possible that the leg-spinners would break through to give England a narrow win. Hollies, Compton and Brown himself exploited unnatural spin to the limit of their considerable gifts, but Donnelly, fortunate to escape being stumped when he had made only 8, extinguished any hopes Brown may have had of forcing victory.

In fact, England had neglected the opportunity afforded by Monday's plumb wicket. Hutton and Washbrook scored too slowly. That Edrich was little faster is understandable, since his loss of form this season had put his Test-match place in jeopardy. It is, however, extremely difficult to excuse Washbrook and Hutton their slowness on any grounds whatever. Each has a particularly impressive record of scoring runs against the clock in a fourth innings on wickets less friendly than that at Old Trafford and against bowling more powerful than the limited attack at Hadley's command. They played perfect batting strokes, always the right stroke to the right ball, never lifting a thing off the ground. In a five-day Test it would have been superb. In a three-day Test it murdered all hope of a finish. Even a belated burst of hitting by Simpson could not save England from having to bat for an hour which they could not spare on the third day.

There are now three opening batsmen in England capable of striking the early blow necessary if we are to win at The Oval. They are Gimblett of Somerset, Clift of Glamorgan and, recently promoted in the order, Graveney of Gloucester. Gimblett is clearly and unmistakably the best of the three. With Charlie Barnett gone from the first-class game and the powers of Denis Smith on the wane, only Gimblett can pulverize an attack at the start of a match, wresting initiative from the bowlers. Unfortunately there is a legend current in the higher circles of cricket to the effect that Gimblett cannot field. In fact, he is a safe catcher and has a throw low in trajectory, accurate in aim and immensely powerful. It may be argued that he is no Mercury on his feet, but the same could be said of both Robertson and Hutton.

Leslie Jackson of Derby showed himself in the Test to be a bowler considerably below the standard of Maurice Tate but reminiscent of the Sussex man in his ability to extract pace from the wicket.

Sutcliffe's century merely placed a statistical seal on something which no one who had seen him play an innings even of twenty could ever have doubted – that he is a very great batsman. On this occasion, because New Zealand's fortunes demanded it, he played, for him, a subdued innings – but even then he was a third as fast again as Hutton. Sutcliffe takes little account of centuries or averages. Cricket is, above all, a game for him. His delight is in stroke-play, and that stroke-play may disconcert the finest bowling in the world. Sutcliffe *in form* would have to be given a place in a World eleven today. Sutcliffe out of form is sad material for any critic with a feeling for the graces of batsmanship.

Possibly the most interesting development of this season's cricket is the new lease of life taken by the game in Yorkshire. It has been said that the great periods of English cricket have always coincided with the periods of Yorkshire supremacy; that England are strong only when Yorkshire are strong. Yorkshire started this season with an eleven which virtually selected itself on a basis of caps already awarded. Some of the older heads in Yorkshire inclined to the view that they had been too easily gained, and that the Yorkshire cap was something for which a man should have to fight. That opening eleven were: Hutton, Halliday, Wilson, Yardley, Watson, Leicester, Coxon, Aspinall, Wardle, Brennan and Robertson – with Smithson also pressing for inclusion. Of the county's most promising reserves, Walker had gone to Hampshire, Jakeman to Northants, and then Barrick went also to Northants. Yet already seven players – Keighley, Lowson, Close, Mason, Trueman, Whitehead and Firth, a wicket-keeper – are worth their places in the side. Close, in the third Test, proved himself a cricketer in manner and a player of gifts. He went out nobly, hitting when England needed runs. He bowled steadily, fielded well and was unfortunate not to hold a catch which he did well to turn into a chance at all. He has not yet been awarded his Yorkshire cap. It seems certain that by next season Mason, Close, Lowson and Trueman must be regular players for Yorkshire, and this will mean that at least three men who have been near to post-war Test selection will find themselves in the second eleven.

In terms of cricketing probability, this new Yorkshire side *must*, within two or three seasons, win the Championship as clearly as any of their great sides of the past. Then, I fancy, we shall see the adage proved true: with a strong Yorkshire county side there will be a strong England side. Close, Lowson, Mason and Trueman of that county should, if they develop as may reasonably be expected, be near to regular Test places, and young players to be seen in other counties – Berry of Lancashire, Graveney and Milton of Gloucester, Preston of Essex, Spooner of Warwickshire, Stephenson of Somerset, Gilbert Parkhouse, May of Combined Services – all have the stamp of the great player. This stamp is not to be mistaken; external factors may condition performances but they can never deny cricketing qualities.

The coming winter will provide a much-needed rest for players like Alec Bedser, Gladwin, Jenkins, Hutton, Washbrook and Wright who are essential to English Test cricket. Thus they should be fresh for the series against the West Indies – who might beat us on a series of hard dry wickets, but look to be ill-equipped to face a damp English summer of slow-turning wickets. No doubt many of our younger players will be 'blooded' against them – Eric Bedser on current form could easily become the second twin not only in the Surrey side, but in an England side too. He has long lacked his brother's confidence but is now scoring runs with remarkable regularity and soundness, and his bowling is little, if any, behind that of Laker. The Bedser twins may easily yet answer our need for all-rounders of Test class.

The great achievement of the season of 1949 lies not in the tense struggle it has provided for the County Championship, but in the promise it holds out for the future of English cricket.

*South Wales Cricketers' Magazine*

SEPTEMBER 1949

The season of 1949 goes down into history only because that is what happens to all cricket seasons. It will fill a volume of *Wisden* but an issue that will never be much sought after, for there has been little in the season which stirs the memory.

1949, I suppose, will be recalled, if at all, as the season when the older generation made its last show and the new generation first appeared. John Langridge, most faithful of cricketers, had a personal triumph and so had Les Berry of Leicester, while Tom Goddard and Emrys Davies denied their age so often that their counties must surely have paused in their anxious search for the successors to those two to wonder if they would ever need successors. The new generation has been recognized in the Championship scoresheets, but those close to every county have seen more young players not yet ready for the three-day game but whose promise is well-nigh unmistakable. We have had our three years of training the younger men and, as always, they have shown themselves full of the essence of the game.

Again Yorkshire have won the Championship. I had hoped that they would fail this year, that one of the lesser counties – Worcester, perhaps – might win it, for, make no mistake about it, Yorkshire are going to be champions now for many years to come until Surrey and/or Lancashire reach peak and dethrone them. The Yorkshire cricketing system is a complex one; it took time to be re-geared after war, but now it is working with something approaching the old flawless smoothness.

Glamorgan have not had a good year. At the start of the season they must justifiably have felt that the weather served them ill and robbed them of many points, while later, the injury to Willie Jones was one the batting could ill bear. Wilfred Wooller, who looked so certain to complete the 'double', failed to make his thousand runs – doubly disappointing because his batting was sorely needed after Willie's injury. The side sadly missed the tonic of John Clay's bowling, which clinched the issue in 1948 and, well as Len Muncer bowled, he lacked the support with the old ball which a county must provide if it is to win the Championship. Again the injury to Willie Jones played a part, for his slow left-arm bowling was just beginning to become effective when he finished for the season. Against this must be set the considerable improvement in the bowling of Allan Watkins who, throughout the season, was steadily 'doing' more and more with the ball. He is still liable to have his bad spell and to try to bowl a little faster, which rarely effects an improvement, but he is a bowler of increasing value. In an effort to cover the deficiencies of the attack Wooller was forced to bowl too much, with resultant effect on his batting. He, too, bowled at slightly slower pace and 'did' more with the ball, but there was too little relief for him against the stronger batting sides. To help Hever with the new ball and Muncer with the old one is too much work for any bowler

– yet he had no alternative except when Stan Trick could play, and even he was not so successful as in 1948.

My greatest disappointment of the season was the Glamorgan fielding. It could still be magnificent at times but it did not consistently produce the miraculous as it did to win the Championship. On some days it seemed to fall to the level of the ordinary – but such days were few, for Wilfred Wooller was always a magnificent inspiration, Phil Clift appeared to love every minute in the field and Gilbert Parkhouse was infallibly game. For the future, Glamorgan must have fewer qualms than ever before. The young bowlers in the second eleven seem to guarantee many years of steady and mature bowling. Would that the side promised a sheet-anchor batsman, so that Muncer, Wooller and even Hever might be left free of batting responsibilities to concentrate upon their bowling. Young Peter Davies, with all his promise, is hardly likely to be regularly available and it is a regular batsman that the side needs. It may, however, yet and well be that Gilbert Parkhouse, Phil Clift and Maurice Robinson will develop the extra degree of consistency their side needs.

Our national cricket, too, has lacked excitement. Our failure to force a win against New Zealand is a four-sided condemnation, of wickets which emasculate good bowling, deficiency of flight in our slow bowlers, the disinclination of our leading batsmen to force the pace to match-winning rate, and the allocation of only three days to each Test. The last, however, is the least of the complaints of the reasonable critic. It was a safeguard to the finances of the New Zealand Cricket Board which gave the side three-day Tests rather than four-day which would have meant the sacrifice of four county-match games.

On the credit side we have little to show. The technical skill of Washbrook and Hutton, the reliability in defence of Bill Edrich and the virtuosity of Denis Compton we knew before, and this season certainly saw no increase of those powers – rather a diminution. Trevor Bailey is an exceptionally fine county fast bowler and dangerous against batsmen of any class when the wicket is lively. I doubt his ability and stamina, however, to take many wickets against the best Australian batsmen in the rarified atmosphere of Australia where the ball swings little, the pitches are never green and the heat sees a man mighty tired by the end of the day. Close looks a good cricketer in the making, possibly one of the great all-rounders five years hence, but he goes now to his National Service and out of Test reckoning, presumably, until 1951. Bedser and Hollies we knew to be steady bowlers, Evans a fine wicket-keeper. We have not, in the past season, found another player who is yet of the calibre of those players. We lack a slow left-arm bowler, a left-hand bat of the quality of Emrys Davies ten years ago, and we lack a genuine all-rounder. It may well be that the end of 1950 season will see Len Muncer a sound on-form selection for the Australian tour. Few of our best youngsters will be quite ready by then – Berry, possibly, or Lowson or Tom Graveney, but only possibly. It may be, however, that Jack Ikin, who was generally considered somewhat lucky to make the last trip, will play himself on merit on the tour next time.

The prospects for next season are that it will show a marked change from the one just ended. Worcester, with a largely veteran side, must surely begin to show signs of a decline. Far too great a burden of bowling has been thrust upon Perks and they have no young bowlers coming along. On the other hand, sides like Hampshire, Northants and Warwickshire have young players who were improving with every game last season. Lancashire, too, have so much talent that they should not long remain in the 'doghouse'.

Surely the time has come for the MCC to take some positive step towards the preparation of fairer wickets for the first-class game. The exceptionally dry summer of 1949 emphasized the general plumbness of county pitches as would not have been the case in a rainier year. Yet who can maintain that the Trent Bridge batsmen – Keeton, Simpson, Poole, Hardstaff, Harris – were quite so good as their figures suggest?

I think we shall see in South Africa this winter a grim proof that a country which produces batsmen's wickets and holds back its young players must crash headlong in the Test arena. I fancy that the veteran South African batsmen will be mown down by the Australian pace bowling and that their bowling may be altogether too lacking in penetration to get out Messrs Morris, Harvey, Hassett and Loxton without assistance from the pitch. Athol Rowan, the off-spinner, seems their best bowler but he needs a little assistance from the pitch and good short-leg fieldsmen if he is to take many of those hard-fought wickets.

Enthusiastic home team selectors may like to toy with the selection of a team of players not picked for England this year to match against the England side. My own eleven would be: H. Gimblett (Somerset), M.M. Walford (Somerset), J.T. Ikin (Lancashire), C.H. Palmer (Worcestershire), H.E. Dollery (Warwickshire), R.O. Jenkins (Worcestershire), W. Wooller (Glamorgan), L.B. Muncer (Glamorgan),

R. Howorth (Worcestershire), A.J. McIntyre (Surrey), D. Shackleton (Hampshire). The bowlers would be Shackleton, Wooller, Howorth, Muncer, Jenkins and Palmer. McIntyre, of course, is the wicket-keeper. The batting lacks real body but it might well produce fast runs right down to number eleven – the *all-round* strength of the batting is not to be ignored, and none of these players would be out of place in a current England XI.

A quiet, unexceptional season, 1949. It will be remembered for its promise rather than for its achievement, I fancy, in that it saw the birth of a great Yorkshire side and the young men who will make a strong England XI in four or five years' time.

*South Wales Cricketers' Magazine*


APRIL 1950

The cricket season of 1950 has already had a disturbing overture in the matter of the resignations of Hugh Bartlett and 'Billy' (S.C.) Griffith from the captaincy and secretaryship, respectively, of the Sussex County Cricket Club. As I write, the matter is still unresolved following the resignation of the President. No one at range and without full information can criticize what has happened – that would be quite unfair to the two sides which apparently exist in the matter. On the other hand, it must be said that it is difficult to think of any two men in one county who are better liked throughout the cricketing world than Messrs Griffith and Bartlett. Together at Dulwich School, at Cambridge (where each won a cricket blue), in the Airborne Division at Arnhem and elsewhere where they served with distinction, and in Sussex cricket, they have been two good companions and good cricketers.

Griffith must have been very close to more Test honours than he has achieved as a wicket-keeper, and no follower of the first-class game will ever forget the century with which he heartened us when, going in first in a Test in the West Indies in 1948, he scored the first hundred of his career. It came, memorably, at a time when most of us were disheartened at Allen's team's lack of success against this season's visitors on their home pitches.

Hugh Bartlett will always be remembered for one of the greatest innings ever played in the long and bright history of the Gentlemen v Players matches. In 1938 he scored a mighty century at Lord's which caused many good judges to compare him favourably with

A.P.F. Chapman, and if he has, since his war service, tended to suppress the free style of that great hundred, he has done so largely in the interests of his side. It is disturbing, in this connection, to recall that so great a cricketer as Maurice Tate left Sussex under such circumstances the he does not now return to his county's grounds. Whatever the rights of the present situation or any other, few with cricket at heart would dispute that cricketers, particularly those who have served county and the game well, are of real importance.

Yesterday our West Indies visitors arrived – a day early – and it may be that they will take us by surprise more than once again before their tour is ended. No good critic, I fancy, would be unduly surprised if this side of John Goddard's – given a summer of hot sun and fast wickets – were to beat us in the Tests. Moreover, if they do do so, it will be for the good of cricket in general. Never, surely, has any country played the game with greater gusto than that which has given us Learie Constantine, George Headley and now, in true succession to them, Everton Weekes and Frank Worrell. For too long Test cricket has been lopsided, with England and Australia too easily beating the other countries. If the West Indies are drawing up to our standard then it is merely a promise, and a heartening one, that India, South Africa and New Zealand will not long remain behind, so that Test cricket will indeed be worthy of its name and no longer an opportunity for the players of the two major countries to score runs and take wickets of purely statistical value.

In a damp summer, one doubts the powers of the West Indies to produce 'natural' spin-bowlers – right-arm off-breakers and left-arm break-away bowlers – or to cope with ours, and then we may win. On fast pitches, however, it is difficult to see that we have a full answer to the magnificent batsmanship of five members of their side and their battery of pace bowlers. One more important factor which may give them appreciably greater success than previous sides is their greater application and increased temperamental soundness, which should enable them to fight back more effectively than their predecessors.

The season of 1950 gives us our last chance to prepare an eleven to meet Australia over there next winter. We need a fast bowler, an all-rounder and a captain. If the last two positions could be filled by the same man, then the selectors would indeed be happy. Therefore we shall watch with great interest the progress of Freddie Brown of Northants and Wilfred Wooller, as well as Norman Yardley. Last season was, for Brown, a year of settling down again to the three-day game from which he had been overlong absent. This year may show us a return to the form of which he was capable in the thirties when he was a Test player in his own right. Again, Wilfred Wooller with his superb fielding, useful bowling and batting in whichever manner best fits the game, must be seriously considered. If he were a little better as a batsman one suspects that he might well lead the side. Norman Yardley is still a sound bet for the captaincy because, particularly on Australian wickets, he is a very useful batsman and his bowling, if not regarded with universal admiration, has nevertheless taken some good Australian wickets at vital times. Brown is probably the best player of the three, Wooller the man most likely to get at the Australians by playing the game harder than usual, and Yardley the most experienced.

For all that, there are many players who would support the captaincy of Tom Dollery of Warwickshire, who is a better batsman than his Test figures suggest and who may be said to be the best captain in England today after the veteran Walter Robins.

And we want a fast bowler. How much we want a fast bowler. Ken Preston of Essex has an opportunity of Test honours rarely before available to a young English player of such small performance. If he can work up to real pace and last the distance he might easily make the trip in September – but, after a first full season of six-day-a-week play, his stamina would have to be great to be relied upon for a full tour. Shackleton of Hampshire, who can also bat and field, is another who stands a chance. Our batting, reinforced by Simpson, ought not to give great anxiety. Watkins will have to fight Jack Ikin of Lancashire for the post of left-hander in the side, but an all-round improvement on a basis of his present fitness is not beyond hope.

Yorkshire, I feel, should again win the County Championship and we have yet to see the best of such players as Lowson, Trueman, Whitehead, Smithson and Lester; if Aspinall is really fit to start the new season then their side should have no difficulty in beating any other in the country.

We are just beginning to reap the harvest of seeds sown at the end of war, and if the English cricketer takes longer to develop than his Australian counterpart, by the same token he lasts longer, and in our younger players now establishing themselves we have the backbone of the county game for some twenty years to come. The shape of that game may easily dictate a lack of leg-spin and fast bowlers – the two types likely to be most effective on perfect wickets – and, if this is so, we must either change the style of our game or stop our groundsmen from producing wickets for batsmen. Today the young off-spin bowler is liable to be put on to bowl on a pitch where the honestly finger-spun ball does not deviate a fraction from the straight. With a new ball, however, the swing-bowler can always 'do' something and the in-swinger, with his battery of short-leg fieldsmen, can always keep down the runs and profit from batsmen's tiredness or error. Thus, those who blame captains and bowlers for the prevailing cult of the in-swinger are in fact blaming the wrong people. If there is a major flaw in English cricket today it lies less in the players than in the wickets on which they play – and that is a flaw which can easily be rectified by county committees.

This can be a great cricket season: there are good cricketers – in every sense of the word – ready for the May wickets, and, if we are tempted to care, we should be very sure first of all that the fault does not lie in us.

*South Wales Cricketers' Magazine*

### MAY 1950

At last we know a little – very little, not half so much as we are tempted to feel we know – about this season's cricket. Snow blurred the outlines of the West Indies' opening canter and slow wickets, pulled muscles and lack of early practice were sufficient for us to assume that some good reputations might be made, but no bad ones allowed to weigh, in these conditions.

Looking to our domestic affairs, with most of our first-team places filled, there are still vacancies for some six or seven young cricketers to travel to Australia – only next September, but that is a lot of cricket away. Young cricketers, I have said before, do not come with a rush, so the men we are looking for are those who have gained experience in the past two seasons or so and whose technique is sound so that they may, this year, fuse the two to produce cricket better than that of their neighbours. At once the two young Cambridge cricketers, D.S. Sheppard and P.H.B. May, moved into their strides, and they and the more experienced old blue Doggart must be possibles for selection. But in these days, the amateur cricketer who can afford to leave his university career to play cricket, even on such a level as that of a Test tour in Australia, is a rare bird. So, unless we have some surprising statement that all or any of these youngsters can make such a sacrifice, we shall be wise to see them as maturing for future years rather than consider them as in the running now.

I thought Gilbert Parkhouse, in the course of his innings at The Oval, looked a very good batsman indeed. He coped with the fastish bowling of Alec Bedser and Stuart Surridge, the off-breaks of Laker and Eric Bedser and the left-arm slows of Lock with utter competence on a wicket which, if it was not difficult, was not perfect for the batsman, and he showed strokes all round the wicket. In other words, he did all that one could hope – and pushed the score along to boot. It is this three-year-experience group that may show the real dividends, and Roley Jenkins and Charles Palmer, now captaining Leicestershire for his first full season of county play, leap to mind as men likely to press their claims.

So Jimmy Langridge becomes, with Tom Dollery, the second of our professional captains. Ripe in experience, tranquil in temperament, rich in skill, Jim knows the game well. It is, indeed, going to be difficult for the selectors to decide – if they ever face the problem – just how much one of these highly skilled skippers would mean to an England side. Not only does Tom Dollery know the job, but he was extremely well liked throughout the counties last year.

In this connection, it does not seem to be particularly well known that, until well into the second half of the last century, many of the most successful teams had professional captains. Thus, in the great days of the Kent XI of the 1840s, Wenman, the wicket-keeper, who was a professional, led the side, although it contained such outstanding amateur players as 'Felix' and Alfred Mynn. Following directly upon the heels of Kent came Notts, who had their great years in the 1850–70 period and who were well led by William Clarke and George Parr – professionals again and among the best players of their day, but whose play appeared unaffected by the responsibility and who were real disciplinarians. Then, among his keenest rivals, W.G. in his heyday was opposed by such Yorkshire professional captains as Allen Hill and George Emmett.

It was a sad day when I was the only person at the Tilbury quayside to see Harold Larwood off to Australia on the *Orontes*. With wife and five daughters and a son-in-law-to-be, he was sailing to begin a new life. What a contrast the family's quiet sitting in deck chairs on the boat-deck made to the full parade of seeing away a Test team, which happened to Larwood twice from the same quayside. Harold was quiet; but then he always was. If he had any bitternesses, they were well concealed; he spoke quietly of his prospects – he would try anything and wasn't afraid. Perhaps the most amazing thing about the whole story is the fact that Jack Fingleton – who was put out for a 'pair of spectacles' in a Test by Larwood, almost unheard of for an opening bat – should be the man who is undertaking to fix accommodation for his former rival's family. Looking at him nearly twenty years after his great days, it was as puzzling as ever to decide whence came the strength to power that terrific bowling. It was a short, slight, quiet, bespectacled, greying man who answered in a quiet voice to the old nickname 'Lol'. What a great fast bowler he was, and how long we shall talk of him. Already legend hangs thick about his name, and we have not his like in our cricket today.

So Denis Compton adds a Cup winner's medal to his other trophies, and thus goes ahead of Patsy Hendren whose career was so much like his. Each was a boy on the Lord's groundstaff who had established himself before the war – that of 1914 for Hendren, of 1939 for Compton. Each lost his best footballing years to war but each played, in wartime or victory internationals, at outside-left for England without qualifying for a full international cap. Each won a County Championship with Middlesex, and each played cricket for England. It is probable that Denis is the greater cricketer, but there was little to choose between them as wingers. Each, too, played under the Corinthian soccer winger R.W.V. Robins for Middlesex.

The West Indians were among my fellow spectators at the Cup Final. They have some capable footballers with them and they seem to have spent the afternoon in a blend of excitement at the game itself and amazement at the combination of speed and skill in the players. This party is a good one, make no mistake of that. Hines Johnson already looks a bowler of immense accuracy for his pace and he is a craftsman of infinite resource who does enough 'off the seam' to keep any batsman playing. Whether 'Sonny' Ramadhin yet knows exactly what he is going to 'do' with the ball is uncertain, but if he doesn't, the batsman won't, and he is halfway to success. Early days yet for the West Indians, but there is a greater temperamental solidity to this team than to their predecessors, and that must count for much.

The sun is shining repentantly over my shoulder as I write; my bag is packed for cricket and the old bug is biting. So my cricket travels begin again – enjoyed by me sufficiently to justify the envy of my friends.

*The Cricketers' Magazine*

JUNE 1950

I write with the season already taking shape, the first Test over, twelve men selected for the England XI in the second Test and the weather threatening to settle after a bout of strong sunshine which temporarily shocked the summer into a bout of thunder.

Ah, that first Test. The wicket was, perhaps, livelier than the powers at Old Trafford had originally intended, but that was obviously due to immense sun without rain – so unusual in Lancashire – which had preceded the game. Now, unfortunately, there seems to be such a scare caused by a Test wicket on which only one batsman made a century that I fear we shall see only marl-tamed monstrosities for the remainder of the series. But, at least, we have seen *one* Test wicket deliberately produced to give the bowlers a chance. And, note and remember, on that wicket which has been deplored, Hutton made over sixty runs after his right hand was so injured as to be almost useless, Edrich played an innings of seventy, Weekes made a fifty and Stollmeyer a superb, almost majestic 78; Bailey, who demonstrated the virtue of a straight defensive bat, scored over a hundred runs without the bowlers ever dismissing him, and Evans made a century. It was a wicket where the batsmen had to battle, but we saw the batsmen of basically sound technique make their mark – and win the game. On plumb wickets the West Indies are a massive batting power, but on a 'turner', all but Rae, Stollmeyer and to a lesser degree Gomez, are at least suspect – they have not the ability (and perhaps it is a virtue) to play their cricket grimly enough – yet.

There is, I fancy, little surprise and much general pleasure at the inclusion of Gilbert Parkhouse in the twelve for the second Test. While, obviously, the doubt as to Compton's future fitness is a major cricketing anxiety, his absence throughout this early part of the season is not an unmixed disappointment. Instead of the new batsmen – Simpson, Doggart, Dollery, Parkhouse – growing up in his shadow, they are being subjected to the sterner test of working out their own salvation – difficult, indeed, but if they come off, conclusive. It seems by no means certain that Parkhouse will play in the Test if Hutton is fit, but his selection must indicate that he has a good chance of making the Australian trip which is apt to make the player. His country-mate McConnon is, obviously, a beginner in big cricket as yet, but already Glamorgan's opponents are talking of him as a young player with the gifts to go far if he continues to learn and to try and, above all, to develop along the lines he has so far followed.

Many young players have already appeared this season who promise to become at least county main-stays – one of the most reassuring signs about our cricket, for far too many counties have been 'carrying' inferior players since the war. Young of Gloucester is at last beginning to redeem his promise of 1946, Gray of Hampshire looks a good young batsman in the making, Dews of Worcester is linking consistent run-scoring to his magnificent fielding, Gardner of Warwick and Spooner are making runs well, and regularly. Angell, of Somerset, has made a huge advance and young Wooler of Leicester is not only bowling quite well but playing some very valuable late innings.

The renewed health of our cricket is apparent in the levelling up between the counties with Warwickshire and Northants high in the table and the bottom counties always liable to disturb the higher ones. The improvement of Leicestershire is a feature of the season and much credit for it must be given to the new captain, C.H. Palmer. Palmer was always a good player, even on a part-time basis, but now, playing all season, he must be considered as a possible for future Test captaincy. He is a quick-footed and stylish batsman with all the strokes, but also has the skill to restrain and restrict them when the game demands. Though his present position in the averages must sometimes make him smile, he can bowl swingers or spinners and keep a length. His fielding, too, is first-class and he goes hard to the end of the day. As yet he lacks experience as a captain but he has a pleasant personality and the current response of his team is an indication of the extent to which he compels loyalty. Under him, the younger Leicestershire players may well realise their full potential, while his contribution to the solidity of their batting enables such a good forcing batsman as Tompkin to play his natural game as he has not always been able to do. Indeed, if the genius of Walsh can be properly exploited, Leicestershire can be a very hard side to beat on hard wickets.

The controversy about the four Cambridge University batsmen appears likely to go on for many years to come. There are good critics to assert that each one of Dewes, Sheppard, May and Doggart is the best of the four. They were not very successful in the Test Trial but, make no mistake about it, barring unforeseeable accidents, each of them is going to make many hundreds of good runs against the best bowling. Perhaps Sheppard is potentially the heaviest run-getter on good wickets, May likely to become the most stylish all-wicket batsman, Dewes the most solid and Doggart the finest stroke-player, but the coincidence which brings them together in one University team is likely to go down into cricket history.

The question of the England captaincy is one which is rarely left alone, and, as in the case of the Cambridge batsmen, there are good critics to support different candidates. Many are for the retention of the personally popular Norman Yardley, who knows the Test game so well. Others, again, would advocate Wilfred Wooller as the strongest captain in the country, a magnificent field and a capable all-rounder. Dollery of Warwickshire is, perhaps, the most subtle and informed of our county captains but he seems to have played himself out of big cricket by his failure to score at Manchester. Insole, of Essex, will gain many supporters with his watchful defence, his willingness to hit when well-set, his all-round usefulness, cheerful good nature and keenness. Charles Palmer has yet to show his best, but that best is going to be very good. And we shall have to consider Hubert Doggart if the Lord's wicket gives him the opportunity to play one of his good and characteristic innings.

The injury to Preston leaves Trevor Bailey as England's fast bowler almost in isolation, for Trueman has yet to add something of pace and experience to his gifts. Bailey, too, has reinforced his position by his two fine innings at Manchester after rescuing the batting at Lord's in 1949. Yet I doubt he is fast enough to disturb the Australians on their own wickets, nor strong enough to be used as a stock bowler. A burden must, it seems, be thrown upon his shoulders which it is hardly fair to ask him to bear – particularly at the moment, with his run-up completely out of gear and the Trent Bridge Test only a few weeks away.

Perhaps the most heartening feature of the Old Trafford Test – after the wicket – was the bowling of Berry. His appearance and his form put an end to all discussion of the position of slow left-arm bowler in the England side: he has flight, length, spin, the ability to take punishment without hurrying or losing length, a sense of humour and, perhaps most surprising in one of his youth, a very real sense of tactics. With experience he should be even better and seems likely, unless some very unfortunate accident befalls him and English cricket, to be our true successor to Verity for many years to come.

I shall end, as I began, with a word about the Old Trafford wicket. To be sure the ball sometimes rose over the batsman's and the wicket-keeper's heads, even when bowled by a slow bowler. But it was the same for both sides: England batted on it when it was at its fastest while breaking up on the first day; West Indies had it on the last day when it was like an ash-heap, but slow. The victory went to the side with most batsmen quick enough of foot, sound enough in basic technique and wise enough in strategy to mould their play to the conditions. It confirms my early impression that we can always beat this West Indies side when the ball is 'doing' something – as indeed we *ought* to do in view of our greater experience of responsive wickets. Cricket followers throughout the world may well sympathize with the Old Trafford authorities. They took a brave step to adjust the balance between batsman and bowler; now, apparently, because the weather took a hand – hot weather instead of rain for a change at Manchester – they are subjected to an outcry. Let us trust it is not such an outcry that all ground committees in the future will pamper the batsmen with plumb wickets, to the end of destroying cricket as a contest and making it into a batting rout, with victory not to the most skilful but to the most patient.

*The Cricketers' Magazine*

JULY 1950

I have just had dinner with Joe Hills, the old Glamorgan batsman and, today, one of our more familiar umpires. Tomorrow the West Indies will play Derbyshire – Derbyshire fresh from the match in which the Hampshire bowlers gave their batsmen more than their due share of worry, and the tourists coming from their mammoth total against Leicestershire. On Sunday the selectors will choose the team for the Nottingham Test. Both these events will be old news by the time this piece is in print, but at the moment my cricketing thoughts turn on them and Joe Hills and, by way of Joe, on to the Old Trafford wicket.

Joe was one of the umpires in the game between Lancashire and Sussex which has just finished at Old Trafford in *one day*. He has one piece of news which is important, for, as an umpire, he is careful not to pass opinions. That piece of news is that the first ball of the match, bowled by young Malcolm Hilton – yes, a slow bowler opened the Lancashire bowling – the first ball turned almost a foot. How, I wonder, will this business of the Old Trafford wicket be resolved? I, personally, am with the Lancashire authorities in principle. I believe that the wicket which sees a match finished within the time limit is a good wicket. It may easily be that the Old Trafford wicket goes a little far on the side of the bowlers but not, I venture to assert, any further than many other wickets; Trent Bridge, Brighton, The Oval in its time, Leicester – and others one could name – have gone in favour of the batsman.

The greatest good the Old Trafford wicket could do for cricket should, in its first stage, be the bringing of the County Championship to Lancashire – then the other counties will begin to think. Consider – if two counties each play four matches of which one wins two and loses two and the other wins one and three times leads on the first innings, they score the same number of points. One win is worth three first-innings leads. Thus, given a side of slightly more than average strength, a county which finishes all its matches in a season stands a very good chance of being in the first three in the Championship, while Notts, for instance, might have the better of every match played at Trent Bridge yet never show enough wins to bring them out of the bottom half of the table.

To be sure, the Old Trafford wicket has begun to favour spin-bowlers for the first time in years, just when Lancashire have no pace bowler of appreciable powers in the side, but that is not strictly relevant. What *is* relevant is that if they are discouraged from producing wickets on which matches are finished, what other county in the country will dare to give the bowlers a chance? They will say, and with reason, that if such a power in the cricketing land as Lancashire dare not do it, then no club dare. Let them, perhaps, and if they can, make their wickets just a fraction better and then no one with the game of cricket at heart can gainsay them and, more important still, cricket will be the game it should be.

Which, we may pertinently ask, is the better wicket for cricket, the one on which a game is played out and won in one day, or the one in which three days of unbroken play are barely sufficient to give a decision on the first innings? Yet the latter has occurred several times this year without protest. The case of the Old Trafford wicket is one of the greatest issues ever brought before the cricketing world and, unless we are such fools as to believe that the purpose of cricket matches is to give batsmen the opportunity to break batting records, then we must say that the Old Trafford ground committee has struck a great blow for the health of the game. And unless I vastly misjudge Lancashire cricket-followers, there will be real and enthusiastic crowds at their headquarters to see cricket matches played to a finish, with only real batsmen making big scores.

Now to the matter of the selection of the England side. The fact that it will be over before these words are read concerns me little because, if my arguments do not reflect the opinions of the selectors, I shall not change them. Well, to begin with, there are two major problems: the first is the captaincy of the England side and the second is Ramadhin and Valentine – against the background of the problematical fitness of Messrs Hutton and Compton, incomparably our two finest batsmen.

The question of the captaincy ought not, if it were decided on a fair and square cricketing basis, to be difficult to solve. I am not of the opinion that a good player, such as Hutton or Washbrook or Compton, would necessarily make a good England captain. After all, those three men are good cricketers, indeed, but would anyone in his right senses regard that as sufficient qualification for making one of them England's wicket-keeper simply because the anticipated wicket-keeper was unable to play? Captaincy is just as specialized a job as wicket-keeping; it is the gossip writers, not the cricketers, who make the England captaincy cheap by suggesting that anyone could do it. There are at the moment three extremely good captains in England. They are Tom Dollery of Warwickshire, Wilfred Wooller of Glamorgan and Walter Robins of Middlesex. No doubt in a season's time one would add James Langridge to that number – when he has had the experience *as captain*. Walter Robins himself would certainly say that he was too old. Tom Dollery has not yet shown his true form in Tests and, while he would be a magnificent start to the idea of a modern professional captain, his past Test failures would, I suspect, inhibit him to such an extent as to impair his captaincy. My own choice would be Wilfred Wooller, a useful change bowler, a fair bottom-half bat and a wonderful field (so that he would not be a passenger), but above all, a captain with heart, courage and experience and one to go for a finish. His selection would, presumably, be a short-term one, designed to let some other captain mature in the game and in captaincy, for the selection of Hubert Doggart or Douglas Insole now would be unfair to the player himself.

The problem of Ramadhin and Valentine may prove a more difficult one. Let us deal with Valentine first. He is a hard slow left-arm bowler: that is to say he keeps a fair length, spins a very great deal and he 'digs it in', bowling at a considerable speed and giving the batsman no time to get to the pitch of the ball. But this, on the other hand, means that he has no real flight to bother the batsman. To be sure, he bowls the ball that goes straight on, and a swinger, but he is, in the main, a straightforward bowler. I do not suggest that he is an easy bowler to play, but I do suggest that, at least once in the course of some ninety overs in the Lord's Test, he might have been hit back over his head at least once. Ramadhin, to my mind, is the more difficult bowler of the two. It is almost impossible to distinguish his leg-break from his off-break. I suspect that the only English batsman who can do so is Hutton. Yet Washbrook made a good hundred at Lord's by playing Ramadhin strictly off the pitch. In the absence of Denis Compton, I believe that the best batting answer we have to this spin-bowling is Harold Gimblett of Somerset, who never fails in confidence even when his colleagues go down about him and, above all, is a batsman who attacks – yet on a basis of defence. The great trouble about selecting a batsman for a specific purpose is that he might always fail on the rub of the green without being any the less the man for the job.

I suspect that there is a prejudice against both Wooller and Gimblett which would not persist if the selectors saw them play a few more times. Certainly, if they played for more fashionable counties they would have had more representative play than they have. At the moment Wilfred Wooller's lack of recent match-play might reasonably mitigate against his selection, but there are no good grounds for failure to choose Gimblett except the fact that he plays for one of the lesser counties.

The recent game between Sussex and Somerset revealed a young cricketer of immense promise in Roy Smith of Somerset. As a right-hand bat and a slow left-arm bowler he has the stamp of the born player. As yet he lacks both confidence and experience, but another two or three seasons should see him a first-class all-rounder on county level at least. The same match saw a double-century by John Langridge who, like John Arnold of Hampshire, is having a batsman's Indian summer at a time when many men are thinking that their days of first-class cricket are at an end. What a calm and mellow batsman he is, master of every push and deflection known to the game and with the innate gift of timing which is the stamp of the born cricketer. From a double-century on a plumb wicket at Hove, he went on to carry his bat for less than a quarter the runs at Old Trafford – which, I wonder, would he regard as the better innings?

*The Cricketers' Magazine*

AUGUST 1950

Fate and the calendar and the editor's printing needs have conspired, it seems, to demand an article of me regularly throughout this summer on the eve of some vital selection. Today I write on the day before the selection of the last five players for the Australian party. Already, after two days' play, it seems that we cannot win the fourth Test against John Goddard's West Indians – if we do so then some cricketer will rise to heights we shall remember after all the remainder of this season has faded in the memory.

Short of that, it seems to me probable that we shall remember the season of 1950 primarily as that in which Ramadhin appeared. He and Valentine have exerted a spell over English batsmen which can only be compared with that of Grimmett and O'Reilly. Yet the two, Ramadhin and Valentine, are not on precisely the same level, similar as their records appear.

Valentine lacks one of the essential characteristics of the great slow left-arm bowlers: flight. On a damaged wicket he can be utterly deadly; on a good wicket he digs the ball in quickly enough to prevent the batsman from using his feet to him, and his pace is always such as to leave little time for a change of stroke or mind. But face him on the plumb wicket and he is no more than steady – though with a steadiness which will never be out of place in a Test eleven.

Ramadhin, on the other hand, would be great in any company. He is characterized first of all by that priceless gift, given only to the very greatest, of real speed off the pitch – every delivery from him compels a stroke more urgent than the initial flight of the ball would argue. Secondly, he has a puzzling flight: many a ball from him has appeared a full toss only for the batsman about to hit it on the volley to find himself in danger of being yorked. It is a combination of pace off the wicket and flight which has meant that, throughout this tour, less than one in thirty of the balls he has bowled outside the leg stump have been hit at all. When, at last, Evans succeeded, at Trent Bridge, in hitting a ball from him that was running down the leg side, it was to be caught at long leg. He spins the ball both ways, and few batsmen in England know which way he is turning until the ball pitches – it appears to me, so far, that only Hutton and Parkhouse can 'spot' him with any regularity. Even if every batsman in England could spot him, however, they would still be faced with the problem of vicious spin coupled with flight and pace. It is not necessarily possible to play a ball merely because you know it is a leg-break – it is one thing to recognize a leg-break and another matter to play it. Thus, while our best batsmen can detect virtually every googly bowled by our leg-and-googly spinners, that does not mean that they never get out to them. It will be found, I fancy, in the end, that Ramadhin spins from his two first fingers but that each of his breaks is spun off a single finger. Meanwhile he has shown us, on all wickets, some most impressive bowling. He himself has been impressed chiefly by the batting of Gimblett, who treated him in salutary fashion at Taunton but never had the opportunity to cross swords with him in a Test.

The West Indies batsmen will be remembered next: Stollmeyer for polish and efficiency; Rae for giving their batting a start of greater solidity than it had ever known before; Weekes and Worrell for stroke-play of contrasting styles but uniform attractiveness and speed of run-getting; Walcott for a massive power off the back foot. The discriminating critic, too, will remember the work of Gomez and Christiani who, on the few occasions when their colleagues failed, made good the deficiency without any great return of glory.

Of the English cricket we shall, I am sure, always regret that Wright was not included in our eleven for all four Tests. Although he has his detractors – chiefly, one suspects, among those who have never seen him bowl – he is clearly potentially the most dangerous bowler in the country. No other player seems likely to get out great batsmen on good batting wickets – as distinct from bowling so steadily that they get themselves out. In an experience of many Tests before and since the war, I have never seen Wright bowl better than in the West Indian first innings at The Oval, when he combined his frequent deadly delivery with a steadiness which gave the West Indies batsmen no peace of mind whatever. Even so great a batsman as Worrell was signally and consistently failing to spot Wright's googly and, after his century, fell to a superb top-spinner.

For the rest we may well remember the triumphal early season progress of the Cambridge University batsmen Dewes, Doggart, Sheppard and May. Doggart proved not of Test class; Dewes, like P.A. Gibb before him, has survived often by sheer courage and tenacity, despite a nervous and uncertain technique outside the off stump. Sheppard must, surely, have a great future unless a bad Test start unsettles him – as I write he awaits his first Test innings on the morrow. If he can play regularly, May might easily prove the greatest player of the four; he is a more varied stroke-player and has a quick-witted cricketing make-up which is the mark of the great attacking player. The early scores of these young men at Fenner's have been set in truer perspective by relative failure on bowlers' wickets, but the *promise* of these cricketers is very real. Whether circumstances – largely financial – will allow them to redeem that promise after their university careers are ended is problematical – as the August successes of M.M. Walford remind us annually.

Much recent conversation between cricketers has treated of the selection of Brian Close to make the trip to Australia. Certainly, despite his magnificent first season, he has given little indication of anything stronger than great promise. That promise, however, like that of the pre-war Edrich, is so strong that it cannot be ignored. Close looks every inch a cricketer in everything he does on the field. Just as Hammond's walk to the wicket made the spectator feel that here indeed was a cricketer, so Close's bearing is undoubtedly that of a man with real gifts for the game. Only next summer will show whether he will return branded as another selectors' failure or as an England player for many years to come. He is going to a hard school in Australia – a school hard enough to break all but the best, but conversely, we may be sure that, if he comes through, there is no subsequent test likely to beat him.

Watkins, after his fine bowling and useful batting against the West Indies in the Swansea match and with his outstanding fielding to support his claims, must stand a strong chance for selection tomorrow for Australia – and his chances may not be the worse for the fact that he has 'come' late in the season. The improvement in his bowling since the South African tour makes him a much safer selection than on the grounds of his batting and fielding alone, and England's present shortage of all-rounders is likely to stand him in good stead.

Shackleton of Hampshire must consider himself unlucky not to have been picked for the Oval Test. At Trent Bridge he was clearly the best of the England bowlers through the period of West Indian domination. He beat Weekes with the best ball of the match when that great batsman was well-set and, all through, he was steady. Test success – if success is to be reflected only in figures – is a risky business. When Bedser broke through, Shackleton was being rested for a few overs before he was brought back into the attack. At the moment Bedser took the first of the tail-end wickets, Hollies was his partner and was left on to the end of the innings. Thus it was that Shackleton's figures did not reflect the excellence of his bowling. The selectors seem, too, to have forgotten the value of his batting, which helped to put a much better face on the English first innings.

Perhaps the greatest injustice of the season has been done to Berry of Lancashire. On his home wicket at Old Trafford, his gifts of flight and strategy are not of such immediate value as the spin and accuracy of Hilton and Tattersall. Berry has even been taken off recently when his figures were one wicket for one run! Yet on a batsman's wicket, there is not a more difficult bowler in the country. The spin-bowler of flight will not always be the most useful one on a turning wicket, but in the long run he will save his side from being submerged on 'plumb 'uns' by good batsmen who do not need to fear spin alone. His eclipse immediately before selection for Australia is unfortunate if it excludes him from the party, particularly since it is not easy to see a satisfactory stock bowler for the tour – apart from Bedser – who may also take wickets. Wright, and to a markedly less degree Bailey, may take quick wickets in Australia, but it is not easy to see who will support Bedser in preventing the Australian batting, once in the saddle, from riding roughshod over our out-cricket.

Shortage of specialist fieldsmen, too, is another point which should be worrying our selectors and which must reinforce Watkins' chances of selection. Without Edrich, the English close-to-the-wicket fielding looked poverty-stricken at The Oval – not, one suspects, without vital bearing upon the game. Moreover, the fact that Washbrook will not make the trip leaves Simpson virtually alone as a class outfield. It is certain that an England side not more strong than Australia in batting and bowling – to express the position only mildly – must be outstandingly strong in the field if it is to stand any chance whatever of winning a Test. Even a single brilliant catch can change the character of a team's batting, and such catches simply are not made by average fieldsmen. The efforts of Bailey at slip to Wright's bowling had a vital effect in the huge West Indian first innings, yet to blame Bailey would be as stupid as to blame a makeshift wicket-keeper for failing to make those leg-side stumpings which are the best efforts of good regular wicket-keepers – the two jobs are equally expert.

It is significant, in assessing first-class cricket today, that visitors to our grounds in the post-war era have found our pitches slow by comparison with pre-war conditions. It is perhaps even more significant that R.H. Spooner, returning to first-class cricket after the 1914–18 war and finding, somewhat to his surprise, that he could still make runs, said that wickets then were slower than they had been pre-1914. Herein, I am sure, lies much of the reason for the decline in driving and in fast bowling. If the long-overdue move to adjust the balance between batsman and bowler is ever made, it must, surely, begin with an instruction to groundsmen to increase the speed of the wickets. It is bad enough to see spin bowlers presented with wickets on which the honestly spun ball will not turn. When the batsman can also be given time to make a second stroke after being deceived into error by flight, then the state of the wicket is criminal – yet it occurs all too frequently.

I must, for my part, admit to something of a feeling of disappointment that the Swansea wicket is now such that three-day matches can be left drawn there. It is interesting to note that the West Indies batsmen found the Swansea wicket more like a West Indian pitch than any other in their tour. That, however, does not lead us towards finished games, which must be the need indicated by our cricket today.

*The Cricketers' Magazine*

SEPTEMBER 1950

So the season of 1950 has ended with a mild splutter and, on the face of it, it has not been a very inspiring cricketing year. However, it would be a dull spectator who was content always with face value, and the season now behind us has contained much to cheer us from the long-term point of view as well as some rousing county cricket – indeed, a healthy cricket can never exist unless the county game is in full blossom.

Perhaps some of the joys of the season are, for me, somewhat clouded by the choice of the final two players for Australia. It should not be assumed from this that I have anything whatever against the selection of so good a batsman as Cyril Washbrook, or of so promising and wholehearted a young bowler as John Warr. I am, however, convinced that selections had already been made on the basis of Washbrook's original refusal of the invitation, so that his reinstatement has given us an unbalanced party – indeed, it is obvious that no party with five opening batsmen is perfectly balanced. Moreover, the choice of Warr is not good when he is recognized as a duplicate of a pace bowler who must be experimental *under Australian conditions* – for Bailey has yet to prove himself on those wickets *and* against Australian batsmen.

If we view the selection in the round, we can see reasons for the selection of each of Brown's men in isolation, but not for the seventeen *as a Test and touring combination*. In a party of seventeen men there is no justification for carrying five players – Dewes, Sheppard, Berry, Close and Warr – who are relatively untried, and all unproven. Berry, perhaps, looks the most likely to succeed at once, and Sheppard must surely do so eventually, but they make the trip with five other men on their first trip to Australia. Even this judgement, perhaps, might have been suspended but for the incredible blunder surely unique in the history of Test cricket – of taking a party to Australia without a first-class slip-fieldsman or, indeed, any man who has regularly fielded behind the wicket in a close position! Parkhouse may well make his place secure by virtue of his gully fielding, but he, even with the assistance of Compton, the only practicable short-leg fieldsman in the team, barely makes it worth the bowlers' while to labour for catches.

The final two places ought, without the slightest doubt – and I say this as one usually only too happy to see eye to eye with the selectors – to have gone to Edrich and Allan Watkins. We shall yet miss the 'guts' of Edrich when we are in a corner, and his slip-fielding might have made a major difference. Allan Watkins ought, in the end, to have been seriously considered for his fielding at short leg alone, but add to that the fact that he has been thought worthy of selection in three separate series as a batsman alone *and* that, over the last six weeks of the season, he was probably the best fast-medium bowler in the country, and his omission is utterly inexplicable. There is an unfailing test of the importance of the omission of these two. Pick a Test eleven from the seventeen men already selected – and then see if there are not two players there whom you would drop for Edrich and Watkins.

It is not impossible for our men to win in Australia, but it depends, it seems, on all our stars coming off together. Hutton must master the fast bowlers, Compton must be utterly fit, Wright must strike his most accurate length, Bedser must be adequately rested and Evans must be at peak form behind the stumps. If all these come off at the same time, I believe we can win a Test with average support from the rest of the side, *if* – and this 'if' ought not to be there – the close-to-the-wicket catches are held.

I fancy that Australia, without Bradman, will not be *quite* the power they were in 1948. On the other hand, I doubt our eleven is any better than in that year except, possibly, in that Simpson or Parkhouse may fill the long-vacant gap at number five in the batting order – but we have ourselves created a fresh gap at number three by the omission of

Edrich, and that is a far more important one, and its satisfactory filling is by no means certain.

Nevertheless, even if we are not successful on tour it is possible, once again, to count a number of young cricketers who are maturing in the county sides – many to reach at least competent county standard and some of them, undoubtedly, more than that. It must be remembered, however, that these young players are not getting so sure a groundwork as their predecessors. Our Tate, Larwood, Hearne, Hobbs, Sutcliffe, Hutton had their two or three seasons of groundstaff and/or minor county experience before they came into full county cricket. Far too many of our young men are being heard of in April, tried the next week, given a month in the nets to rub off the crudest of their corners and then thrown into the County Championship.

There is, undoubtedly, great promise in young Titmus of Middlesex, Trueman of Yorkshire, Heath and Smith of Warwickshire, but they *must* be given time to develop. All of them would be better for two or three experimental years on the groundstaff and in the second eleven, where to try out a new ball is not to present opponents with a winning advantage and where the development of a fresh stroke or the modification of an original does not lead to a series of headline 'failures'. We may take for example Willie Watson of Yorkshire: if he had not lost half the season to his World Cup soccer trip, he must, surely, have been selected for Australia. In 1946 his promise was recognized, but he lacked experience; now, after the bad season which all players experience, he is the fully matured county batsman – but the process has taken five seasons, in the course of which there were times when his place in his county team was doubtful.

So it is, invariably, with all but the very greatest: recall Denis Compton's 'black patch' of 1946. In fact, at least three post-war Test players have come through poor spells and are now clearly and unmistakably better players than when they were picked for England. Ikin of Lancashire has grown up as a batsman; Cook of Gloucester has added flight and subtlety to his original steady left-arm spin; Watkins has developed fresh and more certain strokes and his bowling has improved beyond belief. Yet, picked too soon by virtue of their unmistakable promise, they have, apparently, to suffer for the selectors' errors by being omitted when they have redeemed their promise. These early selections, in fact, do not always do good. Smithson of Yorkshire, taken to the West Indies after only a season's cricket, is now not even re-engaged by his own county! Yet, given a fair run on the groundstaff, he might now have been ready for a county eleven with his deeper technical problems solved at less cost than that of his contract.

That unmistakable aptitude for the game which no great player has ever lacked can always be detected, but while all great players have possessed it, not all those who have possessed it have become great players. Four years should be a fair period over which promise should be confirmed by performance; until then no man should be condemned, nor, except in the most remarkable cases, should he be regarded as fully developed. Such young players as Sheppard and May of Cambridge University are examples of halfway players; neglect or 'over-pushing' could ruin either now. Perhaps May is the most fortunate of the four young Cambridge players – Sheppard, Dewes and Doggart are the others – in that he has not yet had the opportunity to fail in a Test and, therefore, has nothing to live down. Brian Close, however, is the most striking example of the young player with the stamp on him but no achievement behind him – for a single good season in the Yorkshire team is not full proof. The tour of this winter may make or break Close, but I fancy his real friends would prefer to see that issue forced after he had had another year of less important cricket. Next May will show.

My own most heartening experience of the season has been the batting of Alan Rayment of Hampshire. He came late into the Hampshire side, *but* after a fair run with the club and ground side *and* a term on the Lord's staff. His first few innings were not numerically impressive and he could probably have benefited by yet another season with the second eleven. He 'came', however, in the last match of the season, against the severe test of Goddard and Cook, the Gloucester spin-bowling combination, on a turning wicket. With no other Hampshire batsman capable of handling them in either innings, Rayment made a fifty in his first 'knock' and was barely short of his century in the second. The wicket favoured the bowlers throughout, yet he never gave a chance in some five hours' batting. Most impressive of all was the maturity of his method: never once – and I watched him with the utmost care from start to finish of the game – never once did he take a liberty with a good ball, or fail to punish a bad one. No matter how good the bowler, if he bowled a bad ball it was hit – hard – and Rayment has attacking strokes all round the wicket. His two innings answered many questions about him, and certainly proved the wisdom of his two years of groundwork. He has shown considerable promise; 1952 or 1953 should be his year of decision.

The West Indies won the 1950 Test series on their merits. Let there be no doubt of that – it is by no means certain that the combinations of Weekes and Worrell (with Rae for ballast), and Ramadhin and Valentine (with Goddard for a bad wicket) might not seriously disturb the Australians' best eleven today. It was a happy win and a milestone in cricket history. English cricket need not regret that defeat at its back when every county can point to its young men who are to prove the outstanding cricketers of our play a decade into the future.

This winter will be, for us, one of despatches from the other side of the world. They will certainly have good news for us as well as bad; every man's turn comes, and ours is not far away.

*The Cricketers' Magazine*

# −3−

# International Figures

## Typical Bradman: 80 Not Out

*August* 1988.   Sir Donald Bradman is eighty years old today, and much of Australia will be celebrating the occasion. In that country he is far more than a cricketer; he has been a celebrity wherever he has gone, but his own country sees him as something more than that.

W.G. Grace was a great Victorian figure in England; but at the pinch he was simply a cricketer. He was admired, but never knew the adulation that 'The Don' has aroused in his own country. In radio programmes, television, films and books, Bradman has been treated with a degree of reverence that it is hard for people in this country to appreciate.

In 1948 his tour of England as captain of Australia was lightly likened to a royal progress. Crowds flocked to see, not basically the Australian touring team, despite its powers, but Bradman. He did not disappoint them. Indeed, he has rarely disappointed his public: of his 338 first-class innings, 117 were centuries. No one else approaches his figures. In all cricket he averaged 95.14 an innings; in Test matches 99.94.

That last statistic recalls his arch 'failure'. When he came out to bat in the fifth Test match at The Oval, Australia were 117 for one – England had been put out for 52. Fairly obviously it was going to be Bradman's last Test innings – certainly in England. He was cheered all the way to the wicket where Yardley, the England captain, shook hands with him and the England team gave him three cheers.

To the hardest-bitten Australian – and Bradman was not that – it must have been an emotional occasion. His first ball, from Eric Hollies, was played safely and soundly enough. The second was a googly. Bradman, most uncharacteristically, played outside it and was bowled.

Was that wary eye dimmed by emotion? Jack Fingleton refused to believe so, but others would not agree with him. In any event it was the 'failure' that prevented his Test average from being over 100.

Amazing as his figures are – as batsman, captain and member of successful Australian teams (except that of 1932–33) – they do not fully account for his standing in that country. Neither, of course, considerable as they are, do his successes in business go anywhere near explaining that eminence. We must look elsewhere for that – probably, indeed, to Australia's need for a quasi-royal figure. Only that can account for some of the sheer idolatry, which seems often not to be truly connected with cricket, that has been lavished upon him there.

In a way that treatment has served him ill, separating him from his fellow men as it separated him from his fellow cricketers. Why should the boy from Bowral have the *savoir faire* of royalty to bear himself through the social problems of a royal personage without the same degree of protection?

During the English tour of 1948 he was obviously content to accept company which did not make any demands on him. It was then that his character became clear: just how vulnerable he was to what he conceived to be public opinion.

As a single example, dining with him one night, he had a spoonful of soup halfway to his mouth in a hotel dining room when a complete stranger came up and said: 'Will you sign me book?' 'Can't you see I'm eating?' said The Don most reasonably. The interrupter spun on his heel and walked away muttering. 'Now, what will he say about me to his friends?' asked Bradman. Neither was he contented by the comment that his reaction was a most reasonable one.

His ability as a cricketer has not completely satisfied him; rather, it has made him a lonely man. One often wonders whether his fame has proved adequate compensation. That, though, is a matter for his internal and mental make-up.

Let us, for the moment, examine his true importance – as a cricketer – specifically as a batsman, though he was a highly competent fieldsman and might well have made a useful leg-spinner. He was without doubt the most relentless and infallible punisher of the bad ball – and of the marginally imperfect delivery.

Once, in that famous match against Essex when Australia made 721 (and Tom Pearce, the Essex captain, claimed membership of the Purchasers for being the only county captain to bowl the Australians out in a day), Bradman demonstrated his typical gift for punishment. Frank Vigar, the slow leg-spinner, came on. Bradman used his feet to him and, in the course of an over, allowed one ball to pitch; the other five he hit for four apiece. With the ball that did not reach the boundary he was punching his open hand with irritation at his failure to score a sixth four before the fieldsman had stopped it.

He undoubtedly had an extra gift of perception: an ability to see and assess the curve, length and pace of the ball earlier than any other player we have ever seen. His footwork was perfect and extremely fast; he was not tall, but he never seemed to need height and his balance never betrayed him.

He had no distinguishable bias towards the off side or the on, forward or back play. He simply played every ball on its merits and rarely erred in that judgement. In its way, his near-perfection was always spectacular, but once – in the Folkestone Festival of 1934 – he hit thirty runs off a single over from 'Tich' Freeman.

It has been said that he was vulnerable to pace, but when, in 1932–33, Douglas Jardine unleashed his posse of pace bowlers against Australia, Bradman was still top of their batting averages with a figure of 56.57; the next batsman's average was 42.77. The reply to the suggestion that he could not play on bad wickets lies in his figures everywhere, especially in England in wet summers.

This was the master batsman against all types of bowling and on all kinds of surfaces. He never knew a real spell of failure, but his successes were monumental. He more than satisfied even the Australian desire for cricketing success, and at some cost, we may believe, to himself, he has done much to satisfy their hunger for a greater-than-cricketing figure.

*The Guardian*


# Kiwis Touched with Genius

*July* 1986.   The New Zealand series of 1949 in England was, in many ways, remarkable, and something of a moral victory for the tourists. They had expected to play three four-day Tests; but eventually it was decided, for financial reasons, that they would play four of three days each. That shrewd captain Walter Hadlee, smiling grimly, observed: 'Well, that means we can draw all four.' And they did. They achieved it largely because they had the best two left-hand batsmen in the world at that time in Martin Donnelly and Bert Sutcliffe; and they chose, tactically, to play it as a defensive series.

Martin Donnelly was the elder, and the first of the two to appear on the English scene. His talent was early apparent; while he was still at Plymouth High School in Taranaki (six years in the eleven) he was coached by that wise old pro Albert Alderman of Derbyshire, on a winter engagement in New Zealand. While still at school he played for Taranaki against Errol Holmes's 1936 MCC team in New Zealand, and was top-scorer for the local side with 49, made so impressively that Holmes named him favourably in his report to the New Zealand Cricket Council.

That took Donnelly into the Wellington Plunket Shield side; and soon afterwards, only nineteen, he was selected in M.L. Page's team to England in 1937. He was generally disposed to take chances, but at Lord's he helped to save the first Test with a patient innings of 21, in which he dealt calmly with some extremely hostile bouncers from Alf Gover and Bill Voce. His 58 was the top score in the New Zealand first innings at The Oval, when he helped to steer that rather outweighed side to another draw. Returning, he played some outstanding innings for Canterbury until he joined the army in 1940.

As a tank commander in north Africa and Italy, he played virtually no more cricket until, in 1945, he joined the New Zealand Services team under Ken James in England. In the euphoric British atmosphere of peace, his batting, like Keith Miller's, proved splendidly celebratory: Donnelly made 100 not out for New Zealand against Walter Hammond's XI and, within ten days, 133 for the Dominions against England at Lord's and 100 and 86 for the New Zealanders against Leveson-Gower's XI at Scarborough.

In October 1945 he went up to Oxford and, in 1946, became something of a showpiece in that city; after the years of war many who gave themselves some time to watch cricket in The Parks enjoyed him to the full. He played with complete mastery; he equalled Pataudi's record of six centuries in a University season, crowning it, with a superb sense of occasion, with 142 against Cambridge in less than three hours: Lord's Pavilion stood to him. He was top of the University batting with an average of 62.8; the next man's figure was 35.95. In 1947 Donnelly was again top of the University averages with 1144 runs at 67.29.

In the first two post-war seasons he made a profound and much-relished impression on cricket in England. Stockily built, and equable in temperament, nothing seemed to disturb him; he bore the stamp of the great batsman in that he always seemed to have time to play his stroke, however late he might leave it. He was fast on his feet, quick to smother spin, and master of many strokes; and while most of them were elegant, he would, if anyone threatened to pin him down, pull with immense power over mid-wicket. Perhaps his most memorable stroke was an apparently casual flick to send a straight ball of good length wide of mid-on for four. He simply was a batting natural.

He closed his University career with a good degree; a rugby blue; a rugby cap for England against Ireland; and, after the end of the University's cricket season, 162 not out for Gentlemen v Players. In 1948 he played fifteen matches for Warwickshire, then in 1949, joined Walter Hadlee's team touring England. This was only his second Test series; he had played the first at nineteen, and now he bore a heavy burden of responsibility, which he discharged superbly.

Under the heaviest burden of cricket he ever carried – he played twenty-nine matches – he was top of the touring side's averages with 2287 runs at 61.81 and, in the Tests, 462 at 77. Away from Tests he played some quite impudent innings but, outstandingly, he made over fifty in four of his six Test innings and, memorably, completed his 'clutch' with 206 in the second at Lord's. Thus he equalled the rare record for centuries there in the University Match, Gentlemen v Players, and a Test.

That was the end of his Test cricket and, apart from a few matches with Warwickshire in 1950, the end of his first-class career. In fact, cricket saw all too little of him – and England the best of that. Hardly anyone has been dubbed great on so little playing experience: 131 matches in all; in those, he passed the acid test – his average in all cricket was 47.44, in Tests 52.90. He went away to business in Australia; he had never regarded cricket as anything but a game, and he had enjoyed it.

In his early days he bowled a brisk medium, but gave up bowling after the war; he remained, however, a quite superb cover-point. He was also a brilliant tennis player and, at rugby, he played almost everywhere behind the scrum – outside-half for Oxford University; centre-three-quarter for England. He was charming, modest, had a superb dry sense of humour; there have been few more personable cricketers. He was a great loss.

Bert Sutcliffe, too, was a charming personality: modest, enthusiastic and perpetually optimistic. His primary gift was as a batsman, though in his early days he occasionally took wickets with his slow left-arm bowling. Born in 1923, he did not appear in first-class cricket until 1946 – for Auckland – but he already had behind him a remarkable record as a schoolboy at Takapuna where, at thirteen, he scored a century in a house match; at sixteen was captain of cricket; and, against King's College, Auckland, made 133 not out and took seven for 4 and six for 24 in the same match.

During the war he served in the New Zealand Army in Egypt, Italy and Japan, and in north Africa played with Peter Smith and Jim Laker.

Back home with Auckland, he had a fair season and began to show the potential that was to make him his country's leading record-breaker. In consecutive innings for Auckland in the Plunket Shield he made 71, 74, 111, 62 not out; and for Otago against the 1946–47 MCC touring side, 197 and 128 – the first time a New Zealander had performed that feat against an MCC team.

Of course, Sutcliffe was a certain choice for England in Walter Hadlee's touring side of 1949 and, over some twenty years, he broke a whole series of New Zealand batting records. On that first tour he, like Martin Donnelly, proved extremely popular with the English public; and responsibly he made over fifty in five of his seven Test innings. Lean, wiry, fair-haired and invariably cheerful-looking, in those days he opened the innings, and his style caught the eye. He had text-book off- and cover-drives, he hooked fearlessly and, like Donnelly, employed the pull most effectively; like Donnelly too, he was a good field, a safe catcher close to the wicket, and a fine mover in the covers. He was invariably fit, having been a physical training instructor in New Zealand, though subsequently he became official coach to the Otago Cricket Association.

From Auckland he moved to Otago and then to Northern Districts, whom he captained. Bert Sutcliffe played in forty-two Tests and made six overseas tours for New Zealand. Although he never adopted the mentality of a slavish record-breaker – indeed, his determination to get on with the game often cost his wicket – the records seemed to come to him. His 385 for Otago against Canterbury in 1952 remains not only the highest innings ever played by a New Zealand batsman in New Zealand, but also by a left-hander anywhere. With W.S. Haig he put on 266 for the fifth wicket, a New Zealand record, and his stands of 220 and 286 for the first wicket with D.D. Taylor for Auckland against Canterbury in 1948–49 are the only instance in first-class cricket of double-century first-wicket stands in each innings of the same match.

Quite early in his career he moved from opening the innings to the middle order, where the side needed ballast. Returning to open the innings in 1955 against India, he scored 611 runs at 87.28. When he eventually retired, in 1966, Bert Sutcliffe had scored more runs and more hundreds (44) than any other New Zealander, and four times he hit a century in each innings of a match, this despite the misfortune of a broken wrist sustained at Worcester in the opening match of the 1958 tour, after he had scored 139.

He emerged from retirement for the 1965 tour of England and, almost by way of getting his eye in, took a brilliant 151 not out off India at Calcutta. Then, in the first Test at Edgbaston, he ducked into a bouncer from Fred Trueman and was hit on the ear. Characteristically gamely, he resumed his innings after treatment and made 53, but he had to miss most of the rest of the tour.

It is typical of Bert Sutcliffe that, a wholehearted player, he has thrown himself also enthusiastically and most valuably into coaching in his own country.

*Wisden Cricket Monthly*

# Athol Rowan: Cricketer

*December* 1951. On Saturday 18 August 1951, at the end of the fifth Test match, Athol Rowan, then the finest off-break bowler in the world, walked off Kennington Oval and the cricket fields of the world for ever.

We have seen other great players leave the game, but they have done so full of its honours and we have even applauded their wisdom in not lingering in the middle after their powers had begun to decline. Athol Rowan, however, was only thirty years old when his career ended, and he had, that same afternoon, under our very eyes, almost bowled England to defeat. His left knee, originally injured by a barely noticed knock against a gun-carriage in north Africa on war service, had already collapsed four times; he had played on through its pain and strain, but now it had crippled him.

Few cricketers have earned such a reputation as Rowan's so quickly and on so few performances. In his entire career he took 273 wickets at 23.47 and scored 1492 runs with an average of 24.06. He played first-class cricket for only five years from start to finish, and even that included a full year out of action through injury, so that he played substantially less than a hundred first-class matches. Moreover, in the matches he did play, the knee injury which eventually put an end to his cricket was always both a physical handicap and a psychological brake which he had consciously to override with every ball he bowled.

It is not possible to estimate what further triumphs he might have achieved if he had been able to continue the game which was his chief enthusiasm. We can say, however, that a slow bowler of 'natural' spin – that is, a right-arm off-breaker or a left-arm bowler of the break-away – lasts longer than most other types of cricketer. The batsman, as he reaches his mid-thirties, finds that some of the profitable strokes of his twenties are no longer 'business' when his eye loses the full sharpness of youth. The pace bowler loses his most hostile edge of speed even earlier. The slow bowler, however, provided only that he has a sound action and good health, should continue to improve with wider and deeper knowledge of batsmen, increased control, variation and flight.

Indeed, Wilfred Rhodes – also a 'natural' spinner – played a major part in England's Test victory of 1926 when he was only a few months short of forty-nine; while Tom Goddard, the Gloucester off-breaker, had some of his best seasons after he was forty.

That Athol Rowan had bowled better during 1951 – despite his injury – than he had done in England in 1947, does much to confirm the belief that his greatest triumphs lay still ahead of him. Even his measurable achievement, however, demands that he stand – with Vogler, Aubrey Faulkner and 'Buster' Nupen – at the peak of South African bowling.

Athol Rowan's figures, at first sight, appear ordinary enough. In his fifteen Tests – all against England – he took 54 wickets; his average – 38 runs per wicket – may not seem particularly impressive. But nine of those fifteen Tests were played on absolutely plumb wickets where the batsmen of both sides made huge scores, and in only four innings did he bowl on really difficult pitches. Then, if we look further into his figures, we find that, of his 54 wickets, 43 were those of recognized batsmen, that 39 were in the first six in the English batting order, and that only five of them were of batsmen lower than number eight. In Hutton's twenty-four completed Test innings against South Africa since the war, his wicket has fallen eleven times to Athol Rowan.

So much statistics can tell us. They cannot, however, express Rowan's magnificent worth on perfect wickets when he alone prevented the English batsmen from galloping away from the South African out-cricket, nor can they record the number of occasions when the menace of his attack caused batsmen to take their risks at the other end and thus fall to another bowler.

It has been said of the English fast bowler Harold Larwood that only those who saw him bowl in Australia in the season of 1932–33 ever saw him at his greatest. Similarly, much of Athol Rowan's best cricket was played in England. Indeed, he played more first-class matches in England than in the Union; thus, of his 273 wickets, he took 155 in England, while the 273 was made up of 180 English batsmen, 15 Australian and only 78 South African.

This accounts reasonably for the fact that Rowan is as highly esteemed in England as in his own country. He arrived in England in 1947 as one of the lesser-known Springboks, but there was some curiosity, particularly among those who had studied South African reports, to see the young man whose enthusiasm was such that he had played post-war cricket in a leg-iron. His performance in the first match showed that no allowances needed to be made for him. The game against Worcester which opened the tour was played under even worse conditions than those which usually greet the start of an English season. The cold was so intense that snow fell during the match, yet, although his sun-accustomed fingers were deadened by that frozen wind, Rowan was the outstanding player in a losing team: he took ten wickets in the match for 93 runs, made top score in the first innings and the highest but one in the second.

The three musketeers of that tour – Lindsay Tuckett, Jack Plimsoll and Athol Rowan – played in the belief that a long bowling spell was an ingredient of holiday, and that England was their parish. Rowan was the only member of the party to take a hundred wickets in the season; his six hundred runs included a century against Glamorgan, and he held his catches with clumsy, drag-legged speed – but speed.

Like Len Hutton and thirty thousand Yorkshire spectators, I still remember from that tour his bowling at Headingley where, in an atmosphere like a steam-chamber, he bowled unrelieved for three and a half hours on that batsman's wicket to yield only 89 runs to Hutton, Washbrook, Barnett, Edrich and Compton – of whom the two latter were having their greatest run-scoring season. He earned all the five wickets which fell; he took only one.

That humid Leeds atmosphere exaggerated the characteristic of his flight so that he made the ball float away from the bat – sometimes as much as eight or nine inches. He compelled enough false strokes to have taken five wickets had his leg-side fieldsmen been placed near enough to the bat. In that direction, however, his cricketing immaturity was apparent for, in those days, he was inclined to overpitch through sheer anxiety when the short-leg fieldsmen stood in close. I remember how he took his sweater and walked away to cover-point after that spell which would have been phenomenal for a perfectly fit player. Then, such was his concentration on the game, immediately afterwards he produced a racingly fast dive, pick-up and throw-in merged into one action to hit the stumps and run out Hutton.

Rowan was popular with his opponents on that tour; like his friend Lindsay Tuckett he played cricket for the delight of the game, lacking, perhaps, the disposition to dislike his opponents quite as much as the harder schools demand. It was obvious, however, that if he remained fit – and even on that tour his knee troubled him – he would be a major South African Test player for many years to come.

The MCC 1948–49 tour of South Africa gave him the psychological fillip of his elder brother Eric fielding at short leg. It is significant that, during that Test series, South Africa's only three opportunities to win – at Durban, Cape Town and Port Elizabeth – were each created by Athol Rowan taking four or five major wickets in the first England innings. At the end of the series – and after a significantly necessary rest – he bowled sixty overs to take five wickets for 167 in the Port Elizabeth Test where he and 'Tufty' Mann bowled so steadily on a slow wicket that England were rescued from collapse only by George Mann's last-hope hundred.

Transvaal v Hassett's 1949–50 Australians at Ellis Park, Johannesburg was one of the greatest matches in post-war cricket. The Australians – with Morris, Moroney, Harvey, Miller, Loxton and Archer and next to no tail – were put out for 84; Athol Rowan took nine wickets for 19 runs. Then, Transvaal 125 for nine wickets declared – Athol Rowan second-highest scorer with 31 – and Australia batted again 41 runs behind. Australia out in their second innings for 109 – Athol Rowan six for 49 – and Transvaal needed 69 to win. England prepared for a report of an Australian defeat. Instead, the news was that Transvaal lost by 15 runs and that, while Athol Rowan was making his 15 not out – the top score of their second innings – his knee had collapsed under him at the crease. After the amazing all-round feat of taking three-quarters of the Australian wickets and scoring over a quarter of the Transvaal runs for once out, it was said that, not only would he be unable to play again that season, but that his cricket career was almost certainly ended. His absence from the South African eleven magnified the strength of the Australians; he could not, obviously, have reversed the result of the rubber, but I am convinced that, had he been on the South African side, they would have won the Durban Test which, in the event, they so sadly allowed to slip out of their hands.

Reports from South Africa during the 1950–51 Currie Cup season said, sadly but definitely, that there was no possibility of Athol Rowan making the 1951 trip to England. By another minor miracle of determination, at the end of that season he hobbled back into cricket, into the Trial match and played himself on to the ship with the touring party.

Then it was Worcester, 1951, and the opening match of another tour, and there was Athol Rowan batting and bowling in his best form. Miracle or not, he had forced that left leg back into service and, clearly, if he were properly nursed, he might change the course of Test matches. So far from being nursed, however, he was bowled unsparingly – as if the aim were not to find out whether he could bowl, but whether he could break down. He was given more overs than any other bowler in the side in the early matches and, eventually, at Bristol, in such bitingly cold weather as brought out strains and injuries in younger and fitter men, his knee gave out again. Hugh Tayfield was flown over from South Africa to take his place at need, and surely, it seemed, the need was proven. The hours Rowan spent rubbing, treating, building and dressing that knee were a substantial part of his day; it and cricket were never out of his mind. He seemed to think he had, in some way, failed someone – he who above all was a team man. Something bigger than news reporting can contain brought Athol Rowan back again for the first Test, at Trent Bridge. There his bowling – five of the first eight English wickets in the decisive second innings – together with Nourse's batting and Eric Rowan's captaincy, won South Africa their first Test match for sixteen years.

In the Lord's Test he was not a fit or a happy bowler, and at Manchester it was doubtful if he would play at all. His knee was paining him at every movement, he was worried and he was sick, too – infected by one of those sapping germs which always find out a run-down, anxious man. 'Looks like my last Test match,' he said with a transparently assumed smile. He was not, by any standard, fit to play cricket at all. Somehow he took three of the first six England wickets – and took them well.

Then, his knee huge with swelling, packed in a parcel of cotton wool and plaster, painful even to stand on, he went to that slablike bowlers' graveyard at Leeds. The batsman had only to play down the line of the ball to score hundreds of runs, yet Athol Rowan took four of the first six English wickets to fall; in all he bowled 68 overs to take five for 174 in an England total of 505.

Both he and his friends knew it could not last. Yet he came by way of eight for 106 against Warwick – the Champion County – to the Oval Test. There, his 41 was second-highest score in South Africa's first innings of 202. His bowling in the first English innings was better than two for 44 suggests: 27 tight overs, Hutton's wicket again and all the English batsmen played him anxiously. His dour 15 not out in the second Springbok innings of 154 was one of a series of good knocks he played towards the latter end of the tour when he frequently rescued the batting from collapse.

England needed 163 runs to win and Nourse, wisely, brought Rowan on early. Hutton and Lowson had made 53 together when Hutton was given out for obstructing Endean as he was about to catch him off Rowan's bowling – a wicket which the scorebook does not credit to Rowan. With the next ball he had May exultantly taken by his brother Eric at forward short leg, and for the last time a scorebook showed 'caught E. Rowan, bowled A. Rowan' – with all that it implies. Van Ryneveld caught Lowson off him at short leg, and England were struggling. They wanted only 79 runs to win, but Rowan and the tirelessly accurate Chubb were on top of the batting. Two wickets – those of Compton and Watson – went to Chubb to bring in Laker and Brown, the last of England's batting of any quality on a wicket which gave such bowlers the benefit of spin. Both Brown and Laker played strokes off Rowan which were all but catches to the leg-trap, and together they lived a nerve-racking twenty minutes to tea. When play was resumed, the game could have gone either way.

Athol Rowan, without doubt, knew that this was his last match, and he was of a mind to finish well. Brown, never at his best against spin-bowling and obviously resolving to lose his wicket hitting rather than prodding, hit Rowan hard and high, not particularly safely, but for runs. Nourse took Rowan off and brought on McCarthy. At once, against fast bowling, Laker and Brown looked new men, playing firm strokes, and England moved quickly towards a win. Nourse brought Rowan back again, but it was too late: physically he had been finished before the match ever started; psychologically he was finished when he was taken off in face of Brown's attack. For a few moments the tension was renewed, but the margin was too fine, there was not a single run to play with, and England won a Test which Athol Rowan's bowling had that day brought into hazard.

He came off the field alone and quietly, his head a little on one side as is sometimes his manner. 'I shall never play again,' he said. There was nothing to reply.

*The Cricketers' Magazine Winter Annual*

# Farewell to Clive the Colossus

*January* 1985. This week one of world cricket's major figures, physically and in terms of performance, slouched off the scene. C.H. Lloyd of Guyana; Haslingden, Lancashire; and West Indies – Clive to the media, Hubert to his friends – had by then become the most successful Test captain the game has ever known.

Indeed, his record may never be equalled except by another West Indian with perpetually renewed resources of pace bowling. He led West Indies into seventy-four Tests, of which they won thirty-six, lost only twelve, and lost only two out of eighteen series. Until a few days ago they had won an unparalleled eleven successive Tests, had gone twenty-eight undefeated, and had twice won the World Cup. It had all been done in his apparently contradictory blend of the spectacular and the relaxedly calm.

In individual terms he appeared in 110 Tests between 1966–67 and 1984 and – just – 1985; only Cowdrey (114) has played in more. In his 479 matches in all first-class cricket between 1963 and this week, he scored 30,597 runs with 77 centuries at an average of 49.27; took 114 wickets, made 373 catches and was responsible for many run-outs.

If the figures of his success are impressive, the manner of its achievement has been splendidly handsome, the more so for his unhappy start. As a boy trying to stop two others fighting he was hit in the eye with a ruler; that injury, plus many hours of study in bad light, permanently affected his eyesight. Soon afterwards a leg injury was so badly infected by tetanus as to bring him near death. Remarkably, while he was confined to his bed, he grew fantastically – six inches in a month.

Despite those handicaps his cricketing ability was early apparent. Such is the concentration of talent in West Indies, though, that ability is not enough: it must be rapidly backed by achievement. Chosen for Guyana against Jamaica in 1964, Lloyd scored only 12 and was dropped until 1965 when scores of 2 and 17 against the Australians cost him his place once more.

Recalled again in the match against Barbados, he scored nought in the first innings, and there is little doubt that his first-class career was then in jeopardy. In the second innings he made a fine, forcing 107. He did not miss an opportunity again.

When he first broke upon the first-class scene here, he caught the eye by his fielding – perhaps the most effective ever seen at cover point. He had the immense advantage of his height – over 6 ft 4 in – and, even at that, having unusually long arms and legs.

He ambled apparently abstractedly in the field, sun-hat brim folded up like some amiable Paddington Bear, but upon the cue of a stroke played near him he leapt like some great cat into explosive action. His huge strides made his action area immense. In that respect he outstripped the Rhodesian Colin Bland, who may have looked more graceful but could not match Lloyd's vast dives, goalkeeper-fashion, to cut off a ball that seemed far beyond his reach.

Then he returned with a whip of a mighty right arm or, off balance, a strikingly powerful and accurate palm push. In fact, by the hypnotic influence of his fielding presence he scared many batsmen not only out of barely possible runs but out of some that would have been easy. When leg injuries restricted his speed over the ground he took those vast hands and rapid reflexes into the slips where he proved equally valuable.

As a batsman he has always used a weighted bat with extra grips on the handle to hit with unusual force. Against Surrey at The Oval he once pulled a straight ball from Robin Jackman from a wicket on the gasholder side of the ground into the yard of Archbishop Tenison's School, on the other side of the Harleyford Road. Physically his great reach enabled him to drive 'on the up' deliveries to which ordinary men would play back. This combination of reach, enormous strength, natural timing and instinctive attacking urge has made one of the most effective and powerful, controlled hitters the game has known. His 201 for West Indies against Glamorgan in 1976 equalled Gilbert Jessop's record for the fastest double-century.

Once he had found his feet his advance was never checked. In his first Test – against India at Bombay – he made 82 and a match-winning 78 not out. On his first appearance against England he scored 118 at Bridgetown; in his first against Australia 129. He has in his time bowled in three different fashions: slow leg-spin, medium seam-up and, briefly, at quite brisk pace. After his league cricket days, though, he bowled little.

In 1967 he came to England to join Haslingden in the Lancashire League because, he said, 'I thought it would improve my batting technique.' On a bleak London night during the following winter he agreed – exciting for Desmond Eagar and myself – to join Hampshire. He had, though, developed an affection for Lancashire and its people; and when, having been outbid for Garfield Sobers, that county authority approached him, he agreed to join them.

He and Farook Engineer gave an immense fillip to their cricket, especially in the over-limit game with five Gillette Cup wins and two John Player League Championships in seven years; and in 1981 he was appointed county captain.

For the 1974–75 series in India, though, he had already been made captain of West Indies in succession to Rohan Kanhai. From that day until he retired this week he captained his country in every match they played except when injured and, briefly, during the dispute with the Packer 'World Series'.

Captaincy has affected the play of many cricketers, but Lloyd took it in his buoyant stride. In his first match as touring captain, he made 163 at Bangalore; in his first series scored 636 runs at 79.50. As Bill Frindall's valuable figures show, in thirty-six matches as a member of West Indies teams he scored 2282 runs at 38.67; in seventy-four as captain, 5233 at 51.30. As a keynote of his 'captain character' he invariably responded to high challenge. That was apparent in his last innings when in a losing side against Australia, his 72 was both the highest and the most convincing innings of his team.

Lloyd's captaincy has been impressively marked by dignity; firm, unfussy discipline; and cool, realistic strategy. Some among his opponents have criticized him for the ruthless use of his mighty battery of fast bowlers. He, in typically relaxed fashion, has indicated that given the sharpest of cricketing weapons, he will employ it, and that the matter of intimidatory bowling is one for the decision of umpires.

He retires a well-liked and respected cricketer; a philosophic man who managed to play and conduct his matches in a fashion refreshingly free from the acrimony which has infected the cricket of some of his opponents.

*The Guardian*


# Three Men for All Seasons

### THE ALL-ROUNDERS

The phrase 'cometh the hour, cometh the man' passed into cricket lore thirty-three years ago. Cliff Gladwin used it, not too seriously, after the last possible ball of the fifth Test of the 1948–49 series bounced off his hip for the leg-bye that won the match for England.

In the past two years it has proved trebly true. The 1981 season in England offered few such spectator attractions as those of the 1980 West Indians. True, the Australians were the visitors and that fact alone has its own appeal. On the other hand, an atmosphere of some disillusionment and disappointment was engendered by the fact that neither of the two senior Chappell brothers bothered to make the trip; Lillee had unhappily marred his image and, fine player as Allan Border was, he was a grafter rather than a crowd-puller; while Hughes, sadly, did not reproduce his most exciting form.

Everything seemed to conspire to reduce public enthusiasm. Australia won the first Test; the second ended in a draw and crowd disorder; and Botham resigned from the captaincy. So to Headingley, where there was more crowd trouble, and despite a heroic bowling spell by Botham on his return to the ranks, Australia took a first-innings lead of 227. When they reduced Brearley's side to 135 for seven, needing 92 to avoid the innings defeat, English spirits were low indeed. It was the prescribed situation for a highly improbable boy's adventure story. Surely enough, Botham made 149 and gave England a scrap of hope, which Willis seized. Twelve days later Botham did it again; this time, when Australia, 105 for four, wanted only 46 more runs to win, he bowled an all but incredible 28-ball spell to take five wickets for one run: a 29-run win for England. When, within a fortnight, he had followed a first-innings duck with 118 and five wickets, he had turned and won a Test series more nearly single-handed than any man had ever done before. Still he took ten wickets in the final Test at The Oval. He had given cricket in England an amazing psychological fillip – and ushered in an almost gladiatorial era of all-rounders.

England's three Test series since then have been dominated, certainly in the public imagination, by three all-rounders: Ian Botham in all three; Kapil Dev Nikhanj in two; and Imran Khan Niazi in one. Significantly, too, and by happy coincidence for the health of the game, all three are pace bowlers and generous strikers of the ball, the types of players most likely to appeal to spectators.

At the beginning of the 1982 English season which they were to grace and shape, Botham was twenty-six, Kapil Dev twenty-three and Imran twenty-nine. Botham is the most consistent and commanding batsman of the three; Imran certainly now the fastest bowler: sustainedly and resourcefully hostile. All of them will attack any bowling, Botham with the widest range of strokes but Imran most capably for a man whose bowling is regarded as his main strength. All three are 'naturals' with a spirit of adventure.

All three, too, made early marks in the adult game. Botham played for Somerset second eleven at fifteen; for the first team, in the John Player League, at seventeen; and won his first England cap at twenty-one. Kapil Dev, in his first Ranji Trophy match, at the age of sixteen years and ten months, took six for 39 against Punjab; and he first played for India at nineteen. Imran, cousin of Majid Khan and nephew of Jahangir Khan, appeared for Lahore A at seventeen; and for Pakistan at eighteen.

Ian Botham was born in Cheshire and now lives near Scunthorpe; but he learned most of his cricket in Somerset where his father was stationed in the Fleet Air Arm at Yeovil. Immensely physically strong, with a good eye and natural timing, he was desperately keen on cricket from childhood, and utterly determined to succeed in it. He worked his way through various levels of youth cricket to the Lord's staff at sixteen and, in 1974, made his first deep impression on the game in the Benson and Hedges quarter-final against Hampshire. Somerset needed 183 to win; and, almost as soon as Botham came in – at the precarious situation of 113 for eight – he was hit in the mouth by a bouncer from Anderson Roberts. The blow cost him four teeth but, although he was bleeding heavily, he refused to leave the field and his 45 not out, with a final flourish of two sixes, effectively won the match for Somerset and the Gold Award for himself.

He learned quickly, extending his batting from basic strength in driving and square-cutting; under the guidance of Tom Cartwright, improving the control of his fast-medium bowling: adding in-swing to out-swing; developing the bouncer, which sometimes seems to possess him. By 1977 he was recognized as a considerable all-rounder. Yet that summer began and ended with frustration for him: he was relegated to twelfth man for the one-day internationals against Australia; then he suffered a foot injury which kept him out of the fifth Test and almost certainly deprived him of the nowadays rare achievement of the 'double' (in the event he scored 738 runs and took 88 wickets) in the first-class season. In between, however, he took five wickets in the first innings of each of his first two Tests. Before he was twenty-four he had become the youngest player to complete the double in Tests, and had done so in the fewest matches. The first of those records has since been taken by Kapil Dev, but at twenty-five years and 280 days Ian Botham became the youngest – and only the third – cricketer to complete 2000 runs and 200 wickets in Tests.

At twenty-three, Kapil Dev Nikhanj, of Haryana, Nelson in the Lancashire League, Northamptonshire and India, is already a widely experienced cricketer. Lean and wirily strong, he is of the soldierly race of the Jaths (there is a Jath regiment). He is largely a front-of-the-wicket batsman: quick-eyed and aggressive. He bowls at lively pace, primarily out-swing but with what they call in the business a 'nipper backer'; some movement off the pitch, concealed variations and, when the ball is new, an occasional bouncer. He took Ian Botham's record by becoming the youngest cricketer to perform the double in Test cricket, at twenty-one years and 27 days – and in the remarkably short period of one year 107 days. Except when he captains his state from a position close to the wicket, he fields generally in the deep where he is fast and safe-handed.

Imran Khan Niazi has matured and toughened; now he is physically at his peak as a fast bowler and has the essentially combative quality of a Pathan. Capable of genuine pace and a quite lethal bouncer, he regards himself primarily as a swing-bowler and he makes the ball leave the bat as dangerously as anyone in the game – and generally achieves seam movement in both directions. His deadliest weapon, though, is his extra yard of pace which took Botham by surprise at Lord's.

The 1981–82 series in India did not, by its nature and, above all, the wickets on which it was played, provide a platform for Botham and Kapil Dev to appear at their most spectacular; but they both made major contributions. Botham, though, learned much there. He resisted staunchly in the only Test defeat, taking nine wickets and making top score in the disastrous second innings; had an innings of over fifty in each of the other Tests to finish top of the English Test batting with an average of 55. He dominated the third day at Kanpur with 142, his highest score against India. It was a responsible and discriminating innings, though he allowed himself a vivid finish with six, four, six off consecutive balls from Doshi, the third a prodigious pulled drive which struck the scoreboard far beyond the mid-wicket boundary. As a bowler, too, he took most wickets for England, and developed a capacity to contain when the situation demanded.

Meanwhile, for India, Kapil Dev produced a match-winning all-round performance at Bombay, played capably all through and, at Kanpur, struck a spectacular century. His hundred came off only 83 balls. He averaged 53 for the series and took twenty-two wickets – equally highest in the series with Dilip Doshi – at 37.95.

The two were nearer their element in the series in England when, at Lord's, Kapil Dev, highest scorer but one in each Indian innings and taking eight of the thirteen English wickets to fall, was unlucky to be on the losing side. Botham rallied the English batting from potential disaster at 37 for three and then, with five wickets for 46, broke down India to 128 all out, the follow-on, and eventual defeat. In the inconclusive Old Trafford affair in which even the two first innings were not completed, the pair contributed some splendidly entertaining batting: Botham 128 (two sixes and nineteen fours) off 169 balls; Kapil Dev 65 (one six and eighteen fours) off 55.

At The Oval they were top scorers for their respective sides: Botham with a massive 208 (226 balls; four sixes and nineteen fours), Kapil Dev 97 (93 balls; two sixes, fourteen fours). Botham was conclusively top of the English batting in both aggregate and average (403 runs at 134.33) and third in the bowling (nine wickets at 35.56). Kapil Dev was second in the Indian bowling (ten wickets at 43.90); top in aggregate, second in average (292 at 73) in the batting; and his 292 runs came from only 273 balls – a remarkable combination of aggression and consistency.

Reasons other than the quality of the cricket led to an unhappy financial outcome of the series.

So to the Pakistan series: Botham versus Imran Khan. At Edgbaston in the first Test, Imran, like Kapil Dev at Lord's, produced a heroic performance, only to finish on the losing side. To his obvious satisfaction, he bowled Ian Botham – for 2 – with a ball of full length which bit back and, conclusively, was that crucial yard faster to pierce an unfinished stroke. In the second innings, Tahir Naqqash bowled him for nought. However Botham, with five key wickets and, altogether, six for 156, played a valuably dogged part in England's win. Imran took seven for 52 and two for 54; made a determinedly aggressive 22 in the first innings; and, in the face of imminent defeat, a highly resistant 65 (two sixes and six fours) which was by far the highest score for Pakistan.

At Lord's neither had decisive effect. In the long Pakistani first innings, Botham plugged away for 44 overs to take the three good, but costly, wickets of Mansoor Akhtar, Haroon Rashid – and Imran (for 12). When England batted for the first time Botham's 31 was only two less than top score in their 227; and when they followed on, he made top score 69 out of 276 before they went down to defeat. Imran, who did not need to bat twice, took two wickets in each innings; Qadir did the main damage in the first and Mudassar produced his shock in the second. Imran, however, captained Pakistan to only their second win over England since their handsome surprise at The Oval in 1954.

Again, as in 1981, tension and performance were maintained. It was the first time in this country that a series had gone to the final of a three-match rubber all square. Once more, the two all-rounders were at one another's throats. Imran Khan came in at 160 for five, and stayed to take the weight of the innings with top score, 67 not out in a total of 275; Botham took four for 70. He, too, came in to a difficult situation: Imran, with three wickets in nine balls for 2 runs, had cut England down to 77 for four. Botham duly made the highest score but one – 57 – before he was put out by Sikander. Imran's bowling figures were five for 49, and Pakistan led by 19. Once more, like a repeating groove, Imran came in at 85 for four and had made 46 – highest score but one – before he was caught at cover. The bowler was Botham who, for the twentieth time in Tests, took five wickets in an innings (for 74).

Once more the play ran like the script for a Greyfriars story. Imran took Tavaré's wicket at 103 but the English batting seemed to be ambling comfortably to its objective of 219 when Mudassar, again, nipped in: three quick wickets brought them to 187 for four. That was all Imran needed to revive his faith. While Botham stood watching at the non-striker's end, he fired out Lamb and Randall. After Botham drove back a stinging return catch which was too hot for Mudassar to hold, he contented himself with defence until he and Marks had the opportunity to go in for bad light.

So, on the last morning, England, with four wickets left, needed 29 to win, and Botham and Imran were thrown into direct confrontation. It would be quite unfair to suggest that either submerges team to personal interest, but obviously there is rivalry in their opposition. Its outcome would certainly be reflected in Tom Graveney's nomination of the Man of the Match and Man of the Series. Those two decisions were almost certainly settled by a single ball which was not bowled by either of the protagonists. When Botham had scored 4, he followed a ball from Mudassar outside the off stump and was caught by Majid at slip.

Now Imran rose to considerable heights. He bowled to Marks at blazing pace. In the course of a single over – said probably to be the fiercest sent down in the English season – he might have taken all three of those remaining English wickets. Marks, probably without knowing quite how, survived. England came home by three wickets. Imran Khan was named Man of the Match and Man of the Series. No one would dispute his right to those awards; but cricketers have won them for less than Ian Botham had achieved. All very romantic, perhaps; but it has its practical side. The three-match series had virtually balanced the summer's books by drawing in some £600,000 more than the TCCB had expected. That may not be what cricket is played for; but it could not be played without it.

*Guardian Book of Sport*, 1982/3

# —4—

# International Discourse

## Hassett's Australians

*September* 1953.   The touring cricketers who next week leave us to our football will go down in the record books as the '1953 Australian team'. Their captain, Lindsay Hassett, probably fears, behind his quizzically friendly expression, that Australia will remember it as 'Hassett's side that lost The Ashes'. For English cricketers, even those who sought to minimize them because we won the rubber from them, these men will, with the years, become cricketing immortals. Some of them – Hole, Archer, Craig, de Courcy, Davidson, Benaud – will be back to attack us with the weapons forged from their past summer's experience. When the Australians were presented to the Queen, Her Majesty remarked to the barely eighteen-year-old Ian Craig, 'I understand this is your first visit to England.' 'Yes, Your Majesty,' he said, 'and unless my batting improves it will be my last.' He has grown up beyond his figures and gained, this summer, experience for which two generations of English bowlers will pay. Others, in the normal course of Australian Test cricket, may have made their last visit, wherefore we may well recall the sight of them before they become legend.

After all, we did beat them; and that fact alone must give them a certain friendly glory in our memories. Indeed, no statistics can expunge the awe-inspiring effect of nine of them standing in a grim, close crescent around the bats of Englishmen who could deceive neither themselves nor us into a state of confidence. Great batsmen may be ground into quiescent defence, great bowling may, on unhelpful pitches, appear ordinary; but great fielding is the only sustained, minute-to-minute glory of cricket, distilling suspense out of its threat to snatch the uncatchable from the confident stroke, tautening the quiet Headingley afternoon like a fiddle-string by its poised antagonism.

Morris, Benaud, de Courcy, Miller, Hole, Archer, Davidson – all made catches in this past Test series which checked the breath of thirty thousand people. They could draw the last and most fuddled straggler out from the bar when they stood, crouched for the edged stroke, against the new ball as bowled by that unique Ray Lindwall whom we shall not see again in the guise he wore in our summers of 1948 and 1953. The men who propel a cricket ball at a speed faster than the reflex of the practised batsmen do not retain that gift into their thirties. Larwood, Gregory – even the legendary Tom Richardson – once the first young-muscled completeness was past, had to forsake pure pace and, at best, lean upon technique. Lindwall himself, at thirty-two, toyed with medium pace and, by his concealment, variety and control made that loss of concentration a virtue. Thus he could hold back his thunderbolt until batsmen and crowd both bated their breaths against its release. Again and again men were caught off him, with their mouths still half-open with astonishment.

He came softly, steadily, smoothly up his approach like a wind, and his body, mightily muscled at the trunk, swung back and then, on the final stride, forward in a mighty, but understood, surge of impulsion. Custom could not stale the impact of his attack upon player or watcher. For two or three overs he would work up to the stage of ease and looseness when the best deliveries of his life were within his easy command. For a couple of overs he would hold that power which might at any time wreck an innings and then, even in his last over, he might unseat the best. The mothers of English boy-cricketers may well have frightened their children with the word 'Lindwall' as an earlier generation of French women put terror into the name of Marlborough.

Good Test cricketers are present in every period. The player who compels as Lindwall has done in two tours of this country occurs less than once in every generation. He was the siege engine who might at any time blast away all defence; every man who batted against him, every spectator who watched him, not only recognized that fact technically but *felt* it. The years which took away his power to bowl over after over at top speed have informed Lindwall's cricket brain most shrewdly. So, should he care to return in 1956 as a bowler of medium pace who is in full control of swing, length, direction, change of pace and a quick appreciation of the batsman's weakness, a very fine bowler will be needed to exclude him from the touring party.

His fellow opening bowler must almost certainly be a fresh player. That William Arras Johnston who returns to Australia with a batting average for the tour of 102 may well be content to enjoy the joke for the rest of his days in a deck chair. Most amiable and enthusiastic of cricketers, he may accept with his philosophically but humorously raised eyebrow the likelihood that a major knee injury could be a worry to him, his selectors and his captain, and decide to play his cricket in less responsible circumstances. Australia has not had the good fortune to know the bowler Johnston who, in English air and on English turf, made a cricket ball float and curve, nip and turn so that he seemed, while leaving the batsman no moment of peace, almost to bowl for bowling's sake.

In Keith Miller we have seen – and many have misunderstood – the finest all-rounder of post-war cricket and, possibly, one as great as any the game has known. Certainly he has taken catches, played strokes and bowled balls as fine as any living man has seen. Physically a man of amazing animal grace, he is also essentially shy and, even more positively, in his human relationships magnificently generous. In the final Test, at The Oval, he fielded the ball over by the Vauxhall End and, with a single stride, threw it, true as by compass, a full hundred yards, full toss into the gloves of Langley who did not need to move an inch to take it. On a cricket field, Miller is lost in the game: he would bowl with the same fire and prolific repertoire if he were playing on a desert island, for he loves to pit every ounce of himself against the other man. Only, sometimes, when his powers could not lift the game – which is for him always a game – above the pedestrian, he would turn a hungry attention upon the crowd. He could play upon it, with an averted smile, as a busker plays a concertina, with an instant superficial effect which he found laughable. If he can sink his ebullience to the level of cricketing utility – if true competence upon Test level may be so slightingly described – then there is no doubt that Miller could come here three years hence as an elder batsman, playing with amusement as others would give their ears to play. Figures do not show the thoughtful help this sometimes gaily mischievous young man gave to the captain who treated his friendly loyalty with such unobtrusive respect.

Indeed, this departing team should be remembered as 'Hassett's Australians'. Lindsay Hassett bears the two unmistakable marks of the great batsman: he always has plenty of time to play his strokes, and in the perfection of his timing there is a power which he rarely allowed himself to indulge in Test matches. Rather, with consummate perfection of footwork, he moved to a position in which he could wait for the ball to hit his straightly presented bat. The entire concept of the five-day Test might have irritated him; instead, he accepted it as ordained and, with an amused air, demonstrated the type of cricket it demands. He did almost all a captain could do on the field; off it, he talked with understanding, reason and humour to all who came to enquire, beg or importune. In doing so, he set English cricket an example of perfect 'public relations' and set the tone for a team which would still have made its multitude of friends in England even if it had retained The Ashes.

*The Spectator*

# A Test Match is Lost – or Won

*August* 1954.   It happened once before – also at The Oval – when, in 1882, Spofforth bowled out England, including W.G. Grace. On that occasion a sporting newspaper printed an obituary notice of English cricket, stating that the body would be cremated and the 'ashes' taken to Australia.

This time there was less sense of tragedy. 'English cricket' masked its surprise with a sickly grin. It will be good for Pakistan cricket, and for the young Pakistan nation, says your cricketer, swallowing hard and remembering to be high-minded. It will, indeed, be good for Pakistan cricket and for the young Pakistan nation. They would have said so themselves, given time.

Fortunately for that section of the community which takes its sport seriously, the 'disaster' will, by Saturday, have been swamped by the onset of the football season when Hungary will become a greater problem than Kardar's cricketers. In December, too, we shall be visited by a German football team.

Humour could deal no deadlier blow at the sporting creed than that Canada should now defeat Pakistan; but that could be a cruel blow at much simple pride also.

The umbrellas wore an air of well-rolled poise on Monday afternoon. It was then no more than a matter of whether the 'boys' could finish it that night and have a day of rest before their matches on Wednesday. Compton advanced down the wicket, bat raised to threaten such a destruction as he had worked at Trent Bridge. The bowling was too tight a net for him. Wickets fell; unease ruffled the umbrellas. On

Tuesday they did not come. There was more room in the car park.

It had all, in fact, been done on Monday morning. The droll little man Wazir Mohammed, who had plodded so slow and dejected a way back to the pavilion at Old Trafford, batted very seriously: he watched the ball carefully until it met his bat. At the other end, Zulfiqar allowed himself – once – the luxury of a superb late cut. Otherwise, each was determined to show the English spectators that he could lose hard. They ticked off one afternoon train after another. Of course, they were very ordinary players, nodded the umbrellas; they will not last long. They lasted long.

England had what was called a 'pace attack', which is to say that it had two fast bowlers and one medium-fast bowler. In Pakistan, many people bowl as fast as they can – and on fast wickets. No side we have seen is so strong against fast bowling as this from Pakistan. From first man to last they move firmly into the line of the ball and play it without flinching or hesitation. Certainly Mr Tyson from Northants is fast; but his bowling can be seen.

The batting was so slow – almost monotonous. No one knew that the match was being won. Cricket matches are won like that: the scale may be greater in some Test matches – it is often much smaller in other cricket matches – but in essence it is merely the making of runs without the loss of wickets. The process may be called 'hitting out' or 'stone-walling'; unless time forbids it, the result is the same.

The umbrellas liked the Pakistanis: such game, cheerful chaps. They liked Fazal because he could bowl for so long and appear to like it. Now, however, he was engaged upon a process the direct reverse of that put into operation by his batsmen. He was taking wickets without compensation of runs. He was making the ball turn from right to left or from left to right after it bounced. Batsmen do not like this when the ball's landing-point is one from which neither the forward-stroke nor the back-stroke can be played with assurance. Moreover, the ball was being bowled at such pace that there was no time for consideration or exchange of stroke.

There were jokes on the field. Pakistan are not a grim side except when grimness in resistance to defeat is forced upon them. Even then, their manner is that of people (incomprehensibly?) enjoying cricket. Hanif has dared to joke by bowling both right arm and left in the course of the same over: the point of the joke lies in the fact that he took a wicket – with his left arm. On Tuesday he ran out the last English batsman by throwing down the stumps direct from cover point, with his right arm.

Hanif is the finest hooker of fast bowling in the world. He has all the other strokes as well; within two years he might easily be the best batsman in the world. He did not make many runs in this match; neither did Maqsood, on fast wickets one of the most entertaining stroke-players we have seen.

How trite to say that this is a party of pleasant people who, as cricketers, like to score quickly and enjoy the game. The same has been said about teams of whom it was not true; in this case it is quite true. The winners were excited at the result – childishly excited – as excited as the English team after they had beaten Australia last year. Some of them were as near tears as some English cricketers were last year.

The crowd, which slightly outnumbered the police present, and which gathered in front of the pavilion after the match was over, held a large proportion of Pakistanis, many of them students, many wearing horn-rimmed spectacles. There was also a lovely Pakistani girl in a red sari and a matching short coat thrown over her shoulders. They were all very polite: they took their cues as to when to cheer, when to call for a player, and when to be quiet, from the small boys who have been doing this after every final Test since they were big enough to go to The Oval. One such veteran reports that on returning home his mother asked him, 'Has there been a cricket match today then?'

It was an absorbing game of cricket. If only England had just won instead of just losing there would have been no element of surprise – nor quite such deep pleasure.

*The Spectator*

# The South Africans in England

A green tie with a single springbok head embroidered on it, worn every Tuesday, will mark – so long as the ties endure – the members of Jack Cheetham's 1955 South African touring team in England. On Tuesdays, because on Tuesday 12 July, at Old Trafford, and Tuesday 26 July, at Headingley, the Springboks won the third and fourth Tests of the 1955 series – after England had won the first two – to go all square to the final match at The Oval. They lost the rubber, but, at the Savoy Hotel last September, Cheetham, on behalf of his side, accepted the fifth of the annually presented 'County' cricket cups. Four of the cups are awarded for individual achievements by a bowler, a batsman, a fieldsman and a wicket-keeper. The fifth is a 'special award for the year's outstanding performance'. The applause of a crowded room of players, administrators and critics of the game endorsed the judgement of the panel of distinguished cricketers who had nominated the touring side for that distinction.

There were few in the dressing-room or the press boxes to prophesy such success for the South Africans at the end of May. They lost their opening match of the tour to Worcester when, in the first demonstration of their weakness against off-spin, they were bowled out by Martin Horton. The month of May ran on, icy and wet. In such conditions it was understandable that the faster bowlers were not invited to bowl at full pace for fear of muscle injuries. Yet only the accuracy of Tayfield indicated any substantial quality in the remainder of the bowling; the batting was inconsistent and even the side's fielding, which reports of their 1952–53 tour of Australia had made almost legendary, looked no more than ordinary. The bleakness of an English spring meant that the visitors were out of their cricketing element.

At Colchester, however, in the first match of June, the sun at last shone on the tourists' backs; from that day they began to flourish. At last the fast bowlers looked capable of true pace, the ground fielding improved and the batting began, albeit erratically, to make worthwhile runs. In the next match, against Lancashire at Old Trafford, Paul Winslow took his remarkable 40 runs off eight consecutive balls from Jack Ikin and Goodwin and the fielding hinted at its potential. Then to the first Test: an innings defeat in four days.

In the Whitsun fixture with Somerset, Peter Heine amazed even himself by the late sharpness of his out-swing in the close air of the seam-bowler's delight at Taunton. That single match marked the change in him from good county standard to a genuine Test bowler, commanding both swings and an alarmingly steep lift at a pace little short of the fastest.

Heine's bowling and a glorious 142 by McLean gave South Africa a substantial first-innings lead in the Lord's Test. Then Statham smashed their second innings – he presented even McGlew with a 'pair' – and they lost by 71. Cheetham was badly injured by a blow on the elbow from a rising ball by Trueman. Now it seemed to some that the rubber was a foregone conclusion, that public self-satisfaction about English cricket after the Australian tour was justified, and that the South Africans were relatively small beer. The immediate post-war admiration for touring teams, as such, has faded with the novelty of their visits, and much criticism has become sterner, in sympathy with – or possibly, in creating – the change of public attitude.

All this time under the sun, however, the Springboks were finding form and achievement to back the fitness produced by their rigid training. Early in the tour Jack Cheetham had said to me, 'Our fielding is not just a matter of making brilliant catches; it is a matter of hard graft, turning twos into ones, stopping singles, chasing boundary strokes to the last stride; if you are doing that all the time, then, when the impossible catch comes, you get to it and it sticks.' That was beginning to happen in county matches. McGlew was making himself almost a national figure, not only by the devotional courage of his batting, but by the furious speed and enthusiasm of his ground fielding. Heine, Endean, Mansell, Goddard and Duckworth were holding superb close catches; McLean and Winslow were supporting McGlew in the deep.

In the five-day phenomenon of unbroken sun at Old Trafford, sustained and hostile fast bowling by Heine and Adcock put out England. For South Africa the uncompromising opening of McGlew (104 not out) and Goddard (62) brought 147. The middle order collapsed, as usual, but then, while McGlew (retired hurt) was off the field, Winslow made a schoolboy-romance century – completing it with a six over the sight-screen – and with Waite's more sedate 113, South Africa declared at 521 for eight. Lifted by opportunity, Heine and Adcock kept up their pace for over after over and made the ball lift from barely short of a length. May, Compton, Cowdrey, Bailey, Evans – injured and batting one-handed – resisted well, but England's 381 was not enough. Set 67 runs an hour, the South Africans won in a headlong gallop of runs, and suddenly their stature had increased in popular estimation. It was not merely that they had won, but they had won gallantly, by the three most exciting facets of cricket – big hitting, fine fielding and fast bowling.

With their win in the fourth Test at Leeds, gained by steady bowling, superb fielding and a massive second innings, the barely considered players of May became the heroes of July and August. Few defensive batsmen of recent years have so captured the imagination as McGlew, resistance bristling out of his small, hard-trained frame, as he played every ball as if for his life. Goddard, fine slip-fieldsman, dogged bat and bowler of a naggingly defensive length, had grown into a Test all-rounder. Tayfield's mannerisms were known up and down the country as he bowled on and on, dropping his well-flighted and hard-spun off-breaks with the monotonous accuracy of a dripping tap. Every time McLean or Winslow walked to the wicket the little boys returned from their wanderings off-stage to acclaim them with shrill whistles and a high-voiced bubble of anticipation. Less spectacularly, Waite was keeping wicket with neat certainty and batting to confirm the claim that he was the finest wicket-keeper/batsman in the world.

Adcock broke a bone in his foot at Leeds, and upon that cue, Fuller began to bowl his medium-paced variety of swing, cut and spin with steady success. Glamorgan, who had gained a spectacular win over the 1951 South Africans at Swansea, were roundly beaten; so, too, were Warwick before the fifth Test selection from a party in which Cheetham and Adcock were again fit. Time will not see a resolution of the question posed by the South African choice of the diligent Fuller and the phlegmatically experienced Mansell, for that rubber Test, in preference to the livelier bowling of Adcock and the cavalier batting of Winslow. In the event, the side's original weaknesses cost South Africa the series: the middle collapsed (numbers three, four and five made six runs between them in the two innings) and not even batting of elegant judgement by Waite could prevent Laker's off-spin from destroying the second innings.

No Test series could have been more closely fought. The South Africans played with great fire and, by July, their out-cricket was utterly glorious. Spirit lifted their performance far above their technical standard. Except McGlew, Waite, Heine, Tayfield and, possibly, Goddard and Adcock, their players were technically inferior to the English – clearly so by comparison with the English eleven which could have been envisaged at the start of the season. Of that team the selection was deprived of Hutton in five Tests, Cowdrey and Appleyard in four each, Tyson in three, Evans in two and Statham in one: thus, nineteen man-Tests, if the term may be pardoned, were missed by key players. The two Test-winning combinations, Tyson–Statham and May–Cowdrey, each appeared once only.

Down to the end of the tour McGlew batted with utter single-mindedness and – ironically as it must have seemed to the side's batsmen – Tayfield bowled the off-break as well as anyone in the world bowls it today. Heine struck a series of mightily hit innings as the tourists emphasized their superiority over any eleven in England short of Test strength.

Smith, who played in the first Test, had a surprisingly disappointing summer with his leg-breaks in such dry-wicket weather. Murray did not find his batting form, but bowled well enough to suggest that he should have bowled more. Finally, Duckworth, the reserve wicket-keeper, was an attractive stroke-maker.

The 1955 South Africans were a friendly and popular party of cricketers who put cricket first and played it hard. They left with a respect they had earned for themselves and, in their fitness and the unfailing enthusiasm of their out-cricket, they left a memorable example to the cricketers of England. The acid test of any touring side is financial; Cheetham's Springboks came through it triumphantly.

*Playfair Cricket Annual*, 1956

# The New Zealanders in England

The 1958 New Zealanders played their cricket enthusiastically, had few rubs of the green, and achieved as much as a fair-minded critic could ask of them. Moreover, they 'blooded' at least three young players who may become outstanding by world standards.

Hadlee steered his 1949 side shrewdly to draw its four three-day Tests with England. Apparently on the basis of that performance, but certainly not at the request – nor, presumably, the desire – of the New Zealanders, Reid's team was allotted five five-day Tests in 1958. It was unfortunate for them that such an elevation should coincide with an English team so outstanding as not to need the help of the turning wickets which, with almost sinister regularity, fell to the lot of the New Zealand batting.

Over the entire season, the touring side's out-cricket was eager and sometimes brilliant; strong pace bowling, and spin less meagre than their team strategy made it appear, were backed by unflagging ground fielding and consistent catching. It was predictable when the side was selected that, short of remarkable advances by several players, the batting would be weak. Wallace, even at the age of forty-one, probably would have been an asset. Of the capable order of Sutcliffe, Scott, Reid, Wallace, Donnelly, Hadlee and Rabone which mustered over

650 runs in the final Test of 1949, only Reid and Sutcliffe returned.

From a population about as large as that of greater Liverpool, none of whose cricketers can play more than five first-class matches a year, it must always be remarkable if New Zealand musters a Test team capable of matching England's. Ironically, in a match against the touring side immediately before it sailed, Donnelly – completely out of practice – and Rabone, neither of whom, for business reasons, was available for selection, made scores of 48 and 92. On the tour, only three batsmen – Reid, Sutcliffe and Harford – made centuries in first-class matches, and only four – the same three and Miller – completed a thousand runs.

Yet, in the May days, the batting rose above reasonable expectations. Its strength clearly lay in Sutcliffe and Reid. Sutcliffe, in the opening match, promised that he could, and would, modify his former, dashing methods to meet the need for a sheet-anchor to the innings; and Reid soon was batting with effective, controlled aggression. Within the first week, Harford had made fast runs by handsome strokes and the two nineteen-year-olds, Playle and Sparling, had given impressive indications of maturity.

Defeat by Surrey – on a bowlers' wicket at The Oval – was no more than had befallen the last Australian and West Indian sides. The New Zealanders appeared to see it in that light and continued strongly. At Lord's, MCC fielded a side little below Test standard, but its attack was hammered with exciting strokes and the New Zealanders won in a stirring finish.

An amazing win over Glamorgan and an overwhelming defeat of Somerset argued that the tourists were a greater force than had been anticipated, and took them to the first Test with six wins and only one defeat in ten matches – a better record than that of the 1956 Australians at the same point.

This, however, was to prove the peak of the side's performance; never again did it rise to such a level of confidence, aggression and achievement. On the opening day of the first Test, its 'tight' seam-bowling and lively fielding contained the English batting most creditably. On the second morning, its grip was shaken off and from that point onward – apart from the new ball attack – it became a consciously beaten side which went down to a 4–0 defeat in the Test rubber – a record for any series played in England.

Hope must often have drained out of the New Zealand players –

especially the batsmen – on the nights when they heard the rain streaming down to make yet another turning wicket on which their inexperience made them almost abject prey to the spin of Lock and Laker.

Crucially, in the Tests, Reid and Sutcliffe fell far below their form of county matches. Against Somerset and Sussex in particular, Reid was a magnificent punitive batsman, flaying any bowling below the highest class with versatile and fiercely powerful strokes. Sutcliffe, too, could command a county attack and play such fluent strokes as recalled his finest days of 1949. Yet neither showed the five-day-match concentration to make long scores against Test bowling which rarely yielded a loose ball. Thus, Sutcliffe averaged 17.24 in Tests as opposed to 34 in other matches; Reid 16.33 in Tests (a bare 10 until his 51 not out in the final stages of the drawn game at The Oval), but 47 elsewhere. The English bowlers' pace and spin brought out the weaknesses of the other senior batsmen in sharp relief. Miller, a keen cricketer of admirable and cheerful temperament, had a pronounced on-side bias, which found him too often playing across the line of the ball. Harford, initially impressive, lost all confidence; and Meale, as soon as he moved out of dead-bat defence, had no straight strokes and neither his gameness nor his power made good the deficiency.

In almost every Test someone or other batted pluckily but MacGibbon, previously classed as a 'bowler who can also bat', by courage and common sense scored most runs in Tests, using his height and reach to play right forward or right back in defence, driving anything overpitched with firm defiance. The three youngsters, D'Arcy, Playle and Sparling, all played long, correct and determined innings. They began the tour with first-class experience equivalent to less than a month's play in English cricket. Their ability to score from the best bowling was limited, but they recognized their limitations and played intelligently, as well as courageously, within them. All three should be fully capable of Test centuries before the next New Zealand tour.

MacGibbon took most wickets on the tour and, in Tests, three times as many as anyone else, with the best average (twenty at 19.45). Capable of long spells at lively fast-medium pace, he commanded late out-swing and was always likely to 'move' the worn ball dangerously off the pitch. At least one seam-bowler had to be left out of every Test, yet Hayes, of hostile pace; Blair, with his fluent action and occasional sharp swing; and Cave, who, bowling shrewdly and well within himself, had some great days – all were useful, and sometimes more than that.

From the outset the side looked deficient in 'natural' spin. Sparling, however, became a capable, 'flighty' off-spinner of the Ian Johnson type; he might well have been used more, and earlier. Reid attempted to make good the deficiency himself, bowling sharp off-spin at much less than his former pace. He lacked, however, the controlled variety and flight to beat the best batsmen. Moir, apparently lacking his captain's confidence, seemed to lose his own; on his day he turned his leg-breaks and googlies magnificently, but he was never given the amount of bowling a leg-breaker *needs* to win matches. Alabaster, his junior, fell away after a good start, but he has the application and natural ability to make a valuable all-rounder.

The attack was never loose because the fielding was always keen. Playle, Reid, Alabaster and MacGibbon all took good close catches; D'Arcy and Sparling were fine further from the wicket, and everyone did his level best. Petrie, especially when standing back to the faster bowlers, was one of the most reliable wicket-keepers in the country and it was happy that he should have been chosen to play for the Gentlemen against the Players, at Scarborough. His understudy, Ward, produced some performances of bright promise.

There was an unhappy disposition in some quarters to regard the tour as a 'failure' because the side was so roundly defeated in the Test series. Yet the Australians in 1956 and the West Indies in 1957 had done little better. Once more, too, luck was on the side of the big battalions: most of the fortune of the weather fell to the English team. It is by no means certain that the brittle New Zealand batting could have stood up to the English attack even on good batsmen's wickets, but in the event it barely had the opportunity to do so.

Yet even in Tests there were fine and memorable moments for the side. The likeable, boyish-looking D'Arcy fought his way into representative cricket like a new McGlew, his jutting-elbowed defence bristling with defiance; and after his long resistance at Lord's the crowd cheered him, movingly, into the Pavilion. At Leeds, too, Playle resisted for half the last day in poised, imperturbable defence – once startlingly relieved by a cover-drive of true beauty – which changed the entire mood of the match, and, in mid-afternoon, reduced even the English players from certainty of victory to wondering whether this young man would thwart them. MacGibbon's leap of triumph – all six foot six of him hoist high in the air – when he took May's wicket at Lord's is a picture that will remain long in the memory. At Old Trafford, Sparling marked his entry into his twenties with a Test innings which revealed a cricket brain, temperament and all-round capability which probably mark him as a future captain of New Zealand. We may, too, relish the memory of Moir at Old Trafford, batting himself to an artificial position – but one which gave him much wry amusement – at the top of his side's Test batting averages.

Games with the counties produced some fine performances. At Cardiff, for instance, Cave slashed wide the second Glamorgan innings with a magnificent opening spell of seam bowling (8 overs; 8 maidens; 0 runs; 4 wickets) which turned an apparently certain draw into a win for the touring side. Reid, making what was until then the fastest century of the season, hit the Sussex bowling, old ball and new, all over the Hove ground with strokes of such savage brilliance as recalled the 'killer' attacks of Sir Donald Bradman's heyday. On a slow, wet wicket at Southampton, quite unsuited to his type of bowling, Moir baffled and routed the Hamphire batting with as fine a spell of leg-break and googly bowling as has been seen in England for several seasons.

The New Zealanders make the visit to England too rarely to lose relish for it. John Reid's party went about their cricket and the country with a charm which made them genuinely popular. The tour was marked, too, by the players' willingness – indeed determination – to learn all they could from the more intensive and professionalized English game.

*Playfair Cricket Annual*, 1959

# The Indians in England

The Indian tour of 1959 was a sad disappointment. The bright sunlight of a lifetime mercilessly illuminated the tourists' cricket as lacking in both enterprise and fighting quality, and no one can have been truly surprised when they set up the unenviable record of being the first side to lose all five Tests of a rubber in England. They played like sixteen lonely individuals reconciled to defeat, but hoping to salvage some personal credit from the wreckage. The body of cricket in India must have been as dismayed by the tour as English cricket followers; but, outwardly at least, the touring players bore their defeat philosophically and gave no public hint of any dissension – if, indeed, any existed among them.

The Maharaja of Baroda, unusually young at thirty to be the manager of a touring side, carried out his duties with the firmness, judgement and diplomatic public front to be expected from a cricketer, a prince of the old regime and a politician of the new. He, to some extent, disarmed criticism by his declaration that, from the Indian point of view, the purpose of the tour was largely educational and to 'blood' young players for the future. Even on that score, however, the visit was limited in its success.

The side's troubles began even before it was picked. In the 1958–59 'home' series against the West Indies, India had four different captains in five Tests – and three of those four did not make the tour to England. Ghulam Ahmed, who would have been the senior member of the side, withdrew a few days after his selection. The touring captaincy was given to D.K. Gaekwad, who had played in only one Test against the West Indies, and that as a reserve brought in when Kripal Singh had to withdraw because of injury. A mixture of Test form and policy seems to have dictated the omission of the experienced Adhikari, Phadkar, Ramchand and Mankad, so that the final sixteen players included only four who had come in 1952.

The true judgement of any touring side must be based on its performance in Tests. It is essential, however, in assessing Gaekwad's team, to set it in perspective. India has never won a Test in England and not even the most partisan supporter of the 1959 side can have expected it to do so. By comparison with the two previous post-war teams, it must be said that it was markedly inferior to Pataudi's which made so many runs in 1946; but, all factors considered, it probably was little inferior to Hazare's 1952 side which, however, had some few greater moments in Tests and included some better players. Except for limited periods at Lord's and Old Trafford, the 1959 Indians were outplayed by England from start to finish of every Test.

The 1952 Indians unmistakably and crucially flinched from the pace of Trueman. Their 1959 batsmen had had a recent grounding against the pace of the West Indians Gilchrist and Hall. They – though it is important to note, on *far* easier pitches – stood firm, but strokeless, against a sustained English pace attack. The older batsmen – Umrigar, Manjrekar, Roy and Gaekwad – contented themselves with simple defence against fast bowling. Manjrekar seemed to have more time to play his strokes than anyone else, and he batted fairly at Trent Bridge and Lord's; but injury and a cartilage operation kept him out of the last three Tests. Umrigar – apart from his second innings at Old Trafford – Gaekwad and Roy simply did not measure up to the stature of Test batsmen. The younger generation was divided in its approach to this pace bowling which has consistently proved the destroying agent of their country's batting. Contractor and Nadkarni contented themselves with defence – sometimes impressively and for long periods; but Ghorpade and Borde played more freely, looking for runs, but with no greater – indeed, on figures, less – success. In fact, throughout the entire Test series, only one Indian batsman seemed capable of taking a controlled and efficient initiative against the English fast bowling. That was the Oxford undergraduate Abbas Ali Baig, who came into the side after the university term and Manjrekar's injury. Certainly Baig is a young batsman of considerable gifts; English county players had noted him as such at Oxford. But it may well be that his competence, by comparison with the other Indian batsmen, stemmed in part from the fact that he had never had the 'advantage' of playing first-class cricket in India where wickets have long been prepared for batsmen. As a result, record scores have been made there, but the once promising race of Indian fast bowlers has faded away from sheer and inescapable discouragement, while their batsmen have grown up in blissful ignorance of pace.

Indeed, this Indian team, which declaredly came to learn, should have returned home with one crucial lesson firmly instilled – that until India produces pitches which give fast bowlers the chance and encouragement to test its batsmen, its teams will always be routed by pace in other countries.

Apart from Baig's century at Old Trafford, the only feature of the Tests to give any real encouragement for the future lay in the development and sustained performance of the two young pace bowlers, Desai and Surendranath. Desai, who reached the age of twenty during the Lord's Test, commanded a peak of pace surprising in a man only nine stone in weight, and he concealed a disconcerting bumper. It is to be hoped that the heavy and unaccustomed labour of the frequent and long spells he was called upon to bowl has not had an adverse effect on his natural 'nip'. Surendranath, at a pace best described as 'military medium', swung the ball sharply and often moved it off the pitch. Cheerful, tireless and endlessly persevering, he improved considerably as the tour went along, until he became too good a bowler to be wasted on the defensive methods he was apparently ordered (? instructed) to follow.

The spin attack epitomized the entire side – in that its results fell so far short of its obvious potential. Gupte was the greatest disappointment of the tour, if not of the season. Technically as good a leg-break and googly bowler as any in the world, he had studied English conditions in Lancashire League cricket; but although he already had a world reputation, this was his entry into English first-class cricket, and many enthusiasts looked forward to his bowling with considerable interest. He may well have been discouraged by poor support from his fieldsmen, but whatever the reason, he demonstrably lost heart, and within a few matches began to bowl defensively, abandoning flight and losing his life off the pitch. Nadkarni, potentially another Mankad, bowled slow left-arm with subtle variations of flight, pace and length. Competent and thoughtful as batsman, bowler and fieldsman, he could be a very successful player in English county cricket, but his figures for the tour do not fairly reflect his ability. Borde, the second leg-spinner, was easily first in the bowling averages for the entire tour. In Tests, however, he was limited, on average, to less than ten overs an innings by a strategy which, in face of all logic, seemed to set the slowing of the English run-scoring rate above the taking – certainly above the buying – of wickets. Ghorpade hinted briefly at ability to bowl leg-breaks but he was never given enough bowling to demonstrate, to himself or anyone else, whether this was the fact.

It seemed likely before the tour – and the long run of hard wickets ought to have made it more probable – that the Indian leg-spin could seriously disrupt the technique of English batsmen unaccustomed to this type of bowling. Yet it never seemed to be given a whole-hearted chance to do so. Borde, in particular, suffered from his captain's adherence to a policy of limiting the other side's runs.

In a season of turning wickets, Muddiah might have been quite successful. He bowled off-breaks at a pace on the lively side of slow and, although he seemed to be left out of the side too often, he began well. In his three first-class matches at the start of the tour, he had figures of five for 36 against Cambridge University and nine for 145 (in the match) against Glamorgan. After May, however, he barely turned his arm in a match before he fell ill at Leeds and hardly played again.

The wicket-keepers, Tamhane and Joshi, were as evenly matched as their alternate Test selection suggested: each kept diligently to about county standard and proved capable of batting faithfully for half an hour or so. The Test reserves – Jaisimha, Kripal Singh and Apte – made little impression, though Apte suggested that he could develop into a useful batsman.

In their twenty-eight first-class matches apart from Tests, the Indians won six, lost six and drew sixteen. The last figure is the measure of their general lack of initiative and apparent belief that they would save face by avoiding defeat. Five of their batsmen – Umrigar, Gaekwad, Contractor, Roy and Borde – scored a thousand runs on the tour and Manjrekar certainly would have done so if he had been able to play throughout. Borde and sometimes Umrigar – who was a poised and skilful murderer of any bowling short of top pace and class – played entertainingly, and Gaekwad had some handsome cover strokes. Otherwise, the batting crept.

In a summer of batsmen's wickets, the main bowling rarely rose above the pedestrian and the change bowling was bankrupt. Apart from the wicket-keepers, Gaekwad – who seemed to try to keep his brilliance at cover point a secret – Borde, Nadkarni and Umrigar, who held some good catches at slip, the fielding was poor enough to discourage almost any bowler.

It can only be hoped that the tour has stored away some benefit for the future of Indian cricket. On the immediate face of it, however, it would surely mark the end of the Test careers of several of the players but that their juniors on the tour did not seem good enough to displace them. Borde will remain a keen and useful all-rounder; Desai and Surendranath should serve a fair turn as opening bowlers, while Ghorpade observed intelligently and probably to the eventual profit of his cricket.

India's post-war cricket has grown increasingly depressing season by season, but the tour of 1959, surely, marked its deepest trough. If it serves to set in train re-thinking of their domestic game it may prove that, grim as it was, it taught some eventually worthwhile lessons.

*Playfair Cricket Annual*, 1960


# The South Africans in England

The 1960 South African tour was the unhappiest ever made by a party of overseas cricketers in England. But whenever that fact is recalled in cricket history, it should be qualified by the statement that the South African players were not to blame for the side's troubles, which should be laid at the door of the legislators – political as well as cricketing – in their own country. The tourists' misfortunes were emphasized by the setting, for they came at a time when Anglo-South African relations were at their worst for fifty years and when English cricket could ill afford any damage to its standing in the public eye.

Before the side arrived, its selection had been faulted in some quarters on the grounds that a playing strength of fifteen is insufficient to meet the contingencies of a concentrated English tour. There were critics in South Africa who argued that the bowling was badly chosen: certainly Adcock lacked an effective pace-partner, and a leg-spinner of even average ability would have been an asset. Then Winslow, erratic and often disappointing as he has been, did once turn and win a Test match in England. He was passed over in favour of men who patently could never achieve such a feat. In essence, the selection appeared – and ultimately proved – to be based on defensive thinking.

The tour ran into troubles from the start and was never free of them: the anti-apartheid campaign; the Griffin affair; the loss of the Test series outright in the first three Tests; the first financial loss on an English tour reported by any Test-playing country since the 1912 Australians; and, finally, when the time came for them to return home, they were virtually unique among touring sides in being unable to point to a single young player established as of true Test quality.

The extent to which disapproval of apartheid should have been vented upon the cricketers was too lengthily debated at the time to demand treatment here; it is sufficient to say that most cricketers, and a substantial body of non-cricketers, thought the picketing of their matches hard on McGlew's party and, even more definitely, unlikely to further the demonstrators' ends to any degree. Nevertheless, and despite the players' impeccable behaviour in the matter, the campaign must have thrown them off psychological balance from the outset.

Their defeat – without a win to their credit – in the Tests might have mattered less in its effect on the English cricket public had it occurred in a different context. But following immediately upon the hollow victories over New Zealand and India, it was sharply reflected in poor attendances and general lack of interest. Even in county matches, the side had little to attract crowds apart from the spasmodic exuberance of McLean and the bowling of Adcock.

The miserable affair of Griffin – 'called' for throwing so that he did not bowl after the second Test – must be blamed squarely on the South African Cricket Association. Griffin had twice been no-balled for throwing in South Africa. Therefore, to send him to England at a time when unfair bowling was a major issue was, for that reason alone, unwise. To do so after the Association's own categorical statement that no player would be considered for selection whose action was at all suspect was quite indefensible. Finally, when – as is clear must have happened – it was communicated to the South Africans that Griffin's action was not going to be accepted by English umpires, it was utterly unfair to Griffin and the entire party to insist – by refusing a replacement – that he continue to bowl until the issue was finally, and so unhappily, forced.

His opponents, almost all the informed cricketers who watched him and – though they never publicly admitted it – his own team-mates, recognized that, to put it at the lowest, Griffin's bowling action was not uniformly fair. Indeed, many people thought that he broke the law with every delivery. The anxious and sincere attempts of English cricketing authority to handle the matter gently – some said *too* gently – were made, by the recalcitrance of the South African Association, to appear, in the outcome, maladroit.

Griffin was a transparently likeable young man who won immense respect for his impeccable bearing while his whole world was crumbling about his ears; indeed, the entire team behaved quite punctiliously in the intolerable situation into which their administrators had thrust them. The matter generated considerable ill will – much of it enduring – and the full extent of its repercussions still cannot be measured.

Coming at last to the playing side, McGlew had two genuine Test-class bowlers but – by the heyday standards of Bruce Mitchell, Dudley Nourse, Eric Rowan or McGlew himself – not a single major Test batsman. All the side's gameness could not make good that deficiency.

McGlew and Goddard were no longer, at Test level, the reliable opening pair of 1955, and the inevitable early breakthrough found the remainder of the batting struggling abjectly against pace. McLean, as ever, produced the occasional glorious innings; but such brilliance is rarely, if ever, married to consistency. Otherwise, only John Waite – poised but unadventurous – and O'Linn – clumsy and restricted in strokes but with immense guts and patience – ever played Test-length innings against Trueman and Statham. But so long as any match was in issue, even those two merely hung on, never dominating nor seeming to aspire beyond survival.

Fellows-Smith, certainly, batted consistently to due standard in Tests; he is a natural number seven batsman and he duly returned an average of 27 with a top score of 35. O'Linn, though still unprepossessing in style, has improved since his days with Kent; but the other established batsmen all seemed, in varying degrees, less accomplished than in 1955. The young batsmen disappointed. Pithey was always vulnerable to pace, and failed completely to provide the defensive ballast for which he was selected. Carlstein – capable of heady strokes against run-of-the-mill bowling – and Wesley – humorous, game and not without aggressive intent – were both completely out of their depth against a Test attack. Duckworth, as in 1955, hinted tantalizingly at powers which were never realized.

Adcock, on his form in the 1960 series, was, surely, the finest fast bowler South Africa has ever had. Sometimes – and then probably to instructions – he bowled short of a length. But he commanded straightness, awkward movement off the pitch and high pace over some amazingly long and menacing spells. In a losing side, and with no Heine to share the double harness which traditionally brings fast bowlers their best returns, he was never truly mastered by any English batsman.

Tayfield came out of retirement to make the tour, and there were persistent rumours that he was not fit. Perhaps he had lost some of his old nip, but he bowled shrewdly, accurately and with subtle flight. Unfortunately for him and for the Tests as a spectacle, the South African strategy, like New Zealand's in 1958 and India's in 1959, started from the premise that England were the stronger side and set out to confine the English batting by defensive out-cricket. So Tayfield – to his obvious disappointment – was rarely allowed the opportunity to buy his wickets in the manner of the slow bowlers of old. A few aggressive strokes – such as Wilfred Rhodes would have regarded as the prelude to a catch in the deep – were enough for Tayfield to be whipped off in favour of short-of-a-length medium pace. Nevertheless, he took a hundred wickets, and even on plumb pitches he thought out some of the best English batsmen.

Goddard did not at first settle into his old accuracy, but subsequently produced a few spells of penetrative left-arm medium in the Tests. Griffin, until he was finally 'called' out of bowling, was often inaccurate but always quite lively. Pothecary, all but forgotten until called upon to fill Griffin's place, was a county standard medium-pacer who, in the right conditions, produced sharp out-swing and, latterly, in-swing as well. McKinnon bowled over the wicket on the brisk side of slow left-arm and had a few good days at county level. Fellows-Smith, a busy medium-pace trier, was always earning his keep.

The guidance and example of McGlew kept the fielding always keen. At The Oval, Waite joined Oldfield and Evans with 1000 runs and 100 wicket-keeper wickets in Tests; undemonstrative and tidy, he kept as well as ever. Tayfield, Adcock and McLean all held some hard chances, while Goddard, with his quick starting, superb timing and perfect hands, made several of the best catches seen in the English summer of 1960.

In matches with the counties, the South Africans achieved some good wins by sheer team-work, under McGlew's always enthusiastic captaincy. Yet they lacked – apart from Adcock – the type of player expected in touring sides, who stood head and shoulders above the ordinary county cricketers. Against Northants, McGlew made a typical three-day, county-match declaration and the county won in a thrilling and sporting finish. McGlew was never quite so generous again, and the tourists lost only one other county match – against Gloucestershire on a difficult pitch at Bristol, when they were in the deepest pit of their depression after the Lord's Test and the final 'calling' of Griffin.

McLean began spectacularly with a double-century at Worcester, but the side's batting in general was not impressive: only four men scored over 1000 runs and only one made more than 1500 – McLean with 1516 (606 of them in four innings). Carlstein, in a glorious 151 against Hampshire, hinted that he might become McLean's successor, but too often threw away his wicket in amazing loss of concentration. In support of the recognized – if not always recognizable – batsmen, Griffin struck some phenomenal blows and Tayfield often batted with commendable common sense. Yet, except when Adcock was bowling or McLean set, the side's cricket seemed hesitant, as if reluctant to move out of an entrenched position.

Indeed, this attitude – produced by a blend of lack of confidence and the long series of setbacks – was more disappointing than the personal failures. In taking final stock, South African cricket may be most downcast by the fact that the tour established only one new player in the Test team – and that the senior member of the party, O'Linn, who will be thirty-nine by the time of the next Springbok tour to England in 1966. By then all the established members of the side will be thirty-five or over, except Goddard (thirty-four). Yet, while several of them could well be selected for that tour, none of the younger members can be regarded as 'probables' five years hence.

In recalling the South African tour of 1960, most people will remember above all the 'calling' of Griffin. Despite the widespread personal sympathy for Griffin himself, the affair created an unpleasant atmosphere in England; but it seems to have had even more violent effect in South Africa. On his return, there was clear danger that he would be used as a symbol of – at lowest – defiance of the English judgement on him.

*Playfair Cricket Annual*, 1961

# Australian Year

The season of 1961 proffers the recurring cricketing magic of an Australian Year. There are still Australians – and some Englishmen too – who maintain that the term 'Test match' applies only to matches between England and Australia. The rest of us are not quite so sweeping in our judgements, but still an England–Australia series has a quality which, at the lowest, we must call a capacity for making history.

It is, too, the cricket that *makes* players. Talk to an old hand about our younger players – Ted Dexter, Ray Illingworth, Tommy Greenhough, Ken Barrington, Mike Smith, Raman Subba Row, Geoff Pullar, Jim Parks and David Allen – and he will say 'All right, they are good players, but I'll tell you whether they are *real* Test cricketers when they have played a full series against the Australians.'

It would not be kind – nor profitable – to recite their names, but there have been many players of great reputation against all other opposition who have failed against Australia and whom we cannot, therefore, call great. There were – especially between the two wars – cheap hundreds to be taken off the growing Test-playing countries; but never against Australia.

It is not for the purpose of this article, nor to make a debating point, that one says that the Test performances which stand out most in the mind come from matches with the 'old enemy'. I cannot believe that Keith Miller ever bowled *quite* so well as when – particularly at Trent

Bridge in 1948, Melbourne in 1954–55 and Lord's in 1956 – he hitched up his 'strides' and let England have everything he had, in that glorious bowling swing. But did he ever bowl better than Frank Tyson when he reached the climax of his far too short career in Australia in 1954–55? That, surely, was the greatest fast bowling ever seen, with Brian Statham peppering away with his relentless accuracy at the other end, giving the batsmen no respite. Yet the older men will say that it was no better than Harold Larwood's terrific crescendo in the Bodyline series of 1932–33.

Yet none of that senior generation can challenge the bowling of Laker, on those diabolical wickets of 1956 when, from his unforgettable, laconic saunter up to the wicket, he spun the off-break like a striking snake and, for the first time on that highest level of cricket, a whole team of Australian batsmen was reduced to faltering feebleness.

Yet not far behind was that artful spin combination of Grimmett and O'Reilly, its great gift the ability to turn the ball on the deadest of batsmen's wickets and who did turn it, to immaculate length, so that English batsmen floundered.

I was lucky to watch Sir John Hobbs – then simply 'Jackobbs' – stroll about the crease and send the ball wherever he wished; Wally Hammond, murdering 'Chuck' Fleetwood-Smith (that early master of the 'Chinaman'). Every cricket watcher of my age, too, will remember the Bradman of the thirties, that relentless, infallible killer, hitting every ball short of perfection for uncheckable boundaries. Yet, of them all, I remember as vividly two men who broke bowlers' hearts by impregnability rather than by plundering. The post-war cricketwatcher will go down to his grave with the image on his mind of Trevor Bailey's forward defensive stroke which made a cricket bat seem a yard wide. Keith Miller and Ray Lindwall, each and separately, told me that they had had dreams – perhaps nightmares would be the more accurate term – about T.E.B. The English bowlers of his time – Alec Bedser above all – might equally have had their sleep spoilt by the recurrent vision of Lindsay Hassett, diminutive and defiant, moving at sleepwalking pace to allow the ball to drop back from a bat which seemed to be dead straight and in perfect position before the bowler had finished his delivery.

What cricketers we have watched in these post-war years which the carpers have called the decline of the game – Hammond, Bradman, Hutton, Barnes, Barnett, Morris, Compton, Brown, Edrich, Hassett, Bailey, Miller, Tyson, Lindwall, Laker, Bedser, Johnston, Evans,

Tallon, Langley, Trueman, Toshack, Washbrook and Burke. Every one of them produced great cricket at peak level.

Now we are told that cricket is in a pit from which it can never climb back. Yet in the summer of 1961 we can anticipate the bright young O'Neill, Colin Cowdrey, Richie Benaud, Fred Trueman, Alan Davidson, Neil Harvey, Brian Statham, the amazing Ken Mackay and – surely – Peter May. These are men already tested and proved in England–Australia cricket. Make no mistake of it, others will join them – memorably – in the season ahead.

Cricket Spotlight, 1961

# Season of Fellowship

*June* 1988. The greatest English cricket season since 1948 was 1963. It was outstanding on all levels – the Test matches with West Indies, a County Championship gamely won by Yorkshire, and the first season of the one-day county competition.

The Tests were historic in several ways; chiefly, probably, in that Frank Worrell, the first coloured West Indian to captain a side to England, did so so handsomely that he was knighted in the following New Year's Honours. Whereas in their two previous tours of England in 1950 and 1957 West Indies had leant heavily upon spin, this marked their positive switch to the high pace which has characterized their cricket down to the present. Above all, England, for the first time, saw bi-partisan Test cricket on its own grounds: the growing immigrant West Indian population turned up in its thousands to the games against England, and changed the atmosphere completely with its humour and warmth.

Frank Worrell's major triumph lay in creating a winning side of common purpose and good fellowship. Just as they had done in Australia in 1960–61, his team injected fresh spirit into a nation's cricket, and the matches were played in the happiest possible atmosphere.

With the 'luck' that always favours the stronger side, West Indies were able to field the same ten men in all five Tests. The one change was due to experiments with an opening partner for Conrad Hunte, a batsman of vast experience who gave the lie to the old argument that

West Indian batsmen are 'temperamental'. He it was who, in the first Test at Old Trafford, scored the 182 which, with substantial support from Rohan Kanhai, Garfield Sobers and Frank Worrell, built West Indies towards the total of 501 which gave them that match by ten wickets.

It also gave them a tactical advantage in that Brian Statham was so expensive that the English selectors dropped him until the last Test, thus depriving Trueman of a truly fast partner. Shackleton, chosen in his place, was always steady, and sometimes more than that, but without Statham England lacked such a hostile opening pair of fast bowlers as Wesley Hall and Charlie Griffith. Backed by Sobers – who could bowl fast-medium or spin – Worrell and Lance Gibbs, who made the slow bowler's place his own, West Indies' was an enviably balanced attack.

Much of the season was emotionally dominated by the closing stages of the second – Lord's – Test, when, as the last ball was bowled, any one of the four results was possible. In the event, Cowdrey, who had returned to the crease with his left arm – broken by a lifting ball from Hall – in plaster, had not to face a ball. After the ninth wicket fell, when Shackleton was run out, Cowdrey was able to stand at the non-striker's end while David Allen played the two remaining balls of the over and the match. That was, surely, the most tense drawn match in the history of cricket.

Then on to Edgbaston, where Trueman, who had taken eleven wickets at Lord's, returned match figures of twelve for 119, the best achieved by any bowler in a Test at Birmingham. It was a low-scoring match: England, who batted first, 216 and 278 for nine declared; West Indies 186 and 91 (in which Trueman took his last six wickets in the course of 24 balls at a cost of the single four hit off him by Gibbs). For West Indies, Griffith took five wickets and Sobers seven, but England won by 217 runs on a pitch where the first three days were all interrupted by rain.

At Headingley, West Indies batted and built another huge total when Sobers made 102, Kanhai – who averaged 55.22 in the series without either a century or a not-out – 92, the ever-reliable Joe Solomon 62, and almost everyone contributed a few.

Their 397 looked all the more impressive when England lost their first eight wickets for 93 in face of the terrific pace of Griffith, and only Jim Parks, Fred Titmus and Tony Lock at the end lifted them to 174. In the West Indies second innings, when Worrell decided not to enforce the follow-on in case the pitch was affected by the rain which threatened, Titmus took four wickets, but Kanhai (44), Basil Butcher (78) and Sobers (52) scored hectically and set England 453 to win.

Sobers opened with Griffith, and in his first over he bowled Micky Stewart – the kind of event that so often sets a batting side on the wrong foot. Brian Bolus, playing his first Test, made 43, Brian Close 56, and Jim Parks 57, but England were always dropping behind and were eventually put out for 231 (Gibbs four wickets, Griffith and Sobers three each) and lost by 221 runs.

At The Oval, many of the England batsmen got 'in' and then out, emphasizing the fact that, rarely, not a single century was scored for England in the entire series. By contrast, West Indies made four. Nevertheless, West Indies were 29 behind on the first innings. England, chiefly owing to Philip Sharpe's 83, mustered 223; but West Indies, through Hunte (108 not out) and Kanhai (77), scored 255 for two to take the match by eight wickets, and the rubber by three Tests to one.

Only one England batsman – Sharpe (53.40) – averaged more than 34 and, although Fred Trueman took an impressive thirty-four wickets at 17.47, only Derek Shackleton, with fifteen at 34.53, gave him effective assistance. By contrast Griffith (thirty-two), Gibbs (twenty-six) and Sobers (twenty) all took their wickets at less than 30 apiece, and Hall, who bowled 40 overs in the England second innings at Lord's, had sixteen at 33.37. It was then, as later, suggested in some quarters that Griffith threw – especially his immensely effective yorker. Of the West Indies batsmen, decisively, four averaged over 40 in the Tests.

It was fitting that apart from the third Test match, the touring side were beaten only once, and that, despite a narrow escape against Hampshire, was by Yorkshire. This was not one of the county's greatest sides but it was well led by Brian Close and survived injuries to several key players and numerous Test calls to win the Championship. They promoted a young batsman named Geoffrey Boycott, who wore spectacles, from the middle order to open the innings, and he finished second in the first-class averages to M.J.K. Smith, who recovered from a broken wrist to bat with his old confidence.

Fred Trueman was top of the English first-class, as well as the Test-match, bowling figures. In all his first-class cricket for the season he took 129 wickets at 15.15: Ken Palmer of Somerset, who also scored over 800 runs, was effectively second with 139 at 16.07, while the faithful Shackleton took most – 146 at 16.75.

At last authority gave in to popular taste and introduced a one-day county competition, which was called the Gillette Cup. Although it was largely a wet summer, that competition, like the Test series, was little affected by weather and it proved immensely popular, so much so that the final at Lord's in September sold out its full allocation of 23,000 seat tickets before the start. In that final Sussex, captained by Ted Dexter, beat Worcestershire in a tight finish. They won by 14 runs, but the Man of the Match award went to a member of the losing side – Norman Gifford, the Worcestershire slow left-arm bowler, for his four for 33 in 15 overs.

That same year, 1963, marked the centenary of *Wisden*, 'the cricketers' bible', which was celebrated in various fashions. In that year, too, the greatest of all batsmen, Sir John – 'Jack' – Hobbs died just seven days after his eighty-first birthday. It is hard to believe that cricket will ever see a more complete batsman, certainly not one who so combined immense batting skill with the character of a 'verray parfit gentil knight'.

*Wisden Cricket Monthy*

# Young England

Every cricket-watcher loves to 'spot' the coming Test player. Only rarely – in the case of the truly great – is it a really easy matter. Denis Compton, Sir Leonard Hutton and Colin Cowdrey, for instance, were unmistakable Test-match material even in their teens; but, obviously, there are few of such quality. So many others, of high and bright promise, have had some flaw, apparently slight yet, in the end, keeping them from the highest rungs. Still, however, the attraction of identifying outstanding talent at an early age retains its hold on most of us. Forgetting our past disappointments, we count the times when we were right and go out to watch the new year's crop with all the old eagerness.

Who are the young players likely to catch our – or, more important, the selectors' – eyes this summer? So far as the selection committee is concerned, mere promise is not enough in the year of an Australian series. There must be a background of achievement and experience. England's main needs are probably pace bowling, in support of Trueman, and that constantly recurring problem, an opening pair.

There are several young fast – or 'fastish' – bowlers in sight. 'Jess' Price of Middlesex was 'blooded' in county cricket in 1961 but did not play in 1962. Then, in 1963, as a full-time professional, he blossomed out. He is big and strong and he reacted well to the encouragement the Lord's wicket always offers to the faster man. But on less favourable pitches he often surprised good batsmen by sheer pace. He has been debating some changes in his action which would bring him more sideways-on to the batsman, but his success in the testing conditions of India may persuade him to leave well alone for the coming season at least. Despite his limited first-class experience, he is already twenty-six and a fast bowler cannot afford to wait long after that age to make his mark. After his performance in India he probably ranks first of the younger bowlers in the selectors' notebooks.

Jeffrey Jones, of Glamorgan, works up considerable speed for one of his relatively slight build, and he has the advantage of the awkward angle of the left-arm bowler. His is a small – yet important – trouble: he tends to bowl with a tense wrist which prevents him from 'moving' the ball as much as he might do. If he can develop his swing he will be challenging for a Test place very soon. But to win a Test place, either of these two must prove himself better than Statham or Shackleton, which will not be easy.

Of the other young men in this group, David Brown of Warwickshire was set back by injury last summer while Nicholson of Yorkshire and, even more, his county colleague Waring and Cottam of Hampshire, have something yet to learn before they can be seriously considered.

At last, happily, some young opening batsmen have made their marks. The Yorkshire pair, John Hampshire and Geoff Boycott, drew a great deal of attention last summer. They would be the last to pretend that their techniques are yet complete, but if they continue to progress as they did in 1963 they must thrust themselves undeniably forward this year. Each has his advocates as the better of the pair; Hampshire with his air of natural command and power, Boycott with his cool poise and concentration, are contrasted in style but, in their different ways, they have both passed tests stern enough to demand the selectors' consideration. There has been less publicity for Alan Jones, the rather quiet left-hander who opens the Glamorgan innings, but he has had more experience than either of the Yorkshiremen and, playing for Western Australia during the past winter, he had the chance to examine the main Australian bowling strength. He, too, must come into consideration.

Tony Lock's retirement from English county cricket leaves the post of slow left-arm bowler more wide open than for many years. Don Wilson of Yorkshire, a true enthusiast who is by no means a negligible hitter, has been made heir-apparent by his selection for India. But he may find himself hard pressed by Doug Slade of Worcester, who made a considerable impact when he first came into county cricket, suffered the slump so many young men experience in their early county days, and has now settled into a thoughtful bowler of subtle flight.

The improvement of Robin Hobbs, the Essex leg-spinner, on his two minor tours last winter; the unmistakable stamp of class of Tony Lewis, the Glamorgan batsman; the fine aggression of Colin Milburn, who treated the West Indian bowling in such cavalier fashion for Northants; the shrewdly developed technique of Graham Atkinson, the unlucky Somerset opening bat; the unmistakable aptitude for stroke-making of Keith Fletcher of Essex: all these will engage attention – and may well make news – this summer.

*Cricket Spotlight*, 1964

# West Indies Highlights

The England–West Indies series of 1966 will always be remembered for the match-winning cricket of Garfield Sobers. In the first Test he scored 161, had bowling figures of nought for 16 and three for 87, and made four catches; in the second, 46 and 163 not out, one for 89 and nought for 8; in the third, 3 and 94, four for 90 and one for 71: five catches; the fourth, 174, five for 41, three for 39; and at the last, 81 and 0, three for 104. He had a batting average for the series of 103.14 and, bowling in three styles – fast-medium, slow orthodox and slow wrist-spin – took twenty wickets at 27.25. Add to this the fact that he won the toss in all five games and that his temperament at times of difficulty was superb, and you have the picture of the finest all-rounder the game has known.

It says much for the cricket, and argues strongly against the suggestions of the decline of cricket, that there were other players on both sides fit to be mentioned in the next – if not the same – breath as Sobers.

Hunte laid the foundation for the West Indies' three-day win at Old Trafford with a solid innings of 135 and, as soon as the wicket began to take spin, Gibbs, with five wickets in each innings, was the most hostile of off-spinners. On the losing side, Milburn's 94 was a stirring gesture; Cowdrey's 69 a minor masterpiece of defensive play; Titmus bowled usefully, and Higgs with determination and resource but little luck.

Colin Cowdrey took over at Lord's, where a fluctuating game produced a draw of more epic quality than many a match of positive result. Higgs bit into the West Indian innings: Nurse, Butcher and Sobers resisted but a total of 269 and Higgs' figures of six for 91 meant that England had an advantage. It was translated into a first-innings lead of 86 by Graveney's 96 – all class and ease, on his return after three years out of the England side – and a cavalier 91 by Parks.

The crucial moment of the game – perhaps of the series – came on the fourth morning, when Kanhai was out and Higgs and Knight had reduced West Indies to 95 for five – in effect, 9 for five – and David Holford came in to join his cousin, Sobers. Cowdrey set out to contain Sobers and get Holford out for the conclusive breakthrough. A day later, when Sobers declared, they had both made centuries and had put on 274 together. England faltered before Hall and Griffith and were 67 for four; but this was the cue for Graveney, despite an injured hand, to play an innings of cool response while Milburn beat his way to a century of such gusto as to give the final stages an air of bravery and gaiety.

Trent Bridge disproved, beyond all argument, the old belief that the West Indies crumbled in an adverse situation. It is possible to argue that this was a triumph of technique; but it was, even more, one of temperament – such as even so recent a side as that of 1957 could not achieve. They batted first and, before the indefatigable Higgs, John Snow and the emergent Basil D'Oliveira, only Nurse – the new rising power of West Indian batting – Lashley and Kanhai played with effective resolution. For the second consecutive Test they had made indifferent use of winning the toss. Hall and Sobers drove into the England batting, to 13 for three. But then Graveney, making a skilful way to the century he missed at Lord's, a poised Cowdrey and a competent determined D'Oliveira carried England to a lead of 90.

So, at 45 for two in their second innings, West Indies were faced with a searching enquiry into their morale. Kanhai – in a most uncharacteristically defensive innings – and Butcher batted out Saturday. On Monday Butcher went on to 209 not out; Nurse, Sobers and Holford bore him bold company and eventually the declaration – at 482 for five – set England 373 to win. Boycott, Graveney, Cowdrey and D'Oliveira strode bravely, but the balanced attack of Hall, Griffith, Sobers and Gibbs was always in command.

England yielded the rubber disappointingly – apart from a few men, abjectly. Again West Indies batted first; yet at 154 for four they were not in a winning position. Then, however, came the commanding stand of Nurse and Sobers – 264 for the fifth wicket – and a declaration at the round figure of 500 for nine. Griffith and Hall made the initial thrust; Sobers followed up. Only Milburn – returning after injury – and D'Oliveira, reaching true Test stature with an innings of 88, offered any convincing opposition and England followed on. Only Milburn and Barber made more than 25 in the second innings against Gibbs and Sobers, and West Indies were home by an innings and 55 runs: unquestionable champions.

Brian Close took over from Colin Cowdrey; and of the eleven that took the field in the first Test, at Old Trafford, only Ken Higgs now remained.

Snow – playing because Price, the first choice, was unfit – and Higgs broke through on the first morning and, when West Indies were 74 for four, the wickets had been shared between four bowlers. Then, as ever, came recovery: Kanhai's first century in a Test against England and 81 from Sobers. But otherwise, only Hall held up the steady progress of six England bowlers intelligently handled by Close and backed by the best home fielding of the summer.

Yet the West Indian total of 268 looked good enough when Sobers and Hall had cut England down to 166 for seven. At this point on Friday afternoon, Murray – long left out of the England side because, presumably, his batting was not good enough – came in at number nine to Graveney. On Saturday, with the gates closed although it was the first day of the football season, these two went on to 217 for the eighth wicket.

That was staggering enough, but then Snow and Higgs – each making his first fifty in first-class cricket – produced a last-wicket stand of 116 (only 14 short of the record for all Tests) and England had a lead of 259 and their first true psychological advantage of the series. Two fine catches by Murray and West Indies were 12 for two; Close never allowed them to recover and England, to their surprise and delight, won by an innings and 34 runs.

This gave hope – not certainty – for England's Test future. Day in, day out, Higgs bowled like Alec Bedser's true successor; Tom Graveney batted as well as ever – and more reliably; Basil D'Oliveira emerged as a brave and skilful all-rounder; Murray returned triumphantly. Close brought an extra quality of leadership to the side, and perhaps the saddest thought of the final win was that Milburn should have been dropped.

*Cricket Spotlight*, 1967

# One of the Happiest for Many Years

The 1972 English cricket season was one of the happiest for many years. A magnificent Test series with Australia was at the core of it. There were other factors – a fine summer after a grim May, increased prosperity through sponsorship and a distribution of success between several counties – but the England–Australia games were the high peak of it all. Like the weather, the touring side and the Tests began in depressing conditions. The Australians lost a third of their scheduled playing time – including eight full days – before the Old Trafford Test where the attendance, only 32,384 for the entire five days, was a disappointment to everyone, not least the Lancashire club.

From that match onwards the season and the series built up to record receipts and a fine climax. Rarely – indeed never in modern times – has a rubber been so closely fought, so constantly fluctuating or played in a more cheerful atmosphere. The Australians were entitled to be disgruntled about the Headingley wicket – which was the direct negation of their cricket and technique – and could be rueful about the one at Old Trafford. Yet they bore no grudges, generously acknowledged England's retention of The Ashes and, at The Oval, played with immense élan to level the series.

In general the Australians achieved the greater individual success. No English batsman played with Stackpole's aggression and consistency – or luck – and of the regular Test players, five Australians but only two English batsmen averaged over thirty; and, though Underwood won the Headingley match virtually single-handed, Massie did as much at Lord's; while Lillee took more wickets than anyone else on either side – 31, a record for an Australian in England; only Snow (24) came near him for England.

England had the ill luck to lose Boycott – the batsman on whom their strategy was based – from three Tests, the highly capable Arnold from two and Illingworth at the decisive phase of the fifth; Australia, for their part, were without Massie at Old Trafford where the conditions must have helped him.

In essence the 1972 Test rubber saw a young Australian team establish itself, while a long successful English side reached the end of its peak period.

Of the Australian newcomers, Stackpole – surprisingly, he had never made an English tour before – Greg Chappell, Ross Edwards, Rodney Marsh, Bob Massie and Dennis Lillee all made profound impressions. On the English side Lever, Price, M.J.K. Smith, Parfitt, Luckhurst, D'Oliveira and Hampshire all lost their places either during the series or for India, while Illingworth announced that he was not available as captain for that tour and Edrich, also unavailable, had the unhappiest full series of his career.

Lillee was the outstanding personality of the summer. He arrived with a reputation for high pace but doubts as to his accuracy and fitness. He had some trouble with his back early in the tour but by the first Test he was bowling at full speed; his control improved as the summer wore on and he went back to Australia unquestionably not only the fastest bowler in the world but the best fast bowler in the world. Snow, to his immense credit, challenged him hard; he bowled with fire, resource and tenacity and to his obvious delight, he several times batted usefully.

The outstanding success among the newer English players was Greig who played a series of valuable innings, took some good wickets and generally matured as a cricketer as the rubber progressed.

Wood, batting with immense assurance, seemed certain to make a century in his first Test, and 'walked' on to the boat to India only to have an unhappy time against the spin-bowlers there. Arnold bowled well, with his usual ill luck from injuries and dropped catches; Knott was jauntily valuable as ever, and Illingworth, at the age of forty, batted, bowled, fielded and captained the side calmly and capably.

His injury, which at least substantially affected the margin of the last Test, kept him out of the three one-day internationals sponsored by the

Prudential Assurance Company. Brian Close took over the captaincy and England won that series by two to one, due largely to the batting of Amiss, Greig, Fletcher and Boycott and the bowling of Arnold and Woolmer. Stackpole, of course, batted exuberantly for Australia and, after the first game, Lillee bowled effectively and at full pace.

Australia arrived in England an unformed side and went home an effective and well-balanced combination. England set off to India under Tony Lewis to begin a rebuilding process which may well take some years to complete.

*Cricket Spotlight*, 1973

# A Memorable Summer

The 1975 English cricket season must be called successful, though it was by no means one of success for the English team. West Indies worthily won the Prudential Cup for the first international knock-out competition, and assumed the title of World One-day Champions; and Australia took the Test rubber by winning the only completed match against England. Splendid weather for the Prudential games and for most of the Test series, and some stirring cricket, ensured large and enthusiastic crowds and a substantial revenue.

It was economic good sense – though bound to be hard on one of three good teams – to put England in such an easy section of the Prudential Cup that they could be guaranteed a place in the semi-finals. That meant that, in Group B, one of Australia, West Indies and Pakistan – any one of whom could be fancied to win – would be eliminated in the preliminary stages. In the event it was Pakistan, handicapped by the absence of Asif and Imran from their crucial – and narrowly decided – match with West Indies, who were put out.

In group A England beat New Zealand, India and East Africa – Amiss, Fletcher, Old, Wood and Hayes made scores of over fifty; Snow, Greig and Lever bowled well enough for such opposition – and met Australia in the Headingley semi-final. New Zealand, the other A group qualifiers, met West Indies at The Oval. Australia moved with little trouble to the final where, for the second time in the competition,

West Indies beat them – and did so far more decisively than the score might suggest.

East Africa and Sri Lanka were never in the running, though both will have profited from the experience and Sri Lanka resisted staunchly against West Indies. India batted as if for a draw in losing to England. On a bowlers' day at Leeds, Gilmour, brought into the side for the first time, took six English wickets for 14 and, though John Snow (two for 30) and Chris Old (three for 29) contested the issue gamely, Australia won by five wickets. Meanwhile, New Zealand reached 98 for one before Julien, Roberts and Holder swept aside their batting; then Greenidge and Kallicharran had virtually decided the match before the second West Indian wicket fell.

Lord's was full for the final on what was – and needed to be – the longest day of the year. Lillee, Thomson and Gilmour reduced West Indies to 50 for three before Kanhai with a responsible 55 and Lloyd, at his most masterful for 102, took them to 199. Even then Gilmour (five for 48), with his left-arm fast-medium, nearly broke them down again, only for Boyce and Julien to put on a conclusive 52. The Australian innings foundered when three of their first four batsmen – Turner and the two Chappells – were run out by Richards. They still put up a resistance – all but two of their batsmen reached double figures – but they were always crucially behind the asking rate. West Indies simply contained them down to the end when a triumphant West Indian crowd swarmed over Lord's. Their players were to find Australia a tougher proposition in the subsequent Test series there.

Few can have expected other than the sequence of lifeless wickets prepared for the England–Australia Tests. Only once did the Australian fast bowlers Lillee and Thomson find a pitch of any pace, and that was produced by rain at Edgbaston. The storm came after Denness, winning the toss, had put Australia in to bat. All their batsmen except Greg Chappell – who had a surprisingly unsuccessful series – made runs and they scored 359. On a pitch soft on top and hard underneath, Walker and Lillee took five wickets apiece and England were bowled out for 101; when they followed on, the same pair and Thomson (five for 38) put them out for no more than 173 and they were beaten by an innings and 85 runs. Denness did not survive giving Australia first innings and his own scores of 3 and 8. By the fourth Test his main batsmen of the Australian tour, Lloyd, Fletcher and Amiss, had followed him; only Edrich survived. Greig took over the captaincy and, if he could not turn a losing side into a winning one, he made it resistant. They did not lose another Test; indeed, they took the stronger position at Lord's, sighted the possibility of winning at Leeds, and mounted a splendid recovery at The Oval. Greig's own 96 at Lord's – after four wickets were down for 49 – was the first flag of defiance; he was supported by the invariably game Knott; that valuable player of fast bowling, Wood; and then by Edrich with a characteristic 175.

Above all, however, the fresh English spirit was personified by David Steele, the Northants stalwart. Chosen – to the surprise of many – for his first Test at the age of thirty-three, his scores of 50, 45, 73, 92, 39 and 66 made him by far the most consistent England batsman of the two rubbers against Australia. Whether, as many pondered, his front-foot technique would have proved so effective on wickets like those in Australia during the 1974–75 Tests was never discovered. The fact remains that, by steady nerve and sound method, he stepped from county obscurity to the status of folk hero in three weeks. He was even top of the English bowling averages with two wickets at 10.50. But the returning John Snow was by far the most effective English bowler; not so fast as formerly, but controlled, shrewd and purposeful.

Gooch, the young Essex batsman who was the selectors' first adventurous gesture of the summer, could not hold his place. Wherever Amiss went, Lillee sought him out; Fletcher lost all confidence. Edmonds, the Middlesex slow left-arm bowler, had a memorable first Test spell at Headingley, but the Oval pitch had nothing for him. Other successes were Roope, recalled at The Oval; and Woolmer, a natural stroke-maker who, after failing in the first innings, made the highest score of his life and the slowest century ever recorded for England in that massive rescue operation.

Rain on the last day spoiled such chances as England had of winning at Lord's; demonstrators who dug up the pitch might have done so at Headingley but, as it proved, rain would have prevented a result. The Oval Test lasted a full six days – the longest match ever played in England – and England were still batting at the end.

For all these achievements, there was little to suggest that Australia did not deservedly retain The Ashes; certainly none that England could have beaten them on pitches of fair pace. Lillee and Thomson took thirty-seven wickets between them at a substantially lower rate than any of the main English bowlers; while Gilmour, who played in only one Test, then had nine wickets at 17.44 each. Despite the failure of

Greg Chappell, the batting was steady; McCosker averaged 82.80; Ian Chappell 71.50; and the perpetually valuable Ross Edwards 50.50; while Walters, Marsh, Lillee and Thomson all played useful innings.

England will begin their 1976 Test series against West Indies with greater conviction than their predecessors faced Australia in 1975. It has yet to be seen whether they can cope with the West Indian pace bowlers – or if their bowlers can contain the Indian batting. Much is likely to depend on the state of West Indian morale after their defeat in Australia; this has, though, the making of a stirring rubber.

*Cricket Spotlight*, 1976

# New Zealand Test Stars Are in the Ascendancy

*August* 1983. The day when New Zealand could be regarded as a second-rate cricketing power is gone. Their performances against England in the 'World Series' in Australia last winter, in the World Cup, their thoroughly deserved win at Leeds, and the fact that they have beaten every Test opponent, establish that beyond question.

Happily, too, Test attendances, if not of the size of an Australian or West Indian series, reflect a new British respect for them.

It is by no means always recognized here that their cricket has advanced in face of severe handicaps and setbacks. Until well into this century, simple geographical problems of division into two islands, and mountainous terrain, raised problems over a domestic programme. Tours by England, the true source of New Zealand cricket, were generally meagre, tacked on at the end of the major tour to Australia.

Most important, Australia, who might have done so much to foster the game in New Zealand, has treated them with something little short of contempt. While England have played home and out series with them since 1929–30, Australia did not grant them Test status until 1945–46. Then a team under Bill Brown played, and won, a solitary Test at Wellington.

They offhandedly made no further Test contact until 1973–74 when, utterly illogically, they decided on both home and away series in the same season! It was sweet indeed for New Zealand when they won the second of the three-match home rubber.

Glenn Turner scored a century in each innings; Richard Hadlee took seven wickets, his brother Dayle and Richard Collinge five each, their captain, Bev Congdon, three; and they won convincingly by five wickets. Unhappily for the atmosphere of their success, they had to endure a considerable amount of extremely bitter sledging.

Perhaps that was a necessary step to full Test stature. In truth New Zealand has for many years produced players of Test quality; but from a population smaller than the city of Sydney, their problem has been one of quality.

The England side sent there in 1929–30 was not the strongest – one went simultaneously to West Indies – but it did include players as good as Frank Woolley, Morris Nichols, Duleepsinhji, Ted Bowley, Stan Worthington and Maurice Turnbull. They returned much impressed by the batting of Stewart Dempster and John Mills (who made 276 for the first wicket at Wellington), and 'Curly' Page; the all-round cricket of Roger Blunt and the leg-spin of Bill Merritt and the wicket-keeping of Ken James. Dempster, Merritt and James, of course, all later played in the County Championships.

When Tom Lowry brought their first team here in 1931 they were originally allocated only one Test. They played so well at Lord's, though – when they made 224 and 469 for nine declared in an honourable draw – that they were offered two more: they lost one – in the absence of Dempster – and the other was rained off. Subsequently England accorded them short commons with three-, two- and even one-match series up to 1946–47. To the average English follower, though, their cricket was as remote as political Czechoslovakia or footballing Hungary.

The team Walter Hadlee brought here in 1949 effectively marked the crossing of the Rubicon. Offered three four-day Tests, their wise and pleasant manager, Jack Phillips, countered – arguing the economics of wasted days – by proposing four of three days. That granted, he and Walter Hadlee could say with some confidence: 'With our batting we don't think England can beat us in three days.' So it proved.

England, toughened by the visit of the Australians in the previous year, with Hutton, Washbrook, Compton, Edrich, Bailey, Bedser, Evans, Laker, Jackson and Wright, were arguably stronger than they are now. Yet they never looked like winning a match. New Zealand's seven innings comprised 341, 195 for two, 484, 293, 348 for seven, 345 and 308 for nine; they scored more runs than Bradman's Australians had done.

Their batsmen included Martin Donnelly, surely the finest post-war left-hander. Neat, dextrous, unhurriedly perfect in footwork, uncannily certain in reading length and flight, he was quite undisturbed by spin or pace.

He had all the orthodox strokes and the ability to improvise brilliantly; had splendid wrists and timing; conclusively, he was so 'bat sure' that he seemed to middle everything. Donnelly was accorded a special article in the 1950 *Wisden* in which R.C. Robertson-Glasgow wrote 'Donnelly's equipment is complete ... his place is undoubtedly among the few truly great players of the present.'

His departure to business in Australia was an immense loss not only to New Zealand but to world cricket. In the same side was Bert Sutcliffe (one of *Wisden*'s Five Cricketers of the Year), another left-hander, athlete, and record-breaker; Mervyn Wallace, unlucky not to reach a thousand in May; the then young strong man, and subsequent father figure, John Reid; Wally Hadlee, who against Alec Bedser, bowling leg-cutters on a dusty pitch at The Oval, played an innings of utter mastery to make 119 not out in a score of 249 for eight.

They had, too, the tubby Tom Burtt, a slow left-armer of the old school; Jack Cowie, honest fast-medium, who laboured tirelessly to flog pace out of slow pitches. New Zealand continued to produce good cricketers: the dogged Geoff Rabone, the leg-spinner-philosopher Alec Moir; serviceable, seam-up Harry Cave; determined all-rounder Tony MacGibbon. In 1954-55 and 1958, though, their talent was too desperately thinly spread to cope with the strongest of post-war English sides.

By 1965 they had started to build towards their present strength. The batting grew with Bev Congdon, Barry Sinclair, Graham Dowling, Brian Hastings and Mark Burgess. There was a valuable group of all-rounders in Vic Pollard, Ross Morgan and another strong man, Bruce Taylor. Among bowlers, the left-arm pace of Richard Collinge; the fire of Dick Motz; the, alas, all too briefly available left-arm spin of Hedley Howarth, brother of Geoff. At the pinch they have always been one top-class bowler short.

The second historic landmark in the development of New Zealand cricket, though, was the entry and development of Glenn Turner: master batsman who might have given his country's cricket even more than he did. A cricketer of immense application, determination and basic ability, he is the only New Zealander among the few to score a hundred hundreds. He and the power which came with the entry of the two younger Hadlees ushered New Zealand to the phase of power in which they are now finding their feet.

*The Guardian*

# Test Grounds

## The First Test at Trent Bridge

*April* 1951.   There is always an air of bustle and importance about the first Test, with hints and suspicions that one side or the other is going to show us something fresh and startling. There are, too, invariably some players taking their Test baptism, and the batsmen at least must toy with the thought of joining that small and select band of cricketers who made a century in their first Test.

Nottingham has traditionally been the venue of the opening match of each series for so long that it was almost a shock, in 1950, to begin the games against the West Indies at Manchester.

This year Trent Bridge comes into its own again, with the marquees beside the trees behind the pavilion, and an array of old players, which is, of itself, cricket history. To see Sir Pelham Warner, Jack Hobbs, S.F. Barnes, Morris Nichols, George Gunn, the legendary Tom Wass, Reggie Spooner, Herbert Sutcliffe and their old team-mates sitting side by side in the stand reserved for the honoured guests of the Nottinghamshire club is to understand something of the continuity of cricket.

Going even further back, their stand is beside that famous tree – 'George Parr's Tree' – named after the old Notts batsman and All-England XI captain because his terrific leg-hits so often flew over it on their way out of the ground.

This year, too, the visitors' stand beside the pavilion will have all the social gaiety that our South African guests bring with them. Corners of that stand could make the newcomer feel for a moment that he was in the pavilion at Ellis Park, Johannesburg.

For many years now, since long William Gunn and his fragile partner, Arthur Shrewsbury, strolled down the day for their flawless centuries, Trent Bridge has been regarded as something of a batsman's paradise. Of late seasons, however, it has developed a characteristic of 'greenness' on the first morning. On this green-topped wicket, fast-medium bowling comes off at strange and unexpected angles, often even swinging one way and biting back the other.

Indeed, it has been by no means unusual of recent times – the Trent Bridge Test of last year was an example – for the first half of a team to be whistled out by the pacers before lunch on the first day, only for the tail-enders to come along when the wicket has dried out and help themselves to far more runs than the recognized batsmen had made.

Thus, the captain who wins the toss in the first Test of this series may well think very seriously before he takes first innings, for each of the two sides has bowlers of pace and accuracy to exploit a 'green top' impressively.

Once lunch has passed on the first day, the wicket – unless the weather annoys it – plays placidly enough, and there will be centuries to be had there again this time – barring rain.

It was at Trent Bridge in 1947 that Alan Melville saved the last day – when the game was going down to the most certain of all draws – by scoring his second hundred of the match. England will miss him this time, for his strokes – of a consummate elegance – sent the ball away with a power startling from one so slight of physique.

I shall never forget the unfortunate 'Sam' Cook of Gloucestershire coming on to bowl in that game – his first Test – very late into a soundly established South African innings. He was relatively young to big cricket, and the watcher could almost feel his depression when his normal left-arm spin failed to turn the ball on that passive wicket. Almost in desperation, he bowled a swinger: it was a full pitch, and Melville, leaning forward, seemed to do no more than make a gentle pass of the bat, for the ball to fly deep into the car park for a huge six – the beginning of much heavy punishment for the youngster. Poor Sam Cook was dropped from the Test team. Since then, he has developed a longer cricket head and greater variation of flight, but that day has proved a hard failure to live down.

It is late in the day when Trent Bridge is at its loveliest, for then the air seems full of a reflection of the sun off the deep green of the turf. It is in that light, at the quiet end of the last day, that I remember the Test of 1947, with Alan Melville and Ken Viljoen going their easy way down to the finish of the match – a scene in which atmosphere is everything, the atmosphere of cricket.

*London Calling*

# Lord's – Headquarters of Cricket

*May* 1951. The first Test match is usually called just that, or sometimes the 'Trent Bridge Test' or the 'Nottingham Test'. The second Test, however, is always, in cricketing conversation, the 'Lord's Test'. If it is the ambition of every overseas cricketer to play against England at 'headquarters', its attraction is as strong for the Englishman who goes there forty days of every cricketing year.

The red and white bus will bring you from the West End, up Park Road with its walls sun-pale above the shop-fronts tricked on to the ground floor, round the green in front of the church, and there is the wall of Lord's. Such brick-work anywhere else would be called dingy, for its yellowish shade is not pleasing to the eye, but this brick and mortar has supported the shoulders and backs of so many waiting cricket-watchers as to have its own place in cricket memories, if not in history.

Feeling is greater than the chronicles. The first Test ever played was at Melbourne and the first in England was at The Oval. There had been another there and one at Manchester in the four years before – on 21, 22 and 23 July 1884 – Lord's saw its first Test. Yet, though Melbourne, The Oval and Manchester have their backing of history, the Lord's Test is the great event of the cricket world.

Go in through the green doors, or through the Grace Gates, and you are in the little cricket township which has grown out of Thomas Lord's Ground in St John's Wood where, 130 years ago, there were two hollows which each winter filled with water, so that Steve Slatter, who worked on the ground, taught himself to swim in them.

The Tavern has become, through the historic strokes which topped it and the memories of thousands who have watched great games from its hospitable shade, a famous and a cherished home. Indeed, the Duke of Edinburgh is patron of a club – the Lord's Taverners – which includes other famous names among its members, whose common bonds are the practice of the arts, the support of the National Playing Fields Association and habitual cricket-watching from the Tavern.

Self-contained in its possession of its own tavern, kitchens, offices, printing-shop, maintenance staff, workshops – under a Clerk of the Works – gardens and tennis courts, Lord's is even more self-contained in its quality of being a place alone, not to be felt as part of the London which surrounds it.

This velvety depth of grass, the clean concrete, the freshness of the green and white paint, the solidly Edwardian quality of the wrought-iron seats – those do not belong to London. Lord's welcomes Londoners – it houses Middlesex County Cricket Club – but it *belongs* to all cricket.

The present Pavilion is the third. The first Lord's pavilion, built in 1814, was burned down in 1825, with all the original records of the MCC; the second, completed in May 1826, was replaced by the present one only in 1889, yet the new building – for all that it comes from a poor period of English architecture – seems as if it had grown there naturally, and it has its own distinguished contribution to make to the landscape which is Lord's Ground.

Only one man, Albert Trott (on 31 July 1899), has ever hit a ball over this Pavilion; for fifty-two years since then its high balcony has successfully challenged the great straight-drivers of the game.

Lord's has been the scene of great cricket matches – but so have other grounds. Here the laws of cricket have been made – but law-making rarely compels affection. With its nursery, its wide roads, its terraces, stands and outbuildings, it is, for a cricket ground, vast in extent – but others are bigger, and size rarely evokes romantic feelings. Yet it was to Lord's that 'the champion', William Gilbert Grace, a Gloucestershire man and a Gloucestershire cricketer, came as to his cricketing home; and still it arouses a gentle nostalgia in thousands of cricketers, many of whom played the game far less well than they loved it.

If from its amalgam of epic, history, tradition, dignity, and solidity of elegance and pastoral sympathy one single quality is to stand for Lord's Cricket Ground in this age of unrest, it may well be that true graciousness with which it has maintained the temper of the country game from which it grew.

*London Calling*

# Memories of Old Trafford

*May* 1951. The third Test will be played at Old Trafford in an atmosphere compounded, for cricketers, of many great matches played on that constantly changing turf. Once it was a plumb, batsman's wicket; then it developed a 'green-topped' character, and in 1950 it became the centre of much controversy as one of the dustiest wickets on which any modern Test has been played.

The ground itself is not superficially attractive. On windy days, the dust from the ash roads beside the ground blows across the terraces, and the trains go grindingly by. There have been times when those trains have passed more frequently than runs have come from the bats of men battling against the run of the game.

The generous pavilion, however, is a reminder that it stands at the centre of the great wealth of the cotton trade, in a city famous for its civic pride. In fact the ground is not in Manchester at all but in Salford, although it is the headquarters of the Manchester Cricket Club.

My own memories of Old Trafford are memories of cricket and cricketers rather than of their setting. Cricket history recalls the great feat of Tom Richardson, the Surrey fast bowler, who, playing for England against Australia at Old Trafford in 1896, bowled from the start of the day until four in the afternoon without rest. Australia had been set 125 to win but, although the wicket was good, Richardson's terrific bowling threatened to beat them. He bowled overs at full speed to take six of the seven Australian second-innings wickets that fell, for 76 runs.

When they wanted only 9 to win, Lilley dropped Kelly off Richardson. Had that catch been held, England might have won, and Richardson would be even more widely remembered for the greatest sustained spell of bowling in the history of the game. When the winning hit was made off his bowling, Richardson is said to have stood like a man stunned; he never played in another Test at Old Trafford.

Recent years have given us some amazing cricket in Manchester Tests. In 1946, Sohoni and Hindlekar, the last two Indian batsmen, battled courageously to play out the last half-hour and save the game. In 1947, Plimsoll, the South African left-arm pace bowler, exploited the 'green' wicket and, after dismissing Hutton, threatened to run through the English side. Edrich, however, in a brave and skilfully judged onslaught, hit Plimsoll off with a series of attacking strokes, including two huge hits to the long-on boundary. Then came that tremendous stand between Edrich (191) and Compton (115) which gave England the game.

The year 1948 saw Australia facing the possibility of defeat when England, 142 ahead on the first innings, began to build up their second innings through Washbrook and Edrich. Rain probably cost England that match – and added to the sensitivity of the Lancashire officials on the subject of Manchester rain.

Then 1949 brought Hadlee's New Zealanders to one of their best performances in a Test in England when Tom Burtt's six wickets for 162 – in an England innings of 440 for nine – was matched by the batting of Martin Donnelly with 75 and 80, and a century by their own great left-hand bat, Sutcliffe.

Last year saw a series of dusty spinners' wickets at Old Trafford coinciding with a Lancashire attack powerful in spin-bowling. The Test against West Indies was played on a pitch from which the ball turned so violently that a century by England's wicket-keeper, Evans, and other 'long hands' by Edrich, Bailey and, for the West Indies, Stollmeyer, were triumphs of quick-footed batsmanship.

Vast as Old Trafford is, memory of it is concentrated on the 'middle' – the scene of great performances by cricketers whose home ground it was: Archie MacLaren, imperious as captain and as batsman; John Thomas Tyldesley, master bad-wicket player and exponent of the square-cut; R.T. Spooner, whose cutting bore the stamp of cricketing immortality; E.A. McDonald, the Australian who joined Lancashire and bowled for them with a hostility vividly to be recalled even today. There, in the pure Lancashire strain, Barlow, the legendary stonewaller, and Harry Makepeace resisted the bowling of their contemporaries with a hostility which won their county a reputation for defensive cricket second only to that of their Yorkshire neighbours.

Thence, perhaps, stems the tradition of Old Trafford cricket – the game played hard and relished through its rigours.

*London Calling*

# To Headingley for the Fourth Test

*June* 1951. Yorkshire takes the fourth Test, and plays it at Headingley. Headingley, on the edge of Leeds, lacks the elegant distinction of Lord's, lacks, perhaps, the dignity of Trent Bridge, even the prosperity of Old Trafford, but it is a Yorkshire ground, a piece of the strong broadcloth of cricket. Here a Rhodes, a Hirst, a Sutcliffe might take cricket and the winning of cricket matches as a matter of serious importance, and the crowd would be with him even though the question of entertaining them never seemed to enter his head. In fact, a Yorkshire crowd does not come to a Test to be 'entertained'; it comes to watch good cricketers play cricket.

Even at Lord's you will sometimes hear applause for the mis-hit which scurries from the inside edge of the bat, down past the leg stump for four; on a Yorkshire ground such a boundary marks general sympathy for the bowler. The watching of cricket at Headingley is not a diversion, it is a serious matter, demanding unflinching attention and a full knowledge of the game. Airs and graces count for little beside the runs and wickets that win or lose a game; courage will win more admiration than a flashy stroke, and skill is the true criterion.

The 1947 Test between England and South Africa is, perhaps, the best example I can recall of the quality of Headingley. As I came to the ground along the road which looks down on the cool waters of the Aire and the imposing walls of Kirkstall Abbey, an ocean of water fell down, lit by lightning and heralded by thunder.

At Headingley a few minutes later, the rain stood in great pools in every hollow of the ground, yet still the determined thousands stood in their long lines to the turnstiles until, with 30,000 people inside, the gates were shut, and many a man who had looked forward to this day – for was not Len Hutton not out 32? – turned back home. Inside the ground the early-comers had sat out the storm on the terraces rather than lose their places, and now they took the sodden newspapers or dripping macintoshes from their heads and counted their blessings. Those who came later moved down to the grass between the seats and the boundary and stood in the puddles.

'Sit down,' shouted those who held the seats, 'Sit down!' Those in front considered, and saw where justice lay. Dropping newspapers or macintoshes on to the sodden grass, even into puddles, they sat down. There was no quibble that play started late. When it did begin, the scoring was not fast; many stood in uncomfortable positions all day long without complaint – for there were more in the ground than could watch in comfort.

The atmosphere was that of a Turkish bath. At a quarter to one, Athol Rowan came on to bowl at the Kirkstall end: with breaks only for lunch and tea, he bowled until a quarter past six, four hours of bowling, 46 overs, for 89 runs. This was, strangely enough, Hutton's first Test innings in his native Yorkshire; every Yorkshireman there wanted to see him make a century, and Hutton, for his part, was as determined to do so as a man may be. Four and three-quarter hours that hundred took him; it held no mistake, no moment of incaution. The crowd appreciated every run of it and, when he came to his hundred, they stood up from their places and cheered him like an emperor.

There was great batting and great bowling that day. Neither was sensational, wickets were not knocked out of the ground every few minutes, the ball was not hit into the grandstand; but batsmen and bowlers knew their job, did it skilfully, and stuck to it. Yorkshiremen watched, and knew, and appreciated, and if they went home bedraggled they also went home happy.

Not a moment allows you to forget that this is Yorkshire: the broad talk of the county is always in the ear, the tall chimneys stand not far away and so do the strong hills. The pies at the refreshment bars are no niggling south-country snack, but a meal for a hungry man, and the bars where they are sold are long, for Yorkshiremen like their food at lunch-time and tea-time – not in a gentle trickle during the play.

At the back of the grandstand is the rugby league ground, where you may often see the players practising, even during the cricket season. Keith Miller, in fact, went across and joined them there and punted about with them even while a Test match was in progress. That was during the England–Australia Test of 1948, when Dick Pollard, a neighbour from Lancashire, shot out Hassett and Bradman in the same over, so that the crowd saluted him with a roar like thunder which seemed as if it were never going to end. On the same ground, the season before, another Lancastrian, Cranston, had ended South Africa's second innings by taking four wickets in one over for no runs.

Recall Headingley and you recall cricket played hard. Other grounds may sometimes attract the imagination away on flights far from the game, but Headingley is concerned only with cricket and cricketers. Perhaps that is why the real cricketer appreciates Yorkshire applause more than any other: it is to be earned only by good cricket. What better qualification can there be for housing a Test match?

*London Calling*

# The Oval – the Cockney's Own Ground

*June* 1951.   So it is The Oval again – across London, under that long railway bridge whose 'thunder over, rumble under' used to make me think, when I was a boy, that it was a modern inferno. If Kennington is on the 'unfashionable' south side of the river, it makes up for lack of fashion with a huge warmth of humanity.

Here Hayward, Hobbs and Hitch were hailed with none the less enthusiasm for the omission of their initial 'H'. And if there is grime and dust there is also gusto and a humour which is sometimes sadly lacking at Lord's. Many will have to stand to watch the cricket at The Oval, for terraces may not be built which would interrupt the view of the play of certain houses around the ground – that was one of the conditions of the lease when it was first granted to the Surrey club by the Prince of Wales, whose feathers grace the county crest and caps.

The Oval it was which housed the first England–Australia Test to be played in England – in 1880 – and, two years later, the game Australia won and out of which grew the term 'The Ashes'. For me it is personal history, for there I saw my first Test match and two great cricket events which I shall never forget, and it is with The Oval that I associate the finest cricketer I ever saw – Jack Hobbs.

I never saw W.G. Grace, but from my own studies and the word of critics whom I respect, I am perfectly content to accept him as the greatest of all cricketers. After him, however, must come Jack Hobbs. I saw Bradman at his greatest, but I still believe Hobbs to be the modern master. Hobbs specialized in nothing at all as a batsman: good wickets or bad, fast bowling or slow, favourable conditions or back to the wall, his technique was flawless. He had all the strokes in the book.

There was a time when it seemed that Jack Hobbs could make a hundred off the bowling of the then Champion County – Lancashire. John Berry Hobbs was, above all, the King of The Oval.

Hobbs played in what was, by my good fortune, the first Test I ever saw when, at The Oval in 1926, England won The Ashes after that long Australian supremacy which ran back to before the 1914 war. Hobbs, Sutcliffe, Woolley, Rhodes, Strudwick, Tate, Larwood, the young Chapman – it was the flowering of one of the great ages of English cricket, with Gregory, Mailey, Woodfull, Macartney, Bardsley playing for Australia, to prove the win no easy one.

It was twelve years later that Len Hutton, slowly and with a concentration not exceeded even by Bradman, made his 364, the highest of all Test innings – and England won the victory over Australia which was to be her last for thirteen years.

It was there, too, that Don Bradman, in 1948, was cheered all the way to the wicket as he went out to play his last Test innings. Was it, I have wondered ever since, emotion clouding his eyes which caused him to be deceived at once by a googly from Eric Hollies?

It is strange that memories of The Oval should so frequently be of batsmen, for it was the home ground of Tom Richardson, Lohmann, Lockwood and, today, of Alec Bedser. Only a few weeks ago, Herbert Strudwick, whose battered wicket-keeper's hands are now turned to the task of scoring for Surrey, talked to me of Richardson.

'Struddy' was a very young man and Richardson ageing – by cricket standards – when they played briefly together, for Richardson was virtually finished at thirty-two. How fast was he? Faster than Larwood, Bert Strudwick declared.

The trams and buses roll by The Oval, the passengers on the top deck able to look briefly in at the Test. Do they, I wonder, pass the shade of Tom Richardson, huge and heavily moustached, walking, as he always did, up the road from Mitcham, with his cricket bag on his shoulder, observed and admired but never accosted by all cricketing Surrey?

The Oval, like Lord's, has its own tavern on the edge of the ground, but whereas Lord's is an island within London, the Surrey ground is part of Cockneydom, its sparrows pecking with a cockney pertness in the outfield, the roar of the traffic part of the atmosphere of the match, the gasometer and the tall chimneys rightfully part of the landscape.

Here Percy Fender, a London businessman, captained his county with a shrewdness and speed of reaction which the Ovalite recognized as part of himself. He will be watching the Test, and so will that quiet gentleman Jack Hobbs – with *Wisden* to prove that he is rising sixty-nine, although the eye says he is in his fifties.

It is in the last Test of each home series – at The Oval – that we have said goodbye to very many great cricketers – Hobbs among them – as they played their last Test innings. There, too, we say our yearly goodbyes to many who are part of the fabric of the game. Some of them we have seen for the last time on earth at an Oval Test. When the next season has come round, they have not been in their accustomed places. So, perhaps, it is well that The Oval, ground of partings, should have its own perky gaiety, lest we should remember and be sad.

*London Calling*

# –6–

# Notes from the Diary

## John Arlott's Diary

DECEMBER 1960

When cricket talk turns to the subject of young batsmen, it is on sounder ground than with bowlers. A young bowler will often take a crop of wickets in his early days because opposing batsmen do not know his stock-in-trade. But in a second season, the ball which previously took wickets by surprise is already filed in the batsman's mind as a probability. It can be amazing, when a new bowler has had a good start, to find batsmen who have never faced him already 'primed' as to his resources from conversation with their fellow 'professors' in other sides.

On the other hand, the young batsman – our topic here – provided he has made a fair number of runs and against all types of bowling, should be the better for the experience. If he has a particular weakness, of course, it will soon be used against him by opposing bowlers; but otherwise, while, like anyone else, he may have his 'bad trots', he ought not to 'blow up' as so many young bowlers do.

We have little real reason to be complacent about the England batting. After the harvest of runs gathered in the West Indies, all the English batsmen proved vulnerable to a South African attack of lower quality than is to be expected from the Australians.

So there has been some hint of urgency in recent 'shop' talked about the younger batsmen. The year 1960 saw the emergence of several new men, but two of them – A.R. Lewis, of Cambridge University and Glamorgan, and W.E. (Eric) Russell, of Middlesex – were outstanding. At the start, Russell had a clear lead of experience, and that advantage was still apparent by September.

Russell made over 2000 runs, many of them on the Lord's wicket, which is by no means a favourite with batsmen, and he was, of course, for most of the season, ploughing a harder furrow than Lewis, who was batting at Fenner's in non-Championship matches. Nevertheless, each in his different way made a considerable impact on the year's cricket.

In the current era of amateur dominance of our batting, Russell looks clearly the best of his immediate generation of professionals. In 1959 he seemed suddenly to grow up from the typical young Lord's pro, fighting to hold his place, into an assured player, unhurried in manner and smooth in style. Often he appeared to do no more than to lean out to a ball, yet sent it through the covers perfectly placed and at rattling speed. A thoughtful player, he clearly took careful note of the bowling but, nevertheless, maintained a note of aggression, and more than once lost his wicket in the attempt to force the pace against defensive out-cricket. Yet still the recurrent impression of Russell's play is one of poise and time to spare. He has been brought along slowly and there is an unmistakable quality of maturity about his play so that, if he maintains his form, 1961 could see him on the fringe of the England side.

The development of Tony Lewis was more spectacular but, in Glamorgan at least, it did not come as a surprise. Although he had played only fifteen first-class innings prior to 1960, he had been marked down by Wilfred Wooller and John Clay and company in Glamorgan while he was still at school; indeed, he played for the county when he was barely seventeen. He seems marked down as the future captain of Glamorgan – if the business of earning a living allows him to take up the office. Most of us would be hard put to remember Sir Leonard Hutton quite so enthusiastic about any relatively raw batsman as about Lewis after he had played against him. There is little doubt that Sir Leonard appreciated – as many bowlers did more ruefully – Lewis's natural sense of timing, which was more than normal ball sense. Some of those impressed by his early form at Cambridge still held back until they had seen what he would do on wickets less placid than Fenner's. Almost certainly reinforced by that comfortable practice, Lewis proceeded to make runs capably on more difficult pitches and when Championship points were in issue. He has further to go than Russell, but there seems little doubt that even normal progress will bring him to the top of English batting.

Both Lewis and Russell played with others whose promise they rendered a little less bright. There is a frequent – and possibly partly justified – suggestion that a place in the Middlesex side often, and too easily, proves a stepping stone to an England cap. Nevertheless, the ability of the new crop of Middlesex batsmen is obvious. 'The other Russell' – S.E. – is by no means an orthodox bat, but his defence is useful and he punishes the bad ball with unspectacular regularity, shovelling anything short down to long leg with a stroke peculiarly his own which brings him many fours, even when he seems to be going slowly. He has other strokes not strictly according to the manual but to which he lends an air of authenticity. Since he had never played in a first-class match until he came into the Middlesex side as a replacement in 1960, his 1000 runs was a considerable achievement, and he could make many thousands more. Gale, troubled by injuries and perhaps taking his cricket over-seriously, has not yet fulfilled all his promise, but he could yet make many and fluent runs. Parfitt is still walking that precarious tight-rope between shrewd attack and over-venturesome hitting, but he is learning. So, too, are Clark and White, but they may well have to wait to prove themselves.

At Cambridge, Roger Prideaux scored a mass of runs and probably was unlucky not to win a regular place in the Kent side after the University Match. Prideaux takes his cricket seriously and has the temperament, as well as the eye and well-coached method, to go on scoring runs heavily. Whether he can become a dominant player against top-class bowling is not yet resolved, but he has ample time to prove that he can.

In the Glamorgan side, Alan Jones had an undistinguished season; he will do far better when he has finished working out the game for himself – when he will be a very difficult man to bowl against, for he has an attacking instinct which, for the moment, often conflicts with his inherently sound technique.

It has long been difficult to climb from the large Northants groundstaff into the first team, but another newcomer, Crump, made it, and stayed there. Coming into the side late, he made exactly 1000 runs and was second only to Subba Row in the county's averages – with 34.48 although he did not make a century; often, too, he played a major part in salvaging an innings. His team-mate, Norman, again batted with sensitive timing, and Ramsamooj, though he did not live up to his fine start in Championship matches, should prove one of the most consistently entertaining batsmen in the country.

After a tentative season in 1959, Graham Atkinson, of Somerset, missed several early matches through injury, but still came extremely close to a 2000-run aggregate. He used to make most of his runs on the on side but during winter practice he added powerful off-strokes to his repertoire. He can be little more than a stride away from representative cricket. His partner, Virgin, was far less experienced – he had played only twenty first-class innings until last season – but he settled in with a solid defence and a short, but safe, range of punishing strokes. Within a measurable time these two may be the best opening pair in the counties.

The Universities were both well served by batsmen. At Oxford, the Pakistani J. Burki scored steadily – and ended second in the first-class averages – but one would have liked to see him playing in tougher circumstances; the same is true of Dyson and Reddy.

On the harder level, Springall, of Notts, batted with unfailing grit in a losing side; Tindall played some stern, gritty innings when the tide was running against Surrey, and Hall settled into the Derbyshire batting. Sharpe of Yorkshire has something of technique yet to learn, but he has the mind to learn it, and the temperament to make big scores. We may notice, too, that Jim Stewart of Warwickshire, still only twenty-five, continued to hit the ball hard, but so judiciously that he came by 1864 runs.

It would not be fair – though the topic is the younger batsman – to pass by the season without noting Cyril Poole's best year since 1951, and the translation to the century-scoring class of that pleasing stroke-maker H.L. Johnson of Derby.

The year of 1961 may well see two contrasting batsmen realize the hopes they have aroused in good critics: Bolus of Yorkshire and the Nawab of Pataudi had useful seasons in 1960; but substantially greater things, surely, lie ahead of both of them – in 1961?

*Playfair Cricket Monthly*


MAY 1961

Cricket, probably because it has grown up taking its shape from the people who play it on all levels of performance, always seems to have a shaped history. That is also to say that it has been a *growth*, with a social history as well as one of playing events.

We have seen it change with changing times and to meet changing demands in a way that has sometimes seemed uncanny as it developed in time and tune with circumstances and demands.

This year is, clearly, a season of challenge, and could be important in the shape of cricket history. On the one hand is the challenge of

Benaud's side, bent on retaining The Ashes in what promises to be an excitingly even rubber. On the other side, there is the challenge to English cricket to re-establish itself in public esteem and measure up to the great series just completed between Australia and the West Indies. These are the two surface facets of the game's struggle in England. But they are subordinate to the general and internal recognition of the need for a change of heart.

It is useless to expect what is called 'brighter cricket' – or fast-moving play – so long as the main ingredient of the out-cricket is short-of-a-length medium-pace bowling, delivered, over after over, by bowlers who are keeping the game tight and, humanly enough, conserving their energies.

Hinting at historic shape, the Australians bring with them three 'back-of-the-hand' bowlers in Benaud, Kline and Simpson. The leg-spinner – traditionally – and the bowler of the 'Chinaman' – potentially – should speed up play. Can they still do so?

It is simple, but not just, to lump all leg-spinners together. We may, perhaps, take Arthur Mailey and Len Braund as the old-style leg-spinners, giving the ball a huge tweak, tossing it up, taking wickets with bad balls as well as good and, in general, challenging the batsman to hit invitingly curved, but heavily spun, deliveries far out of sight. But between the two wars there grew up a fresh school of leg-spin. Bill O'Reilly was the prototype, bowling to a tight length at all but medium pace and, in the case of his leg-break at least, rolling it rather than spinning it: nearer in technique to the medium-pace 'cutter' than the high-tosser of old. Freddie Brown, in his great period at the beginning of the thirties, was of almost the same type; Douglas Wright was quite medium in pace; even Eric Hollies sacrificed spin to tight accuracy; and Clarrie Grimmett was amazingly accurate.

Nowadays, too, county captains are reluctant to use a leg-spinner so long as bonus points are at stake. In fact, the leg-spinner has been long out of fashion in English cricket. The time came – and could clearly be recognized – in the early post-war years when the average batsman played the leg-spinner defensively and waited for the bad ball before he hit. That was 'business', but it was not adventurous. Moreover, it demanded that the leg-spinner was also a really accurate length bowler – almost a contradiction in terms.

Yet, in that same period, leg-spinners – Ramadhin, McCool, Dooland, Goonesena, Iverson – took good English wickets; all of them, we may note, were from overseas countries.

The leg-spinner could still take wickets in English cricket – say six for 100 in 15 overs instead of the seamer's 40 overs. That makes for faster cricket. It applied in club cricket for years after it died – more or less with 'Tich' Freeman – in the county games. Still, though to a decreasing degree, we can see the club leg-spinner tossing them up to batsmen who are prepared to back their drive against his spin.

The proof for the first-glass game may well lie in the success of the Australian spinners. Used to good wickets, where they must almost tweak their fingers off to take a wicket, they will really turn the ball. In the past, English batsmen have proved tragically foot-tied against Australia's spinners. Now they are even more out of practice against them than ever. For that state of affairs English cricket must take the blame. Bonus points penalize the man who buys his wickets at one every 4 overs instead of one every 10 – which means that, to a large extent, it defeats its own purpose.

Yet we notice that the veteran Dr 'Bertie' Clarke, coming into the Essex side, bowled with marked effect; Greenhough and Barber are beginning to win considerable respect. Perhaps the realization is dawning that a man can be forgiven an occasional bad ball in return for the occasional 'fizzer'. It may be significant, too, that more and more counties have engaged young leg-spinners in the past few seasons. Certainly, Castell, at Hampshire, spins the ball prodigiously, though he may not be ready for first-class play for two or three years to come. Most encouraging of all is the appointment of Ian Bedford to captain Middlesex – traditionally the county for leg-spinners. If he succeeds, in his maturity, in pacing up play, taking wickets *quickly*, Middlesex may shock some of the other counties into a different approach. But the leg-spinner must be allowed a few fours – if only to encourage the batsmen – and captains and batsmen must take their parts.

*Playfair Cricket Monthly*

## DECEMBER 1961

Again with the autumn came changes in county captaincy – some with sad undertones. Yet, harsh as the first report seemed, it could yet prove a happy circumstance for Bob Barber to be relieved of the post with Lancashire. It is a pity that the matter was handled so that the news 'broke' as he was about to leave for Pakistan and India: and that the county's statement did not appear until he was overseas and unable to comment. That was bad public relations, but does not necessarily make the decision a bad one.

A captain who bowls is a constant problem to himself, with the need to assess objectively the subjective matter of the effect of his bowling – or not bowling – both on the match in hand and on his own team. To use a leg-spinner who does, positively, spin the ball, and is therefore liable to expensive inaccuracies, is a delicate decision for the most detached captain. If the captain is himself the leg-break bowler, it is even more complicated. When, as so often was the case with Barber, the decision was not merely whether to put on a leg-spinner, but whether that leg-spinner should be himself or Tommy Greenhough, the other candidate for that post in the England side, the matter became first-class material for a cricket novel, but no help to the smooth running of a team.

Bob Barber is a shy, somewhat introverted and modest young man. In 1960 against South Africa, at Edgbaston, he bowled some of the best leg-spin delivered by an Englishman in a Test for several years. The evidence of the last winter's tour to New Zealand also argues that he is a most effective bowler when he is not captain.

Lancashire had a good neighbouring precedent for the appointment of Blackledge in Barber's place. Like Ronnie Burnet, who led Yorkshire to the Championship in 1959, Blackledge is an experienced club captain, though with no apparent claim to a place in the side on playing ability. But, as Burnet showed, there is a case for the man wise in the basic principles of cricket and the handling of cricketers being a more effective county captain than the gifted but inexperienced player (provided he has a good senior professional to provide the first-class-level expertise). Certainly there are some club captains who handle leg-break bowlers capably, while some established county captains do not.

If, as we hope, the Lancashire committee assured themselves on that point before they chose their new captain, then next season Barber could easily take the narrow step which separates him from the position of the England all-rounder. He is a clean-handed fieldsman, a useful batsman, correct in defence with increasing strokes, and a genuine and thoughtful enthusiast for the game. Thus the change could prove beneficial to him and to English cricket.

No doubt the Lancashire committee will be wondering how the news of Barber's supersession 'leaked'. The fact is that such news as this invariably *does* leak. The lesson to be learnt is simple enough – when such a decision is taken, a statement should be prepared at once, the people concerned should be notified rapidly and the *entire* press informed before one section of it finds out.

The situation at Northampton seems to have developed far differently and more happily. Raman Subba Row's resignation was smoothly announced and carried with it no suggestion of dissension. The decision of Roger Prideaux – a potential England bat – to join them no doubt foreshadows his eventual accession to the captaincy. It was not unnatural that he should want to move from Kent, where the competition for places over the past two seasons has been such that at least two good batsmen were always out of the side. Since Kent made it clear that they wanted Prideaux to stay, his application for special registration seems to fall into line with those of Mike Smith, Peter Richardson and Tom Graveney. Thus he may well have to qualify by a year's residence. Meanwhile, Northants have appointed Keith Andrew to captain the side next season. If they intend that Roger Prideaux should eventually take over, they are fortunate in having a man of Andrew's quality to keep the position warm.

Moreover, Keith Andrew is so retiring that he would no doubt revert to the post of senior professional, in due course, in his usual courteous and unobtrusive fashion. Few cricketers of his considerable gifts can have been quite so modest; had he been more self-assertive he must have played far more often for England.

At Leicester another undemonstrative cricketer, Willie Watson, has moved out of the captaincy with characteristic absence of fuss. The county have David Kirby – clearly the captain-designate – ready to take over. He has the temperament, the approach and the playing ability to develop into a good county captain; but he probably could have profited from a full season under so wise a cricketer as Watson. If Watson plays out his contract, as he is prepared to do, we shall observe him in 1962 with added appreciation for the fact that it may be the last we shall see of a gloriously stylish left-handed batsman. If only for his great innings against the Australians at Lord's in 1953, he must stand among the cricketing immortals; memory will cherish him as the truly handsome batsman.

Neville Cardus has written with his invariable evocative grace on the late Percy Chapman as a cricketer. But a footnote may not be inappropriate from one of the many with lasting memories of his kindness. Few of his actions were more touching, or more characteristic, than his difficult and uncomfortable cross-country journey (with little idea how he might make the return trip) to Maurice Tate's funeral, although he was clearly very ill and looking death in the face. Even as late as last August, from his deathbed, he sent a telegram – which gave no hint of his own tragic plight – to wish Colin Ingleby-Mackenzie good fortune in Hampshire's Championship attempt.

There came, too, news of Bernard Darwin's death. Pre-eminently a golfer and writer on golf, he played a major part in lifting sports reporting to the level of literature. His life of W.G. Grace – in the 'Great Lives' series – is still the best biography of 'The Old Man'; and a number of essays showed his genuine understanding of cricket and his power to write about it with his characteristically sound and humanistic touch.

*Playfair Cricket Monthly*

# Jottings from the Journal

## A Cold, Wet and Windy Start

*29 April–8 May* 1967.   The pre-season skirmishes were given added interest, at least in domestic circles of the counties, by the series of knock-out matches in which each county produced its representative for the final stages of the Single Wicket competition. These games yielded such serious fun and such skills that, apart from adding zest to the usual pre-season practice, they provided entertainment which ought, in subsequent years, to attract and content some substantial crowds. If no one was surprised to find Brian Close emerging as the Yorkshire representative, the margin of his win – 4–3 over Geoff Boycott – was dramatic enough, and who would have nominated Graham Atkinson (a non-bowling batsman) as the Lancashire survivor, leave alone Robin Jackman from Surrey or David Turner from Hampshire?

On the first Saturday of the season, the changing shape of cricket history was reflected by the appearance of two Barbadians (Keith Boyce, of Essex, and John Shepherd, of Kent), a South African (Tony Greig, of Sussex), a Kenyan (Sheikh Basharat Hassan, of Notts), and a Pakistani (Mohammed Younis, of Surrey), all newly qualified to appear in the County Championship. Two players were out to the first ball of the morning and, in the first over of the Worcester v Sussex Gillette Cup tie – what a waste at such an early stage! – John Snow took the wickets of Kenyon and Headley; Tony Buss then had a spell of four for 13 and Worcester never truly recovered. In the other tie of the day, Roy Marshall scored a hundred before lunch for Hampshire who beat Lincolnshire.

By Monday night, Derbyshire had beaten Leicestershire – their first win on their headquarters ground at Derby for five years – and Stringer, a fast-medium bowler making his first appearance for

Yorkshire (and that only as deputy for the injured Nicholson) had taken four good MCC wickets for 10 runs.

The match between Worcestershire and the touring side marks general acceptance of cricket having positively begun and, memory insists, invariably produces bad weather. The Nawab of Pataudi on the one side, Jack Flavell and Jim Standen on the other, were fortunate enough to be confined to their beds with tonsillitis. The remainder suffered viciously cold, wet, windy weather. D'Oliveira made 174 not out, his highest score in first-class cricket, on the opening day when Bedi, a slow left-arm bowler, took three wickets, and bowled with a puzzling flight and some occasionally sharp spin to a steady length. There was virtually no play on the second day and on the truncated third, Engineer – at one time 22 out of 24 on the board – struck the ball generously and Sardesai, his opening partner, batted with cool, professional tidiness. The remainder of the batting collapsed: 106 for eight to Worcestershire's 335 for six declared. Such was the weather, however, that this was a game on which to commend the successful and to withhold any blame from those who achieved less. Only it may be said that there was an obvious disposition among the Indian batsmen – refreshing by comparison with some of their predecessors – to make attacking strokes and that – equally promisingly – their attack is so lacking in pace that it *must* be based on spin.

One of the season's awaited acquisitions, surely, appeared in Tony Greig, the tall South African who, in his first Championship match for Sussex, played an innings of 156 against Lancashire with such power and grace as to prompt comparison with Dexter. A week of horrid weather – but so was the first week of 1947, remembered as the season of sun.

*The Cricketer*


# Deluge at Old Trafford but a Happy Crowd at Lord's

*27 May–2 June* 1967.   The Saturday of the new, anonymous Spring Bank Holiday – with all the traditional Whit fixtures – was completely washed out: not a ball was bowled in any one of the ten games. Someone calculated that this dismal day brought the season's tally to fifty-two utterly blank days out of a scheduled 202. Sunday and Monday were a little better, but the damage had been done. The Yorkshire–Lancashire match – the unlucky Geoff Pullar's benefit – was abandoned without a ball being bowled. Indeed, the deluge upon Old Trafford was so heavy that the match with the Indians, arranged for 3 June – a *week* later – was transferred to Southport.

Understandably, not a single match in the weekend round yielded a finish. It has been, we are told, the wettest May for 194 years; no one disputes the statement.

On the other hand, the series of rain-ruined matches proves that our cricket is more healthy than some think. At any time prior to the last war the financial blow would have been devastating. In the 1930s, such counties as Northants, Glamorgan and Worcestershire might have been reduced to bankruptcy. But in 1967, the weather cannot affect the revenue from supporters' clubs, football pools, radio and television or the vastly increased membership subscriptions.

The Monday crowd at Lord's was a happy one, seeming to cherish its cricket, and as the week grew warmer and drier, the atmosphere at matches was unmistakably happy.

The Indians had a sorry time of it against Surrey. Only Hanumant Singh – who saved them from an innings defeat – Engineer and, to markedly lesser degree, Kunderan and Borde of their batsmen batted even moderately convincingly. Pocock, who grows in capability week by week, bowled well against them; but not quite so well as they made it appear. They play off-spin with what an English professional would regard as naivety.

It would be hard to dispute that the best finger-spinner in England at the moment is Tony Lock. This season, too, he must have dealt out more physical embraces than any other man in the history of cricket: a good catch or a valuable wicket for Leicestershire prompts him to transports of delight and affection, and, beating Kent on Friday, they moved up only two points behind Hampshire at the top of the Championship.

Yorkshire murdered Worcester and are third; but it is a crazy situation in which Notts stand fourth after finishing only one of their seven games; lower down, not one of Warwickshire, Gloucester or Northants has won or lost a match.

The team for the first Test – at Headingley – to be announced on Sunday, has been picked with an eye beyond this summer to the tour of West Indies. Presumably Close, Graveney, D'Oliveira, Murray and

Higgs are certainties; Milburn ought to be; Snow – currently bowling faster than ever before – Amiss, Edrich, Price and – on past evidence – Boycott are probables; but Bob Barber is, apparently, not available. There is talk of Pocock being chosen: he should have a good future; but is he a better bowler now – or likely to be next winter in the West Indies – than David Allen? It is a sad thought that three of the four best batsmen in England – assuming Graveney to be the other – Mike Smith, Colin Cowdrey and Ken Barrington, are all doubtful.

The weather forecast is of fine weather – but possible thunder – tomorrow.

*The Cricketer*

# Boycott Loses His Test Place: Sussex Hit Highest Yet

*17–23 June* 1967.   A week of sunshine and significant activity in the County Championship ended on Friday with thunderstorms over much of the country and India, in the Test at Lord's, in a position which, but for their amazing recovery at Headingley, could only be called hopeless.

The news buzzed round another series of good and lively Sunday crowds that the selectors had dropped Boycott – presumably as corrective treatment for his slow scoring at Leeds – and that Barrington would open the innings with Edrich; Amiss, the heaviest scorer of the season, took the vacant batting position and Higgs, England's only regular player through the 1966 series with West Indies, had lost his place to David Brown of Warwickshire.

In the weekend round, Leicestershire emphasized their new quality and spirit when, having been far behind all through the game against Somerset, they rallied and a stand by Birkenshaw and Tolchard in the last hour gave them a win by two wickets – Lock made the winning hit with no time to spare. After John Mortimore's declaration, Yorkshire – Boycott 98 not out, and Sharpe, after weeks out of touch, 71 not out – won by *nine* wickets.

In the second set of fixtures Yorkshire won again and went above Hampshire – who had no Championship match in the week – at the top of the table. On a couple of difficult wickets at the Nevill Ground,

Tunbridge Wells, Kent beat Sussex and Worcester: Graham took twenty-two wickets for 141 runs in the week and his figures when he routed Worcester in the second innings – seven for 27 – were the best any bowler has produced thus far in the season.

Worcester had Kenyon – as a selector – Graveney and D'Oliveira at the Test and Richardson is out of action through a hand injury; nevertheless they seem to have lost the bright competitive quality which so lately marked the two Championship sides. This evening the leading counties are: Yorkshire 72 points; Hampshire and Leicester-shire 68; Kent 66; Middlesex and Derbyshire 56.

Boycott, as we should expect of him, marked the loss of his Test place with an innings of 220 not out against Northants for whom Milburn, another of the five serious candidates to open the England innings, made 61 in their first innings and, when they collapsed for 99 in the second, an even more impressive 63.

Sussex made the highest score of the season, 450 for six – Michael Buss 150 – against a Glamorgan side still sadly unsure of itself.

In the Test India won the toss and batted first on a Lord's wicket livelier in pace and bounce than that at Headingley. They were put out by Snow – who bowled better and faster than his three for 49 might argue – and Brown, for 152. Edrich, out for 12 and unlikely to have another innings in the match, must now contemplate the wide and varied competition for his place. Barrington batted competently until he was completely beaten by Chandrasekhar – an unlucky bowler – playing with the care of one only three short of his first century in a Lord's Test. Graveney batted stylishly but at easy rate and England, three wickets down, were exactly a hundred in front when the rain came at three o'clock: strong advantage if the weather has affected the wicket, sound foundation for a large score if it has not.

*The Cricketer*

# Majid's Second Century and Lock's Immense Efforts

*1–7 July* 1967.   A week of sunshine has been full of busy cricket, discussion and general interest. It is possible to sense an atmosphere of pleasure through English cricket this season, almost as if the Clark

Report threat to cut the supply of first-class play had made people more aware of it and more inclined to cherish it. Gates on the whole are still not good, but Sunday matches certainly are attracting people who have not been to a county match between Monday and Saturday for years; whether they all pay or not – except at those grounds which have instituted a 'Sunday membership' – is doubtful, but a first step has been taken: more, fresh people are coming to the games.

It was sad that the first Sunday of county cricket at Lord's should have come in a match – Middlesex v Hampshire – which proved desperately unsatisfactory. In three days interrupted only by a stoppage of a quarter-hour for bad light, the two sides failed to reach a decision even on the first innings. Hampshire made 421 for seven declared, Middlesex 371 for seven; neither side took any points at all, but Middlesex retained their two-point lead over Hampshire who now have not scored a Championship point for almost a month.

At the same time Leicestershire, on a dusty wicket from which the ball turned widely and lifted in slow but grotesque bounce, beat Gloucestershire by 103 runs and went back to the top of the Championship table. A generous declaration by Stewart, the Surrey captain, gave Glamorgan their first win of the season and they followed it with their second in the latter half of the week when Tony Lewis, barely even to be described as an 'occasional' leg-spinner, put himself on to bowl and took the last three wickets of Somerset – who were by now playing for a draw – for only 18 runs.

The Pakistanis played Middlesex on yet another perfect – too perfect – slow wicket at Lord's. In the first innings of the touring side, Latchman, the little Jamaican leg-spinner, achieved the best figures of his career: seven for 91. Then Eric Russell and Michael Harris, with an opening partnership of 312, broke the Middlesex record for the first wicket, of 310, set by Syd Brown and Jack Robertson in the county's rich year of 1947. At the last the Pakistanis had no difficulty in drawing the match; Majid scored his second century of the tour – he is full of runs and confidence – and Burki his first. The Pakistanis are, of course, automatically compared with Pataudi's Indians; and in batting they seem sounder in defensive technique. The Lord's pitch, however, provided a searching examination of their bowling. Certainly they have several bowlers faster than any in the Indian side, but they are not truly fast and the gradations of fast-medium are not significant at Test level. More important, their spin-bowling in the Middlesex match included no one so dangerous as Chandrasekhar, so steady as Bedi or who spun as much as Prasanna. They may be grateful for the availability of the two leg-spinners, Mushtaq Mohammed of Northants and Intikhab Alam, who is a club professional in Scotland, and Nasim, slow left-arm, for Tests.

Leicestershire had another turning wicket for their match with Yorkshire. They have made great improvements in playing strength, facilities for staff and spectators and in general atmosphere since they at length acquired the Grace Road ground last year. But these explosively dusty wickets will give rise to complaints from most of their opponents – certainly from those who lose. Yorkshire are always tough opponents on a bad wicket, masters of finger-spin and, on the batting side, of playing it. Illingworth, as successful as any player in the country this season, took six for 52 and five for 27 and scored 60. Despite Lock's immense efforts – he caught four and bowled four of the first eight Yorkshire batsmen – Yorkshire won by an innings and are back in the lead in the Championship, with Leicestershire second, then Kent, Sussex and Middlesex.

Bryan Richardson, younger brother of Peter and Dick, playing his first match of the season for Warwickshire – against Cambridge University – scored a century in each innings. He has never quite made good the immense promise of his schooldays at Malvern during his five years on the Warwickshire staff; perhaps this performance will repair his confidence.

Bob Barber has told the selectors that he is unlikely to be available for the West Indies tour this winter. The selectors, for their part, have issued a writ for libel against Michael Parkinson, who described them as 'palsied twits'. Never a dull moment.

*The Cricketer*

# Superb Gillette Cup Semi-Final; and Eight for 25 by Greig

*15–21 July* 1967. This week has seen English cricket at its peak and at the bottom of the pit. A superbly contested Gillette Cup semi-final between Kent and Sussex at Canterbury drew, and delighted, a crowd of over 16,000. But over the previous weekend, the Championship match between Kent and Hampshire at Southampton did not reach a decision on the first innings until ten minutes to six on the third day.

The Kent–Hampshire fixture was long regarded as a Bank Holiday attraction, but in recent years a certain amount of resentment has grown up between the two sides: too many draws have been played and each has inclined to blame the other for keeping the game too tight for a finish. On this occasion Kent took their first innings through the long first day and an hour into Sunday for 340. Hampshire, no doubt deciding that their only possible objective now was a first-innings lead, ground along even more slowly and scored 82 runs less than Kent from the same number of overs. At the end, Gilliat's first century for the county, a fifty by David Turner – the most exciting prospect Hampshire have had for years – and a brave innings by Timms took them to within four runs of the Kent first innings. But both sides must have lost many friends.

At Newark, where Leicester took first-innings points from Notts, there was no time to begin a second innings, and at The Oval, Pakistan took long batting practice and offered no attempt at a finish with Surrey.

In the fine weather that has followed that ghastly May, more than half the first-class matches played have ended in draws. Billy Griffith, in an interview with J.L. Manning, described this cricket as 'unintelligible'. The short day on Sunday and the new first-innings points allocation are ingredients of the situation. But above all, it seems that the players cannot see the wood for the trees. In fact, they are pricing themselves out of business.

Their situation might be more defensible but for the magnificence of the play at Canterbury on Wednesday. Kent batted first on a hard, true wicket and lost Denness at 3 – the kind of situation which so often produces stalemate in Championship matches. But Shepherd (77) met the crisis with gay attacking strokes; Luckhurst (78), acting as anchor-man, nevertheless scored steadily, and Cowdrey (78) batted with a felicity, ease and certainty such as even he has rarely shown before: indeed, no one on the ground could recall a better innings from him. At one point he took 31 from three consecutive overs of John Snow, and forced Parks to take him off. In face of a total of 293, Sussex batted with too great anxiety, one eye on the clock, another on their wickets; they matched the Kent scoring-rate for a considerable period, but no batsman played a major innings and, despite some characteristically busy runs from Suttle, shrewd aggression by Parks and some big hits by Greig, they were beaten by 118 runs. Kent were without

Graham but Brown, Dixon and Sayer took useful early wickets and Underwood proved too steady for later batsmen who sought to maintain the high scoring-rate asked of them. A day of 468 runs, fifteen wickets, some superb ground fielding and intelligent bowling was enough to please the most captious spectator. Alec Bedser, for all his feeling for bowlers, could but declare Colin Cowdrey the Man of the Match, not merely for his glorious innings but also for his astute captaincy.

In the other semi-final, a rainstorm at Old Trafford delayed the decision between Lancashire and Somerset until the second day. Somerset had made 100 for two before the downpour and that proved a winning advantage on the rain-affected wicket where Ken Palmer – declared Man of the Match – and Bill Alley – a master of this kind of play – bowled out Lancashire for 110. The coach-load of Somerset supporters who set off for the match with forty gallons of cider had much to celebrate. A minor public triumph occurred on the first day when, after a shower, it was decided to restart play at three o'clock; but the slow hand-clap from the crowd of 15,000 brought the players out a quarter of an hour earlier.

Tony Greig of Sussex took eight for 25 against Gloucestershire, the best bowling performance of his career; he and Euros Lewis were given their county caps. Less happily, Tony Lewis, the Glamorgan captain, decided to hand over the captaincy to his senior pro, Don Shepherd, and drop himself from the team because of his unhappy batting form. He will play second-eleven or club cricket 'if necessary' for the rest of the season. This is a truly brave gesture; Lewis has too much natural ability, mental and moral quality to stay long out of the game.

In the Championship table, Surrey, by beating Northants, moved up to seventh place; their resources of talent have not been reflected truly by their low position. Sadly, though, their batsman Mick Willett has announced his retirement because of complications following his cartilage operation; a cheerful cricketer and a useful batsman who liked to get on with the game, he made the decision reluctantly and he will have the sympathy of everyone who understands how the best kind of cricketers feel about the game.

A pleasant day of cricket-watching at Southampton – the touring Indian Schools side against Hampshire Schools. The Indians won easily, with more than one player we can expect to see here on a major tour in years to come: Asif, a stylish opening bat who keeps wicket; S.M.H. Kirmani, a well-organized batsman; A.D. Naik, fast-medium bowler and useful bat, who captained the side; J.M. Bhuta, an extremely hostile fast-medium left-arm bowler – surely a Test player of the near future; D. Sarkar, a leg-spinner who has already played Ranji Trophy cricket; Jasbir Singh, slow left-arm; the two sons of Lala Amarnath, both batsmen, and the elder, Surendranath, an extremely mature medium-pace bowler in the manner of his father.

This weekend Hampshire and Kent meet again – this time at Maidstone; the game assumes an importance beyond who wins or loses: it is as if county cricket itself were on trial.

*The Cricketer*

# The Close Affair – the Buzz of Talk Persists

*19–25 August* 1967.   All this week the cricket 'circus' – to use Brian Sellars' term – and the sporting press have been deeply immersed in the matter of Brian Close and the allegations of time-wasting in Yorkshire's match with Warwickshire. Close was summoned to a meeting of the Counties' Executive Committee at Lord's on Wednesday, where a unanimous decision was reached that: 'The Yorkshire team had used delaying tactics during the second Warwickshire innings, and that these tactics constituted unfair play and were against the best interests of the game. Furthermore the committee held the captain, Brian Close, entirely responsible for these tactics. They have therefore severely censured him and this decision will be relayed to the Yorkshire County Cricket Club.' Meanwhile the announcement of the captain and team to tour the West Indies was deferred from Thursday until next Wednesday; and the Yorkshire committee meets on Monday. Conjecture and argument on the subject have produced an almost unbroken buzz for days. On the face of it, MCC probably would find it difficult to administer such an unprecedented censure *and* award the England captaincy on tour to the same man in the same week. The question will soon be resolved.

Meanwhile, Close has captained England in the third Pakistan Test with no little acumen. Winning the toss he sent Pakistan to bat on an unusually hard, fast and green Oval wicket. First Higgs and then Arnold – five for 58 – dealt with the Pakistani batting, delayed only by Mushtaq who played a shrewd, skilful – and quite uncharacteristically dour – innings of 66. Boycott was unwell – pursued by the virus that has been worrying the Yorkshire side for the past week – and Close opened the England innings in his place with Cowdrey. Asif and Saleem gave the early England batting a hard time of it, making the ball move off the seam and often bounce quickly. But again Barrington made a century – he has made a hundred in each Test of this series with Pakistan – and Graveney played with admirable style for 77 so that, by tonight, England, with 257 for three, are 41 ahead with seven first-innings wickets in hand.

Last Sunday the selectors named the same twelve for The Oval as had been called to Trent Bridge. On the same day Repton Pilgrims, captained by Donald Carr, beat Radley Rangers – despite Dexter's 80 not out – to win the first final of the Cricketer Cup.

In the County Championship there were some surprises. Kent beat Glamorgan by only 26 runs on another of their home wickets – this time at Gillingham – which prompted a complaint from the visiting captain. To the general astonishment Essex, after being put out by Yorkshire for 87 and left 127 behind on the first innings, recovered, and Acfield – five for 32 – and Hobbs bowled them to a win by 9 runs. Hampshire, with two wickets still in hand, drew level with Leicester-shire through a leg-bye from the last ball of the match; Leicester, who led on the first innings and made a well-judged declaration, took six points and Hampshire four.

In the second round, Yorkshire beat Sussex by 83 runs; Glamorgan, in the return of the weekend match, beat Kent by an innings and 157 runs; Jeff Jones again bowled well – he has come to his best form late in the season – too late for the selectors? – while Tony Lewis and – as usual against Kent – Alan Jones made useful scores. (*Daily Telegraph* headline: 'Kent Fail to Keep up with the Joneses'.) Leicester, beating Gloucestershire in the extra half-hour, drew level with Kent in second place. The top positions now are: Yorkshire 25 matches played, 156 points; Kent and Leicestershire both 26 matches and 152 points; Surrey 27 matches, 142 points.

Hampshire followed their level draw with Leicestershire by a tie with Middlesex – who had declared – when Herman (Hampshire-born son of the former Hampshire bowler) yorked Cottam with the last possible ball of the match. It was the first tie in a county match for eight years.

Much other news which would have attracted attention in an ordinary week was overshadowed by the Close affair. Mike Smith announced that he will retire from cricket to take up a business appointment at the end of the season; he had still much to offer to cricket. Dick Richardson, of Worcester, too announced that this will be his last season; he is only thirty-two and, coinciding with the retirement of Don Kenyon, Jack Flavell and Jim Standen, this faces Worcestershire – who have again finished the summer strongly – with weighty problems.

At Eastbourne, against Sussex, Colin Milburn scored the fastest Championship century of the summer – in 78 minutes – and Northants won by ten wickets. The Counties' Adjudication Committee announced that it was 'not satisfied with the basic action' of Malcolm Scott, the slow left-arm bowler of Northants, and barred him from bowling in county cricket for the remainder of the season. Scott, a pleasant person and keen cricketer, has said he will study the films of his action and work to correct it during the winter. Gloucestershire, whose batting has been barely held up by Arthur Milton, announce that they have recruited Sadiq – Hanif's youngest brother – the West Indian Lloyd, and David Green, the Oxford University and Lancashire opening batsman; these interesting cricketers, if they joined the county, would do much to make good its main deficiency.

*The Cricketer*

# Consolation for Kent at Lords

*2–8 September* 1967. Yorkshire are County Champions – for the sixth time in the last nine years – and Kent, runners-up in the Championship, Gillette Cup winners.

Gillette final day has become a genuine cricket occasion giving the end of the season a gay fillip, despite the onset of football. This year the building work at the Tavern–Clock Tower corner of Lord's restricted space but, on an all-ticket day, 18,500 spectators paid to come in and it was estimated that about 6000 MCC members watched also. It was a pleasing day, partisan feeling tempered by good humour.

Kent won the day, in fact, before lunch. Nerves – few of the players except Cowdrey and Brown had ever before played in front of so large a crowd – probably were at the root of some loose bowling by Somerset at the start. Denness – particularly – and Luckhurst made the most of it in a first-wicket stand of 78 and Luckhurst, an industrious anchor-man, continued with Shepherd to 138 before the second wicket fell. Though Somerset first tightened the game and then took six wickets for only 12 runs in early afternoon, the task ahead of them was made decisively difficult by the two young men Knott and Ealham, who put on an extremely sensible 27 at the end.

Peter Robinson, moved up from number eight or nine to open the innings a fortnight before, after Clarkson's injury, played a firm, well-judged innings of 48, but Somerset conclusively lacked a major batsman in the middle of the order. Alley, who had bowled them back into the match by his admirable economy, never found his batting touch; and the promising stand between Barwell and Burgess ended when Barwell was unnecessarily run out. So, although the final difference was only 32 runs, Somerset were always one trick short of a winning position. Shepherd bowled gamely and thriftily despite a leg-foot injury, and Kent's out-cricket was, as throughout the season, highly effective. Denness was made Man of the Match.

Day in, day out, Yorkshire have been the best-balanced and strongest team of the counties. They lost so much play to rain in May that their recovery has been an outstanding sustained performance. Close has directed them single-mindedly towards the top, and if their batting has sometimes appeared fragile, at least one man has usually made runs at a crisis.

Gloucestershire, bottom in the table, had little hope of stopping Yorkshire short of some freak of weather and wicket. That did, indeed, threaten and Mortimore, winning the toss, in yet another decisive match played at Harrogate, put Yorkshire in to bat. An opening partnership of 127 by Boycott and Sharpe before the ball began to turn quickly probably decided the outcome. On the second day Gloucestershire were bowled out twice by Illingworth who had the remarkable figures of seven for 58 and then seven for 6.

One day more of county cricket remained, the third of the match between Somerset and Lancashire at Taunton. In a setting of perfect September, with little of importance at issue, the two sides strove to produce a result, but Lancashire in the end had to choose between throwing away the game or saving it; they rightly made a dignified draw and saved the six points for first-innings lead. The game produced an outstanding innings by Pilling, the shortest player in county cricket, who compensates for his lack of height and reach by quick assessment and footwork. Length is for him a personal matter: often he goes back and cuts a ball to which a taller man would play forward. Here on a wicket which, after rain, was unusually lively for Taunton, he made a century of fine command, mature judgement and crisp, militant strokes, especially the hook which he played with admirable controlled belligerence.

It was a nostalgic time, as final matches always are, and this saw a generous and deserved farewell from crowd and players to Colin Atkinson who is giving up the Somerset captaincy to become Deputy Head of Millfield School. He has been a diligent, sympathetic captain, combative while retaining his ideals.

Now to a weekend of one-day matches – the three Rothmans World Cup games at Lord's and Cavaliers versus a West Indies eleven at Blackheath. What, I wonder, would the elders of the game have said a decade ago, if they had been told that Lord's would house matches sponsored and arranged by Rothmans of Pall Mall, BBC 2 and Bagenal Harvey? Thus has cricket changed.

*The Cricketer*

# −8−

# Three From Three
# Makes Nine

## Glamorgan

ALLAN WATKINS:
THE DISCOVERY OF THE
SOUTH AFRICAN TOUR

*May* 1949. Despite the friendly, even extravagantly, hospitable advances of well-wishers overseas, an MCC touring party must feel itself a single fighting unit in hostile cricketing country. Every player knows that the crowds at Test matches are largely opposition supporters, generous as their applause may be. There is no feeling of personal hostility towards their opponents but there is a closer welding together of the side, so that each member of the party identifies himself with the main body.

So it was with us, players, managers (two of them – one English, Brigadier Green, and one South African, Duggie Meintjies), camp followers and all. I remember the morning when we waited in the passengers' hall while Allan Watkins climbed into the control-tower at Durban airport to listen to St David's Day broadcast by his wife six thousand miles away in Wales. The plane was due to leave the instant the broadcast ended. We waited cheerfully, perhaps a little proud of our fellow traveller for whom planes were held and airport regulations relaxed. When he came down from the tower his face, already unusually reddened by the South African sun, was beaming with delight and everyone of us, I think, shared his happy nostalgia. It was, in other words, an occasion for the entire party, an occasion which we all shared with him.

Often in a Test eleven at home there has been a certain distance between the players. Brought together for one match only, they have not always been so closely knit as an overseas side *must* be. Some of the players in a home Test are near their own homes or have friends locally; the old hands, who know one another well, may make up one party which a new player is perhaps a little shy of joining. Especially if the newcomer has no fellow countyman with him, he can easily feel lonely over a long provincial Sunday in a strange town – which is poor psychological preparation for a Test innings. On a tour it is very different; the players are much together on and off the field. They tend to be particularly friendly with their room-mates but they are all one party and are very close together indeed, physically as well as metaphorically, in the observation coach where they spend the long train journeys. So it is that the team eventually picked for Tests is a unity – made up of men who know one another, and one another's play, intimately. Undoubtedly, on the tour just ended, many of the younger players learned much from the 'old hands'. Len Hutton, for instance, is a wise and tactful adviser and a magnificent model from whom all the younger batsmen must have derived considerable benefit.

I was particularly interested in the progress of Allan Watkins. Early in 1947, I went out on a limb and declared that here was a potential Test player – but found few outside Wales who cared to agree with me. Allan had been unlucky in the matter of injury in his solitary Test against the Australians, and I was anxious for him in South Africa. I felt that he lacked confidence in himself – lacked that confidence which good critics who had watched him knew that he was justified in feeling. At the beginning of the tour he was an uncertain starter and his place in the first Test was by no means assured. The deciding factor in his selection must have been his brilliant fielding. He played at Durban and batted on an almost impossibly sticky wicket to score 9 very impressive runs in the first innings. Those who in the future look back to the scores of that game will hardly be impressed by the bare 'Watkins c Nourse, b A. Rowan 9'. But those of us who saw it will remember that magnificent footwork and a canny dead bat while the wicket was worse than at any other time during the game, and the light poor. We shall remember, too, his catching of Nourse. The South African skipper was bent on consolidating his side's first innings. The wicket, for that first day of the match, was plumb and Nourse was seeing the ball well. Then came a ball from Wright which came in to him a little. Lunch was near and Nourse decided not to risk an attacking stroke but to allow the ball to fall away from his bat on the leg side. He directed it well wide of Watkins and its arc was shallow and short. But suddenly, we saw Allan Watkins at short leg dive, feet higher than head, and seeming to lie in the air four feet off the ground, he coolly reached out and took the catch. Nourse was out – and, by the expression on his face, astounded to boot.

So Watkins came into the second Test, at Johannesburg. He was extremely uncertain for some time against the pace bowlers at the start of his innings, his back-play was hesitant and often he did not even get a touch when he positively played at the ball. His score in that game (7), even backed by his fielding barely demanded his consideration for the third Test. It was, perhaps surprisingly, his bowling which must have tipped the scale for him – he had both Nourse and Wade, the two main-stays of the South African resistance, dropped off him, and actually took the wicket of Tuckett, all for 5 runs in 4 overs. Simpson had not come off at Durban and Palmer was right out of luck so Watkins went to the Cape Town Test, but he had obviously to show improved form there to keep his place. After a useful 27 in the first innings his second innings removed any doubts there were about him. He had, I believe, benefited from 'rooming' and playing with Jack Crapp, and now these two left-handers were consistently playing an almost identical and murderous square-leg stroke which sent the ball for four before the field could move to it. That magnificent eye and sense of timing which make Watkins such an outstanding fieldsman were now enabling him to play this stroke very late and to vary it with a similar stroke which sent the ball very fine indeed to long leg. Scoring his 64 even faster than his partner Denis Compton, he seemed well on the way to a hundred when Mann declared to give South Africa a chance, which was not accepted, of challenging for a win.

I remember, and so will he, Allan Watkins being 64 not out at the end of the first day of the fourth Test at Johannesburg. He had never made a Test century – if he could achieve it now he would be the first Welshman who had ever done so. From six at night to half-past eleven the next morning is a long time to wait with metaphorical pads on and a century still 36 runs away. No man, surely, has ever been so often assured that he would make a century as Allan was that night. I, who perhaps knew him as well as anyone in the party, rather feared that he might be nervous. But there was a firmness about him now which I had never seen before. On that second morning he went briskly about his task – as he needed to do for only Gladwin, Griffith and Young remained to partner him. Gladwin and Griffith did not last long and he was still short of his hundred when Jack Young – the 'Kilburn Slasher' – joined him for the last wicket. Calmly and coolly they added twenty-three valuable runs for that last wicket, saw Watkins' hundred safely past, and the England innings retrieved after a bad start.

With that innings Watkins found himself, and stood out clearly as a player of considerably greater stature than we had ever known in England. Physically he had benefited from South African sunshine and the unrestricted food supplies to become thicker and fitter-looking than during the travels of an English summer. And about his play there was an air of certainty that had been lacking. From the third Test onwards the old suggestion of nervousness and mistiming against swing-bowling at the start of the innings was gone completely. His confidence, too, had increased and strong leg-side play had been added to his always good strokes on the off.

If his bowling through the tour was never very successful it could be quite useful, and his fielding was often bewildering. His work at short leg was so impressive that its effect is difficult to estimate. Certainly he missed some catches which, judging him by his own high standard, we might have expected him to take. Of his effect on the South African batsmen, however, there can be no doubt, but how to assess it? Certainly he and Compton, by their fielding at fine short leg, put the leg-glance out of fashion among South African Test batsmen, who seemed afraid to risk such a stroke when those two were fielding close to the wicket. Thus, while the runs Watkins stopped could be seen, there was no way of estimating the effect on the batsmen of leg-side strokes eschewed. Not only did it deprive them of runs but also, by taking away a stroke automatic to many of them, it must inevitably have affected the entire machinery of their batting minds.

I know that the entire party was pleased with Allan's improvement and all that it promises for the future. It would be a mistake to assume that he is at once good enough to reel off hundreds against the Australians, but it can certainly be said that he has passed through the first filter well. The South African bowling was not outstandingly strong, though possibly better than ours, and it must be admitted that the wickets in general favoured the batsmen. Nevertheless, we watched Allan Watkins grow from a young batsman of promise into a self-reliant batsman of Test class. Two more seasons may easily see him in the Paynter-Leyland class if his improvement continues at a reasonable rate.

Altogether the tour was a success – from a playing point of view in that the team won the Test rubber by two Tests to none and went unbeaten throughout the tour – and also socially, for the team was popular and happy wherever it went. The batting of the side never collapsed, always one batsman came to the rescue, the bowling was steady, if not inspired, and above all, the fielding was magnificent even by comparison with that of Bradman's Australians. A great tour: it was good to be there, good to see the future assets of English cricket being built up in the atmosphere of a happy team.

*South Wales Cricketers' Magazine*

### DAI DAVIES

Dai Davies of Llanelli has been a familiar figure on British cricket grounds for more than fifty years. Within Welsh cricket he holds the historic position of being Glamorgan's first native professional. The story of his first appearance for the county is, in itself, remarkable and, more's the pity, impossible nowadays.

That was romantic; but, whatever the quality of his imagination, he was not a romantic cricketer – Glamorgan could not afford such a luxury. In such a losing side as they were through the sixteen years of his playing career, he had to be competitive, and he was. He was not an elegant batsman to watch, but he played straight, never flinched, and if a ball was short or overpitched, he hit it hard. Above all, whether he had made none or a century, he was always devilish hard to get out. He bowled tight too, usually a fraction short of a length, straight and brisk. In the field he never flagged.

This was the faithful cricketer. His reward did not come in his playing days but, in 1948 at Bournemouth, he was umpiring when Glamorgan won the County Championship for the first time, and it was he who gave Charles Knott out lbw to Johnnie Clay to end the match. Only a few minutes later his voice was a strong influence in the spontaneous 'Hen Wlad Fy Nhadau' of the tiny cluster of Welshmen in front of the pavilion.

He liked to tick off in his mind the necessary ingredients of an lbw decision. Sometimes, indeed, he took so long about the process that the batsman thought he was not out; then Dai, looking almost shyly away to mid-off, would solemnly raise his finger. He called it the 'slow death', and he generally reserved it for batsmen he did not like; they were few.

He was always a good talker, and as an umpire – without relaxing tact or dignity – he imparted much diverting wisdom and humour. My colleagues and I still treasure the Welsh ties we had from him, and cherish them, and even more, the man who has in him the essence of Welsh cricket.

*Dai Davies: 78 not out (Dyfed Publishers, Llanelli, 1975)*

## DON SHEPHERD

Glamorgan have a quite uncommon asset – in lean years their salvation, in prosperity a mighty assurance – in Don Shepherd, for in certain, and frequent, conditions he is the most effective bowler in modern county cricket.

He is essentially what is called an English type of bowler (which must, with apologies and for the purposes of this argument be taken to include Welsh). Two of the most common kinds of pitches on which our cricket is played are the slow 'turner' and the plumb. On a slow-turning wicket, fast and fast-medium bowlers are deprived of their prime asset, while the ordinary finger-spinner turns the ball so slowly that the batsman has time to adjust his stroke. Don Shepherd's outstanding gift – virtually unique in the game today – is positively to *spin* the ball, at almost medium pace, exploiting the turn in the wicket and simultaneously overcoming its slowness. Or, on a sheerly plumb, batsman's pitch, his stamina, good heart and capacity for work, plus his accuracy and variations of pace and flight, make him an ideal defensive stock bowler.

As a man he has graduated, as by nature, to the post of his county's senior professional; he is cast in the mould of those traditional holders of that office who did not merely study and understand the game, but lived it and loved it. He is wise in cricket, unfailingly encouraging and helpful to younger players, respected and popular in his own dressing-room and those of the other counties.

Don was born and bred at Porteynon, in Gower, and at times – especially when Glamorgan have been doing well – it has seemed as if he owned the Peninsula! His progress was followed proudly there when he first came into the Glamorgan side: a twenty-two-year-old opening bowler with a superb high flowing action; and a tail-end batsman with a penchant for uninhibited high long driving. He worked steadily for his first-team place, with out-swing as his chief weapon; and in 1952 – the year he won his county cap – he took 120 wickets.

Moreover, one day of 1954, at Cardiff, when the ball swung about violently, he had figures of nine for 47 in the first innings of Northants. Yet for all this, he lacked the yard or two of speed which would have made him a top-class pace bowler; not all the cricket which obviously was in him had yet come out.

The year of 1955 was not, on figures, a good season for Don Shepherd; but it was the most important of his career for, towards the end of it, after much experiment and discussion, he began to bowl slow-medium to medium off-breaks. It is important that he does not 'cut' the ball, but spins it, using the finger-spinner's grip, with index-finger purchase and a sharply cocked wrist.

This was not a good period for off-break bowlers of any kind; certainly not for a newcomer to the craft, for the limitation of on-side fieldsman – originally introduced to restrict the defensive operations of the fast-medium 'inslant' bowlers – penalized off-spinners savagely in denying them the leg-field their skill demanded on a turning pitch. Glamorgan, especially Wilf Wooller and Shepherd himself, devoted much thought to this problem. As a result, Haydn Davies, who could – and preferred to – take Shepherd over the stumps, stood back, often so far back that the ball reached him on the half-volley. But he became, in effect, not only an extra slip for the 'thick edge' catch, but also the other fine-short-leg which the Laws, on the surface, forbade. There were, too, such fine close catchers as Gilbert Parkhouse, Allan Watkins, Jim Pressdee and Wilf Wooller in support. Don took only sixty-two wickets (at 31 each) in 1955; but the next year, in his new style, he was the first bowler in the country to take a hundred wickets. In fact, on 30 June at Trent Bridge, rain washed out the last day and the Notts second innings when he wanted just two more wickets to become only the fourth man in cricket history to reach the hundred before July. He finished the season with 177 wickets – more than anyone else – at 15.36. That was, too, the first summer in which he bowled over a thousand overs, which was to become the rule rather than the exception through his subsequent career.

For a dozen seasons he has been one of the most effective bowlers in the country: an absolute 'killer' on bad wickets, but also – and more importantly – a match-winner on pitches so slow that normal expectation would be of a drawn game. Given only a little assistance he turns the ball off a perfect length and line, with astute change of pace, adjusting length according to the batsman's propensities and, every now and then, making one go with his arm or, as a legacy from his seam-bowling days, slipping in an out-swinger – which he often holds back – for a catch to slip or the wicket-keeper.

Last year, at forty, he still bowled his thousand overs, still took his hundred wickets, was still accurate when the batsmen were on top, still cheerful under punishment, still coming in, with a spring reminiscent of Doug Wright, in a run-up which, even at the end of the longest spell, has a buoyant, exuberant quality. Indeed, he would probably say that the easing of the on-side limitation had made life simpler for him; and certainly it has made bowling on responsive pitches more rewarding than in his younger days.

So he has gradually ticked off the records: already he has taken more wickets than anyone else for Glamorgan; and this summer he should draw near the figure of two thousand wickets, which only the great bowlers – men of heart and strength as well as skill – have achieved. Thus far, he might pick as his outstanding performance his two spells at Swansea in 1965 when Glamorgan beat Yorkshire – always a relishable feat for any county – in a low-scoring match, by only 31 runs. In the first Yorkshire innings, Pressdee took most of the wickets but Shepherd kept one end savagely tight with 23 overs, 12 maidens, 33 runs, 0 wickets; in the second, he won the match with 27.5 overs, 12 maidens, 48 runs, 9 wickets.

He has taken five wickets in an innings over a hundred times. Few men have been so consistently penetrative without making a Test appearance. During his career England have used bowlers less steady on the perfect wickets which are the Test ideal. Even more certainly, however, there have been many occasions when the pitch has taken turn slowly on the third or fourth day and orthodox spinners have not turned quickly enough to beat the defensive bat; but Don Shepherd, pushing the ball through so much faster, might have bowled out a major batting side. It is a little sad that he never had that opportunity.

Even with the benefit of almost two hundred not-outs, his batting average over his career is still short of double figures, but his innings is eagerly awaited by Welsh spectators, particularly the young. Occasionally, in contradiction of cricketing probability, a series of his huge swings connects consecutively. Then he produces such spectacular innings as that of 1957 when, going in last against Gloucestershire at Swansea, he made top score for Glamorgan, 53, with four sixes – one of them over the rugby stand into Mumbles Road – and four fours; his 73 against the harsh Derbyshire attack, in 1961, when he hit his first fifty, out of 57, in sixteen minutes; or – his most remarkable feat – at Swansea in the Australian match of the same season, when he set a new record with 51 from eleven scoring strokes. If he cannot always produce such results, he never fails through reluctance to hit.

Don Shepherd has taken some two hundred catches, laboured cheerfully in the field, and served and enjoyed Glamorgan cricket for eighteen years. The fresh-faced young enthusiast of 1950, with the mischievous twinkle in his eyes, has not changed a great deal in the meantime: wiser, certainly, perhaps a little heavier, but he still retains his enthusiasm and humour – and the game is full of his friends.

*Don Shepherd*, 1968

# Worcestershire

### R.T.D. PERKS

Seventeen years ago, on 30 April 1930, Worcestershire opened their season with a match against Surrey. One of the opening bowlers was Fred Root, the man who had made the in-swing-leg-theory attack his own, but a bowler now past the peak of his greatness. The other was an eighteen-year-old colt from Hereford, Reg Perks. Already over six feet tall, strong, and with a control which belied his years, he bowled fast from a twenty-yard run. His first victim in county cricket was Jack Hobbs; his second Andy Sandham.

Had Perks been six years older, or Root six years younger, the history of English county cricket, probably of Test cricket, between the two wars might well have been completely different. Each had to combine the duties of spearhead and stock bowler; each in his own way magnificently resolved this apparent contradiction in a compromise which only their captains can praise to the level of its deserts. When Reg Perks began to play for Worcester, Fred Root had completed the greater part of his achievements; by the time Perks' gifts had matured in experience, Fred Root was gone from county cricket. Together they might have matched the achievements of Hallam and Wass, or Macdonald and Sibbles, and have won the County Championship. But a few unbridgeable years barred the way.

So, for most of his county cricket, Reg Perks has borne a burden under which many other bowlers of his type have fallen far short of greatness. When a pace bowler takes the ball to bowl the opening overs of the day on a plumb wicket, knowing that he may well be bowling from half-past five to half-past six that day, there must be a temptation to save himself, to bowl less than all out – with an eye not only to the hours, but to the years ahead. That is a temptation to which Reg Perks has not yielded – he has bowled his best without stint.

Let us face the economic facts of a cricketer's life. Had he played for one of the so-called 'fashionable' counties, Perks could have been nursed. For those 'fashionable' counties are rich in funds and staff with which to preserve the brightest edges of their attack. Worcestershire captains have not dared to rest Perks on fast bowlers' wickets nor on 'plumb 'uns'. The use of the spinners, Peter Jackson and Dick Howorth, as seam-bowlers has emphasized the limitations of their resources in this direction.

So, except on spinners' days, Reg Perks, since 1930, has bowled out of himself much that, in happier circumstances, might have been saved for later years. That is the measure of his service – the service his benefit ought richly to reward.

Conquering his burden of work, he forced his way into the team for the last Test in 1938–39, that historic marathon, and was our most successful bowler both in terms of number of wickets and of average, although Farnes, Wright and Verity were the other bowlers. Again, he was the most successful bowler in the last pre-war Test, that against the West Indies at The Oval in 1939; but for an incredible number of dropped catches which Test fieldsmen should have held, he would have had superb figures. In 1946, only recently recovered from an injury sustained in the Services, short of practice, his cricket restricted by continuing army service, he took his hundred wickets in the season once more. Ill for many weeks of the season, he continued to play when many men would have gratefully and unashamedly rested. He went a sick man to the Test Trial, but can only narrowly have missed selection for Australia.

In the match against Gloucester at Cheltenham, the usually safe-handed Sandy Singleton dropped the catch which would have given Perks all ten wickets. (Peter Jackson still wonders regretfully how he took that other wicket.) Yet Reg Perks never grumbled nor flagged. Throughout his cricket life he has gone his gay, steady, faithful way. He even enjoys his batting! Remember his innings (the winning margin) in Worcester's two-day win over Yorkshire at Stourbridge in

1939 – and his bowling which clinched the issue in the nerve-racking finish to that game?

The mention of Worcester conjures up for me, always, the memory of Reg Perks – all the tanned, smiling broad-shouldered, powerfully lithe six-foot-one of him – that long, rhythmic run-up, accelerating as smoothly as a Rolls Royce – and then the culminating classically high delivery, powerful at half past six as at twelve o'clock. He knows bowling like a master craftsman – he is master of the in-swing and the out-swing, 'seaming' venomously off the 'green' wicket, making his quick off-breaks bite on any responsive wicket. But his deadliest ball is the classic weapon of the true pace bowler, the ball just short of a length yet compelling a stroke which great body-swing causes to lift steeply before the batsman can withdraw his bat – the true 'slip-bait'.

The good nature which lets him accept and forget dropped catches with a smile has never allowed his bowling to be deficient in hostility – yet that hostility has never been spiteful. I have known Reg Perks – and been proud and happy in knowing him – as fellow cricketer, man and friend. Yet I trust, as he would wish, that friendship has not coloured here my thinking or my writing.

You drink, in this benefit year, to a cricketer who has bowled unselfishly into the service of Worcestershire cricket, gifts which might have won him greater personal achievement had his nature so inclined; the service you honour is not only to Worcestershire cricket but to the entire history and tradition of cricket.

*Worcestershire CCC Yearbook*, 1947

### PETER JACKSON

When Worcester take the field, and as Reg Perks prepares to bowl, you will observe a snowy-haired man with incredibly wide shoulders saunter up to the short-leg position. Once there, he will place the two very large hands which end his two very long arms firmly on his knees and survey the batsman. Now short-leg fieldsmen can have a considerable effect upon a batsman. A Yorkshire short-leg, for instance, glares at him with an intensity near to hate and which seems to dispute the batsman's right to be present; an Australian short-leg is obviously confident of the batsman's imminent dismissal. But Peter Jackson is a comforting short-leg: he greets the batsman with a wide grin – he knows everyone in county cricket – and with a 'Good morning' or the continuance of a conversation begun in the pavilion.

The friendliness is sincere as the smile and neither is belied by the brilliance and speed of his catching at short leg, which is often phenomenal.

Nowadays, after Perks has bowled the first over, Peter Jackson will be observed to go, at a gait half roll, half sidle, to the other bowling crease to share the shine of the new ball. As an opening bowler, he bowls medium-paced out-swingers to a precise length and, in the best out-swing technique, he forces the batsman to play at almost every ball. He varies this ball that leaves the bat with an in-swing which is almost pushed in from the edge of the crease. Now his immense length of arm is revealed in his high delivery and easy action.

When the shine is gone, or earlier if the wicket invites, he takes up his main cricket task: the bowling of off-breaks at slow to slow-medium pace. If he now spins the ball a little less than he once did, his precision is greater than ever. This is no place for a dissertation on length bowling but it may not be out of place to remark that many people use the term 'a good length bowler' when they mean no more than that a bowler bowls few full tosses or long-hops. Peter Jackson bowls a very good length within the proper meaning of that term. That is, he bowls, with amazing consistency, the ball to which the batsman cannot play either forward or back with complete certainty. Such a length must be varied for every wicket and for every batsman and it is the measure of the *real* meaning of the expression 'a good length bowler'. He bowls, too, with considerable variation of pace – variation not so much from ball to ball, although that variation is subtly present, but variation of pace to suit the pace of the wicket and its degree of response to spin. In general, his pace is just sufficient to prevent the batsman from coming out to his bowling. On a sticky wicket, or a crumbling one, Peter Jackson's grin grows even broader, and he can hardly get the ball and walk back to his starting mark quickly enough to satisfy his eagerness to bowl. Then he gives the ball air, exploits his length and subtlety of flight to the full, and reveals the hallmark of the true spinner – variation of amount of spin. On such a wicket he will return impressive figures because every ball from him becomes a separate and difficult problem.

As a batsman I have already dubbed Peter the most experienced number eleven in England; he swings his bat with increasing doubt and decreasing hope as the years progress. Since he is a good cricketer, however, there have been times when it has been vital for him to defend and stay, and then he has put his head down, and, sometimes memorably, produced the batsmanship necessary to win or save a game.

But the Peter Jackson I shall remember is the man who has just found a wicket to his liking and who has bowled on it like the first-class spinner that he is. Then, as he comes into the pavilion, there is a happiness in his eye which it is impossible not to share.

It is a modest man who takes his benefit in Worcestershire in 1948: he has played in no Test matches and created few headlines, but he has played good cricket. His modesty is linked with his happiness on his good days, for he is a sensitive man. Because he is a sensitive man he feels keenly anything which he could regard as a failure: he feels the kicks more than most men – which means that it is a more than usual courage which makes him always unflinchingly kind and honest. First-class cricket reveals a man to his fellow players, and it would be hard to think of a cricketer who is better liked among cricketers than Peter Jackson. Peter is a good man, and I sometimes think there is no higher praise on earth than that.

*Worcestershire CCC Yearbook*, 1948

## LEN COLDWELL

If Len Coldwell had to be described in three words, we should call him 'an English bowler' which is, in fact, a precise definition. Of less than the high pace the Australians and West Indies demand in those who open the bowling, he has the steadiness and accuracy of a stock bowler, the ability to swing the new ball sharply and with good control and, given the right conditions – a 'green' or fast wicket – he moves the ball sharply off the seam and makes it lift.

Records rarely tell the full story of a cricketer, but they are at least revealing about Len Coldwell. In the thirteen summers since he first appeared for Worcestershire – in 1955 – he has only three times played in more than twenty Championship matches in a season. He has had more than simple bad luck in the matter of injury; men with less than his combative quality, basic strength and determination might well have given up first-class cricket. But, by sheer application and refusal to be dismayed, he has trained and played himself back into his rightful place at the sharp end of one of the best county attacks.

It is significant, too, that when he has been able to play anything like a full season, he has bowled a thousand or more overs, a tall order for a man with his length of run and of his pace. Yet, for all this willingness to undertake heavy stints – as he has done even in his lean seasons – he has taken his wickets at 21 apiece, an unusually economical rate. For a decade now, he and Jack Flavell have been as consistently hostile an opening pair as any in the county, not merely for the penetrative quality of their best bowling but because of their combination of persistent accuracy, stamina and edge, giving the batsmen nothing and harrying them, over after over, for long spells.

Len Coldwell's chief weapon, technically speaking, is in-swing, often late and abrupt; but it would be an underestimation to regard him merely as a slavish in-swinger. His top pace is on the lively side of fast-medium and, on a wicket of pace, he can make the ball rise menacingly about the batsman's hands, or bowl a disconcerting bouncer. His main strategic weapon, however, lies in change of pace. His faster ball often comes as a surprise, even to a batsman who has played himself in; and his well-hidden slower one frequently elicits a fatally early stroke.

He played in the Minor Counties for Devonshire (his native county, as his accent still indicates) in 1953 and 1954; and he was twenty-two when he joined Worcestershire in 1955. That was Reg Perks' last season; already there was must jostling for the post of his successor and, over the next few years, Coldwell fought for it with Whitehead, Pearson, Aldridge, Jack Flavell, his ultimate fellow survivor, and, in July and August, with the amateur Chesterton.

In 1955 he played in only four matches, but he took three wickets in four of the five innings in which he was given any appreciable amount of bowling. He performed his first hat-trick – against Leicestershire – in 1957, but he did not win his cap until 1959 when he was top of the county's bowling averages with eighty wickets at 20.81.

He reached his highest level of accomplishment in 1961, coinciding with the beginning of Worcestershire's challenge for the Championship. In that year he took a hundred wickets for the first time and, when Jack Flavell was away at the Test during August, he maintained the county's effort with some magnificent long, sustained spells of bowling against Yorkshire and Nottinghamshire.

In 1962 – when Worcester were runners-up – he was fourth in the first-class bowling averages with 152 wickets (only two bowlers in the country took more) at 17.9, won two England caps against Pakistan, began his Test career with the impressive figures of three for 25 and six for 85 at Lord's, and was picked for the tour of Australia and New Zealand where he played in three more Tests.

It probably was no mere coincidence that Worcestershire fell back in 1963 when, through injury, he played no county cricket after the end of May. But in 1964 and 1965, their two years at the top, though he was not always fit, he took 155 Championship wickets at less than 16 runs apiece – match-winning bowling; and, though he missed five weeks in the middle of 1965 through a knee injury, he came back in Worcestershire's spectacular late run-in to take thirty-eight wickets in five matches. Indeed, against Surrey, he took the first eight wickets for only 11 runs – and if Arnold and Harman had not been missed off him, would have taken a remarkably cheap 'all ten'.

He continues his dual competition with injury and Worcestershire's opponents: in 1967 he took more Championship wickets than any other seam-bowler in the side, and this year should comfortably reach the landmark of a thousand wickets.

He is a faithful, rather than a brilliant, field and, though in 1962 he played an extremely valuable innings of 37 against Nottinghamshire, he is not, as a rule, to be found in the first-class batting averages for which the minimum qualification is a rate of 10 runs an innings. His strength is as a combative, resourceful pace bowler, in which capacity he has compelled the respect of the ultimate critics – the batsmen who play against him.

*Worcestershire CCC Yearbook*, 1968

# Hampshire

### NEVILLE ROGERS

To the cricket historian, Neville Rogers is the essentially 'modern' batsman who has been the main strength of Hampshire's post-war batting. For me, he is also a man with whom I have been on terms of argumentative, but mutually reliant, friendship for nearly twenty years.

I have clearly in mind an afternoon at the county ground in the summer of 1939. Jack Godfrey – then on the Hampshire staff, later professional to Cambridgeshire in the Minor Counties competition – and I were bowling in the nets. The batsman was a quietly determined young man whose bat poised warily on the back-lift while he shrewdly assessed every ball before committing himself to a stroke. It was clear that, for him, net practice was no casual fun, but an aspect of a serious profession, a profession too deeply cherished for any detail of it to be regarded lightly.

We met quite often during that summer, but because he was – then as now – inclined to conceal his shyness under a mask of wry taciturnity, I never learned, for instance, the vital element of Neville Rogers' cricket – his family background. Of no player could it be more truly said that cricket was in his blood.

His family has bred cricketers for four generations. His grandfather, Charles Rogers, was the first outstanding professional produced by Oxfordshire: a steady slow bowler, who played for over thirty years at Lords, Kelso and Oxford. Indeed, he deserved some better cricketing memorial than his solitary entry in *Wisden*, which records, under the heading 'Record Hit', that in practice on the Christchurch Ground at Oxford in 1856, he bowled a ball which the Reverend W. Fellows drove the amazing distance of 175 yards from hit to pitch. As the unfortunate bowler's grandson, Neville's characteristic comment on that record was: 'Why do you think I became a batsman?'

Charles Rogers was to make a more substantial mark on cricket through his descendants. His four sons, two of his nephews, four of his grandsons and, already, one of his great-grandsons, were to play county cricket: six of them initially for Oxfordshire, but also ranging over Bedfordshire, Gloucestershire, Hampshire, Worcestershire and Glamorgan.

One of his sons, Alfred, always known as 'Brusher', was Neville's father. He lost one eye in an accident when he was six, but that did not keep him from cricket. At seventeen he went to play in the Lancashire League, but he came back home, became one of The Parks professionals and, as a fast-medium stock bowler, played in every one of Oxfordshire's matches for some twenty years.

So far as cricketers can be bred, Neville Rogers was bred a cricketer, and he was brought up as one. Cricket was the idiom of his family life and his goal, in his mind and his father's, was county cricket. When he was about eighteen, Warwickshire took an interest in him and he felt he had failed in his aim when they did not offer him an engagement. Then, in 1939, when he was just of age, he and Jack Godfrey were asked down from Oxford to Southampton for a trial with Hampshire. This time there was to be no failure. He faced his 'examination' in the nets with determination which may be measured by the jut of his jaw, and the grave regard with which he still looks at the game. The county minute-book says, laconically: 'The Chairman reported that two lads from Oxford had been engaged on the ground staff. Godfrey and Rogers would be qualified next season.' His only regret lay in the fact that his father, who had died in the previous year, could not share in the realization of their mutual ambition.

At Southampton he followed his uncle, H.J. Rogers, who played for the county from 1912 to 1914, and a line of Oxfordshire players in George Brown, Alec Bowell, 'Lofty' Herman and John Arnold. He played out that 1939 season as a club and ground batsman of unrelenting concentration.

Then it was September 1939, and, along with Jack Godfrey and Gerry Hill, Dick Court and others, he joined the Royal Artillery. They were not back from war for the skeleton season of 1945, but in 1946 a man took up the bat that the colt had put down seven years before. Neville Rogers' first county cricket match was against Worcester, at Southampton, on 11, 13 and 14 May 1946. Against a sound Worcester bowling side, he fell only just short of a century on that first appearance. He made 90 in a stand with Jim Bailey (133) of 209 for the fifth wicket; no other batsman in the side made more than 31. He did not maintain that form: his average for the season was a bare 17 for 696 runs, but, batting at number seven or eight, he put together some gritty and valuable scores in the thirties to hold together the tail of the Hampshire innings.

He emerged from the pre-season practice of 1947 as a newly and surprisingly mature player. As Neil McCorkell's opening partner, he made scores of 90, 99, 91 and 90 before, against Cambridge University, on 1 July, his first century declared him a fully-fledged county batsman. Now, too, he embarked upon the steady topping of a thousand runs a season which continued for the nine years down to 1955. By the stern figures which reckon only the runs of County Championship matches, he has five times made more runs than any other member of the side; in 1951 the next batsman was almost 700 runs behind him.

Look at the records, and you will find that these were the lean years of Hampshire run-scoring. Even the entry of Marshall and the development of Horton in 1955 did not make the batting strong. Before that, Bailey and McCorkell played out their cricketing lives, and only Dawson – briefly – Jim Gray and, occasionally, Desmond Eagar and Alan Rayment rose even to good county standard. Yet any county's batting which is to be reckoned strong *must* boast two or even three batsmen of Test class.

Thus, Rogers bore a burden which precluded the delights of batting, for he knew that a single risky stroke from him could precipitate the collapse of the innings. Against this background, he became one of the country's strongest defensive batsmen. The finest bowlers in our post-war game, from the fast to the slow, have described him in virtually the same words – 'as hard to get out as anyone we play against'.

This embattled position seemed to appeal to an essential combative streak in him. Rigidly setting aside any thought of the forcing game he can play, he gloried in being hard to get out. Once, in a match against Somerset at Taunton, travel arrangements for the next match demanded that the match should end at four o'clock on the third afternoon. In fairness to the spectators, however, it was decided to incorporate the extra half-hour in any event, so the scorecards and the press showed the hours of play on the third day as '11 a.m. to 4 p.m.'. The Somerset captain delayed his declaration, clearly to allow Gerry Tordoff, who was batting well, to score his first county century. As usual in this situation, circumstances seemed to conspire against Tordoff having the strike and, by the time he had made his hundred, Hampshire were set to score over 120 runs an hour against some accurate bowling and a tight field. Their initial attempt to race the clock collapsed and left Rogers to carry an innings which could not possibly win – but could, conceivably, lose – the match. The spectators, imagining that the usual extra half-hour was available after the 4 p.m. of the scorecard, began to barrack him as he pottered quietly about, seeing the day out. The out-thrust of his jaw was almost visible from the pavilion. He became impregnable: defiantly not out at the end of play. When he came in, I pulled his leg a little. He gave a grim smile. 'If I could carry this crowd round in my bag, I'd never get out,' he said. Adversity has always provided the final stimulus to his batting.

When he first came to Hampshire, and even as late 1946, his main run-scoring power lay in driving. The challenge of the new ball and the general practice of in-swing caused profound modifications in his technique, until he became the typical 'modern' batsman. His judgement of the swinging ball, his ability to pull his bat away in face of late movement in the air, were masterly in their lack of hurry. He would calmly take on his pads or thigh the ball missing his leg stump by a bare two or three inches, or refrain from 'slip-bait' fractionally outside the off. He decided some years ago that the hook stroke was 'not business', and he rarely used it except in face of the challenge to make runs against the clock. Rather, he exploited a slightly dragged leg-glance for a single, an occasional stroke played behind square leg in which he hit the slightly short ball 'on the rise', or, best of all, he push-drove through mid-wicket. His best off-side stroke was that which he played off a short ball, wide of cover-point's left hand, not quite a square-cut, but somewhere in between it and a square-drive. Against really fast bowling he was unflinchingly – almost belligerently – sound.

To leg-spinners or left-arm breakaway bowlers, he could use his feet, even to play a defensive stroke, but, except to a loose delivery, he tended to push them between the fieldsmen rather than to drive hard. The off-spinner, like the in-swinger, never seemed a problem to him. I always thought it ill luck for him that, being selected as twelfth man for both teams in the England v The Rest match at Bradford in 1950, he should not have been played for The Rest when several batsmen fell out. That was the game in which Laker took his amazing eight wickets for 2 runs against batsmen who were completely lost against his spin on so responsive a pitch. If Rogers had been brought into The Rest team, I fancy he might have played himself into the serious consideration of the selectors. At least, against Laker on a turning wicket in the MCC v Surrey match of 1954, going in first, he carried his bat magnificently for 56 in a total – by a strong MCC batting side – of 126.

He carried his bat through four completed innings in that season – to share with C.J.B. Wood the record for first-class cricket. After Lord's, he made 172 not out in Hampshire's 327 against Gloucestershire at Bristol; 125 not out in their total of 221 against Somerset; and, finally, on a difficult wicket in the Hastings Festival, for an England eleven which included four Test batsmen, he made 101 not out out of 182, on a bad wicket, against Pakistan.

That was his great season and he might, fine close-to-the-wicket fieldsman that he is, reasonably have played in one of the Tests but that a hand injury not only kept him out of several matches but also affected his play for the vital weeks of Test selection.

Lesser batsmen have played for England, and certainly many have done so who lacked Neville Rogers' resolution in face of adversity. I have heard it argued that he is a dull batsman; and, indeed, Hampshire's need has made him a defensive player. Yet, when I remember an onslaught he once mounted on McHugh at Portsmouth, I believe that, in a strong batting side, he might have been a consistently militant punisher of fast bowling.

At the beginning of 1955 he announced his retirement, and afterwards, missing, I believe, the high challenge of opening the innings, he often seemed less than his true batting self. Yet if that was his last season, he ended it memorably, for, when Desmond Eagar fell out from injury, he was the last remaining member of the team of 1946. He had been the one fixed star of the years of failure and it was fitting that he took over the captaincy for the county's stirring run-in to its triumphant third place in the Championship, so that he has the record of never having captained a losing Hampshire side in a Championship match.

Statistics do not tell everything about a player, but Rogers' record in his ten seasons with Hampshire – for which I am indebted to Roy Webber – places him among the county's greatest players.

| Matches | Innings | Runs | Highest score | Not out | Average |
|---------|---------|------|---------------|---------|---------|
| 298 | 529 | 16,056 | 186 | 28 | 32.04 |

Centuries: 28.    Scores between 50 and 99: 75.    Catches: 196.
Thousand runs in a season: 9 times.    Average: 1605 runs a season.
Best season, 1952: 2244 runs.    Bowling: 0–37.

As a cricketer, craggy – tough, perhaps – but something near to being a master craftsman of defensive batting, Neville Rogers, if his decision to finish remains firm, will be missed from the Hampshire side.

As a man, he has used a mock-acid leg-pulling in vain to disguise a very real charm and kindliness. You may rely upon his sense of humour and his honesty; above all, once he accepts you, you may rely upon a friend whose loyalty can be surprising and typically powerful. A Hampshire side without him can hardly hope to make good the loss of such resistant strength. Off the field, his absence will leave Leo Harrison and myself short of a cross-talk partner, and everyone in the pavilion will miss a friend.

*Boscombe Printing Co. (Bournemouth)*, 1956

## C.B. LLEWELLYN

It was as a result of Desmond Eagar's researches that I had in my pocket an address which made a ten-mile detour to Chertsey a tempting prospect one wet Sunday last winter. The address was Charles Llewellyn's, and it took me to the trim bungalow on the edge of Chertsey where he lives with his wife and two daughters.

Charlie Llewellyn, a South African from Pietermaritzburg, played for Hampshire from 1899 to 1910 and appeared in fifteen Tests for South Africa between 1895 and 1912 – more Tests, in fact, than any Hampshire player except Philip Mead. He was a slow left-arm bowler, a forcing bat and a brilliant field at mid-off. For Hampshire he scored 8772 runs at 27.58 and took 711 wickets for 24.66 each. He twice scored two centuries in a match for the county and, against his fellow countrymen, the South African touring side of 1901, he scored 216 (with thirty fours) in 180 minutes and took four wickets for 6 runs in their second innings.

No one from Hampshire, so far as I know, had seen Charlie Llewellyn for many years and I had some doubts about calling on an eighty-three-year-old man unannounced and unexpected. But at least an enquiry at the door could do no harm. I need not have worried, for despite his years, he is as spry as a sparrow – though, he says, too lazy to walk very much, so he makes his local excursions by bicycle. He looks trim and fit and is still recognizable from the photographs taken in his playing days by his wide, high forehead and quick eyes.

Like a number of his contemporaries in the Hampshire side, Charles Llewellyn spent his qualification period at the Training Ship *Mercury*. Then he was, for a decade, a main-stay of the county side.

He is a man of remarkable cricketing 'firsts'. In his first match for Hampshire – against the 1899 Australians, before he was qualified for Championship matches – he scored 72 and 21 and took eight wickets for 132 in the tourists' first innings of 360. He took part in the first Test between South Africa and Australia (1902), was a member of the first South African side to tour Australia (1910–11) and played against the first West Indian side to tour England (1906). He was the first man to perform the all-rounder's 'double' of 100 wickets and 1000 runs for Hampshire in a season (1910); the first – and still only – Hampshire player to score a century and take ten wickets in the same match (v Somerset, 1901); the first professional to play an innings of 200 for the county; and the first batsman to score a century for Hampshire in an hour (v Sussex, 1909).

Unhappily for Hampshire, after the South African tour of Australia in 1910–11, 'Llew' did not return to the county. He went to league cricket in Lancashire (where he acquired a Lancashire accent which he still retains) and continued there until he was sixty-two; at the age of fifty-five he was top of the bowling averages and the only man to take a hundred wickets in the season in the Bolton League.

He might add to his list of 'firsts' the fact that he was the first bowler in English cricket to bowl the 'Chinaman' with any degree of frequency. For, although he was normally an orthodox slow left-arm spinner, he used the left-armer's off-break and its complementary googly variety, employing it quite often – and with considerable accuracy – on plumb wickets where 'natural' spin did not turn the ball.

He explained that he was a product of the 'Schwarz school'; for, when R.O. Schwarz returned from England to South Africa with the trick of the googly which he had learnt from Bosanquet in the Middlesex side, Llewellyn – until then solely a natural spinner – was one of his pupils. The other 'students' – White and Faulkner – were right-arm bowlers but Llewellyn, after two years of struggling to master the googly, proved extremely puzzling to play. Indeed, if he had continued with Hampshire into the fruition period of Mead, Brown, Newman and Kennedy and Livsey (who were all his juniors), Hampshire might have come very near to winning the Championship in 1914, 1921 or 1922 when their signal lack was of a reliable spin-bowler, while a regular player who was also a quick-scoring batsman low in the order and a safe catcher would have been a considerable asset to the team's balance as well as its strength.

So far as the record-keepers are concerned, it was interesting to learn that Llewellyn's entry in *Wisden*'s 'Births and Deaths' section is incorrect. His full name is Charles Bennett Llewellyn but his initials, in *Wisden* and most other records, are given as 'G.C.B.'. The explanation is simple. In his first match for Hampshire – against the Australians in 1899 – D.A. Steele, the Hampshire captain, was making out the batting order when he looked up and said to 'Llew': 'Your initials are G. C., aren't they?' 'No – C.B.' was the answer, and down went the 'B', but the 'G' was never crossed out. It was copied by the scorer and, from him, by the newspapers and, from them, by the chroniclers. But, in fact, it should be 'C.B.' – as in Fry. Strangely enough, his birth date is also incorrect in *Wisden* – it should be 29 – not 26 – September 1876.

At eighty-three, Charlie Llewellyn is certainly the oldest living cricketer who played regularly for the county. Mrs Llewellyn, Dorset-born and, from her youth, a keen cricket-follower, is just a few months older than her husband; she, too, is fit and well and, like him, maintains an interest in cricket.

I hope that, with Desmond Eagar's co-operation, it may be possible to bring them both over to the Surrey–Hampshire match at Guildford in 1960. They will make good company there, for although it is forty years since Charlie Llewellyn bowled a ball or buckled on a pad for Hampshire, he retains his interest in the county's cricket. He is, moreover, full of good – and generous – stories about his contemporaries.

What contemporaries they were, for he enjoyed – and I am convinced that 'enjoyed' is the word – almost as fine a fifteen years in the first-class game as the whole history of cricket can offer. He grew up in the vintage period of South African cricket, when the first flowering of googly bowling lifted them to the top in Test cricket. He played through what Neville Cardus calls the 'Golden Age' of English cricket – bowling against Ranji, Abel, Maclaren, Hayward, Jessop, C.B. Fry, Palairet, Spooner, Warner, R.E. Foster, J.T. Tyldesley, Jack Hobbs, Frank Woolley and even the ageing W.G. Grace. He batted against the bowling of Bosanquet, Tom Richardson, Simpson-Hayward, Hirst, Rhodes, Blythe, Briggs, J.T. Hearne, Lockwood, Neville, Knox, Schofield Haigh, S.F. Barnes, Frank Foster and Braund. He played Test cricket against a whole gallery of Australian immortals – Victor Trumper, Clem Hill, Dr Horden, Warwick Armstrong, Joe Darling, S.E. Gregory, M.A. Noble, J.J. Kelly, Warren Bardsley and Charlie Macartney.

He was lucky in his cricket, enjoyed it then and – without sharing the tendency of some old-stagers to denigrate the cricketers of today – he still relishes those palmy days. He is certainly a lively and contented advertisement for the era.

*Hampshire Handbook*, 1960

LEO HARRISON

There is no more familiar figure – and no more essential one – in Hampshire's perpetually hostile out-cricket than their wicket-keeper, Leo Harrison. Cap peak pointing high, so lean of figure that you cannot imagine a spare ounce of flesh on his bones, trudging with a footballer's walk down the pitch between overs, he has been one of the key men in the Hampshire revival. 'The Lion', or, to give him his full mock-title, 'The Lion of the Forest' – for he was born and bred at Mudeford, on the western fringe of the New Forest – is a cricketer's cricketer.

He catches an opposing batsman behind the wicket and, as his victim turns round disappointedly, says, with dry sympathy, 'Hard luck, mate; it ain't half a blooming game, is it?' The next man comes in and, after an automatic look to check the field, Harrison crouches down again behind the stumps.

He is in every second of the game – yet contrives to go almost unnoticed, as the good wicket-keeper always should. His gloves 'give' in easy timing as he takes the ball and, with a turn of the wrist, he flicks it to a short-leg fieldsman to be returned to the bowler. His short throw is barely halfway through its curve and already, his minimum of movement done, he is relaxed, body straight, feet apart, hands flat against his hips, detached as if the ball had never come to him.

From the pavilion he looks cheekily schoolboyish as the 'young Leo' of twenty years ago. Now, however, he is Hampshire's senior professional and though his thin, rather elfish face is still perched on the brink of the same wide grin, it has been weathered by days in the sun that have set a net of friendly wrinkles round his eyes.

Leo Harrison is one of the best wicket-keepers in England: he has played innings soundly correct and admirable in style against the best bowling; he has been one of the best outfields in the country. By ordinary values of county cricket, that is a happy and wide degree of success. Yet to those who knew him as a boy cricketer in the thirties, and, above all, to Leo Harrison himself, his achievements have fallen short of the high but reasonable hopes of those days. The cricketer he might have been became a war casualty; but he would be the last man to regard that loss as anything but trifling among so many tragedies. His cricketing standards are all but as high as perfection; and sometimes, even when by everyday judgement he has done well, he remains dissatisfied with himself. Any man who loves the game of cricket as strongly as he does must sometimes suffer for it. Indeed, but for his native determination and the fact that the game possesses him, I fancy he might have turned away from the summer-long play-work of the professional player before now. The war came as he seemed about to command remarkable early success. He has had a hard climb to it since then.

News of Leo Harrison came to the county ground early in his cricketing life. At twelve he was a successful batsman for Mudeford in club cricket. During the winter of 1935–36 he went – as a left-handed batsman – to the indoor cricket school at Bournemouth run by C.C. Brockway and Fenley. By the spring of 1937, still only fourteen, he had been converted into a right-hand bat good enough to be taken on to the county staff. Pale, physically even slighter than now – indeed, he looked almost fragile – and with his characteristic flop of hair falling over his right eye, he seemed altogether too young for a county groundstaff. Yet once he took a bat in his hands, he killed every possible doubt: a single stroke convinced his elders that he needed no charity from bowlers. In club and ground matches, his innings were vignettes of perfect style; they ended less because bowlers beat him than because, like the young Hutton, he was so tired by an adult-length innings that after an hour or so he had barely the strength to lift the bat.

The Hampshire staff of those days was still run along stern lines: credit was not easily won, and competition for team places was hard. Leo Harrison began the club and ground season of 1938 with three successive 'ducks'. Within a month, however, he was going in first with Arthur Holt, ahead of men much his senior in years and service, and when the two put on 236 for the first wicket against Romsey, Harrison's talent was unmistakable. In 1939 he was top-scorer for the Hampshire second eleven in a losing game with Sussex II and his claim to a trial in Championship cricket was undeniable.

He was brought into the county side in the August of 1939, at Bournemouth. In his first county match – against Worcester – he made 9 and 12 in totals of 191 and 131. Against Yorkshire with three England bowlers – Bowes, Smailes and Verity – he scored nought in the first innings. In the second innings, Hampshire were put out for 116 and soundly beaten. Only two players – Pothecary and Harrison – made double figures. Their partnership of 31 was easily the highest of the innings, and Harrison batted with amazingly mature solidity and calm for so young a player. Here, unmistakably it seemed, was one who, with experience, would become not merely a good, but a great county batsman. War closed that chapter.

He joined the RAF and played little cricket between 1939 and 1946. Yet, when two strong sides were raised for a one-innings charity match between Hampshire and Sussex, he was easily top-scorer for the county with 38 in a total of 87. Again, he returned to play an innings of superb strokes in a match against a very strong Civil Defence eleven: twice he hit James Langridge over extra cover for six with strokes of majestically easy timing.

It was a pleasant passing thought for Hampshire supporters that the end of the war would add to the side a player who had grown from colt to a major batting power. In the meantime, however, a defect developed in his eyesight and, in the press of weightier matters, it was given little attention. During the summer of 1946, while he was still in the Air Force, he was asked to keep wicket in emergency and, although he was obliged to wear spectacles, 'kept' so successfully that he was chosen as wicket-keeper for the strong Combined Services side of that year. In 1947 he came back to the county staff, where, with McCorkell available, there was no possibility of his keeping wicket. He could not command a regular place in the county team, for his batting was patchy – he averaged 20.34 with a top score of 61 not out (against Yorkshire) – but his fielding in the deep was superb. In 1948 McCorkell injured his hand in June, and for the rest of the summer Harrison kept wicket in his place – with thirty-eight catches and eleven stumpings. Apart from a valuable match-winning 56 not out and a gritty resistance against Yorkshire, his batting fell away completely. In 1949, with McCorkell fit once more, Harrison played only seven matches and a batting average of 24.2 was not enough to keep his place in the team. In 1950 he played in only eight matches; his batting figure fell to only 9.21 and he had little but a wonderful day in the field against the West Indies to justify his continuing to fight with his form and – though he did not realize it at the time – his eyesight. He put on a grin he did not feel, and prepared to fight for his cricket career which, clearly, would be made or ended by his play in 1951.

It was saved: third in the county averages and aggregates, a thousand runs in a season for the first time; and his first century in county cricket – against Worcestershire – won him his county cap. *Wisden* said of that innings: 'Polished stroke-play and reliable defensive methods removed any doubts as to his batting skill.' In 1952 Prouton came back from the Lord's staff to keep wicket. Harrison fielded finely wherever he was placed; again he scored a thousand runs, and he made three centuries – more than anyone else in the side. The 1953 season was an in-and-out summer: he shared the wicket-keeping with David Blake and Prouton but, after some good early scores, his batting failed and he did not hold a regular place in the county team.

It was not until 1954 that he kept wicket regularly: 'Harrison improved as a wicket-keeper,' said *Wisden*. He made 822 runs but, in that slump season of Hampshire batting, only two members of the side scored more, and many of his best innings were played when the side was in trouble; he took thirty-two catches and made ten stumpings. By 1955, after less than two seasons as a regular wicket-keeper, he was clearly among the best in the country – probably second only to Evans – and was chosen for the Players against the Gentlemen at Lord's.

This was the season that lifted Leo Harrison from the level of a loyal county cricketer, struggling for his place in the team, almost to the heights he had promised eighteen years before. Some weeks before his selection for the Players eleven, there was admiring talk of him in the soundest circles of cricket criticism – the county dressing-rooms. The finest of his wicket-keeping was – and is – in standing up to Shackleton, for 'Shack', more than any other seam-bowler in the country, constantly is making the ball move late off the pitch. On 'green' and lifting wickets, Harrison 'takes' him with such unobtrusive ease as to minimize the technique which enables him to do so. Undoubtedly he was worth a place in the English team in either the fourth or fifth Test of 1955, when Evans was injured and unable to play. Certainly, too, most of the first-class players in the country would have chosen him.

He is the least showy of wicket-keepers, but he has the high technical ability to leave his movement until the ball has 'done' everything and still get to it without hurry. His handling is sweetly clean and, while the Hampshire attack lacks bowling of the type which normally pulls a batsman out of his crease, some of his stumpings off Shackleton – and, even more spectacularly, one-handed off Gray's in-swinger down the leg side – have been superb. Unfortunately, except for two innings – of 43 and 17 not out against the South Africans, which were as sound as could be wished – his batting in 1955 became almost negligible. Wicket-keeping probably is the hardest strain in cricket, and he has never been strong: some recession in his run-making was to be expected; but, in addition, although he had given up glasses after 1947, his eyesight had grown much worse.

In 1956 he took to glasses again; his wicket-keeping was as good as ever, and, if his batting figures still appear unhappy, he played so soundly during August as to be not out in five of his ten innings, which suggested that he was growing used to his new lenses. Indeed, those of us who remember his pre-war stroke-play, even if we had not the confirmation of 1953 and 1954, would still find it hard to believe that he will not yet delight us with his run-making. When he is seeing the ball properly, his footwork is so perfect that he bats with quite masterly ease, and at his best, his driving is a triumph of timing and fluency, the speed of the struck ball much greater than the swing of the stroke would promise. He might yet become as fine a batsman/wicket-keeper as McCorkell. Already, I fancy, while esteeming his predecessor's batting as far more effective, Harrison must emerge as the better wicket-keeper of the two. Indeed, he, George Brown and Walter Livsey must stand as the finest wicket-keepers in the history of Hampshire cricket.

Of Leo Harrison the man, I find it less easy to write. What shall we say of our friends, particularly 'the men who were boys when I was a boy'? On the field his dry humour is never quenched; and he is the best-hearted of men when the game is running against his side. The post of senior 'pro' fits him as well as he fits it: he must be *in* a cricket match – however minor the game, it absorbs him completely and his interest extends, keenly and unselfishly, far beyond his own personal performance. Revealingly enough, if Hampshire need a bare dozen or so runs to win and no one is keen to bat, as often as not it is Leo who, with a wrily funny reference to his average, volunteers for the innings with a chance of failure but none of success. He is a perfectionist and, as a Hampshire man, he has a burning feeling for the county side. He came to the ground at Southampton as the legendary era of Mead, Brown, Kennedy and Newman was ending, but, by personal contact, he inherited from those great players. So the performance of the new, young Hampshire men positively matters to him.

He is wise in cricket and shrewd about people. Honest as the day and a trier to the last gasp himself, he finds it hard to forgive anything which is not straight or any cricket played with less than full effort. Know Leo Harrison and you must trust him and like him. For my own part, I have never known a cricketer whom I liked better. I can but hope that he will forgive me for saying so. I fancy he may fall back on that remark of his which has become one of first-class cricket's catch-phrases: 'It ain't half a blooming game.'

*Boscombe Printing Co. (Bournemouth)*, 1957

# Hants and All That

## Noble Butchery

*June* 1967. Basingstoke (and North Hants) was our team; but we had another, and bigger, one out beyond. That was Hampshire, so great a team that even Mister Butler, the professional – and so far as we were concerned, presiding genius – of the Basingstoke ground and club, had not played for them.

But between 1914 (the year this writer was born) and 1935 (when he left Basingstoke), Hampshire never played a match north of Southampton. None of us boys could go even there – thirty miles away by train – and pay to go into the ground, even on a generous eightpence a week pocket money.

The year 1921 was Hampshire cricket's *annus mirabilis*. It was not merely that the county finished sixth in the table – with a single, one-place exception, the best they had ever achieved – but they made a considerable impact on the Test scene; and on Basingstoke.

To be sure Australia, with the legendary fast-bowling pair of Gregory and McDonald, beat England all too conclusively, by three Tests to none. For Hampshire, though, it was a summer of glory. After the second Test, our Honourable Lionel Tennyson was appointed captain of England. In the third – at Headingley – he split his hand in the field, yet, batting virtually one-handed, he scored fifty in the hour – 63 and 36 in the match. He and George Brown – who kept wicket – were first and second in the English batting averages. Philip Mead, of course, was the great success of the series. He was not called in until the fourth Test, when he made 47 in his only innings. Then, in the last, at The Oval, he scored 182 not out, until then – and for seventeen years afterwards – the highest individual innings ever played for England against Australia in this country.

For us, all this simply led up to the match on May's Bounty,

Basingstoke's own ground. Straight from their last fixture, in which they beat Warwickshire to take sixth place and Mead reached 3000 runs for the season, Hampshire came to play Fifteen of Basingstoke. In the words of Harry Lauder, 'It was a splendacious affair'; indeed, it was an all-day game and we took sandwiches – ham for lunch and jam for tea.

The visiting side called itself Hants Club and Ground but it was, with three quite important exceptions, the full county team including, to quote the *Hants & Berks Gazette*, 'the three great England players, Tennyson, Mead and Brown'.

The ground was crowded. Old men said it had never been so crowded before; and, despite subsequent county matches there, it never has been since. Tennyson won the toss, and airily sent Basingstoke in to bat. Rex Lamb, the Basingstoke captain, boldly declared with twelve wickets down, and left Hampshire 254 to win in just over two hours.

Then, there they were – 'Major the Hon. L.H. Tennyson' and 'Mead (P.)' as the little typed slips said – THEMSELVES. The Basingstoke bowling was soon routed. When Mead was lbw to Bert Butler – the men all round said he was not really out because he hit it – George Brown came in. He drove fiercely. Tennyson, though, was to our eyes – and, looking back, by any standards – magnificent. He was a class – probably two classes – above anyone normally seen on the Folly, and he was in immense form.

Cap crumpled on his head, shirt open almost to the waist, in his mighty physical prime, powerful – not so portly as he was to become – and exuberantly determined, he kindled the imagination by the sheer joyous strength of his hitting. He struck the rosy-faced, sturdy 'Erby Knowles, the local stock bowler, for two sixes, three fours and a two in a single over. Again and again the cleanly struck ball flew flat as if it had been fired from a gun; or buzzed across the grass and, as people pulled their legs away, cracked and rattled about the woodwork of the benches. The bowling was simply butchered.

Three strokes remain in the memory. A straight drive off the front foot from the Bounty Road end flew low – it hummed, and seemed to shimmer in the sun – and a young man went running and running the full length of Castle Field football pitch to fetch it. From the other end, off the back foot, he hit over the sight-screen over Bounty Road and so far into Mares' gardens that the umpire simply called for another ball.

Late in his innings, he moved his left leg out of the line of a full-length ball on the leg stump, simply put his bat in its place and jabbed a casual six into the allotments at square leg.

It was all so generous, so spectacular and – though it may seem an extravagant thought – so noble. The 254 runs to win were made in a bewildering hectic hour and twenty minutes. The county batted on to entertain the crowd, and Tennyson made 169 before he was caught from what seemed a surprisingly gentle stroke after all that had gone before. They had scored 308 by half past six; and the little boys, their brains crammed and seething, could let the air out of their lungs.

Not all went well in the life of Lionel Hallam – later Lord – Tennyson, grandson of the Laureate. He did not always behave with a dignity befitting a peer of the realm. On the other hand, he was never mean or little; and his humour, like most of his capacities, was large.

As a captain, he was by no means a master tactician: he was idiosyncratic, erratic, hasty, at times simply and wildly reckless. Yet – or consequently – at Edgbaston in 1922, after Hampshire were put out by Warwickshire for 15 and commanded to follow on, 208 behind, he took the quite ludicrous bet – said to be a tenner at a hundred to one – that they would win the match. In the most improbable recovery in the history of cricket, they did so.

Twenty-five years afterwards, talking face to face as he sucked approvingly at a large scotch and soda, he did not fail.

'Basingstoke, wemember it distinctly, dear boy: bloody tiny little gwound, though; sixes pwetty easy. Wonderful day; gweat party afterwards; nice chaps. You there? 'Mazing; gweat summer for me, o' course; bloody ball hit the middle of the bat all the time. Always liked fast stuff, yer know; came on to the bat so damned sweet. In the Tests, too, yer know; Bwown – great feller, no fear, yer know, no fear – hit McDonald, Gregory, weally fast fellers, back over their bloody heads like wockets. Old Mead, too; they couldn't wowwy him; when they aimed at his head he just bent slowly inside it. Just pushed 'em awound, like he always did evewyone; no bother to old Mead; just pushed 'em awound.'

Club and ground sides came to Basingstoke regularly after that, but they never matched the excitement or the effect of that 1921 game.

*The Observer*

# A Hampshire Vignette of 1928

Thumbing over old Hampshire yearbooks, the eye is caught, again and again, by the score of a match seen long ago, yet still sharp in the memory – compelling a pause to read it through; and often subsequently, something of a reverie. Fifty-two years ago – in 1928 – the train journey from Basingstoke to Southampton seemed, to a fourteen-year-old schoolboy, both long and expensive.

It was, though, the season of a West Indian tour when, in a single match against Middlesex at Lord's, in June, Learie Constantine had captured the public imagination. First he rescued West Indies from the follow-on when, against five England Test-match bowlers – Jack Durston, Nigel Haig, Jack Hearne, Ian Peebles and 'Gubby' Allen – he scored 86 out of 107 in fifty-five minutes. He went on to take seven for 57 – six for 11 in his second spell – and put Middlesex out for 136. Even then West Indies, wanting 259 to win, were stumbling at 121 for five when Constantine once more took the game by the throat with a savagely struck but chanceless 103 – out of 133 – to win it by three wickets. Top-scorer – and in such vivid fashion – in both innings, and by far the most successful bowler of the match, he had created a lasting reputation in a couple of days.

Everyone wanted to see him; certainly Hampshire cricket-followers turned up in substantial numbers at the county ground for the midweek match with the tourists in August. For the young it was imperative to be at the ground early. Then, even more than now, cricket was unique among top-level sports in that the spectators could feel some degree of intimacy – or at least contact – with the players. When they came out to take a net before the start, they were generally happy to let a youngster who had fielded a ball, bowl it at them; or, if they were not, they never discouraged him from fielding. They would, too, invariably sign their autographs and, often, in response to a question, pass a casual remark that was treasured for a fortnight and repeated round the classroom *ad nauseam*.

The spectators of that time were, perhaps, less tolerant of boys, especially when their impromptu matches on the ground sent the ball dangerously near their elders. The crowds themselves, too, were, by present-day standards, amazingly decorous, even formal. They were almost entirely male; and many of them stood all day to watch – there was little or no terraced seating on the county ground then except by the Northlands Road screen. They were generally sombrely dressed; and virtually everyone wore some form of headgear: in many cases flat caps, but also trilbies, boaters and panamas. Schoolboys dutifully wore caps and ties. Applause was confined almost solely to hand-clapping and, except during intervals, no one dreamt of venturing on to the pitch – if they had, Secretary Bacon would have ensured that they never did so again. Yet there was about it all a quiet warmth.

Lionel Tennyson – not yet 'Lordship' but 'the Hon.' – won the toss, Hampshire batted and Constantine, bounding in, spring-heeled and eager, bowled off a spectacular leap, his long right arm whipping over high and his follow-through hurling him down the pitch.

Before there was time to take proper note of him, he had bowled George Brown – middle stump, through a stroke that was far too late – for a duck. If that quietened Hampshire's schoolboy supporters, when he put out Alec Kennedy in the same fashion and had Ronny Aird caught at slip, he left them incredulous. After all, they *were* only the West Indies; and England had already beaten them twice by an innings. Philip Mead, of course, set things in perspective from the first ball he received, clipping Constantine off his pads, square for four. Even he, though, looked startled when, as he completed a defensive back stroke against Constantine, the bowler, hurling himself forward for a caught and bowled, suddenly arrived in the crease at his feet. When he, too, was late on his stroke to Constantine, his pad was there as the second line of defence; but there was no doubt that he was lbw. Off he went at that peculiar rolling gait of his. Utter silence fell upon the young to whom Mead was the great infallible. Constantine had taken four for 24 and, when Griffith bowled Alec Hosie, Hampshire were 88 for five.

This was the cue for Lionel Tennyson, that vast man, born more than a hundred years out of his time: he would have fitted in perfectly into the life of the Regency bucks, gambling, playing, drinking, living life rather more than life size. Today he wore a cap; often he would come out to bat or field in a huge shapeless brown trilby which he wore, sometimes straight, sometimes crooked, slapping it on to his head and adjusting it with a punch in the crown. Now he had put – not pulled – on his cap, in the manner of the time, so short in the peak that it looked as if it were made for a schoolboy rather than an unusually large man. He took guard, jaw and stern jutting, stomach cuddled about the bat handle. It was vividly impressed upon the fourteen-year-old's memory that, during the North v South match at Bournemouth later in the same season, he and Trevor Arnott, the Glamorgan captain, went into the pavilion for their after-match drink, picked up their glasses from the bar and, as they turned towards one another, their two huge paunches came together and forced both of them to take a step backwards.

Lionel Tennyson could not abide flighted slow bowling; indeed, as the Australian Arthur Mailey delighted to demonstrate, leg-spin baffled, bewildered and infuriated him inevitably to self-destruction. On the other hand, as he showed against the 1921 Australians, he had not the slightest fear of fast bowling and appeared even to enjoy it. Certainly he attacked it with every sign of gusto. With only Martin, steady but unremarkable slow left-arm, to hint at flight or spin, this was to be his day.

He proceeded to play perhaps the most characteristic innings of his life. Constantine and George Francis were unquestionably fast; Tennyson set about both of them; but amiable old 'Sniffy' Browne, straightforward medium, suffered most of all. Jack Newman, in one of his best seasons, keeping the other end steady, gave Tennyson his head – and he took it, thumping and thundering mightily. One huge hook off Francis carried the tennis courts; and more than once, attempting to repeat the stroke, he barely cleared fieldsmen; several times hit fours over the top of mid-off or mid-on, and occasionally swatted irritably at Martin's spin. Mostly, though, he drove cleanly through the covers and mid-off; square cut – quite fiercely – or indulged his highly unorthodox but profitable pull. He had some luck: once, attempting to drag Martin through mid-on, he sliced him past slip off the back of the bat; and he was happy twice to edge Constantine down the leg side. Yet he gave no chance and, when he walked in at the end of the day, his ruddy face shining with sweat and pleasure, he had made 158 – Newman 76 – and Hampshire had reached 312: the whole game had been changed.

Next morning he went on to 217, the highest score of his career – made in only four hours; Jack Newman duly came to a tidy 118. Together they put on 311 for the fifth wicket. No more of the drawn game comes to mind. The book says that West Indies made 413 and when Hampshire went in again with the draw certain, Lionel Tennyson put himself in early and made 23 not out in their 62 for two – presumably to show he could do it again. Although Constantine took two wickets, his 8 overs cost 31 runs. He was not always a hero, Lionel Tennyson; but this certainly was his game – memorably so.

*Hampshire Handbook*, 1980

# The Great Hampshire Elevens

Hampshire's Championship win of 1961 is the peak of the county's cricketing history. But the men who achieved it do not stand in isolation. We should rob them of their inheritance if we failed to place them in their rightful tradition. To Hampshire supporters, that triumph compensated for many lean years; but it also evoked nostalgic memories of the sides which made brave, but less successful, attempts on the summit in other years. Indeed, to the members of those early teams still alive, this must have seemed a glorious justification of their efforts.

Since Hampshire entered the – modern – County Championship in 1895, its average ranking for the 57 seasons played is something worse than tenth. So, by comparison with major counties, even Hampshire's best positions have been neither frequent nor remarkable. The best years have been:

| | |
|---|---|
| 1910 | 6th |
| 1912 | 6th |
| 1914 | 5th |
| 1921 | 6th |
| 1922 | 6th |
| 1955 | 3rd |
| 1956 | 6th |
| 1958 | 2nd |

Those successes were gained by three teams – one could almost say two, for the professionals Mead, Brown, Kennedy, Newman, Bowell and Remnant were the nucleus of the sides of the 1910–12–14 and (with Livsey) of the 1921–22 periods. Moreover, they powered the teams that finished seventh in 1919, 1923 and 1926. So that group achieved the county's eight best Championship positions prior to 1955.

The continuity through the three periods emerges when we set down the sides, thus:

| 1910 | 1912 | 1914 |
|---|---|---|
| Capt. J.G. Greig | C.B. Fry | E.R. Remnant |
| C.P. Mead | A.C. Johnston | A. Bowell |
| Capt. W.N. White | C.P. Mead | A.C.P. Arnold |
| A. Bowell | A. Bowell | C.P. Mead |
| C.B. Llewellyn | Capt. E.I.M. Barrett | J.A. Newman |
| A.C. Johnston | G.N. Bignell | G. Brown |

| 1910 | 1912 | 1914 |
|---|---|---|
| G. Brown | G. Brown | H.C. McDonell |
| J. Stone | J. Stone | E.M. Sprot (captain) |
| E.M. Sprot (captain) | E.M. Sprot (captain) | A. Jaques |
| J.A. Newman | J.A. Newman | A.S. Kennedy |
| A.S. Kennedy | A.S. Kennedy | W.H. Livsey |

Batting order and team composition varied so much in these years that these lists are approximations. Thus, C.B. Fry – who captained the winning England side in the Triangular Tournament of 1912 – H.C. McDonnell, E.R. Remnant, Capt. Johnston, Capt. J.G. Greig and J. Stone all played, though not regularly, in each of the three seasons.

| 1921 | 1922 |
|---|---|
| G. Brown | A.S. Kennedy |
| A. Bowell | A. Bowell |
| A.L. Hosie | G. Brown |
| C.P. Mead | C.P. Mead |
| Hon. L.H. Tennyson (captain) | Hon. L.H. Tennyson (captain) |
| A.S. Kennedy | Lieut. H.L.V. Day |
| Capt. L.R. Isherwood | R. Aird |
| C.P. Brutton | J.A. Newman |
| W.H. Livsey | A.S. Kennedy |
| J.A. Newman | W.H. Livsey |
| E.R. Remnant | G.S. Boyes |

Again, batting order is approximate. C.B. Fry batted well in his few matches of 1921; while H.S. Altham, A.S. McIntyre, H.C. McDonell and W.R. Shirley came in during the August holidays and with few changes, apart from the introduction of P.E. Lawrie, the team went on to finish seventh in 1923 and 1926.

| 1955 | 1958 | 1961 |
|---|---|---|
| R.E. Marshall | R.E. Marshall | R.E. Marshall |
| J.R Gray | J.R Gray | J.R Gray |
| H. Horton | H. Horton | H. Horton |
| A.W.H. Rayment | R. Pitman | D. Livingstone |
|   or H.M. Barnard | H.M. Barnard | P.J. Sainsbury |
| N.H. Rogers | A.C.D. Ingleby- | A.C.D Ingleby- |
| E.D.R. Eagar (captain) |   Mackenzie (captain) |   Mackenzie (captain) |
| L. Harrison | P.J. Sainsbury | H.M. Barnard or D. Baldry |
| P.J. Sainsbury | L. Harrison | L. Harrison |
| D. Shackleton | D.Shackleton | D. Shackleton |
| V.H.D. Cannings | M. Heath | D.W. White |
| M.D. Burden | M.D. Burden | M.D. Burden or M. Heath |
|   or M. Heath |   or V.H.D. Cannings |   or A. Wassell |

These three were regular teams, as their predecessors never were: stable elevens, varying choice, according to the pitch, between Mervyn Burden and an extra seam-bowler, but otherwise – except for some changes in a single middle-order batting place – firm. Their batting order, too, remained steady.

To examine all these teams separately: after five seasons at the bottom of the table at the beginning of the decade, Hampshire gradually gathered strength over four years up to 1910. Its power in that first real success lay in the all-round cricket of the South African C.B. Llewellyn (133 wickets and 1110 runs) coupled with the bowling of Jack Newman (156 wickets), and the runs of Philip Mead, A.C. Johnston, Capt. Greig, George Brown and the improved Jimmy Stone. A little more pace-support for the two main bowlers might have made two places' difference in the final table, despite the strength, that year, of Kent, Surrey, Middlesex, Lancashire and Notts. This was the best first-class season Hampshire had ever had: but, at its end, Charlie Llewellyn made his sad decision to leave the county, to go on the South Africans' tour to Australia and, thereafter, to play in Lancashire League cricket.

Without him, the recovery to sixth position in 1912 – one of Hampshire's most glorious seasons – was a considerable achievement. In that year, three of the county's batsmen – C.B. Fry, A.C. Johnston and Philip Mead – stood first, second and third in the first-class batting averages. Kennedy had come on to fill Llewellyn's place in the bowling and, once more, another bowler capable of sixty wickets in a season (Hesketh Prichard, if only he could have played regularly) might have carried Hampshire into a higher place. The event of the year, however, was the win – by eight wickets – against the Australians, still one of Hampshire's two greatest triumphs. Fry, in only eight innings for the county, averaged 116. But it was Mead (160 not out and 33 not out) and Kennedy (eleven wickets for 181 in the match) who effectively beat the Australians.

By 1914 Mead (2235 runs at 35.87 in Championship matches), Brown (with his best bowling season), Bowell, Kennedy and Newman were all fully seasoned and were joined by Walter Livsey, taking over from Jimmy Stone as wicket-keeper. They had, moreover, the bowling reinforcement they had so badly lacked in 1910 and 1912. A. Jaques – usually regarded as the first leg-theory bowler – added his pace to the attack. The lively captaincy of E.M. Sprot, some useful leg-spin from H.C. McDonell and occasional, but valuable, batting by C.B. Fry,

A.C. Johnston, J.G. Greig and A.C.P. Arnold rounded off the side. *Wisden* noted that 'had things gone a little differently' Hampshire might have finished third; and, on the figures – minutes in two cases and one run in another – the assessment was fair. Arthur Jaques was killed in the First World War and the side never made good his loss; it was just such a bowler that Hampshire needed to lift them the few places to the top in 1919, 1920, 1921 and 1922.

The year 1921, after a bad start, proved a remarkable season for the county. Three Hampshire batsmen – Mead, Tennyson and Brown – stood first, third and fourth in the English Test batting averages. Mead was also top of the first-class batting – with 3179 runs at 69.10 – and, between the beginning of June and mid-July, he scored 1601 runs in nineteen innings. But the new power came from the development as all-rounders of Newman and Kennedy: they scored a thousand runs apiece and took 340 wickets between them. But *Wisden* commented that 'whenever it happened that the two men [Kennedy and Newman] were collared, the attack became commonplace to a degree'. The next bowler in aggregate of wickets for the county was Remnant with thirty-eight, and after him, Brown (who kept wicket for England in three Tests) with thirty-six. There the economy broke down, as it was to continue to do over the years, for lack of a third hundred-wickets-a-season bowler.

The full-strength team of 1922 (which also finished sixth) looks, on paper, the best to play for Hampshire until after the 1939 war. It certainly achieved the most remarkable victory in the club's history – against Warwickshire at Edgbaston. Warwick batted first, made 223 and then put out Hampshire for 15 and invited them to follow on. When Hampshire's eighth wicket fell in their second innings, they were only 66 ahead; but Brown (172) and Livsey put on 175 for the ninth wicket and Livsey (110 not out, batting number ten) and Boyes another 70 for the tenth. So Warwickshire needed 304 to win. But Hampshire had now seized psychological command of the match: Kennedy (four for 47) and Newman (five for 53) bowled them out for 158, and Hampshire won by 155 runs. The quality of the county's play in that season was reflected in the fact that five Hampshire players – Mead, Kennedy, Brown, Livsey and Day – were invited to tour South Africa in the following winter.

In 1932 the new generation of John Arnold, Len Creese, Jim Bailey, 'Sam' Pothecary, Neil McCorkell and 'Lofty' Herman joined the ageing George Brown, Philip Mead, Alec Kennedy and the established link-generation player, Stuart Boyes. In that year Hampshire rose to eighth in the Championship. But, with eight wins and ten defeats, they were never in the hunt with the leaders. As *Wisden* said, they had 'a most interesting if not particularly successful season'. Once more, the bowling was a man short; but it was the county's last single-figure position for fourteen years, until they were ninth in 1948.

The gap between the county's genuine successes was a long one – thirty-three years, from 1922 to 1955. In that period, the club's entire approach to its team structure was altered vastly. The change is nowhere more apparent than in the fact that twenty-four players appeared in Hampshire's Championship matches of 1910, twenty-seven in 1912 and thirty-one in 1921; but only twenty-six in the entire seven seasons from 1955 to 1961, inclusive.

The professional hard-core of Mead, Bowell, Brown, Kennedy, Newman and Livsey, with intermittent support from Remnant, Stone and the unfledged Boyes, had 'carried' – without wishing to put too unkind a word to it – at least two, sometimes four, near-passengers in every match for twenty years. That is not to say that the amateurs in question were not gifted players. But it is to say that no cricketer, however talented, can maintain first-class standard if he plays only five or six – usually scattered – games in a season.

Immediate post-war problems led to some improvisations. But the clear aim in that period was a regular (and therefore largely professional), balanced eleven. By 1955 Desmond Eagar, alternately handicapped by lack of pace bowling and lack of spin, had built up a hard team: sometimes deficient in depth of batting, but capable in the field, with Shackleton and Cannings as persistent and accurate a pair of bowlers as Kennedy and Newman and, with a little 'green' in the pitch, equally penetrative. That team achieved the highest Championship position – third – in Hampshire's history. In the last analysis it did so because it was the best catching side the county had ever had and because the emergence of Heath and the spinners, Burden and Sainsbury, gave a Hampshire captain, for the first time, a complete and regular attack. The advent of Marshall improved the scoring-rate and quality of the batting, but, at the pinch, the side did not make enough runs to catch Surrey and Yorkshire.

Then came the change in the captaincy and the retirement of the county's main post-war batting prop, Neville Rogers. For several seasons the spin-bowlers probably were not sufficiently used or developed. But the side had crucial weaknesses in the middle-order batting, lacked a bowler of true 'killer' pace, and its catching had deteriorated since 1955.

In the wet summer of 1958, Hampshire led the Championship from mid-June to late August, but they finished second, behind Surrey, essentially because they were not so well-equipped on turning wickets. In addition, the middle batting was still patchy, the spin-bowlers suffered from lack of trust, and the catching was a recurrent weakness.

The story of 1961 is told in detail elsewhere. But it may bear the note that it was not only the peak season of most of the players, but also the fruition of a studied team-building programme which the committee – particularly Harry Altham and Cecil Paris – and Desmond Eagar planned and carried out on a meagre budget. The reliable Cannings was gone, but his successor, David White, had the extra pace which gave a long-needed edge to the attack. Wassell brought new strength to the spin-bowling, and the catching improved – slightly, but valuably. Meanwhile, the long-lamented frailty of the middle batting was made good by Livingstone, the maturing of Sainsbury and the fine, late flowering of Barnard as a responsible bat with controlled ability to force the pace. The result was a team deep in run-making power, soundly equipped at all points of attack and in which every man was worth his place – a true Championship side.

The only sad aspect of its triumph was that Philip Mead, Alec Kennedy and Alec Bowell were no longer alive to join Jack Newman, George Brown and Walter Livsey in applauding Colin Ingleby-Mackenzie's side when it attained the goal they had striven so hard to reach those many years ago.

*Hampshire Handbook*, 1962

# Two Teams of Champions

No sooner had Hampshire won the Championship for the second time in their history than the two winning sides were compared. Comparisons can be odious, but some of the differences between the two sides are so intriguing as to demand at least discussion. The team of 1961 were always likely winners: they had been third under Desmond Eagar in 1955, second under Colin Ingleby-Mackenzie in 1958. They had two England bowlers in Shackleton – already established as one of the major post-war English county cricketers – and David White; their batting was long and, at the pinch, solid enough virtually to guarantee against collapse. Above all, they were a mature and experienced group of players.

Richard Gilliat's team, on the other hand, was young almost to the point of rawness: four of its members – Mike Taylor, Tom Mottram, David O'Sullivan and Andy Murtagh – had never played a full season for the county (O'Sullivan and Murtagh still have not done so), Herman only one; while five of them were uncapped at the start of the 1973 season. Moreover, which must be unique since Test cricket became established, they won the title without a single England player.

The most impressive aspect of the side's newness is the fact that six of the regular members of the county team in 1969 – Marshall, Livingstone, Reed, White, Cottam and Shackleton – had gone and been replaced in the space of only four years.

There can be little surprise that the bookmakers quoted 66 to 1 against them for the Championship: they themselves thought the odds fair. Though they – and the bookmakers – fancied they had a better chance in the one-day competitions, if only for the potential, of Barry Richards and Gordon Greenidge in particular, for fast scoring. In the end they proved at least the most unexpected champions since Glamorgan in 1948.

The 1961 title was won by only sixteen players, that of 1973 even more unusually by only thirteen. They were Richard Gilliat, Barry Richards, Gordon Greenidge, Peter Sainsbury, David Turner, Trevor Jesty, Mike Taylor, Bob Stephenson, Bob Herman, Tom Mottram, plus either Richard Lewis or, when the ball might turn, David O'Sullivan, with Andy Murtagh as reserve batsman.

In 1961 Hampshire were among the eight counties who played the ideal thirty-two-match fixture list, meeting every other county home and out; in 1973 all counties played twenty matches – a programme with little margin for error.

Some past winners of the title – often essentially powerful sides – have undoubtedly been lucky. It used to be said that Colin Ingleby-Mackenzie's side would never again be given the declarations that enabled them to win in 1961. On the other hand, he steered them preciously close to losing in order to bring off some skilful but close wins. Under Richard Gilliat in 1973, Hampshire won ten matches and, in all but one of them (when Gloucestershire declared at Bournemouth with nine wickets down), they bowled out the opposing team twice.

That is the very negation of luck – it is doubtful if any other winning county since the third-day declaration became customary could claim as much; and they won the toss in only seven of their twenty Championship fixtures.

If this splendid achievement is to be explained it must be on three grounds: the forcing batting which took so many bonus points (they averaged four a match) and built long totals with time to spare; the side's immense coolness under pressure; and the fielding, which transformed steady bowling into a match-winning force (they averaged four bonus points a match for bowling, too).

Greenidge and Richards were valuable not only for the many and brilliant runs they scored, but for the fashion in which they took the initiative from opponents and passed it on to the later batsmen. At need there was Peter Sainsbury to shore up the innings when it toppled but, though it was not impregnable, it proved sounder than many expected.

In August Northamptonshire, arguably on paper the stronger of the two counties – and with Bob Cottam – came to Southampton for the match which both recognized would probably decide the issue. They won the toss, batted first and, by lunch-time on the first day, were 63 for eight and, in effect, beaten. They were never allowed to recover; Hampshire won in two days and, in a run of six wins in seven consecutive matches (they were only one wicket and half an hour from making it eight out of eight), took the title by 31 points from Surrey in second place.

The fielding – some 160 catches were made behind, or close to the wicket, and Gilliat's record at mid-off was unusual in modern times – was superb. There was no better example of this than during the crucial first morning of the Northants match at Southampton. Tom Mottram, whose height and leanness are hardly the physical attributes of an outstanding fieldsman, was bowling to Roy Virgin, the main opposing batsman. Virgin had taken no chances but, seeing a full-length ball, he leaned into it and drove it, characteristically hard and low – no more than four or five inches off the ground – towards mid-on. Mottram, checking his follow-through and pull-away, changed direction, dived far more than the width of the wicket and scooped up the all but impossible catch. Such concentration bred the confidence which took them through the final run-in.

Nothing then would have been more pleasing than to have beaten Kent in the last match. At the start of the season Kent had been tipped to win all four competitions – and did, in fact, take the John Player League and Benson and Hedges Cup. On the last afternoon, however, Hampshire could not make themselves quite enough time to score the 87 runs they needed to win that match with all their second-innings wickets in hand. It recalled 1961 when, having won against Derbyshire to take the title in the last match but one, they met Yorkshire determined to avenge being beaten into second place, and Marshall, in one of the most impressive innings of his life, was run out after threatening to take them in against all probability.

The common factor of the two teams was Peter Sainsbury, trimmest, gamest and most loyal of cricketers – and far too tactful to make comparisons. His utter devotion, tidy left-arm bowling – tighter than ever now – his dogged batting and – although he stands a little further back at short leg than in his greatest days – his eager fielding made him the ideal cricketer – harking back to the classic days of the great senior professionals.

He found the going harder than on the earlier occasion; but he was too wise to rank one side above the other. Let it be said that both teams were friendly and hospitable dressing-room company. Their two captains, so different in manner, both concealed their very real and deeply felt responsibility – Ingleby-Mackenzie by an extrovert gaiety, Gilliat with a carefully controlled quietness; both had the knack of getting the best from their players. There was no happier gesture than the arrival of Colin Ingleby-Mackenzie on the last day of the match, typically, with a cargo of champagne and a delight comparable to that of his own day, twelve years before.

*Hampshire Handbook*, 1974

# 1958, 1974, 1985
## Hampshire's Runners-Up Compared

When, in 1985, Hampshire, under Mark Nicholas, finished second in the County Championship, it was a position the county has bettered only twice (as champions in 1961 and 1973) and equalled twice. It may be interesting to discuss the three teams who were runners-up – those of 1958, 1974 and 1985 – when the main elevens were:

| 1958 | 1974 | 1985 |
|------|------|------|
| R.E. Marshall | B.A. Richards | C.G. Greenidge |
| J.R. Gray | C.G. Greenidge | V.P. Terry |
| H. Horton | D.R. Turner | M.C.J. Nicholas (captain) |
| R.W.C. Pitman | R.M.C. Gilliat | C.L. Smith |
| H.M. Barnard | (captain) | R.A. Smith |
| A.C.D. Ingleby-Mackenzie | T.E. Jesty | J.J.E. Hardy |
| (captain) | P.J. Sainsbury | or N.G. Cowley |
| P.J. Sainsbury | M.N.S. Taylor | T.M. Tremlett |
| L. Harrison (w-k) | N.G. Cowley | M.D. Marshall |
| D. Shackleton | G.R. Stephenson (w-k) | R. J. Parks (w-k) |
| M. Heath | R.S. Herman | R.J. Maru |
| M.D. Burden | A.M.E. Roberts | C.A. Connor |
| Reserves | Reserves | Reserves |
| A.W.H. Rayment | R.V. Lewis | D.R. Turner |
| D.E. Blake | J.M. Rice | S.J.W. Andrew |
| V.H.D. Cannings | | K.D. James |
| D.W. White | | |

There is strikingly little overlapping – Peter Sainsbury in 1958 and 1974; Gordon Greenidge and, narrowly, David Turner and Nigel Cowley in 1974 and 1985. In 1985 Alan Rayment and Vic Cannings (of the almost legendary 'Shack and Vic' partnership) were nearing the end of their county careers, while 'Butch' White was only starting his. Impressively, they have been most handsomely – and that is the word – served by their opening pairs.

It seems remarkable that the historic sides under Lord Tennyson, with Mead, Newman, Kennedy, Brown, Livsey and Bowell, never finished higher than sixth (twice), though they were also three times seventh in the eight seasons between 1919 and 1926. That is not intended as a reflection on the cricket of recent years by comparison with that of the earlier period, or vice versa, but it is a significant indication of Hampshire's standing in relation to the other sixteen counties.

To revert to the three runners-up, it must be said that the side of 1974 was undoubtedly stronger than that which had won the Championship in the preceding season, notably through the appearance of Anderson Roberts, who was easily top of the national bowling averages with more wickets than anyone else in the country. They led the Championship from May until the last match, but the heavy rain at the end of the season cost them one possible, and two probable, wins before it completely washed out their last match – against Yorkshire at

Bournemouth – while Worcestershire took four bonus points to win the title by two points; it was the more ironic for the fact that, three weeks before, Hampshire had beaten Worcestershire by an innings in two days. In 1958, too, Hampshire led the table until late August, but then they had a bad run and took only four points from four matches. Again in 1985, the weather damaged Hampshire's chances of the title; but their performances showed that, although they need more experience and the hardening that that will bring, they are undoubtedly one of the best sides – if not the best – in the country.

It could hardly be argued that either the 1958 or the 1974 side was as long or as strong in batting as 1985. But the bowling of 1974 had greater depth; and that of 1958, with the immaculate Shackleton at the peak of his powers, had greater variety:

> 1958 – Shackleton, Heath, Sainsbury, Burden and Gray.
> 1974 – Roberts, Herman, Taylor, Jesty and Sainsbury.
> 1985 – Marshall, Connor, Tremlett, Maru and Cowley.

Each of the two previous second places occurred in periods of prosperity: Ingleby-Mackenzie's team, despite a couple of lapses, was third in 1955, sixth in 1956 and champions in 1961, while Gilliat's was first, second and third in the three seasons 1973–75. Looking to the future, Mark Nicholas's side seems to lack only a killer spinner – a gap which Rajesh Maru's further development might fill – and more penetrative pace support for Malcolm Marshall, ideally through the improvement of either Steve Andrew or Cardigan Connor.

All three of these second-place sides have been relatively lucky in that, apart from Gordon Greenidge and Malcolm Marshall in West Indian tours, they lost few players to Test calls (Shackleton, Terry and Chris Smith total sixteen Tests). The county may not be so lucky for long: both Smiths, Bobby Parks, Paul Terry, and perhaps Mark Nicholas and Tim Tremlett, are in the running for England selection; that could expose deficiencies in the reserve strength, and they might then regret the loss of Trevor Jesty and, even more, of the younger Jonathan Hardy.

It is difficult, though, to resist the conclusion that the Smith brothers, Paul Terry, Mark Nicholas, Bobby Parks and Tim Tremlett have their best years yet ahead of them – in a side good enough to win the Championship.

*Hampshire Handbook*, 1986

# −10−
# Obituaries

## Tribute to Philip Mead

*May* 1958.   That monumentally reliable batsman, Philip Mead, is
dead. But those who were boys in Hampshire in my generation – and
for that matter in the two generations on either side of it – we can never
as long as we live see this county ground at Southampton without
remembering him. To us he was not merely the soundest left-hand
batsman in the world: he was *the* batsman. Still, when I buy an evening
paper and turn to the stop-press cricket scores, I have the feeling that I
shall read once more that Philip Mead – 122 not out – has saved the
Hampshire innings.

Two Hampshire wickets would fall and then he would walk out, bat
tucked under his right arm, carefully pulling on his gloves; his cap was
set very straight above his long face. He had a rolling, self-reliant walk,
powerful drooping shoulders, long, heavy, thick, bowed legs. He took
guard, looked round the field, twirled his bat and then, turning to
square leg, touched his cap to him one, two, three, four times; next he
tapped his bat one, two, three, four times in the crease, took one, two,
three, four little shuffling strides up to it. Then the bowler might bowl
– but not before Philip Mead went through that ritual before every ball
he ever received: scores of thousands of them – no wonder the peak of
his cap frayed out so often. Sometimes a bowler would try to hustle him
and bowl before he had completed it; but Philip would just step back,
signal that he was not ready, and begin all over again.

Now he settled down to make runs – notice I say to *make runs*. I do
not believe he was interested in *batting* as such, only in making runs.
Indeed, every stroke he played had the first stride of a run built into its
last stages; and he had – and played – every stroke in the game except
the true late cut. He did not care to bat in the nets – that lacked the

competition for runs that for him was the essence of playing cricket. 'I take my practice in the middle,' he used to say. In 1923 he made a century in his first innings of the season – 106 not out in a total of 255 – against Surrey. When he came back into the dressing-room, Alec Kennedy looked up and said 'Well played, Philip.'

'No it wasn't,' said Philip. 'I wasn't timing it properly.'

'Well,' said Alec, 'when did you last have a bat in your hands?'

'Last Scarborough Festival.' That had been eight months previously.

How many runs did he make? For Hampshire alone he scored 48,892 runs – more than any other man has made for any team in the history of cricket – and he made them at an average of over 48 runs an innings. He qualified for Hampshire in 1906, after Surrey had decided not to keep him on the staff at The Oval, and from then until 1936 he scored a thousand runs every season – more than two thousand in eleven of them, twice over three thousand. Altogether he made over 55,000 runs: once he was set he seemed to stay set, day after day, tireless, relentless, with an unfailing appetite for runs. Four times he scored centuries in each of three consecutive innings. During the July of 1923 he scored 1192 runs in seven consecutive innings. He scored his runs equally well against every type of bowling, from extreme pace to extreme spin; again I recall his contemporary, Alec Kennedy saying to me, 'How many hundreds did Philip make – 153? Then I'll bet he made seventy or more of them on spinners' wickets – the turning ball never bothered him a scrap.' He looked ungainly, but his footwork was so perfect that it took him infallibly to the right position for his stroke.

Nothing ever seemed to bother him much – except perhaps the last run to take him to fifty or a hundred. James Langridge recalls bowling to Philip on a turning wicket – left-arm bowler to left-hand bat – with three fieldsmen close in on the leg side. In those days Hampshire paid strictly a pound talent money for fifty, another pound for a hundred. Philip – on 49 or 99 – would turn the ball through the close fieldsmen and as he played the stroke he would chuckle 'That's another ton of coal for the winter,' and off down the wicket. Then his partner had better be backing up, for his running was faster than it looked.

That applied to his batting, too. I remember talking to an old Hampshire player with some uninvited pavilion bore constantly putting his spoke in. When the talk turned to Philip Mead, the unwanted guest chipped in with, 'Oh, Mead, him; I know he made a lot of runs, but he was so slow. I remember him here one day – against Warwick it was – he came in about a quarter to one and he stone-walled all day until half past six for two hundred.' Two hundred and eleven it was – made in under five hours – a rate of 45 runs an hour – stone-walling? Philip Mead's batting was not slow, but it was completely unhurried: he could not be disturbed. Indeed, he pottered about his crease as calmly and certainly as a man in his own back garden – but gathering runs instead of weeds. It often seemed that he could take a single off any ball bowled to him – especially on the leg side. One day at the end of July 1911, against Warwick at Southampton, he made 207 not out in three hours – a scoring rate of 69 runs an hour. The very next morning, at Portsmouth, he went in first against Sussex, scored a hundred before lunch and, altogether, 194 in three hours ten minutes. In two days, 401 runs (for once out) at an average rate of more than a run a minute.

Eighteen years afterwards – when he was forty-two – against Lord Hawke's eleven, with five Test bowlers in it, at Scarborough, he made 233 in five hours – 46 an hour. Not slow by any means, but he never pressed: he placed his strokes and he murdered every bad ball bowled to him. He could hit with great power, but by timing, effortlessly. *Wisden* said that Scarborough innings was faultless; that is the point: he was so sure. Men who played with him and watched him batting from the other end were amazed that he could go all day and never miss a ball he played at. His bat seemed like a natural extension of his long arms. Pace never disturbed Philip. When the Australian fast bowlers Gregory and McDonald tore through the English batting of 1921 as Miller and Lindwall were to do twenty-seven years later, Mead was not picked for England until the fourth Test; he made 47 in his only innings in that game and, in the next, 182 not out – then the highest score ever made by an Englishman in a Test against Australia in England. He made over 20,000 runs after that but, ironically enough, he never played for England in this country again and only once more against Australia – eight years later when he made 8 and 73 in his one match and then went out of Test cricket for ever (with an average of 51 against Australia – a far better figure than those of many more fashionable players).

For years, though, we schoolboys were very excited when a telegram was brought out to him in the field: we used to think he had been picked for England. It was a long time before I learned that those were cables from the course – horse-racing results and prices – his other consuming interest besides runs.

In 1936, forty-nine years old, he made his customary thousand runs in the season – passed W.G. Grace's aggregate – and then retired. During the war, in a charity match on a wicket so fiery that the ball flew over the batsman's head, or shot along the ground, our opponents' second wicket fell and Philip Mead – now nearer sixty than fifty – came out to bat: phlegmatic, sound as ever. He made top score, more than three times as many runs as any other player in the game – without a flaw – and was not out at the end. Less than a year later we heard that he, of the keen, keen eyes, was blind. Still he always came to the Hampshire matches at Bournemouth where he lived. He had long lost his Cockney accent and he used to sit in the dressing-room and talk about the game with a Hampshire burr. He never compared the cricket of his day with the post-war game; and he was always sympathetic with batsmen out of form. He used to sit and listen to the play. 'That bowler's worrying him,' he would say as his ear caught the sound of ball on a part of the bat that was not middle.

His bat seemed all middle. Maurice Tate used those very words once, talking about his first ball as a fast-medium bowler. He was an established county slow bowler until the day when, stung to fury by Mead's imperturbable defence, he swung his entire body into a fast ball which beat and bowled him. More than thirty years afterwards I asked Philip Mead if he remembered it: 'Ah, that I do,' he said. 'Pitched on the off and hit the top of the leg like a bullet – a beautiful ball it was.'

'Did you say anything to him?' I asked.

'Say anything? – Oh, no – I never encouraged bowlers.'

And he never did.

*Radio Broadcast, BBC West of England Home Service*

# Percy Fender

*June* 1985. Lest the recent Australian Hayes/Schultz film of the 1932–33 England v Australia series – virtually a caricature – shown on BBC television has produced any effect, it may be wise to indicate the truth. Percy George Herbert Fender – known to his friends as Bill – was a thinker as cricketer, footballer, wine merchant, writer and human being.

He was one of those who believed that the Australians there in 1932–33 would be vulnerable to fast bowling. Like his fellow thinkers,

Arthur Carr and Douglas Jardine, he was proved right. The film, which showed him being bullied by Lord Harris into resigning the captaincy in 1931, was completely false – he had already told the Surrey committee in 1930 that at thirty-eight he no longer wanted to play a full season's cricket, and Jardine's succession was merely delayed.

There was no antipathy between the two. Indeed, they laughed heartily together about the outcome of the 1932–33 series, which went exactly as they and Arthur Carr had anticipated in the previous year.

Fender was England's senior Test cricketer. Born on 22 August 1892, he was a considerable all-rounder who played first for Sussex, then for his native Surrey, whom he captained from 1920 to 1931; and in thirteen Test matches for England.

*Wisden* captured his quality quite early in his career (1915):

> 'He is not a cricketer whose value can in any way be gauged from figures or averages. As a match-winning factor he is a far greater force on a side than his records would suggest. Tom Hayward said of him last season that he was the making of the Surrey eleven.'

Tall (6 feet 3 inches), he was an often spectacular attacking batsman who scored the fastest century recorded in the first-class game; a bowler of immense variety, originally at fast-medium but subsequently of wrist-spin; and, with fast reactions and an immensely long reach, a brilliant slip fieldsman. Generally considered the most astute county captain of his time, he was widely considered unlucky never to have captained England.

He began his county cricket career in 1910, a fortnight short of his eighteenth birthday, while he was still at St Paul's School, and continued with Sussex on a residential qualification until 1913, a season in which he had such early successes as to be chosen for Gentlemen v Players at Lord's and The Oval. Sussex, however, did not give him a county cap. That omission was generously made good by Arthur Gilligan many years later; but Fender joined Surrey for the 1914 season.

There he had considerable success as player and as a captain who achieved some remarkable results with limited bowling resources on so good a batting wicket as The Oval. He gave Surrey cricket a newly purposeful, even exciting, character. His reputation was that of an astute observer, with a mental card-index of all his opponents, and who would always take a risk to win rather than play to avoid defeat. In his own words, he was 'always trying to make something happen'.

It is generally believed that his representative career was shortened by a difference with Lord Harris, for many years an autocratic figure at Lord's. Fender incurred Harris's displeasure in 1924 by pointing out – quite accurately – in a press article that his Lordship had been party to breaking playing regulations by arranging the covering of the wicket at Scarborough.

For that Harris sent for him at Lord's and fiercely rebuked him. Fender had been chosen for twelve of England's previous fifteen Tests; but after that disagreement, in June 1924, he played only once more for England, and that at a remove of five years.

Fender was a major personality in English cricket for over a dozen years between the wars. The cartoonist Tom Webster increased Fender's public image by drawing him, unforgettably, slouching along, hands in pockets, moustachioed, wearing heavy (but not strong) horn-rimmed spectacles and a sweater down to his ankles.

In fact, he had a highly original turn of mind. In his early years in business he devised inner and outer cartons for condiments; reinforced bags for coke; new lining methods for hat boxes. He designed light-weight underwear, and larger, shadier, peaked caps for cricke-ters. He was, too, one of the first to link commerce with cricket by inviting customers to county matches when he was playing. His friendship with Jack Hulbert led him into lyric writing, and to backing musical comedy.

As a cricket thinker he was not only tactically sharp, but an iconoclast. He first strove to break the barriers between amateurs and professionals. He was the first captain to break the convention of the two using separate gates and doors, and would have had one common dressing-room if Jack Hobbs had not humorously dissuaded him.

Because he had a sharp mind and a combative urge, held strong views which he voiced in wholehearted fashion, and did not suffer fools – or those who disagreed with him – gladly, he was by no means completely liked in the cricket of his day. Andrew Sandham once observed: 'Mr Fender always seemed to know too much for the others; it did not make him popular but he was too clever for them.' The professionals who played under him, however, both respected and liked him; while he, in turn, was always active in their interests.

Described as 'the best change bowler in England', he would experiment with anything – including full tosses – that he thought might take a wicket, though he could bowl sharply spun leg-breaks with unusual accuracy. He was more athletic than his round shoulders and shambling gait made him appear. At school he was highly capable at rugby football, fives, putting the shot, boxing and fencing. Subsequently he took to Association football and kept goal for Casuals in 1913, when they won the AFA Cup; and occasionally for Corinthians and Fulham. A severe football injury – five fractures of the leg – accounted for a subsequent impression of ungainliness. In his later days he enjoyed shooting and, characteristically, excelled at golf and billiards.

In his entire first-class career, from 1910 to 1936, he scored 19,034 runs at 26.65 (with twenty-one centuries); took 1894 wickets at 25.05; and made 558 catches. He six times performed the 'double' of 1000 runs and 100 wickets in a season; and in 1926, against Essex, the 'match double' of a century and ten wickets. In thirteen Tests for England, 380 runs at 19.00; twenty-nine wickets at 40.86; fourteen catches.

After he was left out of the Test team he often reported for the London evening newspaper *The Star;* and he wrote four typically penetrative books on Test series: *Defending The Ashes* (1920–21), *The Turn of the Wheel* (1928–29), *The Tests of 1930,* and *Kissing the Rod* (1934), as well as the expository *An ABC of Cricket.*

Despite his blindness, he travelled, as by far the eldest member of the English party, to the Centenary Test in Melbourne – his thirteen-year-old grandson, Nicholas Benstead Smith, acted as his guide; and he continued to run his Wine Exchange into his nineties.

*The Guardian*

# James Langridge

*October* 1966.   Anyone who has followed the cricket of the past forty years knew James Langridge, who died on 10 September 1966, as a fine all-round cricketer. To many his death must mark, also, the passing of a type, and of an era of cricket.

He has been described as a model professional; but he was something more – in many ways the personification of the tradition of the English, south-country cricket professional.

Jim Langridge was born in the Weald – the place where, with little doubt, cricket began. He came, to be precise, from the village of Newick, which lies in the Lewes–Uckfield–Hayward's Heath triangle where so many Sussex players were bred.

Although, when the weather was too wet or cold for cricket, he could play a useful game of football, he accepted cricket as his life when he was a young man, and he lived in it, and by it, contentedly for the rest of his days.

As soon as Jim Langridge stepped on to the field, you knew him for a cricketer. Almost six feet, with lean, strong shoulders, he invested the sure, unhurried gait of the countryman with a grace of his own. His turn-out was infallibly trim. He permitted himself, however, one mannerism of appearance: he wore his cap – which memory recalls as always of sun-bleached age – tilted at a Beatty-esque angle towards his left eye. His sensitive face was weathered brick-red, his jaw firm, his eye steady. Merely to see him take a ball tossed to him in the field was to recognize his identification with the game. His eye assessed its flight so certainly that, barely needing to watch it, he would put out his hand and take it with the habitual air of a carpenter taking up his chisel. That is the just analogy, for Jim Langridge was essentially a craftsman. Cricket, in every aspect, was his deeply assimilated study.

His left-hand batting was extremely correct: the unmistakable stamp of the good batsman was implicit in strokes played without hurry. There was quiet style about every movement he ever made with a bat. He was understanding against spin, unflinching against pace and, though his cover-driving was in the classic Edwardian mould, he never struck the ball so hard as to disturb his calm poise. His timing was good, his placing shrewd; and he made his runs steadily.

Langridge first came into the Sussex side – in 1924 – as a batsman, and he did not find a regular place until 1927. Meanwhile, he had been working hard at his slow left-arm bowling. In those early years his length was uncertain, largely because, on the true wickets of his time and his county, he tried to spin too much. By the early 1930s, however, he had become one of the best bowlers of his kind. He rarely – except to the wilder sloggers – tossed the ball up to the temptation length of the half-volley; on the other hand, he never pushed it through at near-medium pace in the manner of Charles Parker and Hedley Verity. In his maturity he was a genuine slow bowler of perfect length who employed slight, but extremely skilful, variations of flight. Even on the easiest of batsmen's wickets, his accuracy was such that he was rarely punished, while on a pitch which took spin, he was quite deadly. Then he whipped the ball so sharply away from the bat towards the prehensile hands of his brother at slip that, for years, 'c Langridge (John) b Langridge (Jas)' was a constant entry in the scorebooks.

He came up from the Sussex nursery to the first team at the time when Arthur Gilligan was making Sussex an outstanding fielding side, and by his concentration and safe-handedness in the gully he helped to establish that standard.

Over a first-class career that began in 1924 and ended in 1953, he scored 31,716 runs (at 35.2) and took 1814 wickets (at 22.56); he did the 'double' six times and, in 1937, scored over two thousand runs as well as taking a hundred wickets. He played for England eight times, which probably was less than his due. He was, however, a modest man, who never seemed avid for records or recognition; cricket satisfied him as thoroughly as he served it.

The true measure of Jim Langridge as a cricketer is most clearly to be seen in his performances in the key matches – against Yorkshire – for Sussex during their great period in the early thirties. Yorkshire were then immensely powerful; Sussex finished fourth to them in 1931, second in 1932 and 1933, and were runners-up to Lancashire in 1934. Langridge's all-round record against Yorkshire in those years was unparalleled by any other player of any county. The out match of 1931 – at Hull – was abandoned without a ball being bowled; but, at Hove, he scored 12 (out of 106) and 37 (top score, out of 165) and, of the eleven Yorkshire wickets that fell, he took seven for 108. At Leeds in 1932 he made 13 not out and 53 not out and took none for 88; at Hove, 12 and 47 (top score) and two for 75. In 1933, at Hull, he made 159 not out, the decisive score, in his only innings, and took five for 87; at Hove, 20 runs in his only innings and six wickets for 38; thus he was the most effective player in his county's two wins over the champions. The next year he scored 21, did not bowl in the first innings of Yorkshire but, in the second, returned the best analysis of his career – nine for 34. This, over four years, is a quite outstanding level of performance against the strongest county team in the Championship.

He himself, if pressed – for he was modest and always loath to discuss his own doings – most cherished his bowling spell against Derbyshire at Chesterfield in 1938. Derby, in the last innings, needed 208 to win and had made 178 for two – only 30 short – when there was a shower of rain, too slight to stop play for more than a few minutes. It was, though, enough to arouse life in the pitch. Most of the Derbyshire players had already changed into their everyday clothes, and were sitting in their cars, expecting to watch a comfortable finish before they drove home. Until then the two faster bowlers of Sussex, Nye and Duffield, had done most of the bowling. Jim Langridge had bowled one over for 5 runs when he had Stan Worthington caught at the wicket by 'Tich' Cornford for 119. That was the beginning of an amazing spell of eleven balls in which he took five wickets – including a hat-trick – for no runs. The last eight Derbyshire batsmen – many of the later ones hurrying to the crease in flannels and pads hastily dragged on over street socks, shoes and shirts – were put out for 9 runs and Sussex gained one of the most amazing wins in the history of the County Championship.

The year 1946, the first post-war season, found Jim Langridge one of the elders of the game and one of the major all-rounders in English cricket. Once during that summer I discussed with him the subject of fast bowling in England. He looked at me quizzically and said, 'Last week I took my thigh-pad out of my bag and I was starting to tie it on when I said to myself – "But who do you need to wear it for nowadays?" and I put it back.'

He was chosen for Hammond's team to Australia in the following winter and, after being initially neglected, was chosen among the twelve for the third Test, but pulled a muscle during fielding practice. Returning before he was fully fit, he scored a century but so aggravated the injury that he never played again on the tour.

In 1950 he was appointed captain of Sussex, the first professional to hold that office. He had never sought the post; indeed, it was possible to feel that he sensed that the appointment ended the line to which he belonged – that of the great south-country professional cricketers. Nevertheless he carried out the duties with characteristically unassuming wisdom and courtesy until 1952. Then he became the county coach until he took over the cricket at Seaford College. Up to a few weeks before his death, Jim came to watch at the county ground at Hove – friendly, wise and patient as ever. This was a rare man.

*The Cricketer*

# Leslie Compton

*December* 1984.   Leslie Compton, who died in his sleep two nights ago aged seventy-two, was a considerable all-round sportsman. Although he lacked the charisma of his brother Denis, he was a solid performer at both cricket and football with his two clubs. Something of a physical giant, strong, stern and determined, he was one of the early stopper centre-halves for Arsenal and a seam-bowler, wicket-keeper and serviceable batsman for Middlesex.

He played county cricket from 1938 to 1956. When Middlesex won the Championship of 1947 under R.W.V. Robins, he made a notable advance from a stop-gap to a regular wicket-keeper. Although he looked unusually large behind the stumps, he became tidy and dependable.

At the side's needs he turned his arm at right-arm medium; and in that Championship season, emerging as a free-striking batsman, he scored his maiden century. Overall he had precisely the talents Middlesex needed in 1947, and a loyalty and character to exploit them when they were most needed.

Compton was a member of the Arsenal team which won the FA Cup of 1949–50. Originally a full-back, he became a centre-half in that powerful line of varied talents, Forbes, Compton, Mercer; Scott and Barnes were the backs. Denis Compton, at outside left, and Lewis scored the two goals by which they won. The following season Leslie Compton, at thirty-eight, became the oldest player to be called for England: he appeared against Wales and Yugoslavia and played well enough to have kept the place.

As a footballer he was powerful, purposeful and utterly ruthless – a mighty man at the last ditch. Strongly incisive in the tackles, dominant in the air and physically fearless, he was more nimble than he looked and extremely hard to pass. He was over six feet tall and in later years put on immense weight. He was further hampered by having a foot amputated. He became a publican in north London, and much relished the successes of his former clubs.

*The Guardian*

# Mervyn Burden

*December* 1987.    It is a happy fact that the unluckiest of all Hampshire cricketers should also have been the merriest. There must, surely, have been a fairy godmother overlooking Mervyn Burden's entry into the world who decreed that he should be so resilient as to laugh at setbacks which would have broken some cricketers' hearts.

When he retired, in the autumn of 1963, he was – despite the boyish air emphasized by a floppy fair forelock – the senior member of the county staff, apart from Leo Harrison. He had been a professional since April 1947. He made his first appearance in the County Championship in 1953, and was capped in 1955; yet he had played in only 174 county matches in eleven seasons. He has long been something of a byword in the other sixteen counties, where he is regarded as a prophet without honour in his own country. That may or may not be the case; but it is certain that, when he was one of the twelve from which the ultimate eleven were chosen, over and over again, he was included in anticipation of rain (and a turning wicket) which did not eventuate; or left out, only for the ball to turn so much that his off-breaks might well have been decisive.

All this had an effect on his performance and, indeed, on the entire quality of his cricket. In a side which, through most of his career, was wedded to tight seam-bowling, he could never be sure of his team place. So he never felt that he could take a risk: throw the ball up, experiment with one tossed wide, or one spun out of the back of the hand – anything which invited being hit for four could see him taken off. So he was never quite the attacking bowler he might have been (for he was a game gambler). He tried to bowl tight, which, in its turn, led to over-anxiety and the loose ball sent down out of tension. He genuinely spun his off-breaks; his weakness lay in the fact that he tried to bowl the same – unhittable – ball every time.

Let us, however, not become too profound about Mervyn Burden – there could have been no more certain way of moving him to laughter. In fact, no one ought to presume to write a biographical note about him: to hear the entire story in his own words is to realize just how much laughter a man who has played the game with his whole heart can find in cricket – if he has a sense of humour.

The odds must have been strongly against Mervyn Burden ever becoming a county cricketer. He was at King Edward VI School,

Southampton, where Jimmy Gray was four years his senior. Unlike Gray, though, he never made his mark as a schoolboy player. For most of his time the school was in evacuation quarters at Poole, its accommodation for games limited by shared facilities. He did achieve a place in the under-fourteen cricket team, but his main sporting ability seemed to be as a footballer.

When he came back to Southampton after the war, as a sixteen-year-old, football was still his chief sport; and it was as a member of the ATC football team that, partly to keep fit and partly in preparation for some cricket the ATC boys were going to play between the soccer seasons, he went to the indoor cricket school at Cunliffe-Owen factory at Swaythling in March 1947. There his cricket career had a fairy-tale beginning. He bowled in those indoor nets on only three evenings. With little experience, he simply ran up and bowled at about medium pace, concerned more with amusement and exercise than with any expectation of serious technical development. Solely by coincidence, on his second evening Desmond Eagar and the – then – county coach, Sam Staples, were there, in hope of discovering some talent that would help to solve some of Hampshire's serious post-war playing problems.

They saw, among others, a sixteen-year-old lad, somewhat slight and short to be reckoned a pace bowler. Sam Staples, always a shrewd judge of a cricketer, and Desmond Eagar, whose eye was sharpened by the fact that Hampshire had no money to spend on engaging half-chances, were content that this young man was a worthwhile prospect for the county. What Mervyn Burden, who had not played in an organized match since he was thirteen years old, considered mild exercise was, to their judgement, accurate medium-pace in-swing bowling.

This was by far the highest praise Mervyn Burden had ever received for any of his sporting activities and he went home pleased enough, but satisfied that the whole matter had ended at the complimentary stage. Only the expression on his face when he recalled the event adequately conveyed his amazement at receiving the letter asking him to join the Hampshire groundstaff, and to report to the county ground on 1 April 1947.

He accepted without hesitation: 'I knew I knew nothing about cricket, but I reckoned they were the experts – they ought to know; and if they thought I was good enough to earn my living playing cricket, I wasn't going to argue.'

Mervyn Burden's account of his first appearance at the county ground is one of the masterpieces of spoken autobiography.

'I'd never been on the county ground in my life before. Leo Harrison (I thought he was the boss) took me to the groundstaff room to change. I didn't have any bat or pads; but I did have whites, and my father's boots and a white plastic belt to keep my trousers up. When I came out, they sent me to bowl in the first net. The batsman was a little chap I didn't know: it turned out afterwards that he was Neil McCorkell.

'I've never felt so nervous in my life. I went up and bowled my first ball and it flew clean over the top of the nets and smashed one of the windows in the old dining-room. Someone gave me another one and as I walked back to bowl my next ball I was wondering what the dickens I should do this time. But I didn't have to worry. Johnny Arnold was batting in the next net and, as I turned to run in, he hit an on-drive. I had my back to him and never saw it coming; it caught me a terrific crack on the ankle and I couldn't bowl for a fortnight. Still, I thought I had better show willing, so I turned up the next morning to see if there was anything I could do, and they sent me out to help Ernie on the pitch. You know, I hadn't been there a couple of minutes before I kicked a bucket of whiting across the square. So they sent me home until my ankle was better.'

Not even Mervyn Burden at his unluckiest could maintain quite that standard of disaster. He was top of the club and ground averages that year, with forty-seven wickets, as a seam-bowler. Another good season in 1948 and he went to do his National Service – in the Army – in February 1949. While he was there he played regularly for the Southern Command as an opening bowler and – which may surprise even his best friends – a number three batsman.

He came back to Southampton in August 1950 to find that Shackleton and Cannings, with Gray as third string – plus Carty on 'green' wickets – were bowling medium pace for the first team; Carty, for more than half the matches, Heath, Pitman and Ransom in the second eleven and club and ground sides. 'I didn't fancy *my* chance.' After a talk with Arthur Holt he decided to try bowling off-breaks. He had an un-encouraging time in his new style at Alf Gover's school in the spring of 1951, but he took 120 wickets in club and ground and second-eleven matches that summer. Moreover, he averaged 24.16 as a batsman for the second-eleven; he made the highest Hampshire score of the match against Middlesex II (69) and Sussex II (71). At Hove he hit Jack Oakes, a useful off-spinner with considerable Championship experience, murderously hard, and made his 71 in fifty minutes. After that innings Jim Langridge, then the Sussex coach, congratulated Arthur Holt on having discovered so good an attacking batsman. Indeed, in 1952 Burden almost played for Hampshire as a batsman. He had just made 60 for the club and ground when Cliff Walker was injured in the match with Essex. Desmond Eagar telephoned for an 'in form' batsman from the staff to be sent to join the side at Trent Bridge for the game with Notts. So Burden was on the fringe of his first county match when the cricket grapevine brought the news that 'the ball is turning square at Trent Bridge these days'; so Charlie Knott was sent instead. The wicket proved so plumb that only fourteen wickets fell while 805 runs were scored!

His chance came in 1953: his first match was against Worcester at Worcester – one for 86 in 33 overs on a good batting wicket. His second appearance was against Surrey, in Hampshire's last match of the season at Bournemouth: Surrey needed these points to remain champions and Burden proved the main obstacle to their eventual win, tying down their batting and taking six wickets – including those of Peter May, Subba Row and Tom Clark – for 70.

So he came to the summer of 1954 in good heart; but he played only one match before July and in that he did not bowl. He came into the side at the start of July and went a fortnight without a wicket: then, though, he had forty-six in the rest of the season, including seven for 48 against Leicester.

The year of 1955, until then the most successful season in Hampshire's history, was the best of Mervyn Burden's career; therefore – or, we might say, because – he played in more matches than in any other year. Without achieving any remarkable figures, apart from seven for 53 against Oxford University, he bowled steadily, finished with seventy wickets and honestly earned his county cap. It was then apparent, too, that by sheer effort and enthusiasm, he had turned himself from a below-average fielder into an unflagging chaser of the ball, a quick thrower and, at times, a catcher so surprisingly brilliant that he confessed to amazing himself.

For the rest of his career he became the 'extra' bowler, giving way to a third seam-bowler at Portsmouth or wherever the wicket half-promised pace. Yet, from time to time, he was a match-winner. In 1956, at Portsmouth, Surrey, the champions, put out Hampshire for 191: Fletcher and Clark made 90 for their first wicket, then Burden came on; Surrey were all out for 126 and Burden's six for 23 had made Hampshire's narrow win (by 28 runs) possible. In 1959, when Hampshire finished for the first time as runners-up, Burden played in only seventeen matches: but he took forty-five wickets and effectively won the close games with Notts at Trent Bridge and Northants at Southampton.

The season of 1961, Hampshire's Championship year, marked, as we can now see, the beginning of the end of his career as a regular county player, for it was the season when Alan Wassell elbowed him out of his position of 'extra spinner'. Mervyn Burden played in only fourteen matches; yet he took fifty wickets at 22.92, which made him second in the county's bowling averages and, by taking twenty-two wickets in the two matches against Somerset, virtually won them both. His figures of eight for 38 in the first innings at Frome were the best achieved by any bowler in the Championship that year. But, with typical Burden luck, he missed the £100 award for the best bowling performance of the season because A.J.G. Pearson took all ten in the Cambridge University–Leicester match.

In that great year, at Northampton, he caught Crump in each Northants innings – once running at full tilt and once with a leap to full stretch – off strokes that seemed certain to go for six: two 'impossible' catches which would have been magnificent whoever had made them. He ought to have played in the match with Derbyshire that decided the Championship at Bournemouth. He usually bowled well there, and the pitch would have suited him far better than David White, who was robbed of all pace by the slowness of the wicket. But Mervyn was, once more, twelfth man. As he sat in the dressing-room, suffering the tortures of the helpless with the game in a crucial state, I turned to him: 'Wouldn't you sooner be out there, even if you dropped a catch or bowled a bad ball, than in here, just watching?' 'Not half I wouldn't; but that's the way it is – they do the playing, I do the chain-smoking and nail-biting.'

In 1962 he took sixty-five wickets in seventeen matches. In 1963, picked for only three games, he decided the match with Gloucester, with six for 84; and in his last match, when he took three for 90 against Glamorgan, two catches were dropped off him, one of which would have got rid of Alan Jones, who made 121, when he was on only 20.

Mervyn Burden's most unusual contribution to the Hampshire cricket of his time was one that cannot be reckoned in figures – his humour. The week-in, week-out concentration of county cricket can produce – especially in a team with a chance of winning the Championship – considerable strain. Often, when the Hampshire dressing-room was painful with tension, Mervyn Burden made a joke – usually with an admixture of wisdom – which dissolved the entire company in laughter. Was he ever reduced to a state in which he could neither joke nor laugh? Once – in the match with Sussex at Eastbourne in 1955. After waiting two hours with his pads on while Sainsbury and Cannings put on 55, he went in last with the scores tied and even took guard before he realized that Sainsbury had been out to the last ball of the over. Cannings did not survive the new over, so Burden's batting in such a crisis was not tested. He recovered sufficiently on the way back to the pavilion to play a few jaunty strokes at an imaginary ball.

Infallibly good-natured, a cheerful loser, that rare creature a genuine non-grumbler, a willing and helpful twelfth man, he was one of the salt of the cricketing earth. The game did not deal kindly with him. In 1962 another county asked to sign him. Mervyn was reluctant to leave Hampshire, but 'They were uncovering wickets for 1963; that had to be my chance and I wanted to take it with Hampshire; it just didn't go that way, that's all.' Seventeen seasons on the staff, with only one season – 1955 – as a regular player. He was not given a benefit, but he cheerfully and gratefully accepted a testimonial. He was once asked whether, if he had his time over again, he would still take up professional cricket. 'Of course I would. I've had all these years of fun, and I've had my days; I wouldn't change it.'

Neither would anyone who ever shared a day's cricket with Mervyn Burden have wished to change him. With a laugh full of teeth, he could reduce the tensest cricket match to its true stature – a game. In his acceptance of ill luck – and the whole-heartedness of his effort – he was a model for any cricketer. To which high-falutin' sentiments his response would have been, 'Hey, what's goin' on then – gettin' after me?' But on one could get after Mervyn Burden – without ending up laughably in the wrong.

*Hampshire County Magazine*

# –11–

# Reflecting the Game

## Art

The field of cricket art extends from the masterpiece to completely 'popular' – or folk – art; from Paul Sandby's 'Landscape with Cricket Match in Progress' to naive Staffordshire figures of cricketers: from a work in which cricket is merely incidental to the unsophisticated jumble of cricketana, important for its subject rather than any 'pure' artistic quality.

In Sandby's superb gouache, and the oil (*c.* 1850) by an unknown artist of 'Cricket Match with a View of Christchurch Priory', the game of cricket is merely an ingredient of the landscape: either would grace any art collection and it would not be quite just to call them 'cricket pictures'. The same applies to a number of eighteenth- and early nineteenth-century portraits, usually of youths shown holding a cricket bat. Essentially these are portraits of the persons: the picture, as a work of art, would not be affected if a riding whip or a fishing rod were substituted for the bat.

Most of the major oil paintings of the game are, in fact, landscapes, the cricketers tiny figures in the broad setting. Among the best are 'Village Cricket' (1855) by John Ritchie, 'A Cricket Match on Parker's Piece, Cambridge' (*c.* 1861: artist unknown), 'A Match between the Army and the Navy at Portsmouth' (?H Ladbrooke: 1800–1869), 'Kent v Hampshire 1774', 'The Cricket Match' (?L.R. Boitard, *c.* 1740), 'Gentlemen v Players at Brading, Isle of Wight' (*c.* 1749, attributed to Francis Hayman) and 'A Cricket Match' (George Morland). There are numerous paintings in this style between 1750 and 1850, of varying degrees of excellence; there are also, undoubtedly, a number of copies and some downright forgeries. In recent years some pleasant oil paintings have been made of cricket grounds by Charles Cundall (Lord's and Hastings), Arthur Mailey, the Australian Test cricketer

(Sandringham), Col C.T. Burt (Edgbaston), Olive Sharp (Brockton Point, Vancouver) and Mildred Smith Amandoz (Queen's Park Oval, Trinidad).

Oil paintings of players exist in fair numbers but it would be hard to describe any of them as great; among the best – most of them hanging in various county pavilions – are W.G. Grace by A. Stuart-Wortley, Len Hutton by Henry Carr (in the possession of Sir Leonard Hutton), A.C. MacLaren, Sir Jack Hobbs, Lord Hawke, Wilfred Rhodes, S.F. Barnes and Denis Compton. There are also some few 'character' paintings in oils, mostly produced about the middle of the last century, which have a genuine cricket feeling.

The most important is that called 'The Scorer' – actually William Davies, who was scorer to Lewes Priory Cricket Club – painted in 1842 by an artist of whom little is known, Thomas Henwood: the study of the old rustic, bespectacled and bearded, wearing a wide-brimmed straw hat and sitting at his table with his book, bottle, glass and churchwarden pipe, has been many times reproduced. James Hayllar was a little later than Henwood and there is, perhaps, a hint of sentimentality about his portrait studies; nevertheless, his 'Brewer's Drayman, a Cricketer', 'An Old Cricketer' and 'Her First Lesson' have true human – and cricket – sympathy.

In the field of watercolour, crayon and pen-and-ink drawings there have been far more numerous contributions to cricket art. It includes the most historically important item of all cricket art, a single page, 7¾ by 9¾ inches, from the notebook of George Shepheard senior (1770?–1842), himself a cricketer who played for Surrey. The sheet contains twelve watercolour drawings of cricketers of whom nine are named. Probably executed at a match at Lord's in about 1790, the studies are of Lord Frederick Beauclerk, the Hon. Henry Tufton (11th Earl of Thanet), the Hon. Charles Lennox (4th Duke of Richmond) and the Hon. Edward Bligh – all amateur cricketers of the period – two of Thomas Lord, founder of the famous ground, and the only existing action portraits of three of the greatest of the Hambledon players, Tom Walker, David Harris and William Beldham. Its survival is surprising and happy; it is now in the possession of MCC and has been reproduced, entire and in detail, many times.

George Belcher's 'Impression of Jack Hobbs', 'Herbert Strudwick' by Frank Eastman, 'The Saffrons Ground, Eastbourne' by G. Prowse, several sketches of county grounds in about 1900 by W.A. Bettesworth, 'The Cricketer' by W. Hunt, 'The Oval in 1849' by C.J. Basébe, 'The Long Room at Lord's' by Dennis Flanders and 'Cricket at Phoenix Park, Dublin' by John Powell provide a good cross-section of this work.

Cricket art, however, has reached most people, and done so most happily, through engravings. The best known of the early prints is 'Cricket on the Artillery Ground, Finsbury' (1743), engraved on copper by Benoist after a painting by Francis Hayman, one of the series he and Hogarth executed for Vauxhall Gardens. It is said that the wicket-keeper in the scene is, in fact, Hogarth. This print has remained popular for two centuries. Another well-known eighteenth-century engraving first appeared in *The Sporting Magazine* in 1793 with the title 'Grand Cricket Match played in Lord's Ground, Mary-le-bone, on 20th June and following day between the Earls of Winchilsea and Darnley for 1,000 guineas'. For many years, however, the most widely circulated cricket prints were those – in some cases near-copies of the Hayman engraving – that appeared on the broadsheet, or handker-chief, reproductions of the early codes of laws. Another popular work of the pre-1800 period was the – usually – coloured engraving of John Collet's painting 'Miss Wicket and Miss Trigger'.

In the period of the popularity of aquatints – roughly 1775 to 1825 – some characteristic work was done in that manner on the theme of cricket. In their time most of them were issued in both coloured and uncoloured versions, but nowadays they are generally found coloured, often by a later hand. Two of the best are rather naive – 'Cricket at White Conduit House: 1784', published by Bowles and Carver, and 'Ireland's Royal Gardens, Brighton', drawn by H. Jones and engraved by G. Hunt, which was one of the plates in Sicklemore's *Views of Brighton* (1827). 'North-east View of the Cricket Grounds at Darnall, near Sheffield, Yorkshire', after Robert Cruikshank and R.J. Thompson, and Pollard's 'Cricket Match' are genuine cricket pictures; but, in most of the others, like 'Salvadore House Academy, Tooting' (F. Jukes after J. Walker), 'Laytonstone Academy, Essex' (J. Merigot after T. Atkins), 'Rugby School' and 'Hackney School', both by R. Reeve, and those in the Ackermann books, the game is incidental. A famous colour print of the same period is by Thomas Rowlandson – 'Rural Sports' (1811) – of a match between elevan women of Hampshire and eleven of Surrey. It is drawn in Rowlandson's characteristic fashion, accurately observed, and with robust humour. The cricketer may say it is not *seriously* a cricket picture; the art critic would counter that it is good Rowlandson and that good Rowlandson is by artistic standards very good indeed.

The most popular cricket print of any age was issued by the Brighton publisher and cricketer W.H. Mason. It is titled 'A Cricket Match between the Counties of Sussex and Kent, at Brighton'. Announced in 1843, it was first published in 1849 and reprinted from the original copper-plate thirty years later. Each of the eight-guinea subscribers received a 24-page prospectus and key which is now one of the major rarities of cricket-collecting. The title-page of the prospectus described the picture as 'Introducing characteristic portraits of players engaged in the match as well as many Noblemen and Gentlemen, Patrons of the Noble Game of Cricket'. It continued: 'The Portraits are all taken from life by Mr W. Drummond and Mr C.J. Basébe: engraved by G.H. Phillips.' Prices were: prints three guineas, proofs six guineas, artists' proofs (upon Indian paper) eight guineas. The players represented never appeared together in a Sussex–Kent match, though all of them took part in the fixture between 1849 and 1851. It is, in fact, a fine collection of portraits of seventy-one of the main figures of the game at that time, and it was finely executed. Despite its popularity it was almost the ruin of the unhappy Mason. During the thirty years the plate lay idle, the picture was constantly 'pirated', copied, misattributed and wrongly described, but it was, meanwhile, becoming the best known of all cricket prints – and still is to be met with in cricket pavilions all over the world. Though the original – Mason – plate was engraved on copper, its most attractive form probably is the 'pirated' lithograph – found both coloured and uncoloured – by S. Lipschitz. The unmistakable difference between the two versions is that, in the original, there is a central gap between the foreground figures; in the Lipschitz version, with no loss of artistic quality, the gap is closed. The engraved surface of the Mason is 42 by 30 inches; of the Lipschitz, 23½ by 17¾ inches.

The great period of cricket art undoubtedly was the middle of the nineteenth century when the technique of lithography had been mastered. The output of cricket lithographs consists of less than a hundred, of teams and individual players. They are delicate, decorative, and contemporary judges considered the majority to be good likenesses. They continue to appreciate in value. The finest of them – probably the finest of 'pure' cricket art – are eight lithographs by G.F. Watts. Their titles are 'Play', 'Forward!', 'The Draw', 'The Cut', 'Leg

Half-Volley' and 'Leg Volley' – all drawn direct on to the stone by the artist – 'The Bowler' (Alfred Mynn) and 'The Batsman' (Fuller Pilch). 'Felix' (Nicholas Wanostrocht) is said to have been the model for the first five of the strokes and the Hon. Fred Ponsonby for 'Leg Volley'. Watts' pencil studies for these lithographs – six are in the possession of MCC – show, in several cases, the process of Watts' translation of Felix from a left-hand batsman to right-hand. They capture balanced movement and a quality of vibrant life quite magnificently.

Three major lithographs of the period are of team-groups. The rarest is 'The Two Elevens of the Town and University of Cambridge in 1847', drawn by Felix (Nicholas Wanostrocht); the other two are 'The Eleven of England Selected to contend in the Great Cricket Matches of the North for the year 1847', also by Felix, and 'The United All England Eleven' (*c*. 1852). All of them are carefully made portraits of the players, pleasing in their period fashion. The remainder of the group consists almost entirely of portraits of individual players, most of them by John Corbet Anderson. Virtually the only other artists credited are Felix, C.J. Basébe and W. Drummond. Anderson's warm line and delicate colouring lent itself perfectly to lithography and he invariably drew on the stone himself. The engraved surface of most of his portraits measures about 13 inches high by 9 inches; but the series called 'Sketches at Lord's' consists of twelve portraits, 7 inches high by 5 inches, which were issued in three sheets with four pictures on each.

Felix published the studies of G.F. Watts, who for a time was an evening pupil at Felix's school, and several others, some of which were from his own drawings, though a lithographer transferred them to stone. Apart from the two team groups, his most popular print was one of himself with Alfred Mynn. Felix was a prolific painter and did some work in oils. The three editions of his book *Felix on the Bat* were illustrated with different sets of lithographs. There is a considerable collection of his work, mostly in watercolour and ranging from self-portraits to views of cricket grounds, in the MCC collection at Lord's. Basébe, who also employed a lithographer, was responsible, too, for the series of eight sensitive aquatint portraits of players used to illustrate *Lillywhite's Hand Book of Cricket* and they were also sold separately; they now tend to be more rare than the lithos. He and Drummond were, of course, the artists employed by Mason on his 'Sussex and Kent' print.

Most of these lithographs can be come by with fair ease through the better print dealers – perhaps Hankey and Nixon are the least common. A few years ago their price was usually about ten shillings; nowadays ten pounds is sometimes asked. Originally they were undoubtedly issued plain – in a uniform sepia or yellowish shade – as well as coloured; now most of the plain prints have been coloured to meet taste and demand.

Immediately upon the heels of the lithographs came an even more widely distributed and popular series of cricket illustrations. No. 1 of *Vanity Fair* was published on 6 November 1868, as 'a weekly show of political, social and literary wares'. On 30 January 1869, it increased its price to sixpence and included its first 'full-page cartoon of an entirely novel character printed in chrome-lithography'. For some thirty years *Vanity Fair*, through its weekly cartoon and the – sometimes libellous – prose commentary which accompanied it, was an important ingredient of the British social and political scene. After 1900 its power waned, though it continued under its own name until 1913 and some reference books credit it with continuing to exist, after amalgamations and in changed forms, until 1929.

Selection as the subject of the *Vanity Fair* cartoon conferred a stamp of importance – sufficient importance to be publicly praised or attacked – and, since the choice was taken from all fields of activity and from all countries, cricketers were not portrayed very frequently. The first, of course, was W.G. Grace – in the issue of 9 June 1877. Between that date and August 1913, when E.W. Dillon, the captain of Kent, was selected, thirty-one cricketers were portrayed *as* cricketers in *Vanity Fair* cartoons: a rate of less than one a year. But some forty celebrities who had also played first-class or major public-school cricket, or held high office in the game – such as President of MCC – were included primarily for their eminence in some other field. C.B. Fry, for instance, was drawn as a runner; the Hon. Ivo Bligh, after he had become the Earl of Darnley, was shown in a city suit.

Only two of the cricketers *qua* cricketers – the Hon. Alfred Lyttelton and G.J. Bonnor – were drawn by the earliest and most savage of the *Vanity Fair* cartoonists – 'Ape' (Carlo Pellegrini). Most of them were done by 'Spy' (Sir Leslie Ward), but there were two by 'Stuff' and one each by AJS, OWL, WH, Lib and CG. The style of the drawings varies considerably between Ape's mischievously astute exaggerations and the mild near-portraiture of Spy and most of the other later artists. All, though, make gay and colourful contributions to the walls of a cricket pavilion or club. The earlier prints – from the paper's heyday of wide circulation (once even a 'third edition' in a week) – are relatively easy to come by; those post-1900 are not quite so simple to find. Once more, prices have risen. *Vanity Fair* cartoons in 1939 cost a shilling; now they are expensive.

In 1905 the Art Society published, in weekly parts and later in a bound edition under the title *The Empire's Cricketers*, a series of forty-eight drawings by A. Chevallier Tayler, with text by G.W. Beldam. The drawings, folio in size, are printed on dark grey paper and make heavy use of chinese white. They are not unpleasant but lack movement and character; nevertheless they enjoyed a period of popularity.

Cricket was sometimes employed as a vehicle of political satire by nineteenth-century caricaturists. But the first of the popular cricket cartoonists was the man who signed his work 'Rip'. His drawings can be found in the *Evening News Cricket Annual* (1897–1907), his own sporadic volumes called *Kricket Karicatures*, and a number of periodicals. The master of all this kind was Tom Webster who, shortly after the First World War, began to draw for the *Daily Mail* and continued with *Tom Webster's Annual* and for other papers until about 1960. Webster was an original, with a happy sense of humour and an inventive pencil, but he could sting. He spread his attention over most sports but produced some imperishable cricket drawings; his favourite cricket 'characters' – Percy Fender, Patsy Hendren, George Duckworth, Maurice Tate and Jack Hobbs – come sharply back into the memory as Webster drew them.

Arthur Mailey, the New South Wales and Australian Test leg-break bowler, ranged from oil-painting through charcoal portraits to caricature. Between 1920 and 1953 he published some half-dozen booklets of cartoons of cricketers of his time and the well-known separate drawing of Bradman. He illustrated his autobiography *10 for 66 and All That* with sketches simple, perceptive, evocative and humorous. Roy Ullyett, of the *Daily Express*, who also produces an annual volume of drawings, has followed Webster's method closely, and his 'Fred Trueman' is an awe-inspiringly funny creation.

The term cricketana covers a wide area, of broadsheets, postcards, posters, silver-work, pottery, trophies and other ephemera too varied to list. We may be concerned here largely with items of 'popular' or 'folk' art. Notable in this kind are the two large – 13-inch – coloured Staffordshire pottery figures of about 1855, usually said, though not on completely conclusive evidence, to represent Julius Caesar (Surrey) and George Parr (Notts). There is more certainty in describing a smaller figure as Thomas Box and a rather poor piece of modelling as W.G. Grace. There are, too, a number of rather sentimental Staffordshire pieces of children holding bats, or bowling. A Bow china figure of W.G. Grace is more sophisticated and there are numerous plates commemorating Grace's career. Two unusual items of some charm are 'Stevengraphs', one of Grace, the other entitled 'The First Over'. These small pictures, embroidered in coloured silk, were manufactured by T. Stevens of Coventry and had something of a vogue in the latter part of the nineteenth century. From the 1890s onwards many series of cigarette cards and trade cards have been issued, frequently in colour, depicting outstanding cricketers of the day. Since 1948 Miss Mary Mitchell Smith has been responsible for some firmly modelled pottery figures. For some years, too, the Royal Worcester factory made a limited number of bone china plates with a gilt border and reproductions of the signatures of the touring sides, with a special 'Ashes' plate bearing facsimile autographs of the Australian and English teams of 1953.

In 1941 Messrs B.T. Batsford Ltd published *The Noble Game of Cricket*, a large quarto book with a hundred reproductions, some coloured, of famous cricket paintings and prints, almost all of them of considerable significance, from the large collection of Sir Jeremiah Colman. Unfortunately the edition was limited to 150, only 100 of which were for sale, and copies have become hard to find and expensive when found. Happily, in 1955, the same firm produced *The Game of Cricket* with thirty-four reproductions of major cricket pictures, a distinguished essay by Sir Norman Birkett and notes on the illustrations by Miss Diana Rait Kerr. *Cricket* by Horace G. Hutchinson in the *Country Life* Library of Sport (1903) has 100 plates of sensitively chosen cricket pictures, and is usually described as the best illustrated book of its kind. *Green and White*, subtitled 'Fenner's Observed', consists of high-quality drawings and photographs of ten students of the Cambridge School of Art.

An exhibition of modern paintings under the title 'Play the Game' at Frost & Reed's Gallery in Bristol in 1976 showed some interesting developments in cricket pictures. Period-primitive portraits and team groups by Gerry Wright had a strong Victorian flavour. Roger Marsh showed some historically sensitive portraits taken from photographs. Strikingly strong, large oils full of action, by Rosemary Taylor, of modern player-groups captured much attention. Outstanding, though, was the work of Laurence Toynbee. He does not by any means confine himself to cricket; though a preponderance of his work is on sporting and outdoor subjects. He would want to be known as a painter with a liking for cricket. Neither is the quality of his work entirely even. He is, though, as highly accomplished a painter as any who has produced any bulk of work on cricket; and he ought to be collected by the cricketing establishments.

The greatest recent advance is among the photographers, inheriting directly from G.W. Beldam and the Devon-born Australian emigrant Herbert Fishwick, working with more sophisticated and advanced techniques; Patrick Eagar, Ken Kelly and Bruce Postle have, with high professional skill, illuminated the game in a way that has not been done before with the camera.

For the rest, reference to cricket pictures is largely through catalogues, such as *Catalogue of the Imperial Cricket Memorial Gallery, Lord's; MCC Catalogue 1912; Two Centuries of Cricket Art* (Graves Art Gallery, Sheffield, 1955); *Cricket Exhibition* (National Gallery of British Sport and Pastimes, 1953); and *Catalogue of the Collection at 'The Yorker'* (Whitbread & Co. Ltd, nd).

*Barclays World of Cricket (Collins Willow, 1980)*

# Cricket Images

*November* 1982. The illustration of cricket is a long-standing exercise, stretching back, now, for well over two hundred years.

By 1800 there were many cricket prints in existence. By 1850 artists as important as Thomas Rowlandson and G.F. Watts had turned their hands to it; and work in copper, aquatint and lithograph was available in some volume. Indeed, about 1850 a peak in cricket art was reached in the hand-coloured lithographs of, notably, C.J. Basébe, John Corbet Anderson and 'Felix' (Nicholas Wanostrocht, himself an outstanding player for Kent, the Gentlemen and Clarke's All-England XI).

Subsequently the popular journals of the day – especially the weekly *Cricket* – were responsible for many woodcut illustrations, mainly players' portraits, of varying quality but in many cases capable professional likenesses.

As the game increased in popularity its public needed the urgency of the photograph. Surely enough, in 1857, a certain Roger Fenton –

better known for his photographic reporting of the Crimean War – produced the first cricket 'action' photograph, of a match between the Royal Artillery and Hunsdonbury.

Fenton was fortunate in dealing with a club match which he could approach far more closely than a normal news photographer could come to, say, a Test match. Since the telescopic lens lay still in the future, the main chronicling photographs were often simply a wide view, encompassing crowd, field and background in such a perspective that the details of play and players were unidentifiable.

Nevertheless some extremely sharp and clear – though posed – portrait photographs were produced in the years up to the end of the century. Richard Daft's *Kings of Cricket* (1893) was illustrated with reproductions of lithographs, woodcuts, portrait and team photographs. Four years later, Ranjitsinhji's *Jubilee Book of Cricket* was generously illustrated with (posed) photographs by the monumentally prolific E. Hawkins of Brighton. Hawkins (& Co) took posed studies of virtually every first-class player who came to the Hove ground over a considerable period of the 1890s and up to the First World War. G.A. Copinger relates how, as a young man in the 1930s, he might have bought the entire store of the Hawkins plates for a few pounds. He had not enough money at the time, and returning with it later, he was told they had been sold – never, so far as anyone can ascertain, to be heard of again.

Meanwhile, G.W. – George – Beldam had appeared on the scene. He was a capable and, above all, thoughtfully analytical, all-round games player. As a cricketer for Middlesex he batted soundly enough to average 30.16 from 1900 until he lost form in 1907; and was an intelligent slow-medium bowler. He appeared several times for Gentlemen against Players and, at The Oval in 1903, played a decisive part in their win. A Corinthian soccer player, useful at golf and tennis, he virtually created the sporting action photograph. He had not the benefit of the long-range lens and worked close to his subjects in contrived situations. Nevertheless he did photograph them in motion. By using high shutter speeds and the fastest plates then available he was able to arrest the action. His main publications – all sub-titled 'Their Methods at a Glance' – were *Great Golfers* (1904: with 271 photographs); then *Great Batsmen* (1905: 600 photographs) and *Great Bowlers* (1906: 464 photographs), both in collaboration with C.B. Fry; followed by *Great Lawn Tennis Players* (1907: 198 photographs) with P.A. Vaile. The last of these four books includes matches in actual play taken at close quarters. Beldam's work was simultaneously so precise and so perceptive that it became possible for the first time to illustrate technique and to analyse it with certainty.

Those four major works are now extremely hard to come by but the slighter *Cricket Illustrated*, '60 Photographs by G.W. Beldam of famous cricketers in actual play', is more readily and cheaply to be found. So, too, is *Golf Faults Illustrated* (a useful stroke of gamesmanship if planted at the bedside of a guest staying for a golfing weekend).

His best-known study is probably that of Victor Trumper jumping out to drive; but others, notably of Ranjitsinhji – also available in large sepia prints, signed by subject and photographer – are extremely desirable items of cricketana.

Beldam was limited only by his equipment; and he was not excelled in the field of cricket until the long-range lens gave his successors an advantage he never enjoyed.

The first important name in that development is Herbert Fishwick: born in Barnstaple, he was taken to Australia when his father emigrated, and grew up there. At some point shortly after 1918 he went to England on a visit from which he returned with a long-range lens, and was one of the first to recognize and exploit its possibilities. Fishwick was a general rather than a specialist cricket photographer; he covered the visit of the Fleet to Australia as well as Test matches. His career in cricket was relatively short; but his work on the Australia–England series of 1924–25 and 1928–29 was outstanding. He produced one of the classics of the cricket gallery – Hammond leaning after his mighty cover-drive, spotted handkerchief protruding from pocket, all smooth, purposeful power.

The names of many of Fishwick's skilful successors are lost in the anonymity of acknowledgement to Australian News and Information Bureau, Keystone Press Agency or, in England, Central Press and Sport & General. One of the major performances in cricket photography was that of Ken Saunders and Brian Thomas of Sport & General, who between them caught and preserved every one of Jim Laker's nineteen wickets in the Old Trafford Test in 1956.

One who, however, became well known was Denis Oulds, who worked for Central Press at major cricket matches in the 1930s and continued until the 1982 season. He and his vast 'long tom' were a part of the Test-match scene for many years and his work appeared not merely in newspapers but in many cricket books, especially in the post-war period.

Central Press and Sport & General were, of course, in an extremely strong position when, after the film 'war' of 1930, the Board of Control gave them a monopoly of photography at alternate Test matches. That was not broken until 1972, when professional photographers were allowed into the grounds and considerable competition developed.

The long-range cameras now became almost as great a handicap as they had once been a boon. The average man had considerable difficulty in transporting a 'long tom' and even the fifty plates which were generally regarded as his day's ration – and, therefore, his maximum output. Indeed, in the famous Australia–West Indies tied Test of 1960–61 at Brisbane, the last two photographers with plates left – Ron Lovitt of *The Age* and Harry Martin of the *Sydney Morning Herald* – at the end of that amazingly tense day, had to plan to divide their remaining plates to share the last ball – and what happened to it – to ensure a complete photographic record of a unique occasion.

That same Harry Martin is regarded as the finest Australian of his time in this field: the true successor of Herbert Fishwick. It has been said that many of the younger men had their eyes not on the play but on Martin, and when he pressed they pressed.

The big camera is being superseded; the remainder of the photographers miss Denis Oulds personally in his retirement; but they are grateful for the resultant spare space. It is possible nowadays to use as many as six different small motor-driven camera bodies loaded with different films (as Patrick Eagar does). Converters, in fact, render the larger focal length lenses completely unnecessary. It is possible, too, to take the action from two completely different angles by remote control. Meanwhile black and white and colour pictures may be shot simultaneously by electric linking.

Ken Kelly is one of today's old hands; Yorkshire-born, Midlands-based, but fairly ubiquitous, industrious and conscientious, he has a nose and an eye for a cricketing picture story.

It would be a sorry mistake to label Patrick Eagar a young photographer: he took his first professional photograph in 1965 while still at University. At thirty-eight, he is in full stride, and feels he is still learning. Already, though, he has added a new – but splendid – dimension to cricket photography.

His first book was *An Eye for Cricket* (1979); that was followed by *A Summer to Remember* (1981), an account of the England–Australia series of that year, with text by Alan Ross. Now comes *Test Decade 1972–1982* (World's Work), a generous quarto. There is a neat, perceptive, accompanying account by Graeme Wright, but the 219 pages are preponderantly a pictorial record – in colour, and black and white – of many splendid moments of the Test matches in those ten years of all the Test-playing countries in England, Australia, West Indies, India and Pakistan. This is the work not merely of a sensitive photographer – Patrick Eagar has revealed that aspect in other fields as far apart as vineyards and war – but of one attuned and timed to the game of cricket. He has, in short, the knack of waiting long enough – but not too long – for the exactly right picture.

The value of his equipment (he invented his own long-distance control) is considerable. Having once persuaded him, against his conscience, to a glass of wine in the members' bar at Lord's, and seeing a wicket fall, the only possible response was, 'Oh, Patrick, I *am* sorry – I cost you that photograph.'

'Oh no you didn't – I got it twice.'

'What do you mean?'

'With this.' Opening the palm of his hand to show a miniature electronic device, he said with that widely happy smile, 'I took it from the top pavilion balcony and beside the scoreboard – but, before the next batsman comes in, I will get back to the balcony.' He often laments having missed so many good lunches – and after-lunch drinks – through his need to be by his camera. Yet he rarely misses a ball. *Test Decade* is evidence of that fact; but also of much more. Ponder the picture on the front of the dust-wrapper. It tells a complete technical story in the single moment it captures. Again and again, too, the character of a cricketer emerges, not merely in his facial expression, but in his spontaneous playing reaction to a situation. The spectacular, the humorous, the contemplative, the violent, the warmly human, and the stark: all are caught here in a lens capable of recording at a greater speed than the eye can attain – in the right hands, that is.

*Wisden Cricket Monthly*

# −12−

# Cricket Writers and Books

## How to Build a Cricket Library
### (Part 1)

*November* 1964. Cricket has one of the richest literatures – arguably *the* richest – of British sport. Yet, often the invitation from a good friend and cricketer to 'come and see my cricket library' strains tact to the limit. Again and again the 'library' consists of 'ghosted', so-called autobiographies of famous players, books so distressingly alike in matter, illustration and style of writing that, merely by changing 'I' to 'he' and vice versa, whole chapters could be interchanged between them without anyone noticing the difference, for almost invariably they have been collected from identical news reports and reference books.

The Editor has suggested that, in this and the next two issues of *The Cricketer*, I should offer a few notes to the enthusiast who wants to build a collection of cricket books or extend the scope and interest of an existing collection. These notes, however, are only suggestions. A collection – of anything – is personal, made by the collector's inclination, not according to outside dictation. But where a collection of books is limited, it may be so for one of three reasons:

1 that the collector wants it so limited;
2 that he does not know of the existence of other books;
3 that he does not know how to find the other books.

In the first case, any advice would be presumptuous. The second and third cases are quite widespread. They stem from the assumption that 'books' are *new* books. This is by no means so. For every cricket book now in print and obtainable new, at least a hundred are out of print; but the one is by no means necessarily better than the hundred.

Virtually any second-hand bookshop has a row of books on cricket –

half a dozen of them forecastable to be found anywhere, the best-sellers of old: not necessarily bad books – often, indeed, good – but common because so many copies were printed. But some book dealers have specialized in cricket books, notably at present Epworth Second-hand Books, whose manager, Mr L.E.S. Gutteridge, is also the vice-chairman of the Cricket Society. Their catalogues – often listing several hundred different titles – are informative as well as tempting.

The aim of these essays is to suggest a few books – a dozen to twenty – varied enough to help the new collector discover the direction he favours, for to collect *all* cricket books would face him with a target of some eight thousand titles, demanding a deep pocket – and a lifetime of searching.

My first title is simply *Cricket* – a small book, by Neville Cardus, which Longmans Green published in 1930. In less than two hundred pages it gives a perspective of cricket from earliest to modern times, catching tradition and character, its depth, its differing facets, its pleasures. Any man who reads it must enjoy the game a little – or a lot – more. In fact, Neville Cardus, apart from reporting cricket suberbly, has also increased people's pleasure in the game to a greater extent than any other writer. Reading his other books usually follows automatically.

For those who prefer their cricket more practical we may turn to one of the game's sternest realists – Sir Donald Bradman – noting, as we do, the mutual respect which exists between him and Neville Cardus. Sir Donald's *The Art of Cricket* is the finest analysis of modern techniques, astutely argued and demonstrated from first-hand and top-level experience, superbly illustrated. At one point Sir Donald writes: 'Every prospective international captain should be an avid reader. . . . It is astonishing how many great players make no attempt to enlarge their knowledge. They are the losers.' Certainly the best of them could profit from reading *The Art of Cricket*.

*The Brighter Side of Cricket* is by R.C. Robertson-Glasgow, a fast-medium bowler with Oxford University and Somerset, and a witty and observant match reporter of the game, whose two books *Cricket Prints* and *More Cricket Prints* are perceptive and evocative biographical sketches of two generations of great players. *The Brighter Side*, illustrated by A. Savory, is uproariously, yet always humanly, funny – 'Crusoe' does not make fun of cricket, but *reveals* its humour.

The first cricket classic was *The Young Cricketer's Tutor* by John Nyren, 'Collected and Edited' by Charles Cowden Clarke and published in 1826. The first edition is not quite so rare as it might be but it is usually an expensive – £10 – item. Fortunately it has been so often reprinted that it is easy to pick up some edition or another of it. The really important part of the *Tutor* is its second half, called 'The Cricketers of My Time', in which Nyren recalls the great players of Hambledon in a series of studies at once shrewd and poetic, which bring those men to vivid life across two centuries. This is arguably the finest passage written about any game in the English language. The best edition, in which it is all reprinted, with illuminating additions and some charming links by that fine essayist and genuine cricket enthusiast E.V. Lucas, is called *The Hambledon Men*.

Anyone who has read these four books will, I fancy, recognize the truth of the first sentence of this essay.

*The Cricketer*

# How to Build a Cricket Library
## (Part 2)

*December* 1964.   Any 'foundation' collection of cricket books, such as these notes describe, ought to include one title from each kind of cricket writing, and merely to find how many books that involves demonstrates the great extent of the literature of the game.

Our first batch included no major history so we may lead off here with the Altham and Swanton *A History of Cricket*. It originally appeared in 1926 as a single volume by H.S. Altham covering the subject up to 1925, a book of impressive vision, proportion and perspective. In subsequent editions, E.W. Swanton provided additions to keep it up to date, but the modern spread of the game and its many different levels meant that this could be only a makeshift method. So, in 1963, the *History* reappeared in two volumes, the first *From the Beginnings to the First World War* by H.S. Altham, the second *From the First World War to the Present Day*, by E.W. Swanton. No other book challenges it in its field: it makes absorbing reading and affords unique reference, and each volume contains an excellent book list for its period.

The good cricket library would contain two contrasting companions to the *History*. The first, *Cricket Highways and Byways*, is less ambitious in scope but it must rank among the best of cricket study. It is a collection of the essays of F.S. Ashley-Cooper, probably cricket's most distinguished annalist. Many of his books of statistics were issued in limited editions and are now rare; but this book, and his history of Nottinghamshire cricket, show the extent of his scholarship and the gentle ease of his style.

The second companion to the *History* would be *The Book of Cricket Records* by the late Roy Webber, or the shorter version of it called *The Concise Book of Cricket Records* since brought up to date by his former collaborator, Michael Fordham. This is quite the best modern collection of statistics.

Here, it should be said that it might be regarded as cheating to include *Wisden* in our short list of titles, but its 101 annual volumes afford the fullest chronicling any game has ever known.

In the field of fiction, one book stands alone. *The Cricket Match*, by Hugh de Sélincourt, is an admirably rounded piece of writing by purely literary standards; for the cricketer, its constant sounding of the right note gives it added importance. Mr de Sélincourt wrote several other cricket books, some of them quite amusing but none of the stature of *The Cricket Match*. *The Son of Grief* by Dudley Carew is a somewhat harsh but compelling novel; and the two titles – of an intended trilogy – by William Godfrey are the best modern fictional writing on the game.

There are, of course, hundreds of life-stories of great players, many of them compiled by 'ghost' writers of no great literary distinction and often with little technical knowledge. There are, however, a few outstanding contributions to the section of genuine autobiography from which, if we are to take only one, we might select *10 for 66 and All That* by Arthur Mailey, the Australian leg-break bowler. It is a wise, amusing, modest and, sometimes, surprising book, delightfully illustrated by Mailey's own witty drawings.

Among biographies there is none better than *W.G. Grace*, a physically slight book by one of the most graceful of all sporting writers, Bernard Darwin, better known, of course, in the sphere of golf but here equally at home with cricket, giving his subject due dignity, humanity and significance in a polished piece of writing.

*Kings of Cricket by* Richard Daft is something of a source-book for students of the unique mid-Victorian period, with some rich anecdotes; but it contains, as preface, a long essay by Andrew Lang which is often, and with good reason, described as the finest appreciation of cricket ever written.

To complete this budget with a technical book, the choice must be *The MCC Coaching Book*. The result of the thinking, and re-thinking, of a group of good players and analysts of the game, it first appeared in 1952 and at once towered high over all previous instructional books. It has since been revised and the photographs have been brought up to date in that later players are included. On the subject of how to play, 'The MCC Book' will, surely, remain the classic.

None of these titles should prove difficult to find. Perhaps *Cricket Highways and Byways* will prove the rarest, for it is doubtful if many copies were issued, but it can usually be run to ground in some good catalogue or other. Darwin's *W.G. Grace* – in the 'Great Lives' series – is liable to pop up in any second-hand bookshop, and *Kings of Cricket*, though old, was something of a best-seller in its day and is quite easy to come by.

*The Cricketer*

# How to Build a Cricket Library
## (Part 3)

*January* 1965.   Eight more titles will round off this little basic cricket library with a total of twenty books – enough, and varied enough, for the collector to decide on the direction of his subsequent buying.

*Australian Cricket* by the late A.G. – Johnnie – Moyes rounded off his studies of the game in his own country with a major work. It is amazing that the subject was never truly tackled until so late as 1959, but that fact does bring a considerable bulk of information and reference in good order within a single cover; and it must belong in any proportioned library of the game.

As an important aspect of cricket history, and to give an example of the work of one of the game's most important figures and writers, we may choose *Lord's 1787–1945* in which Sir Pelham Warner, out of his long experience – he was 'chaired' off the ground at Lord's in 1890 – and patient research, wrote with feeling about the place which was his spiritual home. It is a handsomely produced and authoritative book.

*They Made Cricket* is one of the books of the poet, critic and researcher G.D. Martineau, in which the major developments in the game and the people responsible for them are set in perspective. It is a charmingly readable view of history and change.

*Beyond a Boundary* by the West Indian C.L.R. James is a book of great sweep and depth. It is partly autobiographical, partly history – particularly of West Indian cricket – partly appreciation. Its essential theme, however, is 'What do they know of cricket who only cricket know?' and it places the game in a setting of art, philosophy, social history and wider consciousness. In the intellectual sense, it is quite the 'biggest' book about cricket or, probably, any other game, ever written.

Australian cricket has not produced so many books as English, but they have been of uniformly high standard. *Between Wickets* was the first published book of Ray Robinson, who has brought the building of composite portraits of outstanding players to an extremely high level. *From the Boundary* and *The Happy Season* (called *Green Sprigs* in Australia) follow the same method equally happily.

*Masters of Cricket* is a somewhat similar book by J.H Fingleton, the former Australian Test player and a professional journalist. He has written several books, many on tours, but also giving his views on the modern game. His writing is technically informed and penetrative, and he has a good sense of narrative with a strongly flowing style.

There have been many cricket picture books, of widely different kinds. The most ambitious is *The Noble Game* which, however, was issued in a limited edition of 150 copies and only 100 of them were for sale, so that – when it is to be found at all – it now fetches £40 to £50. More recently, however, many of the best pictures of that earlier book and others from the MCC collection were reproduced in *The Game of Cricket*, with a long and characteristically urbane essay on the game by Sir Norman Birkett and scholarly notes on the pictures by Miss Diana Rait Kerr.

With one title left, the choice must be a symposium – *The Cricketer's Companion* in which Alan Ross brought together a considerable bulk – 548 pages – of the best writing on the game from all periods and in all kinds – history, fiction, poetry and profiles in a handsomely produced and decorated book. In addition to being a delightful bedside book, it will set the reader off on countless trails of other books and authors.

So much for the twenty books on which the new collector might base a collection. Every other collector would list a different twenty. But if these will not do for everyone they will at least do to argue about. Happily, too, every year brings at least one, sometimes more, fresh candidates for the list. When the Cricket Society utters its bibliography of cricket there will probably be some seven thousand titles in it, enough to show the extent – and the hopelessness – of a complete collection!

*The Cricketer*

# Introduction to
## *The Young Cricketer's Tutor*

A single word is enough for the unassailable classics – 'Pickwick', 'Hoyle', 'Bovary', 'Aubrey', 'Jude', 'Selborne', 'Whitaker', 'Gulliver', 'Romeo'. So, although the title page of *The Young Cricketer's Tutor* by John Nyren runs to twenty-three lines, it is known simply as 'Nyren'.

This is the enduring work of cricket literature. Before it was published – in 1833 – the few cricket books had been of scores or elementary instruction. After it, nothing of comparable imaginative or literary standing was written on the game until Sir Neville Cardus's early reports in the 1920s. It is arguable that there is no more evocative writing in English about any sport. Yet Nyren has from time to time been allowed to fall out of print, and has not now been generally available since the limited edition of 1948.

Crucially, it has the validity of true literature in the accuracy of observation, sensitivity of feeling and sympathy of expression which makes the Hambledon village cricketers of the eighteenth century credible and relishable human beings in the twentieth – even for a reader with no knowledge of cricket.

It is surprising to find such qualities in a book which is padded – yet still physically slight – hybrid, and 'ghosted'. The first edition, even with its verbatim printing of the Laws, rambling index and list of MCC members, ran to only 126 pages of small octavo. It falls into two separate halves: the first, though unusual for its early date, is no more than simple – if often illuminating – technical advice to boys aspiring to play this game; the second, upon which its reputation rests, is the series of sketches entitled 'The Cricketers of My Time' which had already

appeared as feature articles in *The Examiner* during 1832. According to
the Introduction they were 'collected at the desire of a few friends and
published here'. It is impossible now to know how the *Tutor* was
originally envisaged: whether as an instruction manual – on the lines of
Boxall's earlier and successful booklet – bulked out by reprinting the
reminiscences; or as the 12,000 words of recollection filled out by as
much again of 'how to play'.

The title page modifies 'by John Nyren' with 'The Whole collected
and edited by Charles Cowden Clarke'. Nyren had an almost unique
knowledge of Hambledon cricket. His father, Richard, was captain of
the club during its formative and finest period, and John himself grew
up among its players to become one of them.

The son was a keen and knowledgeable, but not a great, cricketer.
He was only fourteen in 1778 when he joined the hired players of
Hambledon as 'a sort of farmer's pony'. He remained there until 1791,
the end of the club's great days, when the family went to London. He
was a left-handed batsman and considered a brave and good field at
point or mid-wicket. On his first recorded appearance he was the
highest scorer in a match between 'Five of Hambledon and Five of
West Kent (with Minshull)' in which the other nine players were all
outstanding performers. He certainly played in two eleven-a-side
matches for Hambledon and possibly in two others – where the
omission of initials renders it unclear whether 'Nyren' is John or his
father – without making any appreciable score. After he went to
London he played in some thirty matches – generally for Homerton,
though once for England against Surrey – important enough for the
scores to have survived, and, by the standards of the time, often batted
valuably.

Clarke, in the second edition of the *Tutor*, described him as

'a remarkably well-grown man, standing nearly six feet, of large
proportions throughout, big-boned, strong and active. He had a
bald, bullet head, a prominent forehead, small features and little
sunken eyes. His smile was as sincere as an infant's. If there were
any deception in him, Nature herself was to blame in giving him
those insignificant shrouded eyes. They made no *show* of
observation, but they were perfect ministers to their master. Not
a thing, not a motion escaped them in a company, however
numerous. My old friend was a "good Catholic": I mean "good"
in the true sense of the word, for a more single- and gentle-

hearted yet thoroughly manly man I never knew. He possessed an instinctive admiration of everything good and tasteful both in nature and art. He scarcely ever spoke of himself and this modesty will be observed throughout his little Book. He had not a spark of envy; and, like all men of real talent, he always spoke in terms of honest admiration of the merits of others.'

Leigh Hunt, in his review of the *Tutor*, wrote: 'He is still a sort of youth at seventy, hale and vigorous and with a merry twinkle of his eye, in spite of an accident some years ago – a fall – that would have shattered most men of his age to pieces.'

Nyren made friends easily; he found it less easy to make money. He was a calico printer, at one time in a substantial way of business, but he never recovered financially after his factory was burnt down. He died on 28 June 1837 in the old royal palace at Bromley-by-Bow, in Middlesex, where he had been living with his son and where he walked in the garden on the last morning of his life.

Charles Cowden Clarke (1787–1877) was a well-known literary lecturer, critic and essayist, notably a student and – in the best sense – popularizer of Shakespeare. The son of a schoolmaster, at fifteen years old he taught the much younger John Keats, then a pupil at his father's school and who later wrote his appreciative 'Epistle to Charles Cowden Clarke'. After his father's death he set up in London as a bookseller and publisher and became friendly with Leigh Hunt – through whom he met Charles and Mary Lamb, Shelley, Hazlitt – and the musician Vincent Novello. He made a notably happy marriage with Novello's daughter Mary – who compiled the well-known *Concordance* to Shakespeare's plays – went into partnership in publishing with his son, and met the musically inclined Richard Nyren. Clarke became an outstandingly successful lecturer and public reader, and a faithful and perceptive editor – of most of the major English poets – before he retired first to Nice and then to Genoa, where he died in 1877.

Nyren was sixty-seven when he recalled the cricket and cricketers of his youth and early manhood within Clarke's hearing. Whether the quality of the *Tutor* stems from the original speech or the subsequent editing cannot be known. Certainly both wrote independently – Clarke widely, Nyren in Leigh Hunt's *London Journal* – without approaching the excellence of 'The Cricketers of My Time'. In the preface to the second edition of the *Tutor*, published after Nyren's death, Clarke called him 'the amiable Father' of it and said it was 'compiled from unconnected scraps and reminiscences during conversation concerning his old playmates'. The result, though, has a greater unity than any 'scraps', and, as must be important, if not conclusive, Clarke was unable to invest the instructional part of the book with the vivid evocation of the player-sketches.

It is easy enough to detect Clarke's 'scholarly' approach in the quotations from the Saxon and from Strutt, in the first couple of paragraphs of 'The Cricketers of My Time', but that past, the collaboration achieves complete fusion of matter and style.

Clarke's feelings about Nyren's modesty and generosity are borne out in his book; and whatever share Clarke may have had in writing it, only Nyren could have contributed the subject matter. The 'innovation of throwing instead of bowling' which provoked his indignation was the so-called 'March of Intellect system' – roundarm bowling. Until 1835 the ball had to be bowled from below the elbow. In that year the law was altered to 'below the shoulder', despite the opposition of the older generation, many of whom never became reconciled to it. This change, perhaps the most technically important in the history of the game, resulted from the efforts first of John Willes and, finally, the performances of the two Sussex roundarm bowlers William Lillywhite and James Broadbridge, in the 'Experimental Matches' of 1827.

When the *Tutor* first appeared, the Hambledon cricketers and their opponents were mostly dead and all but forgotten. Nyren's sketches gave them and their club a degree of immortality unusual in any sport. The impact of his descriptions led some subsequent writers to call Hambledon 'the birthplace of cricket' or 'the cradle of cricket' when, in fact, it was neither. The game was earlier and more strongly established in Kent, Sussex, Surrey and London than in Hampshire. Such towns and villages as Addington, Mitcham, Slindon, Henfield, Dartford and Chertsey had flourishing teams before the Hambledon club was founded – at some time between 1750 and 1760. It did not at once become established – its major successes were achieved between 1763 and 1787 – and by 1793 fashion had carried the Grand Matches away from the bare hills of the Meon Valley to London; and the club simply expired.

At Hambledon cricket first reached maturity, through straight bat strokes, length bowling and highly organized fielding. These were not new ideas; but 'Old' John Small, the Petersfield cobbler – who 'found out cricket' – was the first orthodox batsman. His shop sign read:

> Here lives John Small
> Makes bat and ball
> Pitch a wicket, play at cricket
> With any man in England

– and he fashioned a straight-sided and shouldered bat to play straight down the line of the ball. David Harris was coached by Richard Nyren to bowl with such accuracy that he is said once to have delivered 170 balls to Tom Walker for one run. The sides of Windmill Down, the club's second ground, sloped so steeply away from the wicket that only outstanding and immaculately placed fieldsmen could prevent attacking strokes from piercing the field and racing away to the bottom of the slope (there were no boundaries then: all strokes had to be run out).

Hambledon cricket is a phenomenon within the history of the game. Until its time cricket had been growing from a children's play to one for the poor – first of the country and then of the cities – to a diversion which wealthy patrons – some of whom played, while others merely wagered on the result – staged on their private estates. Now a group of gentlemen formed a club in the unlikely setting of Broad Halfpenny Down, a bleak hill some two miles out of Hambledon, the Bat and Ball Inn the only building near it.

It is generally accepted that the Reverend Charles Powlett – son of the 3rd Duke of Bolton by Lavinia Fenton ('Polly Peacham') – vicar of Itchen Abbas, founded the club. Prominent members and backers were the Earl of Winchilsea, Philip Dehany, Jervoise Clark Jervoise, the Hon. Charles Lennox (later 4th Duke of Richmond) and Henry Bonham.

The gentlemen members paid a subscription of three guineas a year. They were accommodated for lunch and sometimes dinner – on meetings and match days – by Richard Nyren – secretary of the club, captain and master tactician of the team, and father figure to the players, landlord first of the Bat and Ball Inn and then the George down in the village.

The most remarkable historic coincidence of Hambledon cricket was the simultaneous emergence of so many outstanding cricketers among the countrymen – small farmers, cobblers, carpenters, builders, gamekeepers and potters – of so small an area. Some of them, like Beldham, Francis and the Wells brothers, came from Farnham, and the Walkers from Churt, all on the Hampshire edge of Surrey; while Noah Mann and Barber were Sussex men. The majority, however, came from Hampshire: most lived and were buried in Hambledon, Catherington or Petersfield, or in the even smaller Alresford–Ropley–Bishop's Sutton area.

Nyren ends his memories by naming the best Hambledon team of the great period with the comment, 'No eleven in England could have stood against these men; and I think they might have beaten any two-and-twenty.' In 1772 they did, in fact, beat twenty-two of England at Moulsey Hurst.

Their cricket was clearly recognizable as the game played today, though with some marked differences. Bowling was all underarm – nevertheless it could be extremely fast – and batting tended to be statuesque. The third stump was introduced – only gradually, for sporting fashion changed slowly in those times – from 1775, after 'Lumpy' three times bowled through the gap in John Small's two-stump wicket at a crucial stage of a match between 'Five of the Hambledon Club and Five of All England'. The players wore leather shoes, stockings and silk breeches. 'You would see a bump heave under the stocking and even the blood come through: I saw John Wells tear a finger-nail off against his shoe buckle in picking up a ball' said Beldham. They played in sky-blue coats with black velvet collars – the letters CC (Cricketing Club) engraved on their buttons – and in the early days velvet caps, but when they were engaged by Lord Winchilsea, silver-laced hats.

It is clear that this team appeared under various names. They are sometimes called Hambledon and at others – usually when Beldham, Mann and Francis were not included – Hampshire; or in the colours of patrons.

A minute of 1788 runs: 'Ordered that the Players who are Paid for Practising on Windmill Down are hereby forbidden to engage themselves to play in any County or other great Matches without the Permission of the Stewards of the Hambledon Club unless such Players shall be desired to Play for the Duke of Dorset, Sir Horace Mann or any member of the Hambledon Club. Ordered that Nyren do acquaint the Players who give in their names to play in the County Eleven with the above order.' The specific reference to 'County Eleven' confirms that the titles 'Hambledon' and 'Hampshire' were virtually inter-changeable; though it does not detract from the achievement of the Hambledon club in mustering such a corps of cricketers. This minute was a clear indication that London – effectively Lord's, although MCC was in only its second year – was already exerting attraction to the leading players.

In 1923 the club's manuscript minute book and account book covering the period 1772 to 1796 were made available for publication. They show the simple, near-feudal economics of the club. The waiter – named in six variations of Hunstead – was given a black hat and paid five shillings a day. Members' dinners cost two shillings – ten with wine – port was two shillings a bottle, sherry three; the Windmill Down ground was rented from farmer Garret for £10 a year.

Crowds were large and enthusiastic. (In 1772, when Hambledon played England at Bishopsbourne, the *Kentish Gazette* reported an attendance of 15,000 to 20,000.) Stakes were huge. Nyren says that Hambledon generally played England for five hundred guineas; but they undertook some matches for as much as one thousand guineas – vast sums for those times – with invariably high side stakes. Nyren estimated that between 1772 and 1781 the club had fifty-one matches against England and won twenty-nine of them. F.S. Ashley-Cooper, the eminent early student of cricket history, calculated that on the minimal basis of published reports, Hambledon won £22,497 and lost £10,030 – exclusive of side-betting – on those games.

Against this spendthrift background, the player's pay was abject. For a one-day practice game – which for the Farnham players meant a return ride of fifty-four miles – they were paid 'four shillings if winners and three shillings if losers'. Before an away match, the club advanced one guinea for the entire team, presumably for their accommodation. When they returned, the account books show they were paid between seven and nine shillings a man for a three- or four-day match. A few years afterwards, at the beginning of the new century, when the best of the surviving Hambledon players were engaged in London, they expected – for wager matches, as almost all of them were – £5 if they won, £3 when they lost.

They also may have been tipped by successful backers, and probably sometimes backed themselves to win. Nevertheless, the ludicrous discrepancy between their match-payment and the amounts they were winning for their 'patrons' could only appear an invitation to take a separate profit; and so it proved. Nyren could write:

'No thought of treachery ever seemed to have entered their heads. The modern politics of trickery and "crossing" were (so far as my own experience and judgement of their actions extended) as yet a "sealed book" to the Hambledonians; what they did, they did for the love of honour and victory; and when one (who shall be nameless) sold the birthright of his good name for a mess of pottage, he paid dearly for his bargain. It cost him the trouble of being a knave – (no trifle); the esteem of his old friends, and, what was worst of all, the respect of him who could have been his best friend – himself.'

There was not, however, only one man involved. The bookmakers – who were making as much as the backers – searched out the raw young countrymen in 'The Green Man and Still' in Oxford Street, where the professionals stayed when they were in London – though their pay could barely compass its prices. In his old age, 'Silver Billy' Beldham recalled playing in a strong Surrey side which seemed to have a match against All England well in hand, when he discovered the bookmakers were laying seven to four against them. 'This time, though,' he said, 'they lost: they laid in the belief that some Surrey men had sold the match; but then Surrey played to win.'

This was a ludicrous situation and it came to its inevitable conclusion in 1817. Lambert – the finest all-round cricketer of the period – and one of his associates began to quarrel outside the pavilion windows at Lord's, each blaming the other for 'selling' matches. Their allegations fitted so closely with the events – especially the then recent and amazing defeat of England by Nottinghamshire – that the listening MCC members called them into the committee room. There they continued, in high anger, to make such convincing accusations of corruption against one another that MCC could do no other than ban them from the first-class game for the rest of their lives. At the same time bookmakers and betting were also barred from cricket grounds.

That event lay far into the future from Hambledon's great days. Their cricket then seemed a mixture of the convivial, epic and idyllic. The social side was a major aspect of club activity for the members. In 1772 Winchester, Salisbury and London newspapers carried the advertisement: 'The Gents of Broadhalfpenny Cricket Club are desired to meet at Dick Nyren's at the George at Hambledon on Saturday the 7th November on Special Business. N.B. Dinner on Table at 3 o'clock.'

At the front of the earliest surviving minute book there is a list of:

Standing Toasts

1 The Queen's Mother
2 The King
3 Hambledon Club

4 Cricket
5 To the Immortal Memory of Madge
6 The President

All is admirably terse and obvious except 'Madge', which gave rise to much airy and inaccurate speculation until a diligent researcher discovered, in Grose's eighteenth-century *Dictionary of the Vulgar Tongue*, that it meant 'the private parts of a woman'.

The records show a faithful observance of that line of the club song which runs: 'He's best who drinks most.' A wine cistern was one of the first amenities installed on Windmill Down. The classic entry in the minute book runs: 'A wet day: only three members present: nine bottles of wine'. Although the members bought their port and sherry, the table wines were generally contributed. When William Barber was landlord of the Bat and Ball he was allowed a corkage charge of 'sixpence per bottle for drinking the club wine'.

'September the fifth 1782 – An Extra Meeting to Eat Venison & Drink Bonhams and Fitzherberts Claret.'

By a decision of 1774, 'If any dispute shall arise among members, should they not be silent after being desired to wave the subject of conversation by the President, the Gentlemen so disputing shall forfeit one dozen of claret to the club.' In 1795 it was decided 'on account of the high price of provisions the gentlemen present have thought proper to allow Nyren two shillings a head for each dinner instead of one'. Still the bill for forty-nine members was £39 4s – including wines. The President provided venison for the annual dinner; when J.C. Jervoise failed to do so in 1782 he was fined a buck.

The annual dinner which wound up the season apparently resulted in some accidents in the unlit countryside in 1790, for the following year the meeting 'ordered that the last meeting of the Hambledon Club be in future of a Moonlight night'.

The most historically important entry in the Hambledon minute book is not concerned with cricket. Late in the club's history – on 29 August 1796 as its last meeting but one – it is recorded that there were 'Three members and twelve non-subscribers (including Mr Thos Pain "Author of the Rights of Man") present. No business noted.'

This is a matter of some significance. It is not, I believe, elsewhere suggested that Tom Paine ever returned to England after 1792. In that year, having issued the second part of *The Rights of Man*, he managed to take ship from Dover only half an hour before the warrant for his arrest reached the quay. In August 1796 he had been released from prison in France; recovered from illness; completed part two of *The Age of Reason,* and written the savage letter of attack on Washington which must then have made it appear improbable that he would ever again be happily received into America. He may well have wished to explore the possibility of being accepted back into England. Henry Bonham, the secretary of the Hambledon club, was a Radical; and the 'twelve non-subscribers' in contrast to the mere 'three members' – a most unusual imbalance – pose an intriguing situation which presumably will never be explained. It gives the story of the Hambledon Cricket Club an end as unique as its main course; for, less than a month later, the last entry in the minute book – for 21 September 1796 – reads 'No Gentlemen'.

For some five years since Hambledon so nearly won their match against Twenty-two of Middlesex at Lord's, the great players and Grand Matches had been moving to London or to fresh patrons. In its subsequent matches in the eighteenth century, Hambledon is called 'Hambledon Town': the greatest of all village clubs had reached the end of its greatness. Men in Hambledon continued to play cricket; there is still a Hambledon team now, but simply another village team, distinguished from others only by its historic name.

By the middle of the nineteenth century Broadhalfpenny had been put down to plough and Windmill Down to conifers. In 1924, however, Winchester College bought Broadhalfpenny Down and devoted it once more – and in perpetuity – to cricket. The Bat and Ball Inn still stands and opposite, on the edge of the old ground, there is a stone memorial to the Hambledon Cricket Club – but its living memorial is 'Nyren'.

*The Young Cricketer's Tutor, John Nyren (Davis-Poynter, 1974)*

# The Author of *The Cricket Field*

Later Victorian Bath – Bathwick and the Lansdown Club in particular – was familiar with the sight of a tall, white-bearded old gentleman in an Inverness cape: the Reverend James Pycroft, author of *The Cricket Field*. Pycroft was born in Wiltshire but, as a small boy, came to Bath to go to school in Grosvenor Place. In 1824, when he was eleven, already a cricket enthusiast, he contributed from his weekly pocket money to what he describes as 'a fund for bats and balls'. The schoolboy contributors to the fund played cricket on summer half-holidays on Charmbury Down, above Swainswick. More than one adult, apparently, was attracted by their play, and they were, Pycroft says, 'joined by gentlemen in the neighbourhood'. With this influential support they moved to Lansdown (which Pycroft always spells in the older manner – 'Lansdowne'), half a mile beyond Beckford's Tower, and became the Lansdown Club.

Thirty, or even forty, miles the new club might post for a match with one of the few clubs available as opponents in the West Country of the 1830s – Clifton, Teignbridge, Sidmouth, North Devon, or even as far afield as Stalbridge, in Dorsetshire. They were often outplayed, particularly when their opponents introduced such a player as E.H. Budd, one of the half-dozen greatest figures in the cricket of those days. Pycroft, however, found reinforcements for the club. At Oxford, where he revived the match with Cambridge as an annual fixture in 1836, two of his contemporaries were R. Price and F.B. Wright, both Wykeham-ists. Price was top scorer, with 71, in the first University Match in 1827, and both he and Wright, a famous hitter, played in the second game in 1829. In Price and Wright, Pycroft brought back to Bath a pair of cricketers whom Budd described as 'the two best men I ever met outside London'.

Pycroft himself, although he became a curate, first at Chardstock and then of St Mary Magdalen, Barnstaple, still managed to play cricket, sometimes for the Lansdown. He also captained North Devon.

He was an unhappy man when his duties at Barnstaple kept him from the Lansdown's greatest match: twenty-two of the club against the All England XI in 1852. As was its custom, the club played no professional in its team and refused the aid of 'given' bowlers. These bowlers were usually supplied by Clarke, the All England secretary and captain, to opposing local sides (at their expense) in order to make the game more even.

The twenty-two batted first and scored 99; only three of them scored double figures and Clarke took twelve wickets for 54 runs. The England XI batting was immense, almost Olympian: George Ander-son, first choice for Yorkshire; George Parr, the 'Lion of the North'; William Caffyn, the finest Surrey batsman of the day; timid Julius Caesar, who was frightened of fire but of no bowling; Joe Guy, 'all ease and elegance, fit to play before Her Majesty in Her Majesty's parlour'; the mercurial and masterly 'Felix'. This was the finest batting in the land. The Lansdown opened their bowling with George Yonge, the Eton and Oxford University fast roundarm bowler. Yonge bowled forty-five balls to the first five All England batsmen – Anderson, Caesar, Martingell, Parr and Box – without a single run being scored from him – and, in the spell, he dismissed two of them. He took six wickets for 36 runs against the finest cricketers in England, and the side was out for 91; the Lansdown twenty-two led on the first innings by 8 runs. Clarke, Bickley and Grundy went grimly to work in the Bath second innings and put them out for 78. Lansdown needed 87 to win. But the game was, in the words of *Scores and Biographies*, 'Unfinished owing to the wet'.

Yonge played very little cricket after he came down from Oxford; almost all his games were for the Lansdown, until he gave up the game and went to live at Windsor. Playing for Hungerford Park against the All England XI again, he took five wickets for 3 runs, and the great team was all out for its lowest score – 12. His greatest performance, however, was for the Lansdown – against West Gloucestershire in 1847 – when he took all ten wickets for 2 runs, one of the most impressive bowling feats ever recorded.

Pycroft's last cricket match was for the Lansdown against Kingscote in the 1850s. The old man found himself missing balls which he would once have hit, but he kept his wicket up. Although a number of balls passed very near the stumps, he was satisfied to have the stumps covered and refused to be disturbed. One of the fieldsmen, however, said several times, and loudly enough for Pycroft to hear him, 'What a shave,' and 'What a fluke!' At length Pycroft turned with, 'I'll tell you what, gentlemen: I am here to guard three stumps, not five, so I claim to play accordingly.' The field was silenced and the old man made 39 not out and then put away his bat and pads for good.

The All England XI came again to the Lansdown – this time to play against eighteen of the club – in 1864. The number six batsman for the great England side was a tall, gangling boy of fifteen, William Gilbert Grace, from Mangotsfield. It was the lad's first 'big' match, and he made 15 careful runs before John Lillywhite ran him out. 'I did not mind that,' said W.G. afterwards. 'I had played for the All England XI.' If the cricket-minded curate and the boy who was to personify cricket met – and they must at least have seen one another – neither took any great impression. Pycroft was looking back nostalgically to the days of Mynn and Pilch, the boy was looking ahead – to a future peopled by great cricketers whose names were yet unknown.

Pycroft watched the club he had helped to found through its moves – Sydenham Field, the riverside, and finally to Victoria Park, at Weston. He retired from his Barnstaple curacy in 1856 and returned to Bath, to read and write about cricket and to press for the Lansdown Club's Jubilee Dinner in 1874.

Pycroft was a prolific writer. Besides *The Cricket Field* he wrote a novel, books on Greek and Latin grammar, on English literature, on the Public Health Act. But conversation was his glory – and autobiography approaches more nearly than any other literary form to conversation. So it is in his several volumes of autobiography that we find the real Pycroft, with his gentle courtesy, his brittle anecdotes, and his rolling phrases. And there we find his cricketing friends of the West Country: his Charlie Golightly, Henry Kingscote, Sainsbury, Gomonde, Stothert, and Dr Falconer from Bath belong there. And Pycroft himself is as ever talkative, friendly, polite, repetitive, unendingly talking about cricket.

Author of *The Cricket Field* and *Cricketana,* a founder member of the Lansdown Club of Bath, responsible for reviving the University Match – that his biographer must say of the Reverend James Pycroft. He died in 1895; thirty years afterwards, people who had been small children when they met him for the only time recalled him with remarkable affection: no one who knew him has ever placed on record an unkind word about him. Few people now alive remember the elderly parson in the Inverness cape; but the books he wrote, more 'period' than literary in quality, contain something of a lovable, very minor Victorian.

*Concerning Cricket* (*Longmans,* 1949)


# Frederick Lillywhite and His Tent

Wherever William Clarke's travelling eleven went, their chronicler, occasional umpire, emergency player and chief printer, Frederick Lillywhite, pitched his tent and sold his scorecards. And, in 1849, Lillywhite issued, from Lord's, the first edition of his *Young Cricketer's Guide* which ran to 1866 as the only adequate cricket annual. Lillywhite is for me the most digestible of all cricket historians. Never, surely, could any man impart to such painstaking cricket records such perfect unconscious humour. The set of twenty-two editions of the *Guide* is one of the rarest of all cricket sets, and one of the most entertaining books ever published on any game. By the third edition it had attained to sixty-six pages. This paralysingly stylized passage comes from the editorial essay 'On Cricket' in the third edition:

'If the assertion of celebrated writers be true, that the character of a people may be discovered by observing the nature of their amusements, every Englishman must feel gratified that the sport denominated "Cricket", after having been for a number of years the favourite pastime of the inhabitants of many parts of England, has at last become national. "Cricketing", by common consent, has gained the appellation of noble. The qualities necessary to those who practise it are courage, activity, and perseverance; and we may justly be proud, if foreigners judge of our national habits and disposition in reference to an amusement of such an excellent character. The objections which some men raise against the public practice of sports, that they are generally too puerile for the adult, and perpetuate the pastimes of our infancy, cannot be applied to "Cricketing". Manliness is the characteristic of the game; and in the practice of its various parts, those qualifications which form and adorn the soldier are necessarily cultivated and acquired by the player. The batsman must learn to meet, with firm nerves, an object propelled against him with great force, and, by the union of strength and skill, strike it with his utmost force amongst his antagonists. The bowler must acquire the art of pitching a length ball; and in doing this must alternately depend on stratagem and strength and the fielders, like sentinels, follow the ball with the rapidity with which it cuts the air, and grasp it in the hands, though at the risk of being overturned by the impetus with which it falls. The highest pleasure which is felt by generous persons contending in sport against each other arises from the knowledge that they are the cause of gratification to those who behold them. Amongst cricketers, the pleasure is heightened by the conviction that their pastime is untainted by vulgarity and cruelty; and that their fair countrywomen may witness of prowess of a brother, a lover, or a husband, without a blush, or the painful sense of impropriety. He, indeed, must hold pleasure to be a thing altogether forbidden – must be insensible to the charms of nature, and the beauty of manliness – who could behold a village green, where the young contended and the old admired, without acknowledging that a cricket match, with its attendant circumstances, formed the most pleasing picture which the holidays of the people of any country can produce.

'Most sports in their decision, create heart-burning and jealousies, and, in proportion as the winner triumphs, the loser becomes splenetic and depressed. This, however, cannot be said of "Cricketing". The defeated party leaves the field without diminution of honour or reputation; for the winners may have been indebted for their superior score to chance, or the good fortune of one man; or, perhaps, the play might have been pronounced better on the losing than the winning side, notwithstanding the result.

'It is likewise worthy of remark that "Cricketing" is seldom made the object (at least among "Cricketers" themselves) of gambling speculations; it being notorious that the best players contend merely for honour; while the game, including so many as twenty-two persons, prevents the unfair sportsman being enabled, with the least tolerable certainty, to bet on any positive event, unless it could be supposed that the players, as a body, were all dishonest, and that an individual, if he possessed the inclination, could find a purse of sufficient depths to bribe them all.'

The whole book is of considerable topographical interest and, within the shape of cricket history, invaluable, while unconscious humour is always lurking over the page. Here are a few random items from the section headed 'Celebrated Cricket Grounds':

*'Birmingham* Cricket Ground is a field of about seven or eight acres, and is situated at Edgbaston, about two miles from Birmingham; it is enclosed with a hedge, which, if properly kept in order, would be an excellent enclosure.

*Bradford.* – This ground is an excellent piece of turf, well enclosed with a brick wall, but very small.

*Canterbury.* – This celebrated ground, under the management of Fuller Pilch, is about a mile from the town on the south, in the parish of Lawrence.... It does not afford any excellent views, being surrounded by trees; but, on the occasion of a grand match, it presents a scene of animation and brilliancy. The surface is without any inequalities, and cannot be surpassed by any cricket ground in England. It is patronised once a year (return Kent and England match) by the nobility and gentry from Lord's.

*Derby* Cricket Ground is about half a mile from the centre of the town, and is surrounded by water. It is an excellent piece of turf, and is partly supported by the gentlemen of Burton-on-Trent.

*Leamington.* – The two well known cricketers, Wisden and Parr, are the proprietors of this ground, which, in the winter of 1849 was levelled and the turf relaid at a great expense. It is a most excellent ground and kept in good condition. Its situation is good, being but a very short distance from the town. It contains about nine acres. A splendid Indian tent is erected by the proprietor of the Bath Hotel, which is kept standing during the whole summer. The erection of this tent alone costs the proprietor seven or eight pounds.

*Lisbon.* – The Club here meets for practice at Campo Pegueno, about three miles distant from the city; and when any ships of H.B.M.'s navy are in the Tagus, the Club engages in making matches with the officers. This Club is exclusively English, with the exception of the President (The Marquis of Playle), and two other members, who are Portuguese. It was established in the commencement of 1849 and varies from 20 to 35 members (owing to the residents retiring to England).'

Precisely what mixture of motives actuated the shrewd Lillywhite in his *Brief Remarks Upon 150 of the Celebrated Players at the Present Time* is not always apparent, but it contains some of the most back-handed compliments ever printed about any sportsmen, after an introduction which runs:

'It will be seen in perusing the following pages, that there are "players in former times" playing at the "present time" in all our first-rate matches. Several young players have of late years "shot up" especially since the "Eleven of England" have shown their skill by their "Northern circuits". The game has now become much more popular, and has been instrumental in bringing many young players into notice. Those whom I have thought promising, and others, too, who are worthy the space they will here occupy, I have inserted; and shall, during the ensuing season, closely watch the play of all young practitioners, in order to publish the names in a future edition.'

Here are some extracts from the list:

'BARRETT, HUGH. – This player was born at Harewood, in the county of York, in the year 1811, stands 5 ft 8 ins, and weighs 12 st. He has a moderate defence, is a good hitter, and an excellent slow bowler. He now resides at Leeds, and is the worthy host of the Haunch of Venison, where all cricketers make it their rendezvous during a match; and the manner in which they are entertained is highly creditable to the "slow bowler of Leeds".

BATHURST, SIR FREDERICK, BART. – This baronet is a staunch supporter of the game of cricket, particularly in his own county – Hampshire. He is the first gentleman bowler in England, and stands about 6 ft. As a batsman he is very hazardous. The Hon. Baronet is from the Winchester School.

BROWN, CHARLES, was born at Nottingham, on the 15th of December, 1815, stands 5 ft 10½ ins and weighs 12 st. By trade he is a dyer. He commenced cricket at the early age of 15, by playing in a grand match. It is extraordinary the facility he possesses in delivering the ball behind his back. He is a good cricketer being a very fair bowler, an excellent wicket-keeper, and a very fair batsman. Brown's restlessness alone is the cause, no doubt, of his being left out of many of our first-rate matches.

DEWDNEY, MR, is a member of Islington Albion Club, and an excellent batsman, considering his age, which is between 50 and 60 years.

FELLOWES, MR H.W., is the fastest bowler in England. As a batsman, he is a hard hitter, but not very steady.

FENNER. F., was born at Cambridge in 1811, and stands 5 ft 10 ins. He is an excellent batsman and bowler, but has not played in any of the England matches since 1843. He is now lessee of the New Cricket Ground at Cambridge, and likewise carries on an excellent business in the cigar line.

LILLYWHITE, FREDERICK, a "Still younger brother" is a professional bowler during the term at Cambridge. When cricket matches commence he attends the ground of every grand one in England with a printing press, and publishes statements of the game. He also supplies gentlemen with a statement of the game each day by post; and has with him, when travelling in the country, every description of cricketing apparatus.

MORSE, MR C. – This gentleman is better known by his name being spelt backwards. He is very tall, has great command over the bat, and is likewise very scientific.

ONSLOW, MR F. – This gentleman plays with the Hampshire Club, and is a great teaser to the bowlers.

ROBERTS, MR. – This gentleman is a member of the Surrey Club, and a good supporter of the game. Another season's practice will, no doubt, greatly improve his play.

WALKER, MR JOHN, is also from the Cambridge University, where, from the professional bowlers who visit that town during the term, he has nearly learned the art of batting.'

This volume of the *Guide* harks back to give us a sound memoir – much of its contents not to be found elsewhere – of 'Brown of Brighton', the first of the legendary fast bowlers and of whom we have heard before. The essay comes appropriately here because it serves to emphasize the value of the information contained in the *Guide* – which earlier selections may have left open to doubt:

'This veteran is 67 years of age. He came out at Lord's in 1818, in a single wicket match, opposed to Mr Osbaldeston, who was then considered and publicly known as the fastest bowler in England. Lambert was then in his prime, and open to play any man in England; and such was the confidence in his play, that Mr Osbaldeston and Lambert, challenged any four men in England; and the match was played at Lord's in 1818. Brown bowled the whole of the time, and astonished the spectators by his swiftness; so well, however, did Mr Osbaldeston and his partner play, that Brown bowled six hours at them in the first innings, but the latter were eventually beaten in a single innings. Mr Osbaldeston and Lambert had two to field for them, Baker and John Sherman. From this time Brown played in most of the great matches; and the velocity with which the ball shot from his hand has struck many a young and really skilful player with terror. Every one of the field (with the exception of Brown himself when bowling) have frequently been seen behind the wicket, it being next to impossible to drive his balls forward. Perhaps his greatest cricketing feat on record is that which took place in Goodwood Park in 1818, the same year that he went to Lord's. He was playing against Lillywhite and James Broadbridge, a man renowned as a cricketer in Sussex. The side on which Brown played had lost seven wickets in the second innings, and had to get four runs to tie their opponents' first innings. Brown went in with a relation of Lillywhite's. The veteran (at that time a fine young hearty player) said to his colleague. "We must go to work now"; and to work they went accordingly, the last three wickets scoring enough to put their opponents in upon 108 runs. Brown himself got between 60 and 70 runs. It was not at all times judicious to let Brown bowl, there being the danger of "byes" but in this match, the opposite party were getting runs so fast from moderate bowling that Brown was put on. Six balls were then an "over". All the men were placed behind the wicket, when Brown began, and in six balls he lowered five wickets. Perhaps there is not such another feat on record. Suffice it to say, that his side won the match by 40 runs. Brown has thrown a ball farther than any man in England. He once threw a cricket ball 137 yards on Walderton Down; and the distance is recorded in the *Sporting Magazine* of 1831.

'He first went to Brighton in 1825, and a few years afterwards became lessee of the Royal Brighton Gardens, where he lived several years; but not answering his expectations, he left them, and now keeps a respectable lodging house in Middle Street. He is also scorer to all matches played at Brighton.'

*Cricket – Pleasures of Life*
*(Burke, 1953)*

# Foreword to *The Weaving Willow*

There are some cricket books to which I should hesitate to write a foreword, for reasons varying between humility and disinterest.

This, however, is one for which I am the natural foreword-writer. J. Marshall and myself are cricketers of identical calibre. Under the helpful laws of the games boys play, and assuming the names of the great – Hobbs, Tate, Douglas, Macartney – we have both performed great deeds. Indeed, we have both played games in circumstances which would baffle Messrs Hutton and Bedser. I read that Mr Marshall's characteristically anxious style of batting originated in many childhood innings played with a sitting-room window immediately behind the wicket. For my part, my peculiar – nay, incredible – bowling action was developed by an eight-foot pitch on which I tried to bowl overarm off-breaks.

J. Marshall performed two hat-tricks at Broadwater Green; I once took six for 10 at Tylney Hall; but there was never, alas, any great competition for our services in first-class cricket – nor, for that matter, in the Minor Counties Competition: there is little profit in continuing.

Both of us, however, can wag our heads sadly at the moment of aberration in which a Test batsman loses his wicket after batting a mere three hours – which would probably represent our total combined batting times in any given season.

The author disclaims any serious contribution to cricket literature. Yet, how many of the books published about cricket are literature? They may contain scores and statistics, advice and technical analysis – but how often can we ordinary cricketers really share them, how often are they concerned with the stuff of literature, which is human character? How often are they warmed by charitable humour? This book meets all three of those demands.

This year – an Australian year – will centre attention on the Tests. Because we have become conditioned to it, we shall be in danger of believing that the winning or losing of The Ashes is the crux of our cricket. So John Marshall's book is at once salutary and comforting. Thirty men, perhaps, will take part in the Test series. Thousands, up and down the country, will roll their sleeves and swing at a cricket ball, and miss – or edge it gloriously past the leg stump. Almost – alas, the tragedy of my life lies in the fact that it *is* 'almost' – *almost* as many men will bowl, to see their favourite delivery thrashed cross-batted out of sight, or even more sadly, edged into the hands of first slip, and dropped. With Providence, however, it will be a four – or the middle stump knocked backwards. The ingredients, however, are not important.

I have known fine players – one of them among the dozen greatest practitioners of all time – who did not enjoy cricket. But *all* bad – what a silly word – cricketers enjoy it.

Some of us *need* this book, to remind us that cricket is not just an international competition, but a game: its purpose, enjoyment. Moreover, the cricketers who gave us the first, and still the finest, of all cricket writings – Nyren's *The Cricketers of My Time* – were village cricketers, the village players of Hambledon, not so very far across the Hampshire border from Broadwater Green. Incidentally, in the days of

Hambledon – September 1771, to be precise – Broadwater Green played their earliest recorded match against Henfield.

Much airy-fairy nonsense and condescending bunk has been written and spoken about village cricket. Village cricket, like gardening, or walking, or just sitting, is something men do in their free time because they enjoy it. Once, *all* cricket was like that. Whether England beats Australia or not, the importance of cricket lies in the pleasure that the greatest possible number of people derive from it, irrespective of their skill. After all, if the bad players are not allowed to play, who would provide the cars to take the good players to away matches?

*The Weaving Willow, John Marshall (Hodder & Stoughton, 1953)*

# Centenary Tribute to Neville Cardus

*April* 1988. The centenary of Sir Neville Cardus's birth falls on 3 April 1988, even though he himself gave his date of birth as 2 April 1889. He was, above all, an individualist. He left school at thirteen, worked as a pavement artist, delivered laundry for his grandparents who 'took in washing', as an assistant in a printer's workshop, as assistant cricket coach at Shrewsbury School and (completely – even intensely – self-educated in the local public library) as secretary to Dr Cyril Alington, the school's headmaster; then as music writer for the *Daily Citizen*, as assistant to Samuel Langford, music critic of the *Manchester Guardian* – as he steadfastly called it long after it became *The Guardian* – and he claimed to have worked in virtually every department of that paper before he became its music critic and, by accident, its cricket correspondent. He was, too, the author of twenty-eight books: two of autobiography, nine on music and seventeen (five of them posthumous collections of essays) on cricket.

The confusion about his date of birth undoubtedly stemmed from his uncertainty about that event; he was the son of a prostitute – about whom he wrote most movingly – by, so he claimed, or at least trusted, an Italian musician. In 1964 he became a CBE and in 1967 he was knighted.

He was the most delightful of companions, gentle and considerate, and a bubbling, if somewhat overriding, conversationalist. He claimed to have married Edith King, a local schoolmistress, in Manchester because she helped him so far along the road to literacy, and he once wrote disclaiming real interest in sexual matters. He did, though, undoubtedly have affairs, but certainly he was an oddly considerate husband. Even after he withdrew into the bachelor seclusion of the National Liberal Club, he never failed to visit his wife every day.

Of his journalistic enthusiasms, the first, and probably the most enduring, was music, and certainly he regarded his period working under Sam Langford as the key experience of his life. His major fame, though, is as a writer on cricket. It is not reasonable that such standing is based on the respective merits of his work in the two fields. In fact, the explanation is relatively simple. Throughout his early lifetime there were a number of highly capable and literate writers on music, while cricket writing was, on the whole, pedestrian. Neville Cardus had watched cricket at Old Trafford as a little boy, to whom the county players seemed little gods. His spell of coaching under Attewell and Wainwright at Shrewsbury had given him some technical background in the game, but essentially, when he was sent, during a period of convalescence, to cover cricket for *The Guardian*, he contrived to write of the players as romantic figures, rather more than life-sized. In doing so, he created an entirely fresh attitude to the game; it was precisely that kind of hero-worship that possessed the average cricket watcher. Neville Cardus put that point of view into heroic language.

He himself used to refer to his early cricket writings as his 'greeny-yallery' period. If, though, his work later became more 'hard', he nevertheless retained his early command of language and the feeling of those days. There is no cricket writer in the world since his day who does not owe something, if not almost everything, to the work of Neville Cardus.

Within a year, publishers had recognized his outstanding talent and, although he began to write about cricket only in 1919, by 1922 as perceptive a publisher as Grant Richards put out his *A Cricketer's Book*. At once, and constantly, he was imitated; but none of his imitators had that mastery of language he had acquired in all those years in the public library and, later, at the *Manchester Guardian*. He became, if not a cult, a major influence and, so far as literature was concerned, Longmans in their 'English Heritage' series, later Collins in 'Britain in Pictures', turned to him as the literate authority for their volumes on cricket in series which ranged widely over human activities and experience.

It is easy to see that, in a way, he created a mythology of cricket. The clearest example of that lies in his series of pieces on the clash between the fast bowler Ted McDonald, of Lancashire, and the graceful, tall, left-hand batsman Frank Woolley, of Kent. There were, though, many cricketers whom he elevated to considerable heights in the minds of those who followed the game.

Once he was chided for a 'quotation' from Dick Tyldesley of Lancashire with the suggestion that Tyldesley would never have made such a statement. Cardus's response was simple and direct: 'That is exactly what he would have said if he had thought about it, because that was what he felt.' Certainly, too, Cardus knew his Lancastrians, their reactions and their language.

At first in his career as a cricket writer he used to fight shy of the players, largely, no doubt, through his natural modesty and a fear that they might look down on one who lacked their cricketing skills. Soon, however, that barrier was broken down. Cricketers became proud to know him and happy to talk to him, while he reflected them as truly, yet as kindly, as ever. Suddenly they found themselves, through his writing, as the hero figures they were in the eyes of boys, yet it was all most maturely expressed: the language of literary sensitivity used to write of sport. Throughout it all, too, he maintained his sense of humour, which may have had its basis in a poor Lancashire family but which had been digested in his eager early hunger for literature.

When he was knighted he wrote most firmly and separately to his friends insisting that to them he was 'still Neville'. That Neville, of course, was an adopted Christian name. When he first went to the *Manchester Guardian* he was known as 'Fred'. He was, though, very conscious of value, of the difference between the two names for a writer; and similarly he was aware, though he rarely, if ever, expressed it, of the fact that music was a more 'elevated' subject than cricket.

His writings on music were sensitive and perceptive (when young he took some singing lessons, but subsequently he worked solely by listening and reading). His *Ten Composers* is a most scholarly work; *Talking of Music*, characteristic in manner; *Gustav Mahler; His Mind and His Music*, perhaps the most influential of his writings in that field; while his *Kathleen Ferrier, a Memoir* is peculiarly personal, for her singing affected him deeply – so deeply, indeed, that he once confessed that he was not an objective critic of her work.

*Autobiography* (1947) is probably the most mature of all his writings, revealing his deep appreciation of character when he talks about other people, of a mixture of veracity and romance when he writes about himself.

Neville Cardus was a character deeply to be appreciated as both man and writer. Perhaps his 'slum' was in fact an honest suburb; perhaps many of his characters – cricketers and others – appear of greater stature than they actually were. From the start to finish, however, he was an enthusiast, not simply for music and cricket, but for life and people. It was, and for his readers remains, a matter of zest. There is no more vivid example of that fact than the manner in which his cricketers still become alive to readers too young ever to have watched them. He will be read with relish so long as people read.

He is one of the great characters of *The Guardian*, of which he once wrote 'A dear tyrant, the MG; I have never been able to break free from them.' That proved true: he went away for some years to Australia, where he worked for the *Sydney Morning Herald*, and he returned to England to work for another paper, but he came back to *The Guardian* – despite its change of name. Still, too, after a cricket match or a concert, he could be seen at a nearby café, writing his copy in that immaculate handwriting which reflected the sensitivity of one who had made his own way – an enthusiastic individualist.

*The Guardian*

# Poets and Peasants

## A.C., Cricket Rhymster

The Middlesex men neither falter'd nor blunder'd
And yet Dr Grace got a well-earned two hundred.

Craig wrote that – Albert Craig, the Surrey poet or, as he later called himself, the 'Cricket Rhymster'. It is hard to describe it as poetry – or, for that matter, competent verse – yet it was one of the couplets Craig himself chose to print at the head of a broadsheet. It could not be much worse by literary standards, could it?

But there are better couplets that I don't recall. Craig did not seriously claim to be a poet. One of his best-remembered retorts was made when someone shouted at him, 'Any fool could write this stuff.' 'Yes, sir,' said Craig, 'but it takes a clever man to sell it.'

For over twenty years, from the early 1880s until 1908, Craig peddled his wares round the cricket grounds – and occasionally the soccer and rugby grounds – of southern England. His main stock-in-trade were single sheets of doggerel celebrating some cricketing feat or anniversary, with 'Written by A. Craig', or later, simply 'A.C., Cricket Rhymster' at the bottom, and sold at a penny each.

Craig was part of the cricketing scene of his day. Before a match started he would be selling his verses among the spectators, informing them – in confidence – that the home side had won the toss – though the toss had not taken place, or, if it had, he did not know the result. But in the days before the public-address system he used often to promise the crowd that he would be there in front of the pavilion – 'and, if England or Surrey, or whoever it might be, have won the toss, I'll throw my hat in the air – and if they have lost, I'll jump on it'.

He was born in Yorkshire and was a post-office clerk in Huddersfield until some verses he wrote on William Bates – the old Yorkshire batsman – had a little local success in Dewsbury. Then he came to

London – he used to say he never used the return half of his ticket. He must have been about thirty at the time – no one seems to have seen any of his rhymes dated before 1882; and he settled in Kennington and made The Oval his headquarters.

Craig's pieces were, above all, topical – usually with long rolling headline-type titles. One is headed:

WELL DONE SURREY

The Surrey Champions
beat the
Nottingham Cracks by 158 runs
June 1887

Composed immediately after the victory, it begins:

> Hurrah! hurrah! the task is done!
> Shout, lads, both loud and hearty!
> The famous fight is fought and won,
> Let's toast the winning party.
>
> Notts struggled hard to avert defeat,
> But Surrey fairly beat 'em.
> Throughout the match they had them sweet,
> And will when next they meet them.
>
> *Chorus*
> Here's to Surrey's famous team
> Cheer them Saints and Sinners!
> Let us all take up the theme
> Give credit to the Winners.

His introductory patter varied according to the ground he visited: 'Good old Yorkshire, the county of my birth'; 'Dear old Surrey, my favourite county'; 'Grand old Kent [or Essex, or Middlesex], my future home'. And he could always break down sales resistance with such little jokes as: 'They asked me at Lord's last week about the Oval crowd: "What do you mean?" I said. "They are not a crowd – nothing so vulgar – you are an accumulation of intelligent and cultivated people."'

Craig was a period figure – and a public figure too: he called himself 'the captain of the spectators', and as soon as he set foot on a ground he would be hailed on all sides. There were even picture postcards of him – he sold them himself.

One of Craig's early effusions – printed on pink paper – was titled:

'The Coming Man'
An Old Pro's Opinion
of
George Lohmann
The Famous Surrey Cricketer

It starts with this stanza:

> I met a nice old gentleman at Beckenham, this day week;
>> The Kent and Surrey men were playing there.
> On passing by, I noticed he seemed inclined to speak –
>> Such people in the South are somewhat rare.
> Said he – 'I love the grand old game, and our men, I love them all;
>> And I've come today from Sydenham to see George Lohmann bowl.

The closing stanza is even flatter and yet even more human:

> When our mutual friend had had his say, I grasped him by the hand;
>> I told him I was proud to hear his views,
> And that a glass of something neat I really meant to stand.
>> He saw I meant it and could not refuse.
> We wished all professionals long life, success and wealth,
>> And, before we parted company we drank George Lohmann's health.

Scansion was not a strong point with Craig, and in his hurry to be up to date, the same couplet used to appear more than once – so that, at a loss for a start, he often fell back on:

> We've merrily scribbled our homely rhymes
> In honour of cricket a thousand times.

A recurrent theme is the success of a coming man – Craig loved to hail a new player of promise – and, surely enough, he came out with a poem when, in 1905, Jack Hobbs, playing only his second county match, made a century. It is pure Craig:

> Joy reigned in the pavilion
> And gladness 'mongst his clan,

Whilst thousand breathe good wishes round the ring;
   Admirers dubbed the youngster
As Surrey's coming man;
   In Hobbs's play they saw the genuine ring.
'Twas worth going miles to see
   Illustrious Hayward's smile,
Whilst Razor Smith and Walter Lees
   Cheer'd with the rank and file

Alas, characteristically, Craig ended on a note of bathos:

   Against the Essex favourites
      He gave some rare displays;
   One veteran whisper'd fervently
   'Another Ernie Hayes'.

Most of Craig's hundreds of rhymes were thrown away and, indeed, by literary standards, they hardly warranted saving; but you could call him a folk poet of cricket, and after his death – in 1909 – the game had nothing similar until the 'Cricket, Lovely Cricket' calypso in 1950. Certainly the affection in which he was held is underlined by those who frequented English cricket grounds before the First World War and who so warmly recall the chirpy, chatty, grey-haired little man, always streaming with sweat, who, when the weight of coppers he had taken threatened to drag the pockets out of his coat, trotted off to unload them into some secret cache behind the pavilion at The Oval.

*Radio Broadcast, BBC Home Service*, August 1961

# The Slaughters at Dairy Lane

*Opening music and background sound effects*

*J.A.:* Lord's – for cricketers all over the world, headquarters, representative of the best. (*crowd effects*) Representative despite its modern mob scenes of the game's peak, not really of its roots – for cricket's roots are in the country. (*music*) Through the centuries times have changed and today, through the Haig National Village Championship, even country cricketers can play at Lord's. (*crowd applause*) But only a few do that (*applause*) and those who don't remain the grass-roots of cricket. (*church bells ring*) So come to the country, to the Cotswolds a hundred miles west of Lord's and London, and to two nearby villages: first The Slaughters, Sunday 8 May.

*The Vicar:* The Service next Sunday will be Evensong at 6 o'clock. Now may we wish all good fortune to our village cricket team in their match next Sunday against Dumbleton.

*J.A.:* Now Dumbleton – same day, same time.

*The Vicar:* You may be interested to know that in the next round of the Haig Cup, Dumbleton plays The Slaughters – and we wish them well.

*J.A. (with church music):* Two communities, a dozen miles apart in the Heart of England, drawn together in the Haig Championship, an evocative bearing – Dumbleton versus The Slaughters at Dairy Lane. For both, this week feelings will run high and fingers will be crossed. The next day – Monday – and you can sense the character of the rival villages: The Slaughters, Upper and Lower Slaughter, are picture-postcard villages, all sparkling water and Cotswold stone. The tourists flock through, but being largely foreign and therefore ignorant of our eccentricities they miss the cricket ground hiding behind the houses. The Slaughters are a traditional local team – butcher and baker and candlestick maker. The butcher is Richard Austin – how could you have a team called The Slaughters without the butcher? The baker: Martin Collett, a bowler and tail-end bat; and the candlestick maker: Paul Lockey, restorer of antiques and a destroyer of bowling. The captain: Ray Mossen, works in a TV shop. Gerald Hathaway, the number three bat, is a newsagent – drives a mobile store; and Andy Poole – the wicket-keeper and opening bat – does, well, precious little it seems – not in the summer anyway (though he might dispute it): for him winter's for working and summer's for cricket.

(*short interlude of music*)

*J.A. (with music):* Dumbleton's an attractive village, unspoilt, uncluttered by tourists, basically farming land in the shade of Dumbleton hill. The cricket ground's concealed from the main road behind a farm up Dairy Lane and this – next Sunday – will be the battle ground. The pavilion – a proud edifice this – bought from a neighbouring club in 1900 and it was second-hand then, and while Dumbleton strangely has no pub, the cricket club would make one almost redundant. Which leads me to mention, if you'll pardon it, the 'gents' – connoisseurs reckon it boasts the finest view from any 'convenience' in the land. The trimmings and trappings of village cricket of course include religion – which reminds me Vicar Giles is a player himself: safeish bat, if a bit slow. (*moo*) This is farming country and Denis Baker, the opening bowler, is a farmer. But times and manners change. Chris Hawkins, the all-rounder, is a barman at a golf club; John Evans, a middle-order batsman, a school teacher; Josh Allen, a promising bowler, is a schoolboy, and for both villages Tuesday is selection night. (*background talk*) Presiding at Dumbleton, the captain, Alec Hopkins . . .

*Captain:* Can anybody play?

*Reply:* Not really – we had a very good hiding. (*laughter*)

*J.A.:* None of your stuffy formalities – Dumbleton select in their kitchen within easy reach of the bar. The Slaughters are rebuilding their pavilion – formerly a wooden hut.

*Captain:* You know – so somebody's got to be fortunate.

*J.A.:* Problems aren't merely of technique and temperament but of chance; Vicar Giles of Dumbleton has been showing good form, but then Sunday is a busy day for vicars.

*Team Discussion:* Stuart – he played well last Saturday didn't he? – He had a good game, even if it wasn't mature.

*J.A.:* But the policy is usually the same – first write down the definites.

*Captain & Team:* Calling names of those selected.

*J.A.:* Charity, you see, tends to begin at home. Put your own names down then you'll have a clear mind to think about the others.

*Team Discussion:* You've got him in – you've got him in – what about Jim – are you going to put him in?

*J.A. (and background discussions):* These are in inner corridors of power – making decisions that may wreck careers and transform devoted husbands into wife-beaters and lost souls. Mind you, if you want an excuse for losing there's one as old as cricket itself – blame the umpires.

*Members:* Well, it would be nice to have neutral umpires because we have had to get 'em out twice on umpiring in the past – haven't we? (*Chorus of assent*). Our old umpire couldn't count up to six last year.

*J.A.:* And eventually it's all decided . . .

*Selection:* A. Hopkins, captain; K. Mitchell; C. Hawkins; D. Watcott; D. Chandler (*fade*)

*J.A.:* And now the Committee face their critics . . . (*background discussion*) Life may now proceed for the rest of the week. The match

will be discussed everywhere – from country pub to village fete.
(*short musical interlude*)
*J.A. (with music):* Village life does go on, but it's never been the same since some humourless souls invented railways and motorcars and others began patronizing and sentimentalizing about it; and the same goes for its cricket. These days you don't often see fast-bowling blacksmiths in braces nor slogger farmers with binder cord around their trousers. (*sheep bleats, dog barks*) Take Dumbleton – until recently Dumbleton were a team of farmers like Albert Slater, now sixty-four. Now Baker and Albie's son Jeff are the only farmers and the pitches are truer and the cricket more text-book than cowshot, and some players are like Drinky – David Drinkwater, the man Dumbleton nearly dropped (a decision surely mischievous which could have caused a peasants' revolt). (*car starting*) Drinky's a trendy, a pillar of the county club, commuting to business in the nearest big wicked city – well Redditch actually. Yes, times have changed. (*music*) The fete just up the road from Dumbleton seems almost an anachronism (*music over*), a quaint, once-a-year caricature, but cricket, village cricket, goes on every Saturday and Sunday, and indeed mid-week too. Because while your blousy town club cricketer's trapped in the rat race, your village player has his priorities right by established tradition and commuters or not, they're very much part of village life: wherever there's something on, the cricketers are there too (*background talk*) – the characters, the social swingers . . .
*Spectators:* What do you reckon?
Well – they're a bit out of my territory this lot.
*J.A.:* And Chris Hawkins, the barman . . .
*Chris Hawkins with friends:* Yeh – well there's Denis Baker who is a bit useful, and then there's this lad . . . have you seen this lad John Evans, have you?
No . . . he's been with us what – twor or three years now. He's a schoolmaster over at Winchicombe, you know . . .
*J.A.:* Talking this week and every week, about players, prospects and opponents, for news of The Slaughters' deeds travels fast and grows in the process as it comes down the grapevine.
*Supporters:* The chap that really is the danger, I suppose, as far as we are concerned, is this chap Andy Poole.
Yeh, doesn't he take a while to get his runs though?
Well, no he doesn't – he gets on with it . . .

*J.A. (with background talk):* This week the obsession affects supporters as well as players, among them the Vicar of The Slaughters . . .

*The Vicar & Supporter:* They've got to get the odd one haven't they? Yeh – batsmen here aren't bad, but they've also a pretty good side.

*J.A.:* The match involves everyone . . .

*Supporters:* What have they got? They've got Andy Poole and this other lad Richard Bailey, butcher, who does his bit but may come off, may not.

*J.A.:* In the Coach and Horses near The Slaughters, down on the Dumbleton farms, and up at The Slaughters bakery . . .

*Supporters:* Steady bowling side, steady batting side, batting right through to number eleven, we shouldn't do too bad.

*J.A.:* In Cotswold spinnies and woods . . .

*Supporters:* It should make a good game.
Well, I hope it will keep fine for it.
Yeh.

*J.A.:* Where butcher Austin of The Slaughters goes shooting. Indeed, everywhere. (*shotgun goes off*) What absorbs the cricketers, you see, has nothing to do with the sentimental aspects of village life (*sound of horse clopping down road*) . . . it's the question of winning or losing . . .

*Supporters:* Oh rubbish – we've got the bowlers – they've got no bowler at all. (*heated arguments*)
They're useless – how often does a side come to Dumbleton and get 200 runs against them?
That's absolutely rubbish.

*J.A.:* And so it's Sunday 15 May – the day of the match.

*Organizers:* Now the fence along here and along here and all along there and on top of the pavilion is six – yeh – all right, not hitting against the boards that's four – over the top is six – into the boundary for four. Right – out we go.

*Umpire & Captains:* Heads or tails? It's a tail – we'll put you in to bat then.

*J.A.:* The Slaughters will bat (*background chatter*) and now just savour the lovely, yellowing, sweat-stained impedimenta. (*applause*) And now to open, Andy Poole the winter worker, the summer cricketer, one of The Slaughterers Dumbleton respect and fear. Drinky, the city commuter, bowls to him. (*sound effects*) Oh – you wouldn't see that at Lord's, would you? Swinging clean across the line and the first bowl. Skipper Alec Hopkins, the wicket-keeper, David

Drinkwater the bowler. (*sound of ball being struck*) And that's better, down towards the pond behind the 'gents' (*applause*) – four runs for Andy Poole. (*spectators chatter, birds sing*) Well, he's bowled him (*applause*), so the great Andy Poole out – the bowler David Drinkwater. (*applause*) In comes Gerald Hathaway, the newsagent (*applause*), a member of a famous Cotswold cricketing family. (*birds sing, sound of bowling*) Six – yes, off the mark. (*more applause*) And soon Slaughters climb to the dizzy heights of double figures – ominous. Meanwhile, bowling from the other end, the farmer – Denis Baker. (*sound of bowling*) And there's another one, but is it a run-out? (*applause*) No . . . (*applause*) . . . much local concern. The farmer bowls to the candlestick maker, Paul Lockey (*background sounds*), and becoming a bit of a problem to Dumbleton is Mr Lockey, the restorer of antiques. I wonder if he includes his pads among his antiques. Alan the schoolboy fielding, Baker the farmer bowling to Hathaway. ('*Well bowled!*') And he's bowled him! (*loud applause*) Well, Dumbleton's umpire trying desperately hard to look neutral and Slaughters' counterpart as though he were at a funeral. And in comes the number four. (*birds singing*) Beautiful bit of country, isn't it, Dumbleton Hill? ('*Out!*' *applause*) Out! He's castled him as well, and if this were a Test match I could see the headlines now: 'Harvest for Farmer Baker'. (*applause*) 20 for three and a deep depression over The Slaughters; but the candlestick maker's still there, Paul Lockey, and going well I must say. (*applause*) Eric Giles, the Dumbleton's vicar, is here between services, but his presence seemingly induces no fear whatsoever in Mr Lockey. (*sound of bowling*) Four more, surely. (*applause*) Time for Dumbleton's Alec Hopkins to get concerned, as indeed is his Uncle Vic in the pavilion – local postman now, but in his day a player for Gloucestershire with the great Wally Hammond. (*crowd chatter, sound of bowling*) That's part of the joy of village cricket of course, the characters on the periphery. (*birds singing*) Look at him – Russian they tell me – and some are too young to understand, and some just stand and wait. Dumbleton's bowling really being put to the sword now, and of course when you're down your critics tend to open up.

*Supporters:* Of course, Alec stands up, which is all very well and you get an occasional stumping, but it's not so good for catching. (*applause*)

*J.A.:* And with tea on the stove and by the time Lockey is out The

Slaughters have built up a total by village standards not inconsiderable – 72 for six.

*Supporters:* That bloke has come in and kept doing that all the time – he's batted bloody well.

In the realms of respectability, yeh.

*J.A.:* The 72 for six you understand relieves the pressures of life, and young men's fancies can turn to other things . . .

*Spectators:* Is that the one you said had . . .?

No.

*J.A.:* Out in the middle, Dumbleton call on their schoolboy Alan to rally the ranks.

*Umpire:* Out!

*J.A.:* The appeal unnecessary. (*applause*) The batsman's departure almost indecent in haste, and in comes The Slaughter's captain – Ray Mossen. (*applause*)

*Spectators:* Well, it should be getting down now. (*indecipherable asides*)
Here, dog! (*yelp*)

*J.A.:* Never mind the dog madam, just look at this for an attitude; they shall not pass. Two captains in brown pads – a tableaux of sartorial elegance. (*sound of bowling. 'Out!'*) And another run for The Slaughters. (*dog barking*) A duck with three wickets still to fall. (*cows mooing, sound of bowling. 'Out!'*) And there's one (*applause*) – genuine cowshot, justly rewarded. (*background chatter*) And the schoolboy bowls again. (*bowls*)

Bowling in the finest tradition of schoolboys – a yard too fast – so he's not bad. Here he comes again. (*bowls*).

*Captain:* Go on, go on!

*J.A.:* Slaughters' captain exercising his prerogative issuing stern orders to run to the baker, Martin Collet.

113 for 8. (*birds twittering*)

*Captain:* Out! (*applause*)

*J.A.:* Captain Hopkins, a healthy baritone, announces that it is now 113 for 9. Last man in. (*applause*) Notice that black-band bat – reckon I've seen at least five Slaughterers using that bat today. (*bowls*)

*Umpire:* Out! OUT!

*J.A.:* An encore for the schoolboy and his captain. (*applause*) The Slaughters all out 114 and everything and everyone stops for tea. (*announcements, mooing, chatter*) And after tea, back they come. Dumbleton need 115 to win. I suspect he'll have to do his stuff, if

The Slaughters are going to stop them. Farmer Baker opening the batting as well as the bowling – a privilege normally reserved for captains. (*bowls*) And bang! There, you see, you wouldn't get that at Lord's, would you? First ball and hit it as hard as you can. And now Baker has the strike at the other end. (*bowls*) Oh dear! (*applause*) Yes, another actually authentic cowshot, and from a farmer as well. (*applause*) So now Andy Poole, tail up now of course, to Chris Hawkins the barman (*bowls*), who immediately redresses the balance and reviews generally to give The Slaughters a bit of the stick. (*applause*) For a time Dumbleton are riding high, then Hawkins gets out and now they're 49 for two.

*Umpire:* Out! (*applause*)

*J.A.:* 49 for three. (*applause*) And here's the skipper, Alec Hopkins, and a mighty man is he. (*applause*) Hypercritical applause from The Slaughters – Captain Mossen to bowl and now Hopkins the non-striker . . .

*Umpire:* Hopkins in ground. (*bowls*)

*J.A.:* Well, take that as a warning. That's something generally frowned upon as not cricket, but then this is village cricket and no holds barred. Now he bowls to Hawkins (*bowls*), and Alec may well scowl at the wicket because that ball never really left the ground after it pitched. (*applause*) Groundsman would be for the chop, if there was a groundsman, which there isn't – they do it themselves. (*more applause*) And in comes the schoolmaster John Evans. 61 for four, 54 more needed, and now it's the turn of the Dumbleton folk to worry. (*bowls*)

*Umpire:* One!

*J.A.:* But Eric Giles back in his robes before Evensong, restoring some semblance of tranquillity (*bowls, and applause*), and apparently providing some sort of divine inspiration as well: because I must say this schoolmaster looks good. (*bowls*) And so does his partner, David Watcott. (*church bells peal*) Now I'm beginning to get slightly concerned about Eric, the Vicar: you can hear the bells calling him to his own service, but he shows no signs of leaving . . .

*Supporters:* Remember when we played before and old Eric stayed to the end and he had to run like hell 'cause he was twenty minutes late?

*J.A.:* It appears he has a reputation for this sort of thing.

*Supporters:* Looking for overtime see – double time – you want to take it when he starts running at the last five minutes, two minutes before the service – made off to a fine art. (*laughter*)

*J.A.:* Well I agree, it would have meant almost a sacrilege, wouldn't it, for a Dumbleton man to leave at a moment like this, with the game in the balance and Evans and Watcott still there. (*sound of bowling*) There's another nice shot, almost worthy of a county player. (*applause*) And now, as the shadows start to lengthen, there seems a new mood over the cricket ground. (*music over*) It's village cricket with its teeth drawn, Dumbleton surely on their way to a win. Local superiority, peace and pleasure.

(*music*)

*Supporters:* I bet Eric's trying to get that service over real quick in church. (*laughter*) He'll just tell them that one joke, ring the bell, sing a hymn and away back again.

(*sound of bowling, applause*)

*J.A.:* Dumbleton are 113 for four and they need just 2 to win; and Evans to take the bowling. (*bowls*)

*Supporters:* Oh, well caught! (*applause*)

*J.A.:* Well, there you are, you talk about what a good player he is and he gets out like that when they need just a couple to win. (*applause*) Still, he's today's hero. (*applause*) 2 to win, Watcott facing ... (*bowls*) and that's it, and Dumbleton have won. Glory be! (*hymn singing, applause*) And now back at the ranch, if I may make so bold about Dumbleton's pavilion, another cricketing convention gets under way – the beer-up. (*background chatter*) Yes it is. The match they analyse in such loving detail wasn't a particularly good match at all by neutral standards, but this is part of the eccentricity. The match doesn't really matter now; it's become just the excuse, and the extroverts last the pace best.

(*music*)

*Supporters:* (*cheers*)

*J.A.:* Dumbleton may well acclaim themselves, for this is their night. (*applause*) But in the huge Haig Championship, winning matters merely tonight and not at all for the future, and Dumbleton's time will come. (*sound of bowling*) In the next round they visit a team called Stinchcombe Stragglers, and now Dumbleton get beaten and soon Stinchcombe will lose too, then those who beat Stinchcombe will be beaten, and so on across Britain until two teams out of 850 emerge, to the final at Lord's.

(*music*)

*J.A.:* Village players tread where Hobbs and Bradman and Hutton trod. In 1977 the privilege was accorded to the cricketers of Lindle Moor in Lancashire and Cookley from Worcestershire. (*applause*)

Watching Cookley become national champions (*applause*), this is an occasion, village cricket in the shop window . . .

*Supporters:* Fantastic!

*J.A.:* Yet somehow again not quite its heart: the heart of the village game remains in the villages; there it beats fiercely and naturally every weekend (*background chatter*), where those who succeed go home late at night. (*music over*) In the manner of the man in that often quoted country diary handed down to us: 'last Monday your father played at cricket and came home pleased enough, for he struck the best ball in the game and wished he had not anything else to do, he would play at cricket all his life.'

(*music – fade out*)

*John Haig & Co. – Trans World International Film Library*, 1979

# Lloyds, Lillees –
# Products of the Permissive Society

*February* 1985.   If, at my first Test match, fifty-nine years ago, I could have looked forward to cricket in 1985, I should have been staggered. Now, at seventy-one, looking back on the game then and as it is now, I am not the least bit surprised.

Life changes, the world changes, and, as those who grow near to it understand, cricket is pre-eminently the game of change.

It is not instantly obvious that a print of an eighteenth-century match played on the bare down at Hambledon – with underarm bowling; curved bats, two-stump wickets; players wearing velvet jockey caps, nankeen breeches and buckle shoes – is the same as the game now played in vast stadia by men hurling bouncers at one another with straight bats and three stumps and in helmets and light-weight boots.

Yet the same they are: unmistakably so; and we can trace every phase of the development – steady development – that took the game from that to this.

Cricket, though we do not always realize it in youth, truly reflects the society in which it is played. The reason for this mirroring probably lies in the length of matches: not the hasty hour and a half of a football match, but five or six days; even at club level, five or six hours, so that the players change together, spend their time when not batting or fielding together, eat together and generally drink together afterwards. In other words, cricket fits into their life pattern and, therefore, reflects it.

Not only were those Hambledon players as unmistakably Georgian as their modern counterparts are the product of a permissive society; but the cricket of different countries reflects national characteristics – as is apparent to anyone observing the differences between India and Pakistan at play.

Such ideas, though, were remote from – even beyond – a twelve-year-old boy going to the first Test match of his life, at The Oval in 1926. A Test match then was a rare occasion. Before that England–Australia series began, in June 1926, no country had played a Test since the same two countries met in Sydney in March 1925. After it ended, in August 1926, no country played a representative game until South Africa and England at Johannesburg in December 1927. By way of contrast, between September 1983 and April 1984, twenty-eight Tests were played; and, in its home season of 1979–80, India alone played eighteen home Tests.

Even the 1926 Oval scoreboard would seem strange today; amateurs were accorded the title Mr, but professionals were not; just as, in those days, gentlemen addressed their grooms – as Sir Pelham Warner addressed professional cricketers – by their surnames.

There they were, the cricket idols, their brilliantined short-back-and-sides hair, topped by caps with peaks so narrow that they accorded virtually no protection against the sun. Some of the aristocrats of the game played in trilby hats, like Lord Hawke (who also affected butterfly collars). Others habitually paraded the ground in straw boaters.

The scorecard reads like a match played on the Elysian Fields: Jack Gregory, Charlie Macartney, Bill Woodfull, Warren Bardsley, Bill Ponsford, Herbie Collins, Arthur Mailey and Clarrie Grimmett were on the Australian side; England had Jack Hobbs, Herbert Sutcliffe, Frank Woolley (completing an unbroken run of fifty-two Tests since 1909), Wilfred Rhodes (recalled at forty-nine), Patsy Hendren, Maurice Tate, Harold Larwood, Bert Strudwick, Percy Chapman.

The match was to be played to a finish to decide the rubber. In the event, although interrupted by rain and slowed by a difficult wicket, it was over in less than four days.

The details are salutary for those accustomed to present-day standards. In 21¾ hours, two fast, two fast-medium and six slow bowlers sent down 482 overs (about 22 an hour); forty wickets fell and 1143 runs were scored (52 an hour). At the end the decorous, dark-clad crowd (some 20,000) moved in orderly fashion to the front of the pavilion and gave cheers for both sides; the captains uttered a few formal words; the spectators gave another round of cheers and then made their way home.

A few boys lingered for autographs; but did not press for them as the Australians went to their charabanc and the English players – except the amateurs who took taxis – made their way to the underground station or buses. They could not afford motor cars on professional cricketers' wages.

The age of stardom was approaching, but had not yet fully dawned. Jack Hobbs had already recommended a specific make of foundation pen, and advocated teetotalism – 'Alcohol dims the eye' – but when, having beaten W.G. Grace's record of 124 centuries, he was offered several hundred pounds merely to be introduced from the stage of the London Coliseum, he refused in some alarm.

The inter-war period, of course, saw the high points of the careers of three of the greatest of all batsmen, Jack Hobbs, Don Bradman and Walter Hammond (W.G. Grace must have been the other) as well as Patsy Hendren, Philip Mead, Frank Woolley and Herbert Sutcliffe, all of whom made over 140 centuries. It was, too, the high point of batting records, first pointed by Bill Ponsford and then dominated by 'The Don'.

This was transformation. Jack Hobbs, whose ability has never been questioned, was little concerned with records. 'How many hundreds did Jack make?' asked Wilfred Rhodes one day. 'A hundred and ninety seven.' 'Well ah can tell thee, if he hadn't given it away so often when he had made 60 or 70, it could have been 297 – or (with a chuckle) 300.'

There can be no doubt – because it is the pattern of cricket – that this challenge by batsmen led first to the fast leg theory known as 'bodyline' – and then to defensive bowling.

Warwick Armstrong, bowling leg-rollers from round the wicket, had checked fast-scoring batsmen as long before as 1911–12. The regular pattern of unambitious bowling to restrictive fields had yet to come. Bowlers used habitually to attack. Indeed, when, at Headingley in 1930, Australia's score during the Bradman–Kippax stand stood at 400 for two, that fast-medium eternal optimist Maurice Tate was still bowling with two slips, a gully and a short-leg.

England first – at Melbourne in 1932–33 – introduced the pattern of unbroken fast bowling with Harold Larwood, Bill Voce, Gubby Allen, Bill Bowes, plus the fast-medium of Hammond. It remained, though, for the West Indies to introduce a routine of unbroken pace (at a deplorable over-rate). Clive Lloyd explained, blandly enough, that, given such a weapon as his pace posse, a captain would be stupid not to employ it; and that, if it contained an element of intimidation, it was the duty of the umpires to curb it.

Fiery pace had already proved the decisive factor in the wearing of protective helmets by batsmen; and, in many ways, the eclipse of attacking spin – or at least finger-spin bowling. That lately has required qualification. When, in the recent fifth Test at Sydney, the wrist spin of Bob Holland and the orthodox left-arm of Murray Bennett exposed, for the second time, a weakness of West Indian batsmen against the turning ball, the rest of the world must have scented hope. No one anywhere can expect that the magnificent sequence of West Indian pace will dry up. On the other hand, it must be possible that their batsmen will continue to be vulnerable to spin until, perhaps, they once more produce a Ramadhin and a Valentine in sheer defence against another Grimmett and O'Reilly.

Many of the changes in the game have crept up on it almost unnoticed. Gradually bowlers became more pragmatic. The one-day game proved conclusive; in some ways violently so. It began, at county level in England, out of sheer economic necessity. The county game was going broke; it needed to draw in those casual spectators who spent Sunday afternoons watching county benefit matches. Soon came the Nat West knock-out trophy in 1963; the John Player (Sunday) League in 1969; and finally, the Benson and Hedges league/knock-out Cup in 1972. The entry of the Packer organization into the international game meant that the over-limit game had come to stay. That was visibly apparent in the horrid coloured garbs foisted on the players; which argued an acceptance of many new values. The over-limit game, though, produced other effects: valuable financially but, most profoundly, damaging technically on English cricket; least in the West Indian game.

Primarily, and with immense benefit to the world game, as demonstrated first by Lancashire under Jack Bond in the early days of the English knock-out competition, it showed that raised standards of fielding could prove conclusive.

Absolute peaks of catching and, above all, of ground fielding were soon demanded in all quarters. Australian and the best of West Indian fielding had always been of high quality. English had not. Indeed, the giants of the English game – men like Hobbs, Woolley, Mead and Rhodes – could never have continued to play into their fifties if such high fielding standards had been demanded of them. In their day it was possible to 'hide' men in the field; the one-day game ended that.

Standards in the field had already been lifted before, and more rapidly after, the Second World War. As Philip Mead, maker of 153 centuries, remarked, in his blindness, after asking the precise placing of Cliff Gladwin's leg-side field: 'Well, that would have cost me a few hundred runs a year; my old leg-glance wouldn't have been much use.'

The exploitation of close catching, especially by Glamorgan which effectively won the County Championship of 1948 through its ability in that direction, was soon taken up throughout the world game. The furious ground fielding performance, however, was almost purely a product of the over-limit game. During the 1920s, Bertie Oldfield and Bert Strudwick could keep wicket at Test level virtually unruffled. George Duckworth, though, began, and the rest of the world, force put, followed, the salmon-leap take and the catch to lift wicket-keeping to new heights – or perhaps widths is a more fitting word.

Whether the employment of plug-away, short-of-a-length defensive bowling is a gain is questionable. The value of flat, speeded-up 'slow' bowling is even more doubtful. The record, for the English Sunday League, of the permitted eight overs for no runs, is held by Brian Langford, the Somerset off-spinner.

One fact beyond question is that, in England especially, the over-limit game has given rise to bad batting habits: the taking of unorthodox and – by Test standards – uneconomic risks. That has undoubtedly disturbed the foundations of the country's batting at three-day and five-day level. The performance of the Australian, Pakistani and, above all, West Indian Test batting has been less affected.

Apart from the mechanics of the game, the seventy-year-old spectator notes with some grief a steep decline in manners. This is the age of Dennis Lillee and John McEnroe; not only of those two persons, but of those who support them. Sheer human good sense will eventually rectify that. In the politics of the game, the shift of power from the establishment of the game to the players is historic. The Cricketers' Association came coolly and acceptedly to power in England, the formerly militant Players' Association more rapidly, but equally effectively, in Australia, where the board of control was routed by Packer. The scars are slowly – if only superficially – being healed.

Financially, cricketers are more fairly rewarded for their skills and efforts than ever before. Still some leading players earn more from endorsing commercial products than from playing cricket; but that is simply a reflection of the world in which we live. Some of the problems of the future are clear to foresee. If other sports – especially the various football codes – pay more than cricket, they will syphon off much talent from the game. If the staggering proliferation of Test matches and, even more, of international knock-out play continues, the value of both will be debased.

In the past, however, it has not only reflected but always, within itself, resolved the problems of its period.

*The Weekend Australian*

## Goodbye

### Imogen Grosberg

All through the cavalcade of daily play
Runs like a golden thread this fur-lined voice;
Lulled by its vintage warmth each summer day
Outpours its drama. Hearing, I rejoice
That I have shared, through seasons of delight,
Treasure of words and pageantry of sound,
Free flowing cadences in swallow flight
Across the splendour of a sunlit ground.
Rare and mature, the Hampshire tone serene,
Earthily spiced with wit and metaphor,
Weaves no more tapestry of white and green,
Enchantment fading now to 'nevermore'.
Life with its paintings, books and wine and arts
Lies beckoning. He bows out and departs.

*Hampshire Handbook*, 1981

# Index

Abdul Qadir, 116
Abel, R., 67
Ablack, R. K., 64
Acfield, D. L., 187
Adcock, N. A. T., 125, 126, 136, 138, 139
Adhikari, H. R., 132
Ahmed, Ghulam, 132
Aird, R., 223
Alabaster, J. C., 130
Alam, Intikhab, 183
Alderman, A. E., 100
Aldridge, K. J., 202
Ali, Mushtaq, 38, 39
Allen, D. A., 140, 143
Allen, Sir G. O. B. ('Gubby'), 222, 311
Alley, W. E., 185, 189
Altham, H. S., 226,
    and Swanton, E. W., *A History of Cricket*, 268
Amarnath, Lala, 38–41 *passim*, 186
Amiss, D. L., 152–4 *passim*, 180
Anderson, G., 282
Anderson, J. C.: lithographs of, 257, 261
Andrew, K. V., 175
Andrew, S. J. W., 235
Andrews, T. J. E., 12, 14
Angell, F. L., 82
apartheid: and Test cricket, 136
'Ape' (Carlo Pellegrini): cartoonist, 258
Apte, A. L., 135
aquatints: of cricket, 255
Archer, K. A., 106
Archer, R. G., 118
Armstrong, W. W., 310
Arnold, J., 87, 151, 152, 186, 207, 228, 249
Arnott, T., 224
art: and cricket, 253–65
Ashes, The, 11, 118, 121, 150, 154, 166, 291
    plate, 260
Asif Iqbal, 187
Ashley-Cooper, F. S.:
    *Cricket Highways and Byways*, 269
Aspinall, R., 59, 62, 70, 77
Atkinson, C. R. M., 190
Atkinson, G., 147, 170, 177
Australia: cricket book on, 270
    leg spinners, 172–3
    Test tours, 21–2, 49–51
    of 1948, 52, 56–8
    of 1953, 118–21
    of 1961, 140–2
    of 1972, 150–2

Baig, A. A., 133
Bailey, J., 207, 228
Bailey, T. E., 62, 68, 73, 81, 83, 91, 92, 125, 141, 163
Banerjee, S. S., 39–41 *passim*
Barber, R. W., 149, 173–4, 180, 183
Bardsley, W., 12, 14, 166
Barlow, R. G., 163
Barnard, H. M., 230
Barnes, S. F., 158 painting of, 254
Barnes, S. G., 49–51 *passim*, 55, 58
Barnett, C. J., 52, 66, 70, 105
Baroda, Maharaja of, 132
Barrett, H., 288
Barrick, D. W., 70
Barrington, K. F., 140, 180, 181, 187
Barron, W., 61
Bartlett, H., 75–6
Barwell, T. I., 189
Basébe, C. J.: lithographs by, 257, 261
Bathurst, Sir F., 288
Bedford, P. I., 48, 60, 173
Bedi, B. S., 178, 182
Bedser, A. V., 39–40, 52, 57, 58, 71, 73, 79,90, 93, 141, 167, 185
Bedser, E. A., 71, 79
Beldam, G. W.: cricket photographer, 262–3
Beldham, W. ('Silver Billy'), 279
Benaud, R., 118, 142, 172
benefit matches, 27–9, 179
Bennett, M. J., 311
Berry, G. L., 62, 71, 72, 83, 91, 93
Bhuta, J. M., 186
Birkenshaw, J., 180
Blackledge, J. F., 174
Blair, R. W., 129
Blake, D. E., 216
Bland, K. C., 110
Bligh, Hon. Ivo: cartoon of, 258
Blunt, R. C., 156
Bodyline series, 13, 141, 310
Bolus, J. B., 144, 171
Bonnor, G. J.: cartoon of, 258
books: on cricket, 166–95
    of cricket paintings and prints, 260
Booth, A., 41
Borde, C. G., 133–5 *passim*, 179
Border, A. R., 112
Botham, I. T., 112–17
Bowell, H. A. W., 207, 225, 227, 229

Bowes, W. E., 40, 311
Bowley, E. H., 156
bowling: changes in, 310–11
    the Chinaman, 44, 172, 212
    leg spinners, 172–3
    natural spin, 76, 104
    roundarm, 275
    and wicket, 85, 91
    yorkers, 144, 187
Boyce, K. D., 177
Boycott, G., 144, 146, 149, 151, 152, 177, 180, 181, 189
Boyes, G. S., 228, 229
Bradman, D. G., 14, 49–51, 54, 55–8, 97–9, 310
    as batsman, 98–9
    at The Oval, 166–7
    Test average, 98
    *The Art of Cricket*, 267
Braund, L. C., 172
Brearley, J. M., 112
Brennan, D. V., 70
Broderick, V., 61, 62
Brookes, D., 61
Brown, C., 288
Brown, D. J., 146, 180
Brown, F. R., 61, 64, 76–7, 172
Brown, G. (1783–1857), 290–1
Brown, G. (1887–1964), 207, 218–20 *passim*, 223, 225, 227–9 *passim*
Brown, S. M., 47, 48, 60, 182
Brown, W. A., 49, 51, 55, 55, 155
Browne, C. R. ('Sniffy'), 224
Budd, E. H., 282
Burden, M. D., 227, 229, 247–52
Burgess, M. G., 157, 189
Burki, J., 171
Burtt, T. B., 65, 157, 163
Buse, H. F. T., 64
Buss, A., 177
Buss, M. A., 181
Butler, H. J., 61

Caesar, J., 282
Caffyn, W., 282
Cannings, V. H. D., 56, 229, 234, 252
captaincy: of England, 83, 86
Cardus, Neville: as writer, 292–5,
    *Cricket*, 267
Carew, Dudley: *The Sin of Grief*, 269
Carlstein, P. R., 138, 139
Carr, A. W., 240
Carr, D. B., 187

cartoonists: cricket, 258–9
Castell, A. T., 173
Cave, H. B., 66, 130, 131, 157
Chandrasekhar, B. S., 181, 182
Chapman, A. P. F., 11–13 passim, 76, 166, 175
Chappell, G. S., 112, 151, 153, 155
Chappell, I. M., 112, 153, 155
Cheetham, J. E.: 1955 team, 123–7
Chesterton, G. H., 204
Chevallier Tayler, A.: artist, 259
Christiani, C. M., 89
Chubb, G. W. A., 108
Clark, E. A., 170
Clark, T. H., 250, 251
Clarke, Dr C. B. ('Bertie'), 173
Clarke, Charles Cowden, 273, 274
Clarke, R. W., 61, 64
Clarke, W., 79
Clay, J. D., 38, 72, 195
Clift, P. B., 63, 68, 69, 73
Close, D. B., 68, 70, 71, 73, 90, 93, 95, 144, 149, 150, 177, 179
'affair' (at Headingley), 186–7
coaching: as job, 32
Coldwell, L. J., 203–5
Collinge, R. O., 156, 157
Collins, H. L., 12, 14
Compton, D. C. S., 39, 42–4, 48, 52, 57, 58, 60, 69, 73, 80, 86, 93, 94, 105, 108, 121, 125, 145, 162, 193, 194
painting of, 254
Compton, L. H., 48, 246
Congdon, B. E., 156, 157
Connor, C. A., 235
Constantine, Sir L. N., 76, 222–4
Contractor, N. J., 133, 135
Cook, C. ('Sam'), 94, 95, 159
Cooper, E., 50
Cornford, W. L., 245
Cottam, R. M. H., 146, 187, 232
County Cricket:
Championship, 85, 181, 187, 188–90
professionals, 23–36
in 1947, 41–9
county cricket teams: at breakfast, 20–1
captains of, 173–6
Cowdrey, M. C., 109, 125, 126, 142, 143, 145, 148, 149, 180, 184, 185
Cowie, J., 60, 68, 157
Cowley, N. G., 234
Coxon, A., 70
Craig, Albert: 'cricket

rhymster', 296–9
Craig, I. D., 118
Cranston, K., 52, 63, 165
Crapp, J. F., 193
Cheese, W. L. C., 228
Cresswell, G. F., 60, 65
cricket: art, 253–61
beginning of, 275, 277
changes in, 308–13
Golden Age of English, 213
grounds, celebrated, 286–7
historian, 284–90
league, 32
literature, 266–95
one-day game, 311
photographers of, 261–5
play, video, 299–308
pleasures of, 14–20
qualities of, 16–17
reporting, 20–2
style of, 171–3
village, 292, 299–308
as way of life, 34–6
and weather, 178–80
Cricket Society, 267
bibliography by, 272
cricketana, 259–60
cricketers: boy, 24–5
and lack of security, 33–4
later employment for, 31–2
professional career, 29–31
rates of pay, 278, 313
in 1949, 25–7, 30, 34
Crump, B. S., 170, 251

D'Arcy, J. W., 129, 130
Daft, Richard: Kings of Cricket, 269–70
Darwin, Bernard: W. G. Grace, 269
Davidson, A. K., 118, 142
Davies, D., 195–6
Davies, D. E., 72, 74
Davies, H. G., 65, 197
Davies, P., 73
Davis, C. P., 61
de Courcy, J. H., 118
de Selincourt, Hugh: The Cricket Match, 269
Dempster, C. S., 156
Denness, M. H., 153, 184, 188, 189
Desai, R. B., 133, 135
Dewdney, D. T., 288
Dewes, J. G., 82, 83, 89, 93, 95
Dews, G., 82
Dexter, E. R., 140, 145, 187
Dixon, A. L., 185
Doggart, G. H. G., 78, 81–3 passim, 86, 89, 95
D'Oliveira, B. L., 148–51 passim, 178, 179, 181
Dollery, H. E. ('Tom'), 52,

74, 77, 79, 81, 83, 86
Donelly, M. P., 40, 60, 63, 65, 69, 100–1, 127, 128, 156–7, 163
Dooland, B., 172
Dowling, G. T., 157
Drummond, W.: lithographs by, 257
Duckworth, G., 125, 127, 138, 312
cartoon of, 259
Duffield, J., 245
Duleepsinhji, K. S., 156
Durston, F. J., 222
Dyson, E. M., 171

Eagar, E. D. R., 111, 208, 210, 229, 230, 248
Eagar, Patrick: cricket photographer, 264–5
Ealham, A. G. E., 189
Edrich, W. J., 42, 44–6, 48, 52, 57, 58, 60, 69, 73, 81, 93, 105, 151, 153, 154, 162, 163, 180, 181
Edmonds, P. H., 154
Edwards, R., 151, 155
Emmett, G. M., 57, 79
Endean, W. R., 125
Engineer, F. M., 111, 178, 179
England: Test captaincy, 82, 86
engravings: of cricket, 255–6
Etherington, M. W., 51
Evans, T. G., 40, 52, 57, 73, 81, 88, 93, 125, 139, 163
Eve, S. C., 68–9

Fagg, A. E., 52
Fairburn, A., 48
Faulkner, G. A., 104, 212
Fazal Mahmood, 122
'Felix', (Nicholas Wanostrocht), 283
lithographs, 257, 261
Fellowes, H. W., 288
Fellows-Smith, J. P., 138, 139
Fender, P. G. H., 239–42
cartoon of, 259
Fenner, F. P., 288
Fenton, Roger: cricket photographer, 261–2
Fiddling, K., 61
Fingleton, J. H. W., 80, 97
Masters of Cricket, 271
Firth, J., 70
Fishlock, L. B., 40, 52
Fishwick, Herbert: cricket photographer, 263
fives: game of, 17–18
Flavell, J. A., 178, 188, 202
Fleetwood-Smith, L. O'B. ('Chuck'), 141
Fletcher, K. W. R., 147, 152–4 passim, 251
Francis, G. N., 224

Freeman, A. P. ('Tich'), 99, 173
Fry, C. B., 67, 226, 227
  cartoon of, 258
Fuller, E. R. H., 126

Gaekwad, D. K., 132–5 passim
Gale, R. A., 170
Gardner, F. C., 82
Garlick, R. G., 61
Ceary, G., 11
Gentlemen v Players, 75
  and W. J. Edrich, 46
George Parr's Tree, 158
Ghorpade, J. M., 133–5 passim
Gibb, P. A., 40
Gibbs, L. R., 143, 144, 148, 149
Gifford, N., 145
Gilchrist, R., 132
Gillette Cup, 145, 177, 183–6
Gilliat, R. M. C., 184, 231–3 passim, 235
Gilligan, A. E. R., 244
Gilmour, G. J., 153, 154
Gimblett, H., 64, 66, 69–70, 74, 87, 89
Gladwin, C., 61, 68, 71
Glamorgan CCC, 72–3, 191–9
Goddard, J. D. C., 76
Goddard, T. W. J., 72, 95, 96, 104, 137–40
Godfrey, J. F., 206–7
Godfrey, William: cricket author, 269
Gomez, G. E., 81, 89
Gooch, G. A., 154
Goodwin, F., 124
Goonesena, G., 172
Gover, A. R., 40, 100
Grace, Dr W. G., 79, 121, 161, 166, 283
  book on, 269
  painting of, 254
  Staffordshire figure of, 260
Graham, J. N., 181
Graveney, T. W., 53, 68, 69, 71, 148–50 passim, 179, 181, 187
Gray, J. R., 208, 248
Gray, L. H., 48, 82
Green, D. M., 188
Greenhough, T., 140, 173, 174
Greenidge, C. G., 153, 231–3 passim, 235
Gregory, J. M., 12, 13, 119, 166, 219
Greig, A. W., 151–3 passim, 177, 178, 184, 185
Greig, J. G., 226–8 passim
Griffin, G. M.: 'calling' of, 136–40 passim
Griffith, S. C. ('Billy'), 75,

143, 144, 148, 149, 184
Grimmett, C. V., 12, 88, 141, 172
Gul Mahomed, 41
Gunn, G., 158
Gunn, W., 158
Gupte, S. P., 134
Guy, J., 282–3

Hadlee, D. R., 156
Hadlee, R. J., 156
Hadlee, W. A., 59, 63, 69, 99, 101, 156
Haig, N. E., 222
Haig, W. S., 102
Hall, W. W., 132, 143, 148, 149, 171
Halliday, H., 70
Hambledon Cricket Club, 272–81 passim, 291–2
  annual dinner of, 279–80
Hamence, R. A., 51
Hammond, W. R., 40, 141, 310, 311
Hampshire CCC, 205–18, 219–35
  as County Champions, 230
  elevens, 225–30, 233–5
Hampshire, J. H., 146, 151
Hanif Mohammed, 122–3
Hardstaff, J. (Jnr), 39, 52, 74
Hardy, J. J. E., 235
Harford, N. S., 128, 129
Haroon Rashid, 116
Harris, Lord, 240, 241
Harris, M. J., 74, 182
Harrison, L., 213–18, 247, 249
Harvey, R. N., 49, 51, 58, 61, 74, 106, 142
Hassan, S. B., 117
Hassett, A. L., 49, 51, 55, 57, 74, 141
  as batsman, 120–1
  and 1953 team, 118–21
Hastings, B. F., 157
Hawke, Lord, 309
  painting of, 254
Hawkins, E.: cricket photographer, 262
Hayes, J. A., 66, 129
Hayllar, James: artist, 254
Hayward, T. W., 67
Hazare, V. S., 39, 40, 132
Hazell, H. L., 62
Headingley: as Test ground, 163–5
Headley, G. A., 76, 177
Hearne, J. W., 94, 222
Heath, D. M. W., 94
Heath, M., 229
Heine, P. S., 124–6 passim
Hendren, E. H. ('Patsy'), 11, 13, 80, 310
  cartoon of, 259
Henwood, Thomas: artist, 254

Herman, R. S. ('Lofty'), 187, 207, 228, 231
Hever, N. G., 63, 72, 73
Higgs, K., 148–50 passim, 186
Hill, Allen, 79
Hill, C., 67
Hill, E., 64, 68
Hill, J. C., 56
Hills, J. J., 84
Hilton, M. J., 62, 84, 91
Hindleker, D. D., 38, 40, 162
Hobbs, Sir J. B., 11, 12, 43, 94, 141, 158, 166, 199, 298–9, 310
  cartoon of, 259
  death of, 145
  painting of, 254
Hobbs, R. N. S., 147
Holder, V. A., 153
Hole, G. B., 118
Holford, D. A. J., 148, 149
Holland, R. G., 311
Hollies, W. E., 52, 58, 69, 73, 90, 97, 167, 173
Holt, A. G., 223
Horton, M. J., 124, 207
Hosie, A. L., 223
Howarth, G. P., 157
Howarth, H. J., 157
Howorth, R., 41, 50, 52, 75, 200
Hughes, K. J., 112
Hunte, C. C., 142, 144, 148
Hutton, Sir L., 39, 41, 52, 57–8, 69–71 passim, 73, 81, 86, 93, 94, 105, 108, 145, 162
  at Headingley, 164–5
  at The Oval, 166
  painting of, 154
  on tour, 192

Ikin, M. J., 40, 74, 77, 94, 124
Illingworth, R., 140, 151, 183, 189
Imran Khan, 113–17
Indian: Test tours, 37–41
  of 1959, 131–5
Ingleby-Mackenzie, A. C. D., 175, 230, 231, 233, 235
Insole, D. J., 83, 86
Iverson, J. B., 172

Jackman, R. D., 110, 177
Jackson, F. S., 67
Jackson, H. L., 62, 68, 70
Jackson, P. F., 50, 200, 201–3
Jahangir Kahn, 113
Jaisimha, M. L., 135
Jakeman, F., 70
James, C. L. R.: Beyond a Boundary, 271
James, K. C., 100, 156
Jaques, A., 227, 228

Jardine, D. R., 99, 240
  and Bodyline series, 13
Jenkins, R. O., 62, 71, 74, 79
Jepson, A., 61, 62
Jessop, G. L., 67, 110
Jesty, T. E., 231, 235
Johnson, H. H. H., 80, 171
Johnson, I. W., 56
Johnston, A. C., 226–8 passim
Johnston, W. A., 49, 55–8
  passim, 119–20
Jones, A., 146–7, 170, 187,
  251
Jones, I. J., 146, 187
Jones, W. E., 72
Joshi, P. G., 134
Judge, P. F., 38
Julien, B. D., 153

Kallicharran, A. I., 153
Kanhai, R. B., 111, 143, 144,
  148, 149, 153
Kapil Dev, 113–15
Kardar, A. H., 37
Keeton, W. W., 74
Keighley, W. G., 70
Kelly, Ken: cricket
  photographer, 264
Kenyon, D., 177, 188
Kirby, D., 175
Kirmani, S. M. H., 185
Kline, L. F., 172
Knight, B. R., 148
Knott, A. P. E., 151, 154, 189
Knott, C. H., 195, 250
Kripal Singh, A. G., 132, 135
Kunderan, B. K., 179

Laker, J. C., 51, 52, 57, 58,
  71, 79, 102, 108, 126,
  129, 141, 209
  photos of, 263
Lamb, A. J., 116
Lamb, R., 220
Lambert, W., 279
Lancashire CCC, 85
Langford, B. A., 312
Langridge, J., 40, 79, 86, 87,
  216, 231, 242–5, 250
Langridge, J. G., 72, 244
Lansdown Cricket Club,
  282–4
Larwood, H., 11, 13–14,
  79–80, 94, 105, 119,
  141, 166, 311
Lashley, P. D., 148
Latchman, A. H., 182
Lawrie, P. E., 226
Lester, E. I., 59, 77
Lewis, A. R., 147, 152, 168,
  169, 182, 185, 187
Lewis, E. J., 185
Lewis, R. V., 231
Leyland, M., 194
Lillee, D. K., 112, 151–5
  passim
Lillywhite, F. W., 284–90

Young Cricketer's Guide,
  284
Lindwall, R. R., 49, 53–5,
  57–8
  bowling of, 119
literature: on cricket, 266–95
lithographs: of cricket, 256–7
Livingstone, D. A., 230
Livsey, W. H., 218, 225,
  227–9 passim
Llewellyn, C. B., 211–13, 227
Lloyd, C. H., 109–12, 153,
  188, 311
  as captain, 111–12
Lock, G. A. R., 79, 129, 143,
  147, 179, 180, 183
Lockwood, W. H., 167
Lohmann, G. A., 167, 298
Lord, Thomas: painting of,
  254
Lord's: cricket ground, 160–1
  Pavilion, 161
  wicket, 68
Lord's Taverners, 160
Lowry, T. C., 156
Lowson, F. A., 70, 71, 77,
  108
Loxton, S. E. J., 51, 56, 58,
  74, 106
Luckhurst, B. W., 151, 184,
  188
Lyttelton, Hon. Alfred:
  cartoon of, 258

McCarthy, C. N., 108
Macartney, C. G., 12, 13, 14,
  166
McConnon, J. E., 81
McCool, C. E., 53, 56, 172
McCorkell, N. T., 207,
  216–8, 228, 249
McCosker, R. B., 155
McDonald, E. A., 163, 219,
  294
McDonnell, H. C., 226, 227
MacGibbon, A. R., 129, 130,
  157
McGlew, D. J., 124, 125–6,
  130, 137, 139
McIntyre, A. J., 75
McIntyre, A. S., 226
Mackay, K. D., 142
McKinnon, A. H., 139
McLean, R. A., 124–6
  passim, 137, 139
McMahon, J. W. J., 51
Mailey, A. A., 12, 13, 166,
  172
  as cartoonist, 259
  10 for 66 and All That, 269
Majid Khan, 113
Makepeace, J. W. H., 163
Manjrekar, V. L., 132, 135
Mankad, M. H. ('Vinoo'),
  39–41 passim, 132
Mann, F. G., 48, 60, 62, 106,
  193

Mann, N. B. F. ('Tufty'), 106
Mansell, P. N. F., 125, 126
Mansoor Akhtar, 116
Maqsood Ahmed, 123
Marks, V. J., 116, 117
Marsh, R. W., 151, 155
Marshall, John: The Weaving
  Willow, 290–2
Marshall, M. D., 235
Marshall, R. E., 177, 207,
  229, 233
Martin, F. R., 224
Martin, Harry: cricket
  photographer, 264
Martineau, G. D.: They Made
  Cricket, 271
Maru, R. J., 235
Mason, A., 70, 71
Mason, W. H.: cricket print,
  256
Massie, R. A. L., 151
May, P. B. H., 71, 78, 82, 89,
  95, 108, 125, 126, 142,
  250
MCC: at Lord's, 161
  and pay, 31, 33
  and professional
    cricketers, 23
  tours, 191–5
  training by, 33
  The MCC Coaching Book,
    270
Mead, C. P., 219–21
  passim, 223, 225, 227–
  9 passim, 310, 312
  obituary, 236–9
  runs made by, 237
Meale, T., 129
Melville, A., 159
Merchant, V. M., 38, 40
Merritt, W. E., 156
Milburn, C., 147–50 passim,
  180, 181, 188
Miller, K. R., 49, 51, 53,
  54–5, 57–8, 106, 118,
  120, 128, 129, 140–1,
  165
Mills, J. E., 156
Milton, C. A., 68, 71
Mitchell, B., 137
Modi, R. S., 39, 40
Moir, A. M., 130, 131, 157
Morgan, R. W., 157
Morland, George: artist, 253
Moroney, J., 106
Morris, A. R., 49–51 passim,
  55, 57, 58, 74, 106, 118
Morse, C., 289
Mortimore, J. B., 180, 189
Mottram, T. J., 231, 232
Motz, R. C., 157
Moyes, A. G. ('Johnnie'):
  Australian Cricket, 270
Mudassar Nazar, 116
Muddiah, V. M., 134
Muncer, B. L., 63, 72–4
  passim
Murray, A. R. A., 127

Murray, J. T., 149, 150, 179
Murtagh, A. J., 231
Mushtaq Mohammed, 183, 186
Mynn, Alfred, 79
  lithograph of, 257

Nadkarni, R. G., 133–5 passim
Naik, A. D., 185
Nasim-ul-Ghani, 183
Nawab of Pataudi (Snr), 38–40, 132
Nawab of Pataudi (Jnr), 171, 178
Nayudu, C. S., 38, 41
Newman, J. A., 224, 225, 227–9 passim
New Zealand: cricketers, 1983, 155–7
  Test tours, 59–60
    1949, 99–103
    1958, 127–31
Nicholas, M. C. J., 233, 235
Nichols, M. S., 156, 158
Nicholson, A. G., 146, 178
Norman, M. E. J. C., 170
Nourse, A. W. ('Dudley'), 107, 108, 137, 192–3
Nupen, E. P. ('Buster'), 104
Nurse, S. M., 148, 149
Nutter, A. E., 61, 64
Nye, J. K., 245
Nyren, John: The Young Cricketer's Tutor, 272–81 passim
Nyren, R., 273

Old, C. M., 153
Oldfield, W. A. E. ('Bertie'), 12, 13, 61, 139, 312
Old Trafford: Test cricket at, 161–3
  wicket, 69, 81, 83–5
O'Linn, S., 137–9 passim
O'Neill, N. G., 142
Onslow, F., 289
O'Reilly, W. J., 88, 141, 172
O'Sullivan, D. R., 231
Oulds, Denis: cricket phtographer, 263
Oval, The: as Test ground, 165–7

Pakistan: Test tours, 121–3, 182
Page, M. L. ('Curly'), 156
paintings: modern, of cricket, 260–1
  oil, of cricket, 253
  of players, 254
Palmer, C. H., 50, 52, 74, 79, 82, 83
Palmer, K. E., 144, 185
Parfitt, P. H., 151, 170
Parker, C. W. L., 243
Parker, J. F., 40

Parkhouse, W. G. A., 71, 73, 79, 81, 93, 197
Parks, J. M., 140, 143, 144, 148, 184
Parks, R. J., 235
Parr, G., 79, 282, 287
  Staffordshire figure of, 259
pay: of cricketers, 25–7, 30, 34, 278, 313
Paynter, E., 194
Pearce, T. N., 51, 98
Pearson, A. J. G., 202, 251
Peebles, I. A. R., 222
Perks, R. T. D., 74, 199–201
Petrie, E. C., 130
Phadkar, D. G., 132
Phillips, Jack, 156
photographs: and cricket, 261–5
  The Noble Game, book of, 271
Pilling, H., 189
Pithey, A. J., 138
Place, W., 64
Playle, W. R., 128–30
Plimsoll, J. B., 105, 162
Pocock, P. I., 179, 180
Pollard, R., 40, 52, 57, 165
Pollard, V., 157
Ponsford, W. H., 12, 14, 310
Poole, C. J., 74, 171
Pope, G. H., 62
Postle, Bruce: cricket photographer, 261
Pothecary, A. E. ('Sam'), 138–9, 228
Prasanna, E. A. S., 183
Pressdee, J. S., 197, 198
Preston, K. C., 69, 71, 77
Price, J. S. E. ('Jess'), 146, 151, 180
Price, R., 282
Price, W. F. F., 48
Prideaux, R. M., 170, 175
professional cricketers, 21–36
  further employment, 31–4
  in schools, 23
  as way of life, 34–6
Prouton, R. O., 216
Prudential Cup: 1975, 152–5
Pullar, G., 140
  benefit, 179
Pycroft, Rev. James, 281–4
  The Cricket Field, 281, 284

Rabone, G. O., 60, 127, 128, 157
Rae, A. F., 81, 89
Ramadhin, S., 45, 80, 86–9 passim, 96, 172
Ramchand, G. S., 132
Ramsamooj, D., 170
Randall, D. W., 116
Ranjitsinhji, K. S., 67
  photo study of, 263
Rayment, A. W. H., 95, 208, 234

Reddy, N. S. K., 171
Reid, J. R., 127–31 passim, 157
Remnant, E. R., 225, 226, 228, 229
Rhodes, W., 11, 13, 62, 104, 166, 310
  painting of, 254
Richards, B. A., 153, 231, 232
Richards, I. V. A., 153
Richardson, A. J., 12, 13
Richardson, B. A., 183
Richardson, P. E., 188
Richardson, T., 119, 162, 167
Ridgway, F., 68
Ring, D. T., 56
'Rip': cartoonist, 259
Ritchie, John: artist, 253
Roberts, A. M. E., 113, 153, 234
Roberts, F., 289
Roberts, W. B., 62
Robertson, J. D. B., 47, 48, 52, 60, 62, 68, 70, 182
Robertson-Glasgow, R. C.: The Brighter Side of Cricket, 267
Robins, R. W. V., 46–7, 77, 86
Robinson, M., 63, 73
Robinson, P. J., 189
Robinson, Ray: Between Wickets, 271
Rogers, A., 206
Rogers, C., 206
Rogers, N. H., 64, 205–10, 229
  record, 210
Roope, G. R. J., 154
Root, C. F., 199
Ross, Alan: The Cricketer's Companion, 271
Rowan, A. M. B., 74, 103–9, 164
  knee injury, 103–9
Rowan, E. A. B., 106, 107, 137
Rowlandson, Thomas: artist, 255–6
Roy, P. K., 132, 133, 135
Russell, S. E., 170
Russell, W. E., 168–9, 182

Saggers, R. A., 51
Sainsbury, P. J., 229–34 passim, 252
Saleem Altaf, 187
Sandham, A., 199, 241
Sardesai, D. N., 178
Sarkar, D., 186
Sarwate, C. T., 38, 40, 41
Saunders, Ken: cricket photographer, 263
Sayer, D. M., 185
Schwarz, R. O., 212
Scott, M. E., 60, 65, 127, 188
selection: of Test teams, 92–6
Shackleton, D., 75, 77, 90,

143, 144, 145, 217, 229,
230, 235
Sharp H. P. H., 48
Sharpe, P. J., 144, 177, 180,
189
Shepheard, George: cricket
watercolours, 254
Shepherd, D. J., 196–9
Shepherd, J. N., 177, 184,
189
Shepphard, Rt Rev. D. S.,
78, 82, 89, 93, 95, 165
Shinde, S. G., 41
Shirley, W. R. de la C., 226
Shrewsbury, A., 158
Sikander Bakht, 116
Sime, W. A., 61
Simpson, R. B., 172
Simpson, R. T., 52, 69, 74,
77, 81, 91, 93, 193
Sims, J. M., 48, 60
Sinclair, B. W., 157
Singh, H., 179
Singh, J., 186
Single Wicket competition,
177
Singleton, A. P., 200
Slade, D. N. F., 147
Slatter, Steve: groundsman at
Lord's, 160
Smailes, T. F., 40, 51
Smith, D., 66, 70
Smith, D. V., 68
Smith, M. J. K., 140, 144,
151, 180
retirement, 187–8
Smith, R., 87
Smith, T. P. B., 40, 102
Smithson, G. A., 70, 77, 94
Snow, J. A., 148 149, 151–4
passim, 177, 180, 181,
184
Sobers, Sir G. St A., 54, 111,
143, 144, 147–9 passim
Sohoni, S. W., 38, 162
Solomon, J. S., 143
South Africa: MCC tour to,
191–5
Test tours, 106–7, 123–7
in 1960, 135–40
Sparling, J. T., 128–30 passim
Spofforth, F. R., 121
Spooner, R. H., 71, 82, 91,
158
Spooner, R. T., 163
Springall, J. D., 171
Springboks: see South Africa
Sprot, E. M., 227
'Spy' (Sir Leslie Ward):
cartoonist, 258
Sri Lanka: cricket team, 153
Stackpole, K. R., 150–2
passim
Staffordshire pottery figures:
and cricket, 259–60
Standen, J. A., 178, 188
Staham, J. B., 126, 141–3
passim
Steele, D. S., 154, 212

Stephenson, G. R., 231
Stephenson, W. H., 71
Stevens, G. T. S., 11, 13, 14
Stewart, M. J., 144
Stewart, W. J. P., 171
Stollmeyer, J. B., 81, 89, 163
Stone, J., 226, 227, 229
'stone walling', 122, 238
Stringer, P. M., 177
Strudwick, H., 11, 166, 167,
312
painting of, 254
Subba Row, R., 140, 175, 250
Surendranath, 133, 135, 186
Surridge, W. S., 79
Sussex CCC, 75
Sutcliffe, H., 11–13 passim,
63, 65, 68, 70, 94, 101–
3, 127–9 passim, 157,
158, 163, 166, 310
as batsman, 102–3
Suttle, K. G., 184
Swansea: wicket at, 92

Tahir Naqqash, 116
Tallon, D., 49, 51, 58
Tamane, N. S., 134
Tate, M. W., 11, 13, 14, 70,
76, 94, 166, 239, 311
Tattersall, R., 91
Tavaré, C. J., 116
Tayfield, H. J., 107, 124, 126,
138, 139
Taylor, B. R., 157
Taylor, D. D., 102
Taylor, M. N. S., 231
Tennyson, Hon. L. H.,
219–21, 223–4, 228
Terry, V. P., 235
Tests: atmosphere of tours,
191–2
with Australia, 21–2
development of, 309
see also under separate
countries
Thomas, Brian: cricket
photographer, 263
Thompson, A. W., 48
Thomson, J. R., 153–5 passim
Timms, B. S. V., 184
Timms, J. E., 61
Tindall, R. A. E., 171
Titmus, F. J., 94, 143, 144,
148
Tolchard, R. W., 180
Tompkin, M., 82
Tordoff, G. G., 208
Toshack, E. R. H., 56, 57
touring sides: and pay, 27
Toynbee, Laurence: artist,
260
Tremlett, M. F., 64–5
Tremlett, T. M., 235
Trent Bridge: Test ground,
158–9
wicket, 67, 159
Trick, W. M. S., 73
Trott, A. E., 161

Trumper, V. T., 43, 67
Trueman, F. S., 69–71
passim, 77, 94, 103, 124,
142–4 passim
cartoon of, 259
Tuckett, L., 105, 106, 193
Turnbull, M. J. L., 156
Turner, A., 153
Turner, D. R., 177, 184, 231,
234
Turner, G. M., 156, 157
Tyldesley, J. T., 163
Tyldesley, R. K., 294
Tyson, F. H., 122, 126, 141

Ullyett, Roy: cartoonist, 259
umpires: as job, 31–2,
pay, 31
Umrigar, P. R., 132–5 passim
Underwood, D. L., 150–1,
185

Valentine, A. L., 45, 86–8
passim, 96
Van Ryneveld, A. J., 108
Vanity Fair: cricket cartoons,
258–9
Verity, H., 243
Vigar, F. H., 98
Viljoen, K. G., 159
Virgin, R. T., 171, 232
Voce, W., 40, 100, 311
Vogler, A. E. E., 104

Wade, H. F., 193
Waite, J. H. B., 125, 126,
137, 139
Walcott, C. L., 89
Walford, M. M., 74, 90
Walker, C., 70, 250
Walker, J., 289
Wallace, W. M., 60, 63, 65,
68, 127, 157
Walters, K. D., 155
Ward, J. T., 130
Wardle, J. H., 51, 62, 70
Waring, J. S., 146
Warner, Sir P. F., 158,
Lord's 1787-1945, 270
Warr, J. J., 92, 93
Washbrook, C., 39, 52,, 57,
58, 69, 71, 73, 86, 92,
105, 162
Wass, T. G., 158
Wassell, A., 230, 251
watercolours: of cricket,
254–5
Watkins, A. J., 52, 62–3, 68,
72, 77, 90, 91, 93, 94,
191–5, 197
Watson, W., 10, 94, 108, 115
Watts, G. F.: lithographs
256–7, 261
Wazir Mohammed, 122
Webber, Roy: The Book of
Cricket Records, 269
Webster, Tom: cartoonist,

241, 259
Weekes, E. de C., 76, 81, 89,
    90, 96
Wellard, A. W., 64
Wenman, E. G., 79
Wesley, C., 138
West Indies: and C. H. Lloyd,
    109
    Test tours, 76, 80, 96,
        in 1928, 222–4
        in 1963, 142–5
        in 1966, 147–50
Wharton, A., 62, 64–5
Whitcombe, P. A., 60, 62
White, D. W., 170, 212, 230,
    231, 234, 251
Whitehead, J. P., 70, 77, 204
wickets, 67–8, 85, 150, 196,
    198
    greenness, 159
    Old Trafford, 81, 83–4,
        85, 162

preparation, 74
    speed of, 91–2
Willett, M. D., 185
Willis, R. G. D., 112
Wilson, D., 70, 147
Winslow, P. L., 124–6
    *passim*, 136
*Wisden*, 287
Wood, C. J. B., 151, 154, 209
Woodfull, W. M., 12, 14, 166
Woodhead, F. G., 52, 61
Woodhouse, G. E. S., 64
Wooler, C. R. D., 82
Wooller, W., 63, 67, 72–4
    *passim*, 76–7, 83, 86,
        87, 197
Woolley, F. E., 11, 12, 66,
    156, 166, 294, 310
Woolmer, R. A., 152, 154
Worcestershire CCC, 199–
    205
World Cup Series, 153, 155

Worrell, Sir F. M. M., 76, 89,
    96, 142, 143
Worthington, T. S., 156, 245
Wright, D. V. P., 52, 71, 89,
    93, 172, 192
Wright, F. B., 282

Yardley, N. W. D., 57, 70,
    76, 77, 83, 97
Yonge, G., 283
Yorkshire CCC, 26, 59
    as County Champions, 72,
        77, 188–90
    fund, 32
    strength of, 70–1
Young, D. M., 68, 82
Young, J. A., 48, 52, 62, 194
Younis Ahmed, 177

Zulfiqar Ali, 122